VISUAL QUICKSTART GUIDE

AUTOMATOR

FOR MAC OS X 10.5 LEOPARD

Ben Waldie

Peachpit Press

Visual QuickStart Guide
Automator for Mac OS X 10.5 Leopard
Ben Waldie

Peachpit Press
1249 Eighth Street
Berkeley, CA 94710
510/524-2178
510/524-2221 (fax)

Find us on the Web at: www.peachpit.com
To report errors, please send a note to errata@peachpit.com
Peachpit Press is a division of Pearson Education

Project Editor: Rebecca Freed
Production Editor: Becky Winter
Development Editor: David Reynolds
Copyeditor: Linda Laflamme
Tech Editor: Mary Norbury
Composition: Jerry Ballew
Indexer: James Minkin
Cover Design: Peachpit Press

ISBN-13: 978-0-321-53935-9
ISBN-10: 0-321-53935-4

9 8 7 6 5 4 3 2 1

Printed and bound in the United States of America

Dedication:

For Jen, Lizzie, and Maddie, who make everything possible. I couldn't do it without you.

Acknowledgments

I would like to take this opportunity to sincerely thank a number of people who have directly led to and assisted with, the creation of this book.

Thanks to my wife, Jen, who spent many a late night reading, proofing, and offering input. Without her, many of the things that I set out to accomplish would not be possible.

Thanks to my two beautiful daughters, Lizzie and Maddie, for your love, support, and above all, patience.

Thanks to Mary Norbury and Chuck Toporek for introducing me to Peachpit at WWDC.

Thanks to my editor, Becca Freed, for doing such an amazing job managing the production of this book, and for everything else she has done along the way, which has been a lot!

Thanks to David Reynolds, Mary Norbury, Linda Laflamme, Becky Winter, Darren Meiss, Nancy Davis, Cliff Colby, Sara Todd, and everyone else who worked so hard to bring this book to fruition.

Thanks to Sal Soghoian at Apple, who has consistently offered helpful input, suggestions, and information about Automator and AppleScript.

Thanks to Kerry Hazelgren for always being willing to answer my questions and listen to my input.

Thanks to the incredibly talented Automator and AppleScript teams at Apple for implementing and keeping alive such amazing Mac automation technologies. Keep up the good work!

Thanks to Tim Davis for giving me the opportunity to learn AppleScript so very many years ago. Without that opportunity, I would not be where I am today.

About the Author

Ben Waldie is president of Automated Workflows, LLC, which offers AppleScript, Automator, and workflow automation consulting services to Mac-based businesses. For years, Ben has developed professional automated solutions for such companies as Abercrombie & Fitch, Adobe Systems, Apple Inc., CNN, Microsoft Corporation, NASA, PC World Communications, and Time Inc. In addition to this book, Ben is the author of *AppleScripting the Finder*. He has also written numerous Automator and AppleScript columns for Apple.com, *Macworld* magazine, MacScripter.net, *MacTech* magazine, and *X-Ray* magazine and is the author of an AppleScript training CD (Virtual Training Company). A frequent presenter at Macworld Conference & Expo and other events, Ben is president of The Philadelphia Area AppleScript Users Group.

www.automatedworkflows.com

ben@automatedworkflows.com

TABLE OF CONTENTS

TABLE OF CONTENTS

INTRODUCTION

With its knack for reliably automating complex, repetitive tasks, the personal computer was supposed to make life easier. But does yours really, or does it just make *more* work for you? For many, the latter seems to be the case, but it doesn't have to be. Your computer's ability to make your life easier depends on how you use it. If you're like me, then you probably use many different software applications during your workday, and you probably find yourself doing the same things over and over again.

Take digital photography, for example. Each time you plug your digital camera into your computer, you need to download the images into a set of folders, import them into a photo catalog, rename them, assign keywords, and more—sounds like a ton of work. Applications such as iPhoto can help tremendously with these tasks by automating much of the process for you. If you look closely at the tasks you do—known as your *workflow*—you will probably see that many are automated by your existing software.

Everything you do on your computer involves software—it provides you with the tools you need to do page layout, image editing, word processing, and more. Sometimes, your software does its job well, however, this isn't

continues on next page

always the case. You may need your software to do things it wasn't quite designed to do. Perhaps an application just doesn't automate those time-consuming tasks that you do regularly. Or, you may need a way to move information between multiple applications. If you're a programmer, then you can write your own custom software, or you may be able to automate your existing software using something like AppleScript.

Figure i.1 Say Hello to Automator's friendly little icon mascot, Otto.

But what if you're not a programmer? Your wish has been granted! Installed with Mac OS X is Automator, a tool for average folks that has one job: to perform repetitive tasks the way *you* need them done.

About Automator

Automator's user-friendly interface lets anyone create custom automated tasks, whether simple or complex. Within Automator, you'll work with two main types of components: *actions* and *workflows* (**Figure i.1**).

- Actions are built by developers, and are installed onto your Mac either by themselves or with an application. Each action's responsibility is to perform a single specific task, such as opening a file, checking for new email, or rotating an image.
- Workflows are designed and built by you: You place a series of actions in order to create an assembly line of tasks. You can save workflows and run them later in a variety of ways, such as from within Automator, from the Mac OS X Finder, from iCal, and more.

Programmers are in luck, too: Mac OS X includes all of the tools necessary to build custom actions. You plug them right into Automator to extend your automation possibilities even further.

Benefits of Automator

Automator is much easier to use than any automation technology that's been available before, while including many of the same benefits. After you've created a few workflows, you'll wonder how you ever functioned without Automator. Its main benefits are:

- **Ease of use.** Automator's simple user interface makes automation easy for anyone with a decent grasp of how to get around Mac OS X. With Automator, it doesn't take a rocket scientist (or a skilled programmer) to build an automated workflow. By putting such an easy-to-use tool directly into the hands of a typical Mac user, Apple ensures that anyone can take advantage of automation.
- **Less stress.** Automator can actually reduce stress. That's right, you read that correctly. Automator reduces stress. By removing the same old repetitive, boring tasks from your workload, you'll feel a renewed sense of energy and motivation, as you become free to focus on things that you actually enjoy, such as graphic design, photography, and more. Spend your time being more creative.
- **Fewer mistakes.** No matter what we might like to think, we all make mistakes from time to time—entering an incorrect file name, accidentally deleting a file, moving a file into the wrong folder, and so on. By automating tasks you can eliminate these sorts of mistakes. A properly created Automator workflow doesn't make mistakes. It performs consistently and accurately day in and day out, like a robot.
- **Do more faster!** An Automator workflow interacts directly with your Mac, eliminating time spent moving and clicking the mouse, pressing keys on the keyboard, and mulling over what to do next. Thus, you accomplish more work in the same amount of time. In some cases, it may even be possible for your workflow to run while you're away from your computer—at lunch or when you leave at the end of a day.

What Can Automator Do for You?

This will vary, depending on your specific workflow needs. Every Mac user's workflow is different, and every Automator workflow you build will be different.

Here are a few of the things Automator can do:

- **File and folder processing.** Quickly create workflows that rename files and folders on your Mac, compress them into archives, burn them to disc, and more.
- **Music- and audio-related tasks.** Build a workflow that simply plays music in iTunes. Or, create a more involved workflow that downloads songs from a website, imports them into iTunes, and syncs them with your iPod.
- **Photo and image conversion and manipulation.** If you're like me, then you probably have thousands of digital photos and images on your Mac. Don't work with them one at a time. Instead, create workflows that batch process photos and images, converting them from one format to another. Quickly and easily manipulate them with workflows that perform scaling, cropping, rotating, and more.
- **PDF processing.** Need to encrypt a PDF, add a watermark, or insert metadata? Built-in PDF actions make it easy to create workflows to batch process your PDF documents.
- **Email- and Internet-related tasks.** Create Automator workflows that download photos from webpages and import them into iPhoto, or upload files to your website, email files, and more.
- **Folder watching.** Create a workflow that watches a folder on your Mac. Simply drop files into that folder to run the workflow, allowing the files to be processed.
- **Scheduled workflows.** Use iCal to schedule workflows to run anytime—even if you're in a meeting or it's the middle of the night!

What Can't Automator Do for You?

Automator can do a lot, but it can't do everything. Like all good software, it still has limitations:

- **Automator can't make decisions.** It can do only the things you tell it to do, exactly the way you specify, in the order that you specify. It can't choose different courses of action based on varying conditions, which more advanced automation technologies (such as AppleScript) can.
- **In Leopard, you can create an Automator workflow that runs over and over again (that *loops*).** But information is still passed through the workflow in a linear fashion. In other words, there's no way to have Automator pass one file at a time through the workflow. For example, let's say you create a workflow that performs three tasks: open a file, make a change, and save the file. If you are processing 700 files, all 700 files will be opened first, then all 700 files will have a change made, then all 700 files will be saved. This can really make processing large numbers of files difficult, as you probably don't want 700 files open at once on your Desktop.

✔ Tips

- To get around Automator's linear processing limitation, you can download my Automator Multi-Item Processing Utility from www.automatedworkflows.com/software/automator_actions/automator_tools.html. This free tool converts Automator workflows to AppleScript applications. After converting the workflow, simply drag and drop multiple files or folders onto the AppleScript application to process them one at a time through the workflow.
- If you occasionally feel limited by the actions available to you, just look around because the list is still growing. In addition to the dozens of Automator actions Apple provides in Mac OS X, more are included with specific Apple applications, such as iPhoto and Keynote. Actions are also being released regularly for many third-party applications. Visit www.apple.com/downloads/macosx/automator/ to see what's available.

When to Use AppleScript

Need to do something Automator can't handle? Try AppleScript. Though it has a much steeper learning curve than Automator, it too can be self-taught. I know because I taught myself AppleScript.

With a little time and practice, you can write AppleScripts to automate virtually any task in Mac OS X. As you'll learn in Chapter 13, "Building Advanced Workflows," AppleScripts can even be plugged into your Automator workflows to extend Automator's reach.

No time to learn a scripting language? Prewritten AppleScripts are a good introduction, and you can find plenty of them online. Visit www.apple.com/applescript to get started.

System Requirements

Automator was first released with Mac OS X v10.4 (Tiger), which is the minimum installation to use Automator. Mac OS X v10.5 (Leopard), however, introduced a completely revamped version of Automator with loads of new useful features and a redesigned interface.

This book focuses on using Automator in Leopard and with the applications installed with Mac OS X. While some of the main principles and topics will still be pertinent to Tiger users, many discussions will be Leopard specific.

Likewise, some of the example workflows provided involve iLife and iWork applications, such as iPhoto or Keynote. If you don't have these installed, simply do your best to follow along.

What's New with Automator in Leopard?

Automator was off to a great start in Tiger, but it was still a 1.0 release. Mac OS X 10.5 Leopard is a giant leap forward. It introduces a number of enhancements, including a few very highly anticipated features. New Automator features in Leopard include:

- **Revamped interface.** Automator sports a slick new interface that's easier to use and customize (**Figure i.2**).

continues on next page

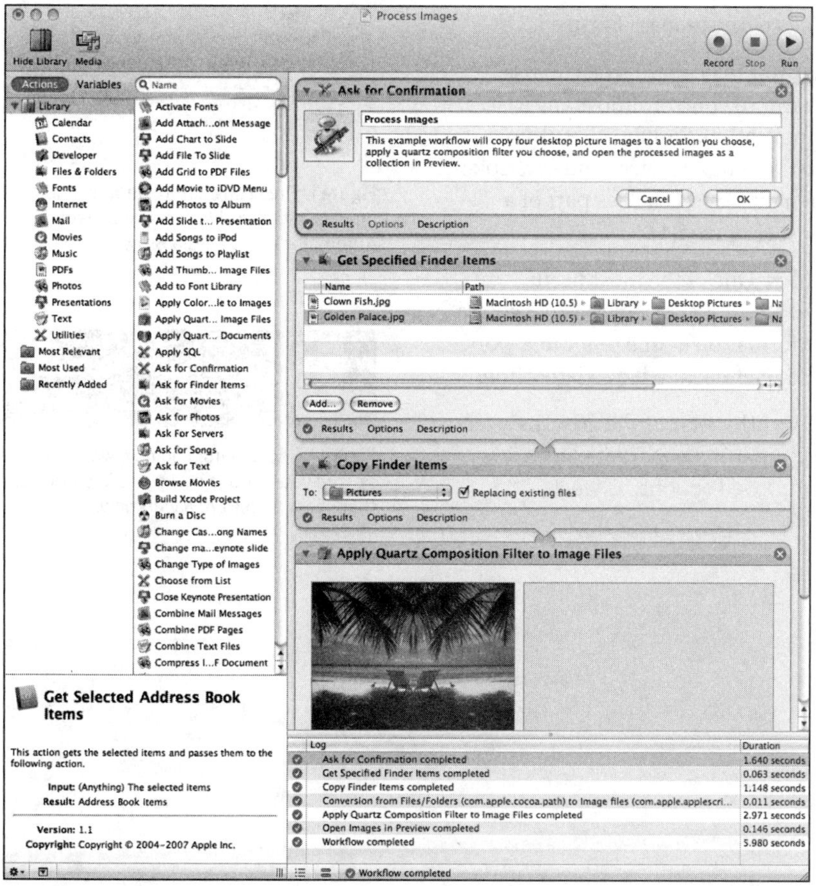

Figure i.2 Automator's interface in Leopard is new, improved, and much quicker than its predecessor.

- **Better performance.** There's no way around it, building Automator workflows in Tiger was a sluggish process. In Leopard, it's now a breeze! Automator's interface is quick and snappy, allowing you to build and edit workflows in a flash.
- **Starting Points.** Creating workflows has never been easier. Starting Points prompts you to choose the type of workflow you want to create, opens a workflow template, and prefills it with actions to get you started.
- **Media Browser.** Automator now makes it easy to quickly insert audio, photos, and music into a workflow with only a few clicks of the mouse (**Figure i.3**).
- **Recording.** In Leopard, you can use Automator to control almost any Mac OS X application. Simply tell Automator to watch your mouse clicks and keystrokes, and then play them back as part of a workflow (**Figure i.4**).
- **Variables.** One of the most useful Leopard additions, variables allow you to store information at one point in a workflow and refer back to it at a later time.

This list is just the start of the great new features of Automator. Leopard includes lots of new and improved actions, as well!

Figure i.3 Inserting audio, photos, and movies into a workflow is a snap with Automator's new Media Browser.

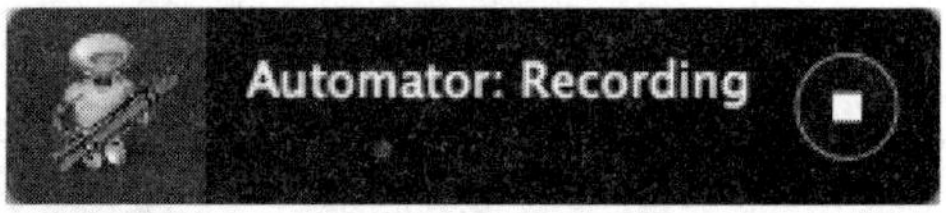

Figure i.4 Automator can now watch your every move. Record your mouse clicks and keystrokes, and play them back as part of a workflow.

About this Book

Automator for Mac OS X 10.5 Leopard: Visual QuickStart Guide is written for any Mac enthusiast interested in learning how to use Automator, regardless of skill level. Whether a beginner or an expert, you'll find that this book covers Automator from top to bottom.

While you're certainly free to skip around, the chapters are arranged in a logical manner. For the best possible learning experience, move through them in order.

If you do, you'll begin by exploring some of Automator's key concepts that you'll use throughout the book.

Next, you'll create some simple Automator workflows. Hands-on experience is perhaps the best way to learn Automator. These workflows are designed to get you familiar with Automator's interface, and help Automator's key concepts to sink in.

The remainder of the book covers Automator in detail. Screen shots and step-by-step instructions carefully walk you through all aspects of Automator, including creating, saving, and running workflows, and much more. You'll be up and running with Automator in no time!

Example Workflows and Companion Website

As a bonus, you can download actual completed versions of all example workflows from the *Automator for Mac OS X 10.5 Leopard: Visual QuickStart Guide's* companion website: www.peachpit.com/vqs/automator. Be sure to register your book here, to gain access to the bonus content. You can also visit the Books section of my website at www.automatedworkflows.com/books/books.html for current information about this book.

1

Getting Started

Automator's purpose is to help you to become more efficient. It works with the files, folders, applications, and the operating system on your Mac to automate time-consuming or repetitive tasks. When using Automator, you'll first think about an overall job you want to accomplish. Next, you'll identify the applications or processes that will be involved, and, finally, specify the individual tasks you want to perform within those applications or processes.

In Automator, each task is called an *action*, and you can link multiple actions together to form a *workflow*. The workflow you create can run within Automator, or you can save it to run outside of Automator in a variety of ways. When run, the actions within your workflow execute sequentially, in some cases passing information between one another.

For example, you might create a workflow that retrieves unread emails from your inbox, converts them to audio format, adds them to iTunes, and syncs them with your iPod, allowing you to listen to your email on the go. You'll soon find that Automator makes it easy to create useful workflows for photos, music, text, and more.

About Workflows

Automator documents are called *workflows*. You build a workflow by gathering and configuring the actions for the tasks you want to automate. You can then perform these tasks at any time simply by running the workflow.

✔ Tips

- Look for example workflows to get you started. A good online source is www.apple.com/downloads/macosx/automator, or you can try other third-party Automator sites.
- Don't be afraid to use or build onto another person's existing workflow.
- Be sure to spread the good word about Automator. Share your own workflows with others, too.

You can run workflows in a variety of ways:

- From within Automator
- As applications from outside of Automator
- As plug-ins for other applications or processes

✔ Tips

- If desired you can schedule workflows to run at a specific time, such as in the middle of the night or while you're at lunch.
- You can add workflow applications as login items, allowing them to run automatically whenever you log into your machine.

About Actions

Most Automator actions are designed to perform a single specific task, such as writing text to a file, opening a URL, or copying files from one location to another. In some cases, a single action may do everything that you need. You also can link Automator actions sequentially, however, to form a larger, more complex, multipart, automated process, such as downloading songs from a website, importing them into iTunes, and syncing them with your iPod.

Determine the Actions to Use

Before building a workflow, you need to figure out what you want to automate. Look for things you do manually that take a lot of time or are repetitive. For example, renaming and resizing image files are both time-consuming and repetitive. Now look for actions that can do these things for you. To get started:

- Think of the tasks that you normally need to perform manually.
- Think of each step in your manual workflow as a single Automator action.

When you build your workflow in Automator, you'll assemble these actions together to form your complete workflow.

✔ Tips

- Try outlining your desired workflow. It's a good idea to step through the sequence of manual tasks, and outline each step as you go.
- Need to create a repeating workflow? Learn how to use Leopard's new Loop action in Chapter 10, "Workflow Looping."

Action Input and Output

In a workflow, an action can get information (input) from the previous action, and pass information (output) down to the next action. For example, you can build a workflow that retrieves photos from a folder, compresses them into an archive, and attaches the archive to a new email message. You would need four Automator actions for this:

1. **Ask for Finder Items (Figure 1.1).** Asks the user to choose a folder of photos. It then passes that folder down (output) to the next action (input) in the workflow.
2. **Get Folder Contents (Figure 1.2).** Gets a list of any files in the folder passed as input, and passes those files to the next action in the workflow.
3. **Create Archive (Figure 1.3).** Compresses the list of files passed from the previous action into a zip archive. The location of the created archive is then passed to the final action in the workflow.
4. **New Mail Message (Figure 1.4).** Tells Mail to create a new email message and attaches the archive passed from the previous action.

Actions can pass a variety of information between one another, such as file and folder paths, text, email messages, and so forth. The task an action performs determines the type of information it inputs or outputs.

✔ Tip

- Not all actions accept input or pass output; whether they do or not depends on their function.

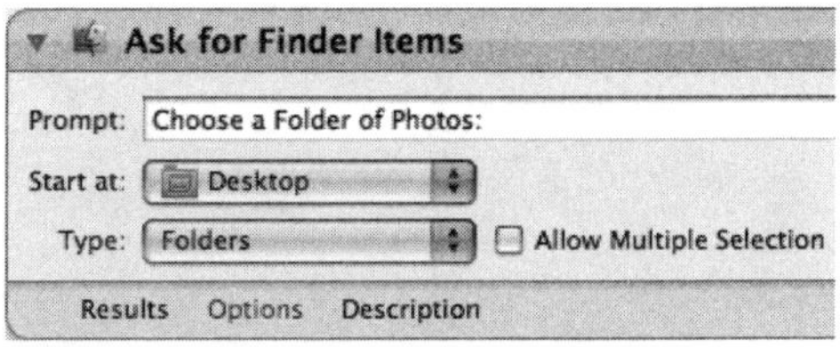

Figure 1.1 The Ask for Finder Items action asks the user to choose a folder of photos.

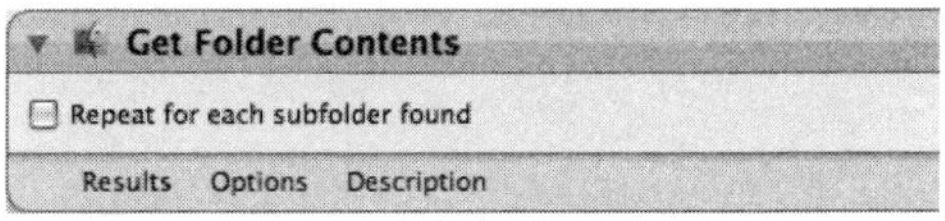

Figure 1.2 The Get Folder Contents action gets a list of any files in the folder that was passed from the previous action.

Figure 1.3 The Create Archive action builds a zip archive containing the files passed from the previous action.

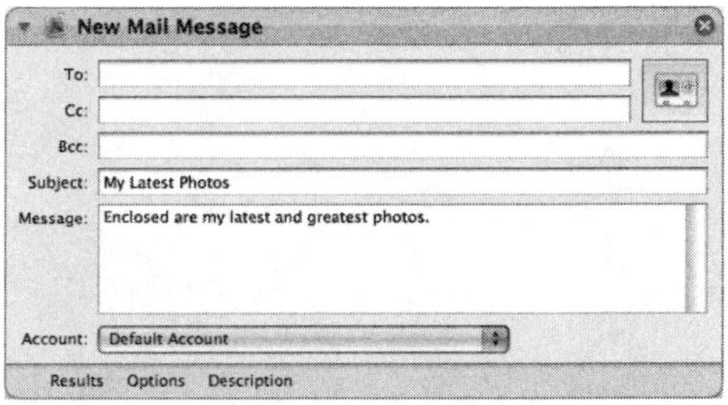

Figure 1.4 The New Mail Message action creates a new email and attaches the archive passed from the previous action.

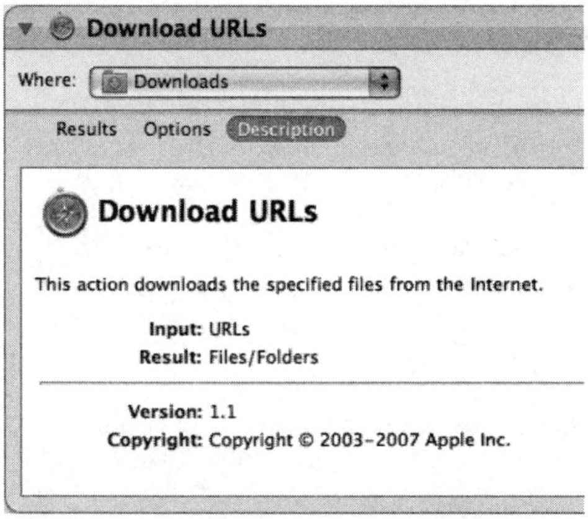

Figure 1.5 The Download URLs action accepts URLs as input, but passes files and folders as its result.

Some actions accept one kind of information as input, but output a different kind. For example, the Download URLs action, included with Automator, accepts a list of URLs from a previous action as its input (**Figure 1.5**). It then downloads the specified URLs and outputs the file paths of the downloaded files to the next action for further processing.

Many actions are designed to process information passed to them by the previous action. When adding actions to a workflow, therefore, take care that each action passes the right kind of information to the next one in a workflow. For example, an action that compresses files into a zip archive can accept only file paths as input from the previous action. Passing the wrong kind of information to an action produces an error, or the action simply ignores the information and does nothing. Chapter 4, "Working with Actions," provides more detail on adding actions into workflows.

✔ Tips

- Just passing through? Some actions don't generate output of their own. Instead, they pass their input down as output for further processing.
- Check an action's description area to see the kinds of input and output it uses.

Conversion Actions

Sometimes, you may need to put two actions together, whose output and input don't match. In these situations, Automator will try to convert the mismatched output from the first action to the right kind of input for the second.

To do this, Automator uses *conversion actions*. Conversion actions are built into Mac OS X, but aren't visible within Automator's interface. You don't need to worry about adding conversion actions into a workflow. Automator automatically does this in the background when the workflow runs.

Whenever Automator finds mismatched actions together, it looks for a conversion action that can change the output to the correct input type for the next action in the workflow. If it finds a conversion action, then the workflow runs successfully. Because conversion actions are not visible within Automator's interface, you probably won't even know that this process has happened. If Automator can't find a conversion action, it may return an error when the workflow runs, or the second action may ignore the output of the first action.

Figure 1.6 shows an example of mismatched output/input values. The Get Selected iTunes Items action retrieves a list of any selected items in iTunes and passes them to the Copy Finder Items action. The Copy Finder Items action accepts files and folders as its input, however, not iTunes items. When you run this workflow, Automator runs a conversion action behind the scenes to convert the iTunes items to Files/Folders, so that they can be processed without a problem.

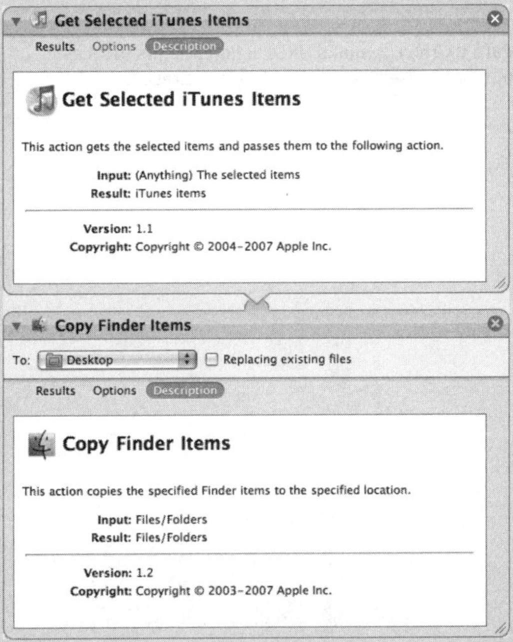

Figure 1.6 Mismatched action output/input. The result of the Get Selected iTunes Items action is iTunes items, but the input for the Copy Finder Items action is Files/Folders. This is handled behind the scenes by a conversion action.

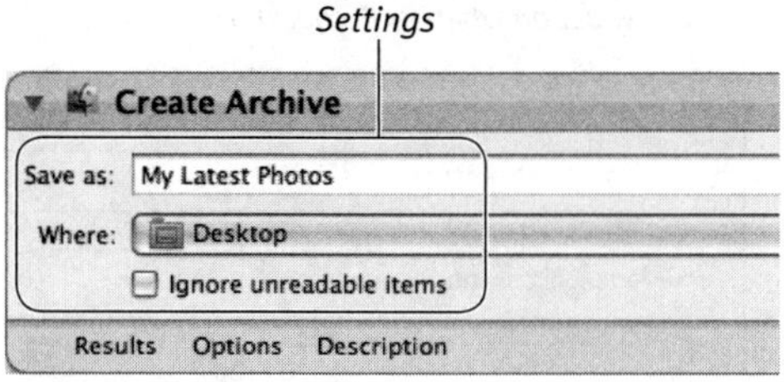

Figure 1.7 The Create Archive action has modifiable settings, including the name and save location for the archive.

Figure 1.8 The Update iPod action has no modifiable settings.

Action Settings

Actions don't always know exactly what you want them to do. Sometimes you may need to tell them how to behave by specifying certain details, such as where to save a file, what name to use, and so forth.

As Chapter 4 details, when you build a workflow, you often have the ability to specify settings for actions. These settings control how the action behaves when the workflow runs.

Remember the workflow that compresses photos into a zip archive and then attaches the archive to a new email message in Mail? Several of its actions have modifiable settings.

For example, the Create Archive action allows you to specify a name (*My Latest Photos*) and output folder (*Desktop*) for the archive, and whether any unreadable items should be ignored (**Figure 1.7**).

Some actions perform a single, very basic task and may not require settings to be specified at all. For example, Automator includes an iTunes action for updating a connected iPod (**Figure 1.8**). This action doesn't require any settings to be specified. It simply uses iTunes to update any connected iPod.

✔ Tip

- If you're unsure of what an action's setting does, check its description for more information, or see if it has any accompanying documentation.

Action Options

In some cases, you may not want to configure an action's settings when you build the workflow. Instead, you may want the action's settings to be specified when the workflow runs.

To allow for this, many actions can be configured to display their settings when the workflow runs. For example, you may decide that you want to change the name of the zip archive now and then in the photo compression workflow. To do this, you can configure the Create Archive action to display when the workflow runs (**Figures 1.9** and **1.10**).

✔ Tips

- Allow for customization. Others may want or need a workflow to run differently than you do. If you plan to share your workflow with others, consider configuring some actions in the workflow to display when run.
- Some actions can be configured to show only specified settings, rather than all settings, allowing you to pick and choose which settings will be modifiable when the workflow runs (**Figures 1.11** and **1.12**).

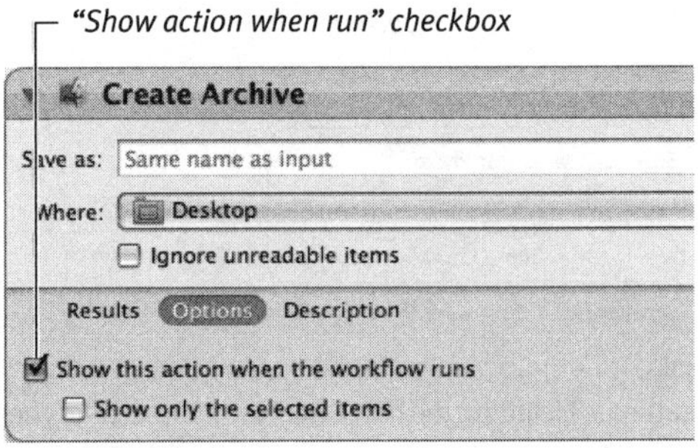

Figure 1.9 Configuring the Create Archive action to display when run.

Figure 1.10 The Create Archive action, as it appears when run.

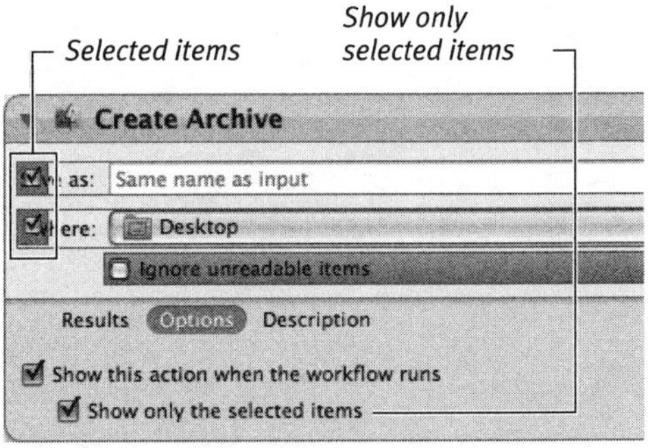

Figure 1.11 Configuring the Create Archive action to display only selected settings when run.

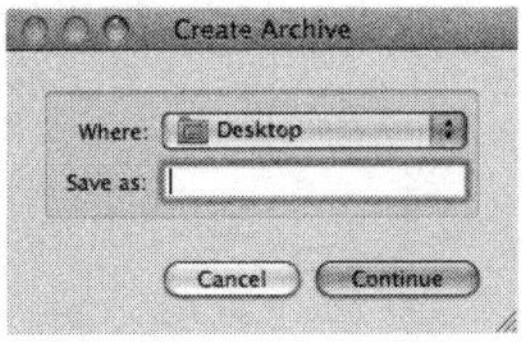

Figure 1.12 The Create Archive action, displaying only selected settings when run.

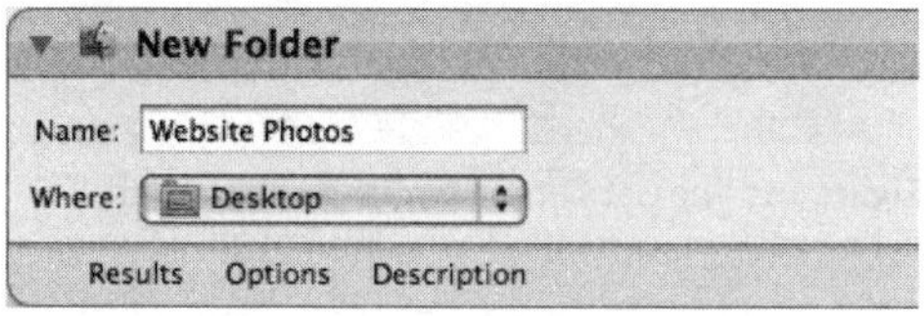

Figure 1.13 The New Folder action builds a folder named *Website Photos* on the desktop.

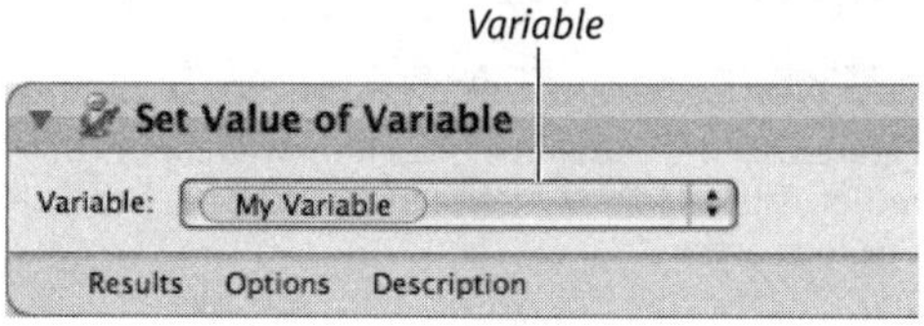

Figure 1.14 The Set Value of Variable action stores the Website Photos folder, created by the previous action, for reference later in the workflow.

About Variables

An action in a workflow can receive information from the previous action, and it can pass information down to the next action. But, what about two actions that don't appear together in a workflow? Can they still share information with one another? In Leopard, the answer is yes! Automator in Leopard includes a powerful feature called *variables* that can help you create much more robust workflows. Variables allow you to store information, such as File/Folder references or text, in memory at a certain point in a workflow, and refer back to it at a later time.

For example, suppose you want to build a workflow that creates a folder on the desktop, gets the current webpage in Safari, retrieves image URLs from that page, and then downloads those URLs into the newly created folder. In this workflow, the first action would create the folder, and the last action would download URLs into that folder. Several other actions fall between these two, however, so how will the last action know about the folder created by the first? The solution is to use a variable to store the folder when the first action creates it. The last action can then reference this variable when it needs to access the folder. The final workflow consists of these five actions:

1. **New Folder (Figure 1.13).** This action creates a folder named *Website Photos* on the desktop, if one does not already exist. It passes a reference to the newly created folder to the next action in the workflow.
2. **Set Value of Variable (Figure 1.14).** This action accepts the reference to the folder from the previous action, and stores it in a variable named *My Variable* for future reference. (Chapter 11, "Using Variables," will cover naming variables.)

continues on next page

3. **Get Current Webpage from Safari (Figure 1.15).** This action ignores the results of the previous action, gets the current webpage from Safari, and passes it down to the next action in the workflow.

4. **Get Image URLs from Webpage (Figure 1.16).** This action locates any image URLs on the webpage passed from the previous action and outputs these URLs to the next action in the workflow.

5. **Download URLs (Figure 1.17).** This action downloads the image URLs passed from the previous action. The problem is that this action received only the image URLs as input. It doesn't know about the folder that was created at the start of the workflow. To work around this issue, you can refer back to the variable *My Variable*.

Preexisting Variables

You can also retrieve values from a number of built-in, preexisting variables that handle dates, times, locations, system information, user information, and more. For example, you might want the name of that new photos folder to include the current date. You could add it by referencing Automator's built-in Today's Date variable in the New Folder action's Name field (**Figures 1.18** and **1.19**). Chapter 11 explores preexisting variables, as well as how to add variables into actions and workflows.

✔ Tip

- If variables seem confusing, don't feel like you need to start using them right away. Get comfortable creating workflows first, and then move on to variables.

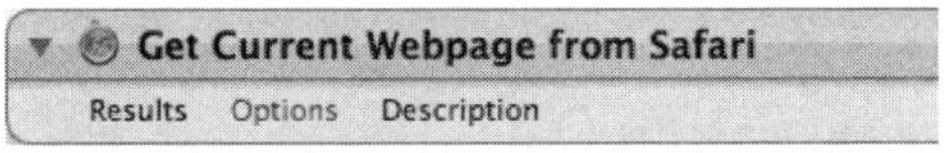

Figure 1.15 The Get Current Webpage from Safari action gets the currently opened webpage in Safari.

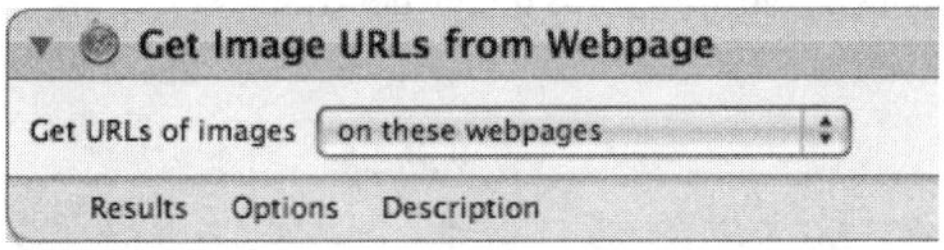

Figure 1.16 The Get Image URLs from Webpage action retrieves URLs to any images in the webpage from the previous action.

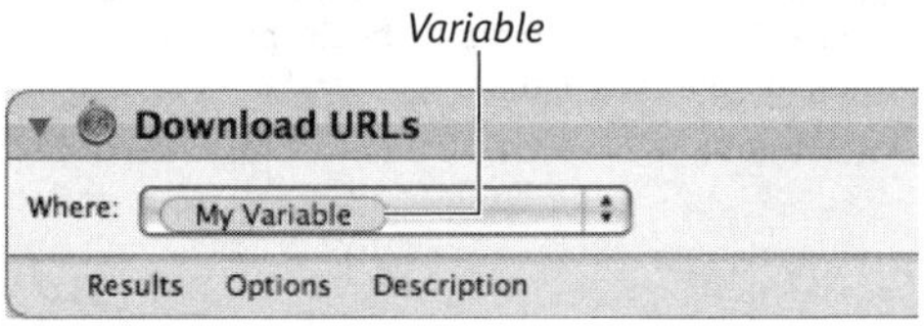

Figure 1.17 The Download URLs action downloads the image URLs from the previous action into the stored Website Photos folder.

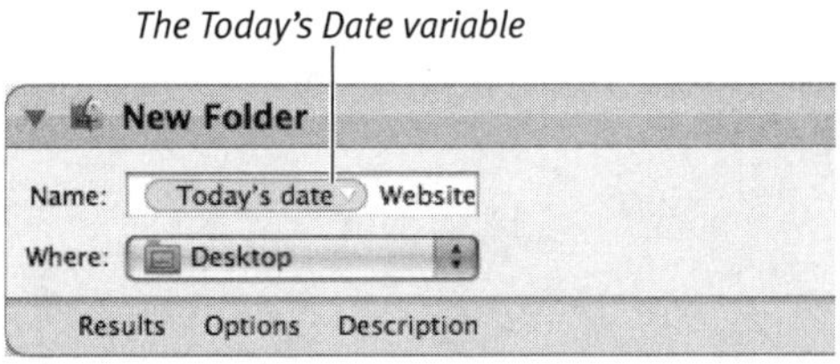

Figure 1.18 The current date variable, to be added to the name of a new folder.

Figure 1.19 A new folder, named with the current date.

Which Applications Work with Automator?

To control an application with Automator, you must have actions for that application installed. Many times, these actions are built right into the application, but sometimes you must install them separately. To get you started, Mac OS X includes hundreds of actions that cover most of the core Apple applications, including Address Book, the Finder, iTunes, Mail, and Safari, as well as application-independent activities, such as manipulating images, setting the audio volume on your system, or taking a screen shot.

As you install other Apple software, you may also begin to see more actions appearing in Automator. For example, iLife automatically adds actions for iPhoto and iDVD.

✔ Tip

- Automator actions are installed with a number of other Apple applications, including Aperture, Keynote, Apple Remote Desktop, and Soundtrack Pro.

Some non-Apple applications also now have built-in actions that automatically appear in Automator when you install the application. In addition, loads of third-party developers are releasing Automator actions for a variety of applications and processes.

BBEdit was the first commercial application with built-in Automator actions, and the list is growing. Third-party applications with built-in Automator actions now include Fetch, GraphicConverter, Microsoft Office 2008, NetNewsWire, Stuffit Deluxe, and Transmit.

Some third-party applications are bundled with Automator actions that need to be installed separately.

Third-party developers have also released Automator actions for applications including Adobe InDesign, Adobe Photoshop, FileMaker Pro, iView MediaPro, and QuarkXPress.

✔ Tips

- For a comprehensive, up-to-date list of third-party Automator actions, visit Apple's Mac OS X download website at www.apple.com/downloads/macosx, or check out www.automatoractions.com.
- Having trouble finding actions for an application? Consider contacting the application developer. Make it known that you want Automator actions for the application and provide some ideas of what you want to do with those actions.
- You may still be able to control an application with Automator even if it doesn't have actions of its own. As you'll learn in Chapter 5, Automator in Leopard now supports recording your manual tasks in lots of Mac OS X applications.
- Are you an AppleScripter? If so, then you can create your own Automator actions for any AppleScriptable application using Xcode. Appendix C will give you the details.

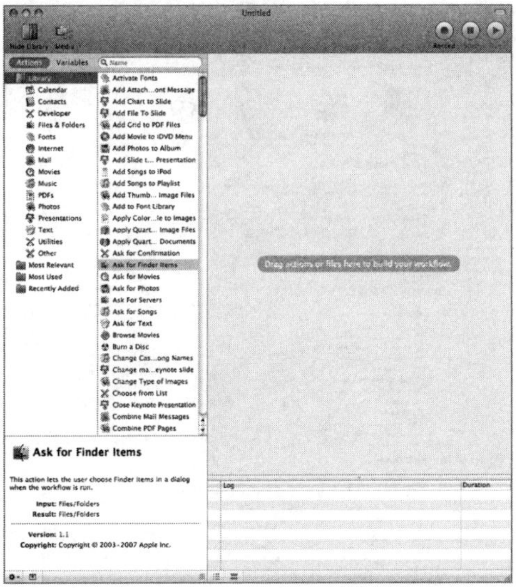

Figure 1.20 Automator's interface may seem complex at first, but you'll soon find that it's fairly straightforward.

Getting to Know Automator's Interface

So far, we've explored some of the key concepts of Automator, including actions, workflows, and variables. Now, it's time to begin exploring Automator in a bit more detail, to see how things all come together. Automator's interface may seem complex at first glance (**Figure 1.20**). Once you get to know it, however, you'll find it fairly simple and straightforward to navigate. Here's a look at Automator's primary parts.

✔ Tips

- Don't expect to catch on to Automator's interface instantly. To learn your way around, build a few basic workflows. Things will start to fall into place and make sense with time.
- You can customize many aspects of Automator's interface, hiding some areas, resizing others, and so forth. Chapter 8, "Customizing Automator," explores this further.

Understanding Starting Points

When you first launch Automator, a new workflow window opens with a Starting Points panel attached. New to Automator in Leopard, the Starting Points panel (**Figure 1.21**) enables you to quickly and easily begin building workflows, making it an excellent way to get started using Automator. Simply choose from a set of common workflow types listed in the panel, and Automator opens a workflow template that's prefilled with one or more actions to get you going.

✔ Tip

- Unfortunately, Starting Points doesn't exist for Automator in Tiger. If you're a Tiger user, you'll have to create all of your workflows from scratch.

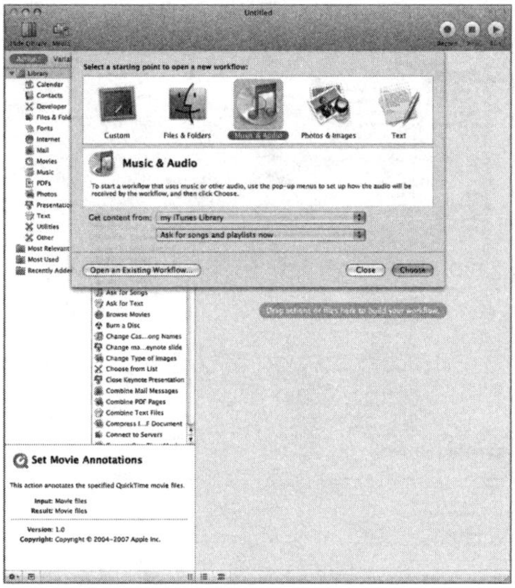

Figure 1.21 The Starting Points panel, attached to a workflow window.

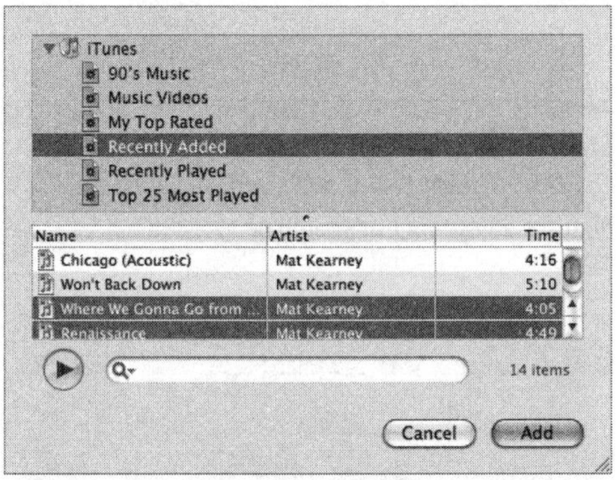

Figure 1.22 Choosing songs to be processed by a music workflow.

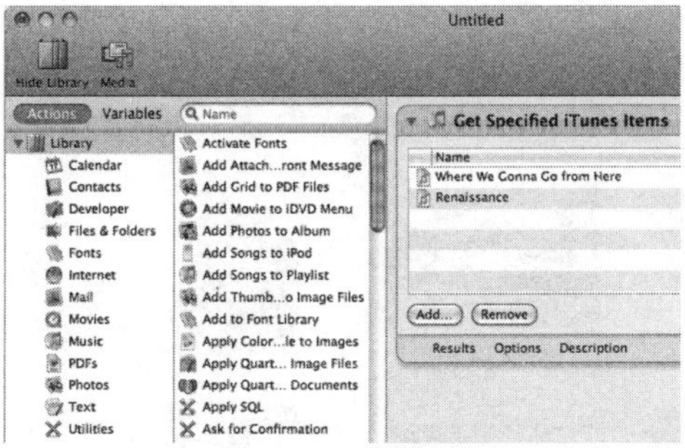

Figure 1.23 The beginning of a music workflow, prefilled with the Get Specified iTunes Items action, as created by Starting Points.

You can use Starting Points to begin creating the following types of workflows:

- **Custom.** Doesn't contain any prefilled actions. It's an empty workflow; you build all of it yourself.
- **Files & Folders.** Contains prefilled actions to locate files and folders on your Mac. You build onto this by adding actions to process the files and folders, such as compressing them into a zip archive.
- **Music & Audio.** Contains prefilled actions to retrieve music and audio content from your Mac, your iTunes library, or the Internet. You build onto this by adding actions to use the music and audio content, such as playing it or syncing it with your iPod.
- **Photos & Images.** Contains prefilled actions to get photos and images from your Mac, your iPhoto library, your computer's camera, or the Internet. You build onto it by adding actions to work with those photos and images, such as resizing, cropping, or emailing them.
- **Text.** Contains prefilled actions to get text content from the user or from TextEdit. You build onto it by adding actions to use that text content, such as inserting it into an email or converting it to spoken audio.

Once you choose the type of workflow that you want to create, Automator asks what you want to process (**Figure 1.22**), and then automatically creates the first part of the workflow for you (**Figure 1.23**). Chapter 3, "Workflow Creation Basics," will walk you through all of the types of workflows that you can create using Starting Points, as well as discuss how you can enable and disable Starting Points.

Understanding Automator's Toolbar

The toolbar at the top of an Automator workflow window gives you quick access to common functions (**Figure 1.24**). Just click a button to begin recording manual tasks, run a workflow, or open Automator's Media Browser to access your music, photos, and movies. As you'll learn in Chapter 8, the buttons in the toolbar can be customized, as well.

✔ Tip

- Can't find an action to do what you need? Click the Record button in Automator's toolbar to begin recording manual tasks within an application, such as selecting menus, clicking buttons, and typing text. You can then play those tasks back as part of your workflow.

Understanding Automator's Media Browser

Often, you may want to create a workflow that processes music, photos, or movies. Automator's Media Browser enables you to preview and navigate these items visually. To process an item, simply drag it from the Media Browser into a workflow (**Figure 1.25**).

Figure 1.24 Automator's toolbar.

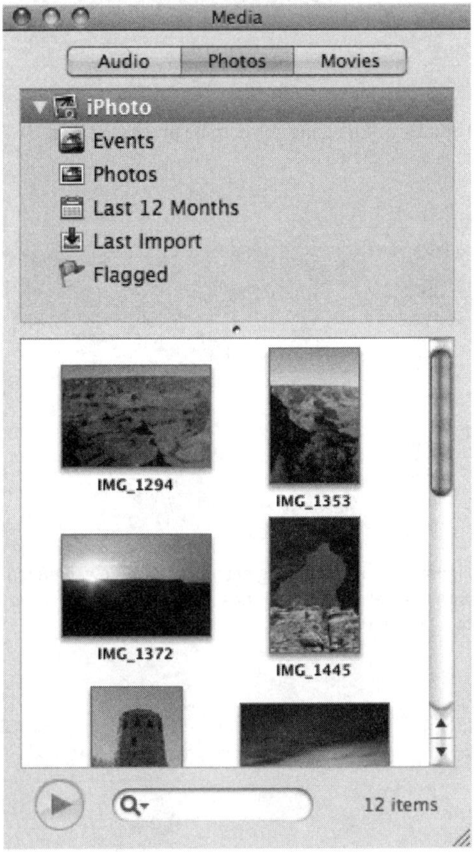

Figure 1.25 Automator's Media Browser window.

Figure 1.26 Clicking the Media button in the workflow window's toolbar displays the Media Browser.

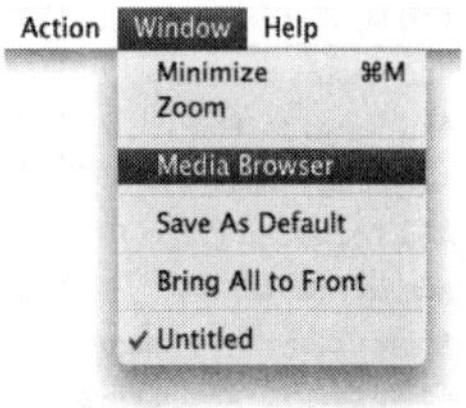

Figure 1.27 Choosing to display Automator's Media Browser window.

Figure 1.28 The Library of actions and variables in an Automator workflow window.

To display Automator's Media Browser:

Click the Media button in the workflow window's toolbar (**Figure 1.26**).

or

Choose Window > Media Browser (**Figure 1.27**).

The Media Browser is displayed.

Understanding the Actions and Variables Library

The left side of the workflow window contains a library of available actions and variables (**Figure 1.28**). The Library is split into two columns:

- **Categories/Applications.** This column lists the categories or applications of actions or variables.
- **Actions/Variables.** This column lists the actions or variables within the selected category or application.

You select actions and variables within the Library list and drag them into a workflow area to form an Automator workflow. As you install more Automator-ready applications, the list of available actions may grow.

To view a list of available actions:

Click the Actions button at the top of the Library area to display a list of action categories in the Library's left column (**Figure 1.29**).

By default, Automator's actions are arranged in categories such as:

- **Calendar.** Actions for performing calendar-related tasks in such applications as iCal.
- **Files & Folders.** Actions for copying, moving, compressing, and otherwise manipulating files and folders.
- **Internet.** Actions for downloading and opening URLs in Safari, as well as other Internet-related operations.
- **Mail.** Actions for creating emails, opening emails, and more.
- **Movies.** Actions for working with movies in DVD Player, QuickTime, and similar applications.
- **Music.** Actions for importing audio files into iTunes, syncing your iPod, and more.
- **Photos.** Actions for resizing or cropping images, importing images into iPhoto, and more.

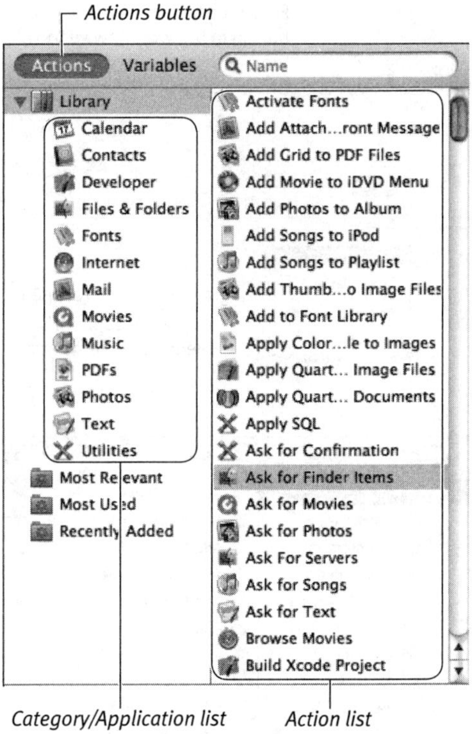

Figure 1.29 The Library list of actions, arranged by category.

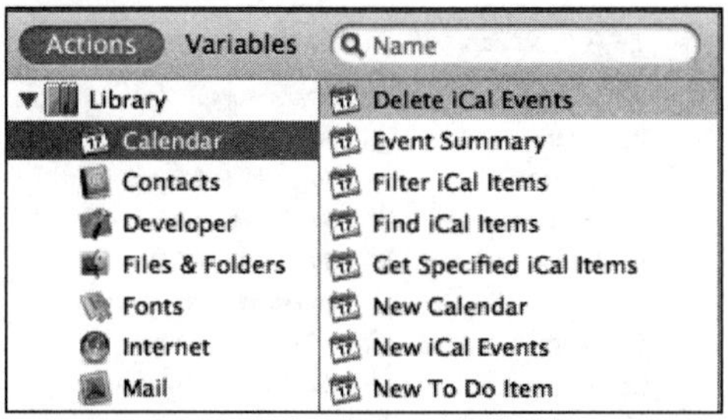

Figure 1.30 Viewing the Calendar category of actions.

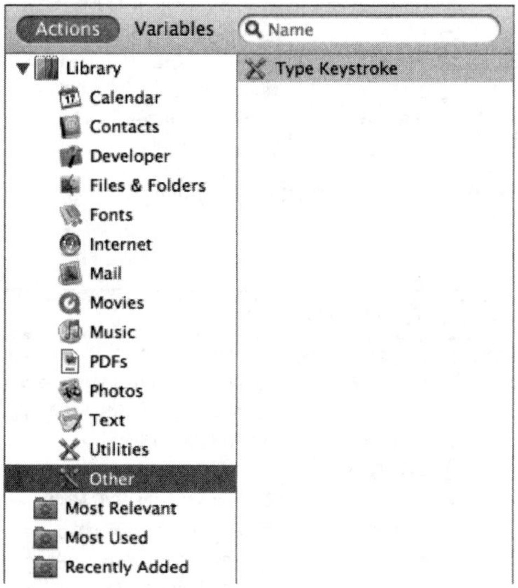

Figure 1.31 The Other category of actions, displaying a third-party action that doesn't fit into a built-in category.

To view the actions within a category:

Click the category name in the left column of the Library list to display the actions within that category in the right column (**Figure 1.30**).

✔ Tip

- If you have actions installed that don't fall into one of Automator's built-in categories, look for them in the Other category, which appears at the bottom of the Library list (**Figure 1.31**). If you don't see this category, then all of your installed actions fit into Automator's built-in categories.

To view all actions:

Click the Library item at the top of the left column of the Library list to display a list of actions for all categories (**Figure 1.32**).

In Tiger, actions were arranged by application only. If you would feel more comfortable with this familiar view, you can arrange the action list by application rather than by category (**Figure 1.33**).

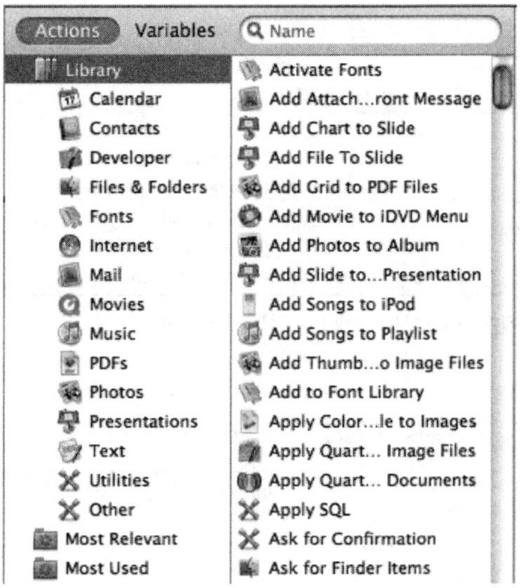

Figure 1.32 Viewing a list of all installed actions.

Figure 1.33 The Library list of actions, arranged by application.

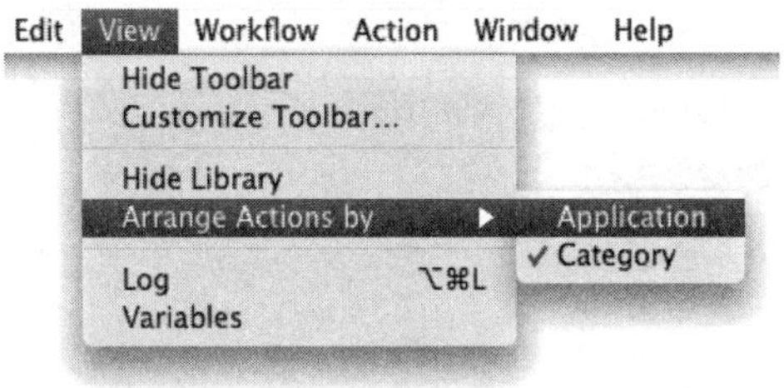

Figure 1.34 Arranging actions by application, rather than by category.

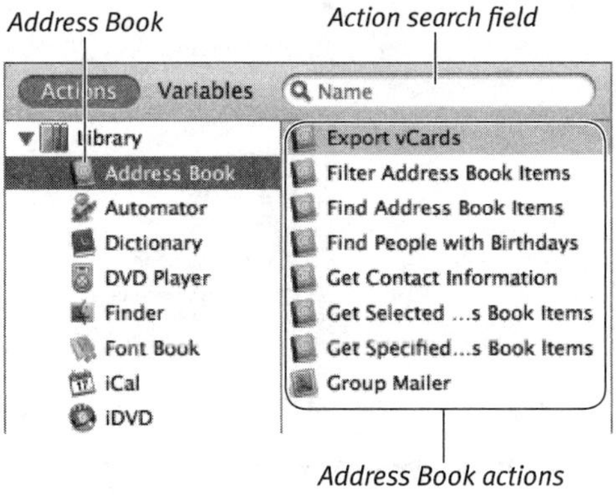

Figure 1.35 Viewing actions by application.

To arrange actions by application:

Choose View > Arrange Actions by > Application (**Figure 1.34**).

✔ Tips

- Automator remembers your view choices. If you configure Automator to arrange actions by application, then actions will still be arranged that way the next time Automator launches.
- When you view actions by application, some actions remain listed in categories, such as PDF and System. These categories are used to organize actions that aren't tied to a specific application.
- Some actions may be listed in multiple applications or categories.

To view the actions associated with an application:

Click the application name in the Library list to display a list of actions for that application (**Figure 1.35**).

Just as you can choose how the Library list displays actions, you can instruct it to display a list of Automator's predefined variables.

✔ Tips

- Need to quickly locate an action? Type its name or a related keyword into the Search field at the top of the Library area (Figure 1.35).
- As you'll learn in Chapter 8, you can create your own custom groupings of commonly used actions in Automator's Library list.

To view a list of available variables:

Click the Variables button at the top of the Library area to display a list of variables and their categories (**Figure 1.36**).

Variables in the Library list are arranged into several categories:

- **Date & Time.** Variables relating to dates and times, such as the current date.
- **Locations.** Variables for various locations on your Mac, such as your Movies or Photos folder.
- **System.** Variables for such system information as your IP address or operating system version.
- **Text & Data.** Variables for storing text content and other kinds of data.

To view the variables within a category:

Click the category name in the Library list (**Figure 1.37**).

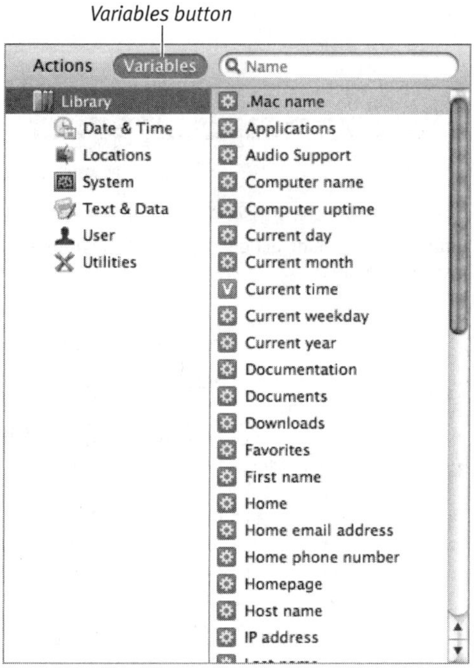

Figure 1.36 Viewing variables.

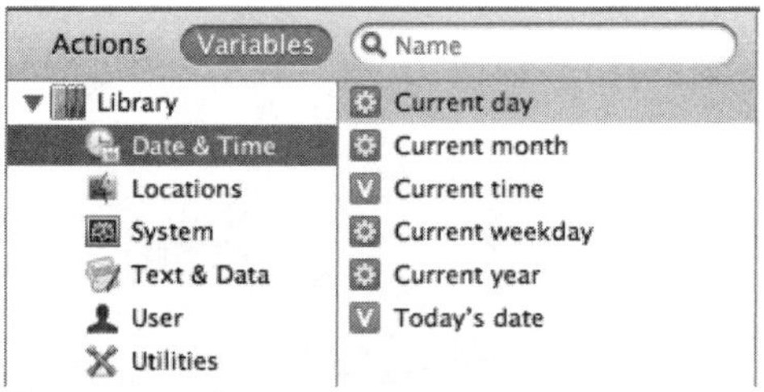

Figure 1.37 Viewing a category of variables.

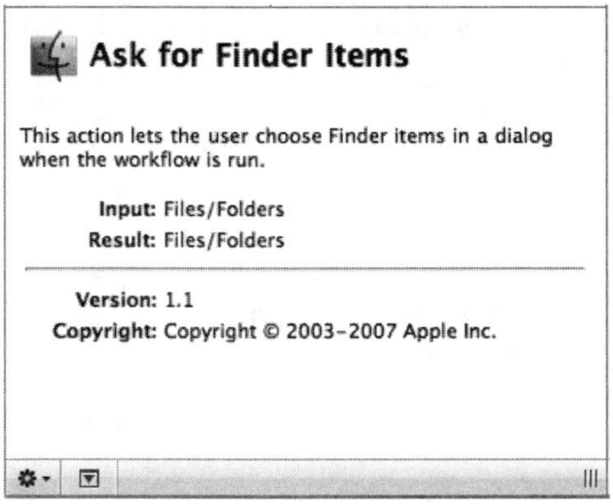
Ask for Finder Items
This action lets the user choose Finder items in a dialog when the workflow is run.
Input: Files/Folders
Result: Files/Folders
Version: 1.1
Copyright: Copyright © 2003–2007 Apple Inc.

Figure 1.38 The description of the Ask for Finder Items action.

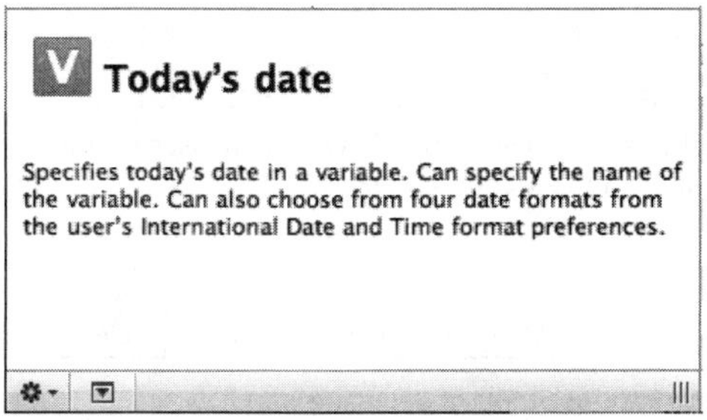
Today's date
Specifies today's date in a variable. Can specify the name of the variable. Can also choose from four date formats from the user's International Date and Time format preferences.

Figure 1.39 The description for the Today's Date variable.

Viewing the Action and Variable Description Area

When you select an action or variable in the Library, Automator displays its description in the bottom-left corner of the workflow window (**Figures 1.38** and **1.39**).

Action descriptions vary in length and content. Some are highly descriptive, but others may contain little information or be extremely confusing.

Action descriptions may include:

- An overview of the action's functionality
- A list of input and output types for the action
- A list of other related actions
- A link to the developer's website
- Alerts
- Copyright notices
- Notes
- Options
- Requirements

✔ Tip

- If you don't know what an action does, consult its description for more information.

Understanding the Workflow Area

We've made it! The main part of an Automator workflow window is the workflow area (**Figure 1.40**). This is where you'll spend most of your time. To create a workflow, simply drag one or more actions from the Library list into the workflow area. A detailed view of the added action appears, giving you access to the action's settings and options. Within the workflow area, actions can be configured, rearranged, disabled, and more.

Viewing the Workflow Status Area

When you run a workflow within Automator, the bottom of the workflow window provides brief status messages that tell you which action in the workflow is currently running (**Figure 1.41**). When a workflow finishes, the status area tells you if it was successful (**Figure 1.42**) or if a problem occurred (**Figure 1.43**).

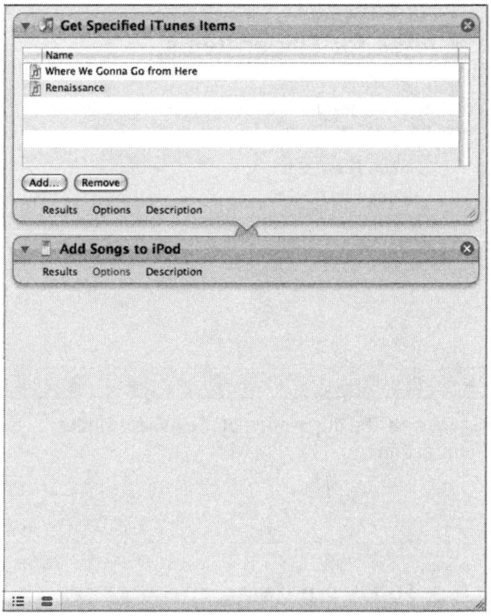

Figure 1.40 Actions, which have been inserted into Automator's workflow area.

Figure 1.41 Status of a running workflow.

Figure 1.42 Status of a successfully completed workflow.

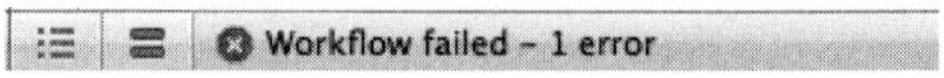

Figure 1.43 Status of a problematic workflow.

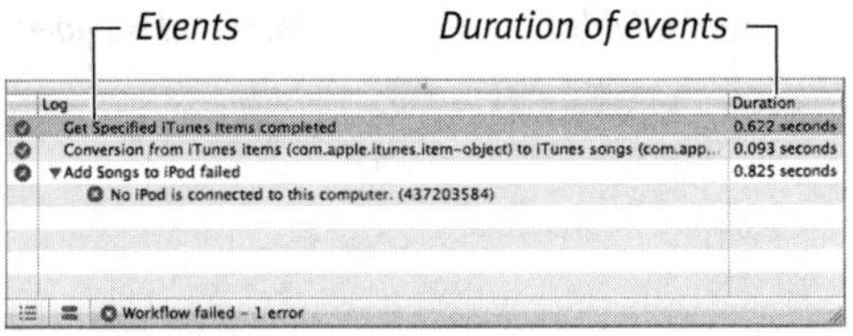

Figure 1.44 Automator's log area.

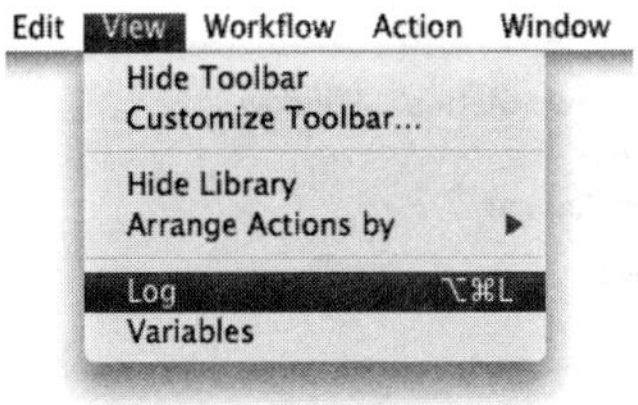

Figure 1.45 Choose Log to display Automator's log area.

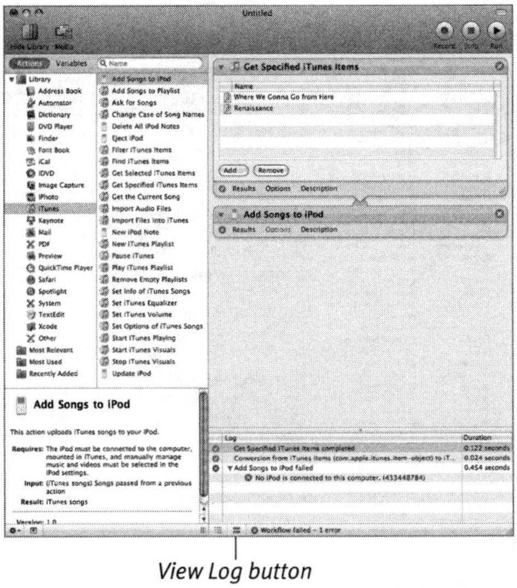

Figure 1.46 Automator's log area, at the bottom of a workflow window.

Viewing the Workflow Log Area

The status area in Automator is great for quick updates. If you want a more detailed account of your workflow's status, however, you can consult Automator's log area. The log, which resides at the bottom of the workflow area, indicates which actions ran, whether they ran successfully, whether any conversion actions ran, and more. It also provides detailed information about any errors that may have occurred (**Figure 1.44**).

To view the workflow log area:

Choose View > Log (**Figure 1.45**).

or

Click the button at the bottom of the workflow area (**Figure 1.46**).

or

Press Option ⌘ L.

The workflow log is displayed at the bottom of the workflow area.

✔ Tip

- The workflow log can be a very valuable troubleshooting tool. Be sure to check it often!

Viewing the Workflow Variables Area

If your workflow uses variables, the bottom of your workflow area can display a list of those variables as well. Here, you can configure your variables or drag them into various places within the workflow. When the workflow runs, the workflow variable area indicates the values of any variables used (**Figure 1.47**).

To view the workflow variables area:

Choose View > Variables (**Figure 1.48**).

or

Click the [button] button at the bottom of the workflow area (**Figure 1.49**).

A workflow variables list is displayed at the bottom of the workflow area.

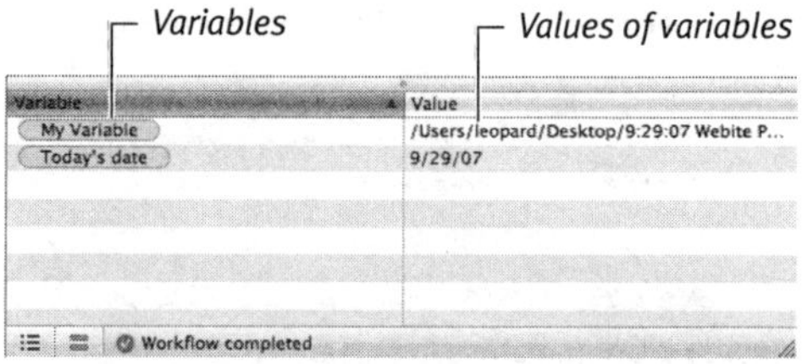

Figure 1.47 Automator's workflow variables area.

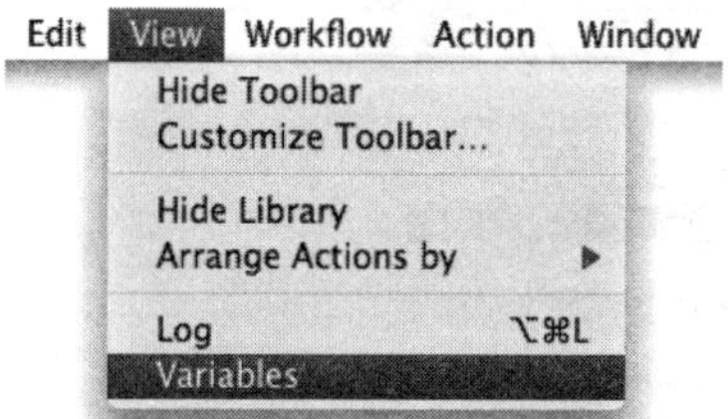

Figure 1.48 Choose Variables to display Automator's workflow variables area.

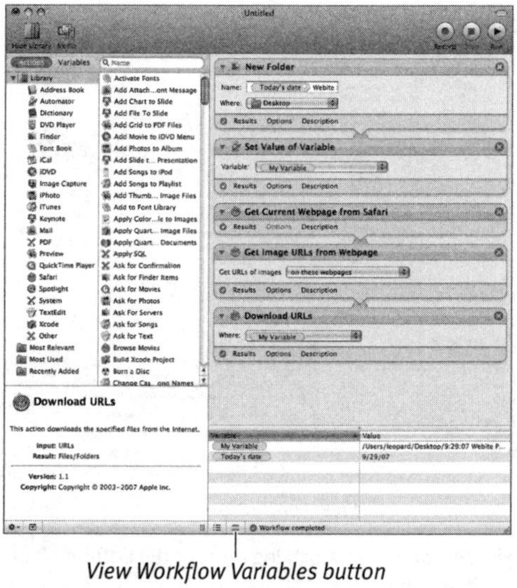

Figure 1.49 Automator's workflow variables area, at the bottom of a workflow window.

2

Building Simple Workflows

The best way to learn to use Automator is to dive in and build a practical workflow that accomplishes something you do repeatedly. Not only will such a project familiarize you with Automator's interface, it will show you how much of a difference the application can make in your unique workflow.

To help you get started, this chapter walks you through creating several simple workflows:

- **Email Daily Birthday Greetings.** Creates birthday greeting emails for anyone in your Address Book whose birthday is the current day.
- **Add Spotlight Comments to Photos.** Adds Spotlight comments to your digital photos, making them easier to search.
- **Email Photo Thumbnails.** Creates thumbnail versions of iPhoto images, and inserts them into a new email message.

For each of these, step-by-step instructions demonstrate how to locate the necessary actions, configure them, and bring them together to form a completed workflow.

Email Daily Birthday Greetings

If you're like me, then you're probably guilty of frequently forgetting people's birthdays. Have no fear, Automator can help! With only two actions, you can create a simple workflow that sends birthday greetings automatically.

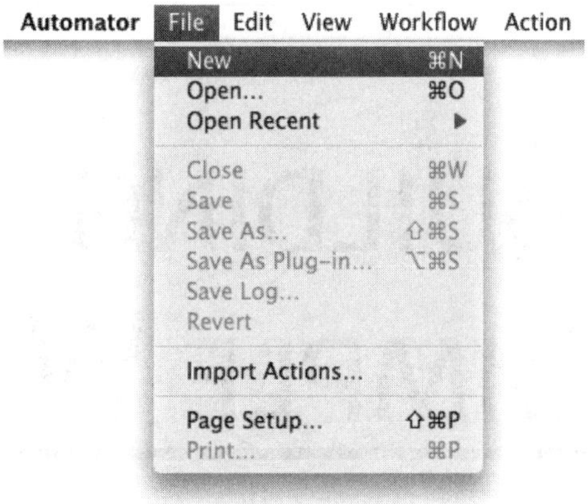

Figure 2.1 Creating a new workflow.

Actions used:

- Find People with Birthdays
- Send Birthday Greetings

To build the workflow:

1. Choose File > New (**Figure 2.1**).

   or

   Press ⌘N.

   A new workflow window and Starting Points panel appear (**Figure 2.2**).

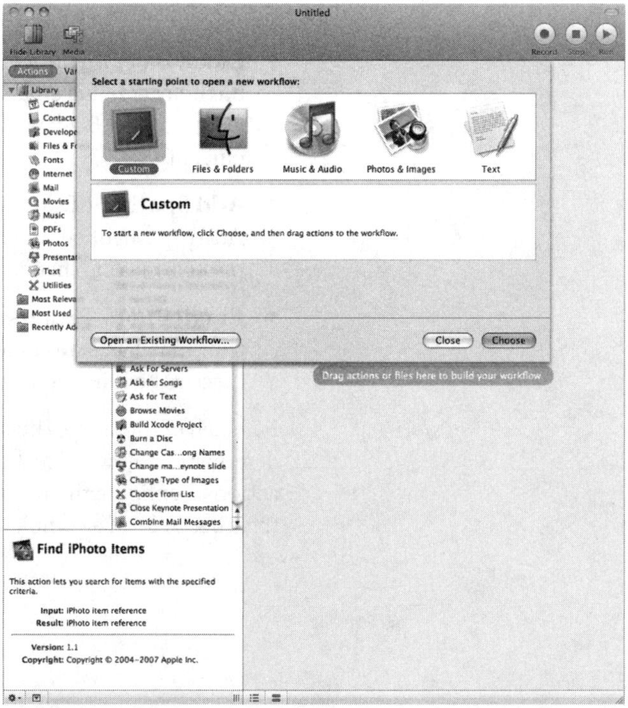

Figure 2.2 A new workflow window with the Starting Points panel.

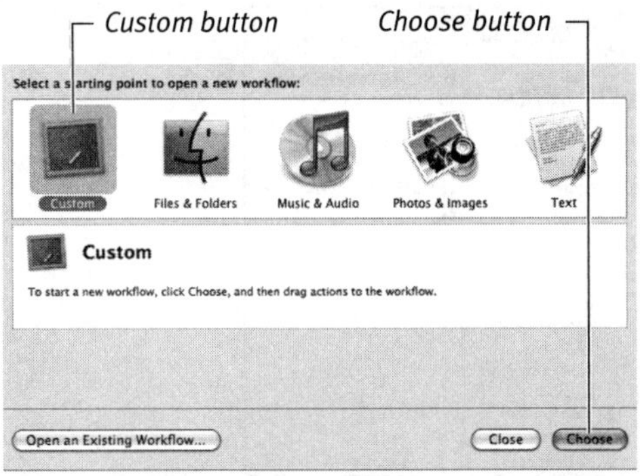

Figure 2.3 Choosing the Custom option in Starting Points to create a custom workflow.

2. To create a custom workflow, click the Custom button in the Starting Points panel (**Figure 2.3**).
3. Click the Choose button in the Starting Points panel to create an empty workflow window (**Figure 2.4**).

Now, you're ready to begin adding actions to the workflow.

✔ Tips

- If you notice an action in a screenshot from this book, but don't see it on your own machine, don't worry. My machine has more than the default set of applications and actions installed.
- The example workflows in this chapter feature actions arranged by category. If your actions are arranged by application, choose View > Arrange Applications By > Category (**Figure 2.5**) to match the examples.

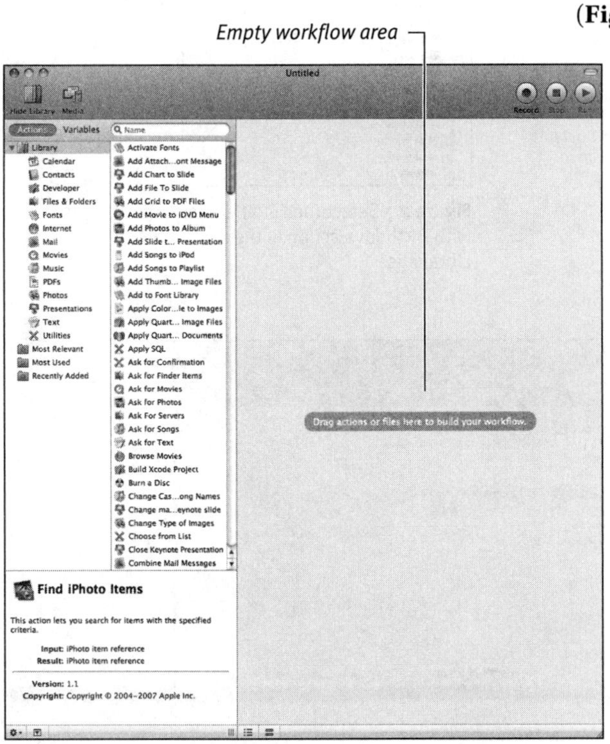

Figure 2.4 A new custom workflow window, as created by Starting Points.

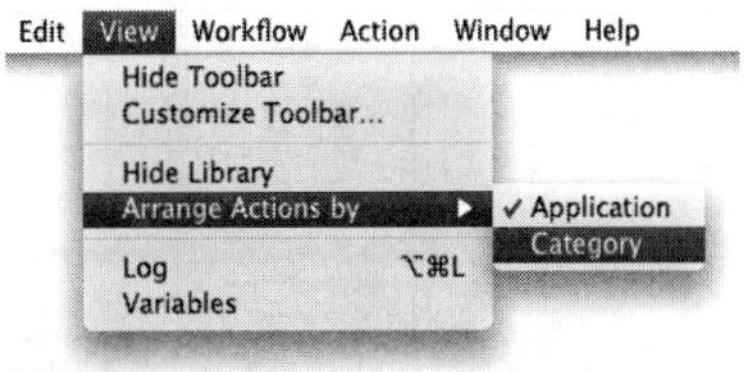

Figure 2.5 Setting Automator to arrange actions by category.

To add the Find People with Birthdays action:

1. Click the Contacts category in the left column of the Library list (**Figure 2.6**).

   Automator lists that category's actions in the right column.

2. Click the Find People with Birthdays action in the right column of the Library list (**Figure 2.7**).

3. Drag the Find People with Birthdays action from the Library list into the workflow area (**Figure 2.8**).

   Automator displays an interface for the action within the workflow area (**Figures 2.9** and **2.10**).

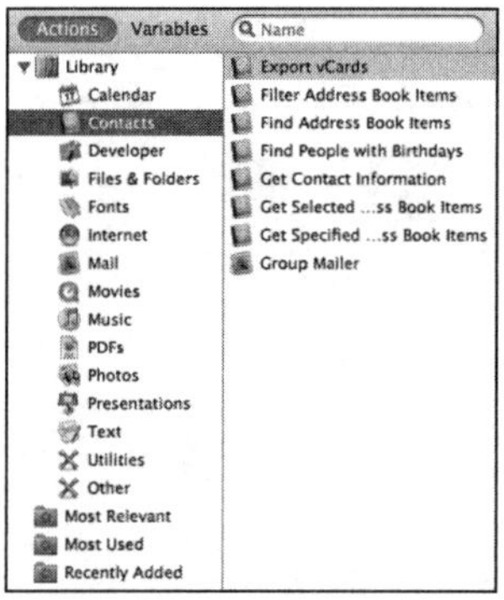

Figure 2.6 Select the Contacts category in the Library list.

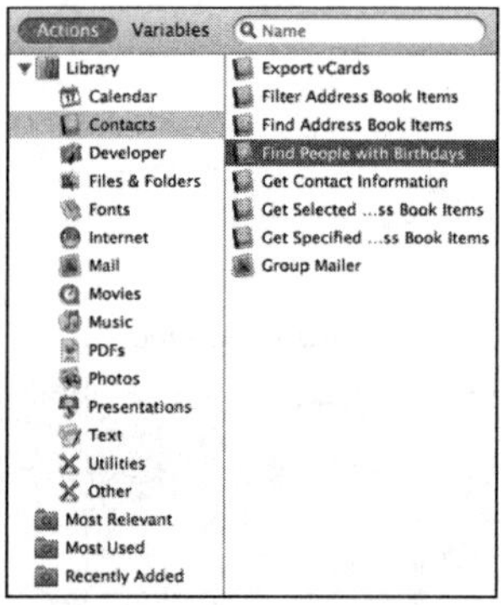

Figure 2.7 Select the Find People with Birthdays action in the Library list.

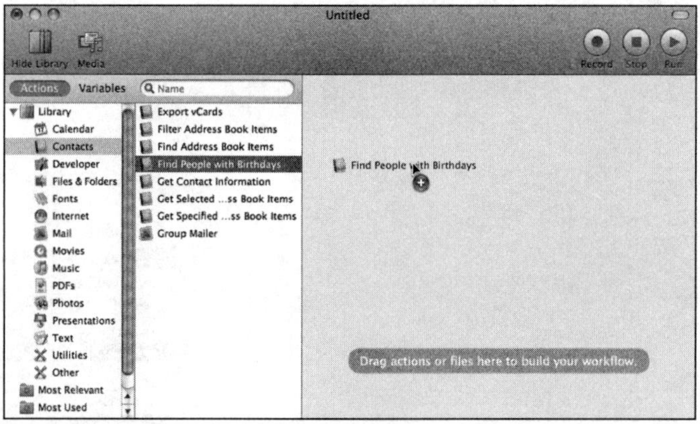

Figure 2.8 Dragging the Find People with Birthdays action into the workflow area.

4. Choose Today from the pop-up menu on the action's interface (**Figure 2.11**) to limit the action's results to birthdays for the current day only.

✔ Tips

- Actions are listed in alphabetical order in the right column of the Library list.
- You can quickly navigate to an action by entering the first few characters of its name in the search field at the top of the Library list.

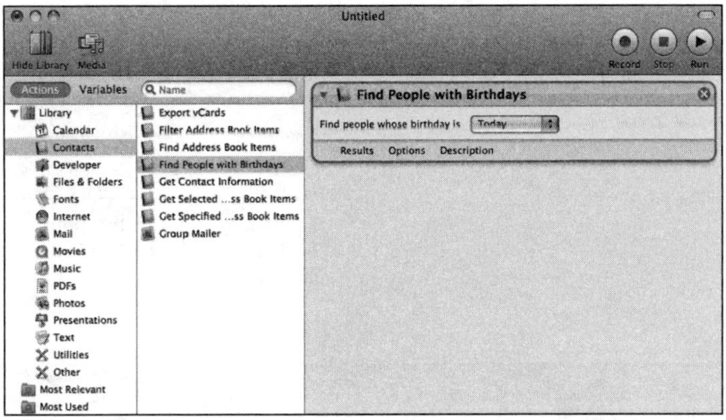

Figure 2.9 When added to the workflow area, the Find People with Birthdays action's interface is displayed.

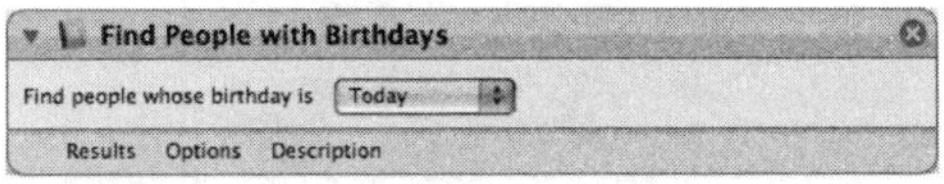

Figure 2.10 The Find People with Birthdays action's interface.

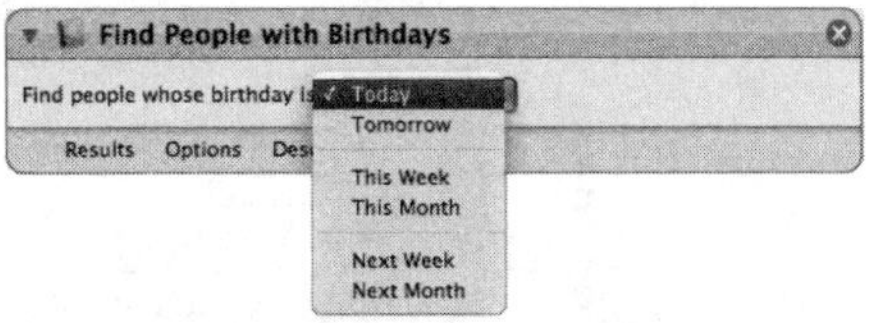

Figure 2.11 Configuring the Find People with Birthdays action to locate people with a birthday on the current day.

To add the Send Birthday Greetings action:

1. Click the Mail category in the left column of the Library list (**Figure 2.12**).

   In the right column, Automator lists the actions in the Mail category.

2. Click to select the Send Birthday Greetings action in the right column of the Library list (**Figure 2.13**).

3. Drag the Send Birthday Greetings action from the Library list into the workflow area and drop it below Find People with Birthdays.

   Automator displays an interface for the action within the workflow area (**Figures 2.14** and **2.15**).

Figure 2.12 Selecting the Mail category in the Library list.

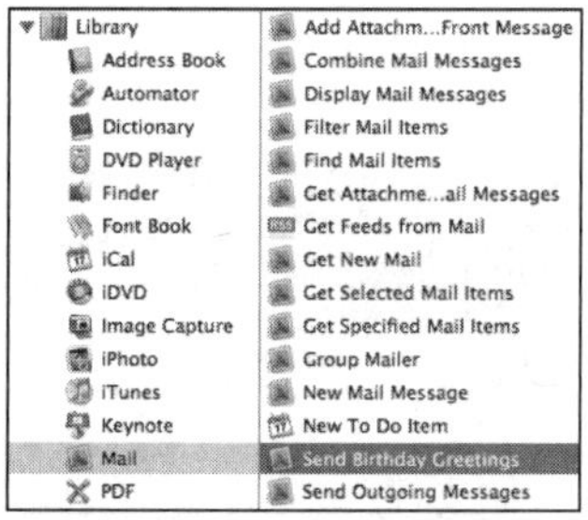

Figure 2.13 Selecting the Send Birthday Greetings action in the Library list.

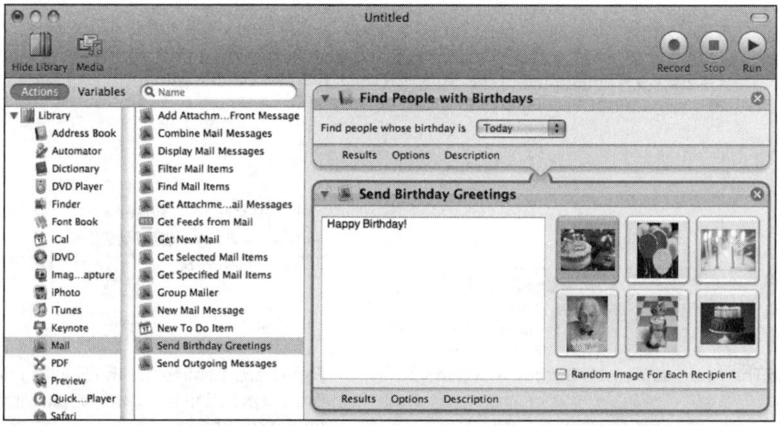

Figure 2.14 The Send Birthday Greetings action, once added into the workflow area.

Figure 2.15 The Send Birthday Greetings action's interface.

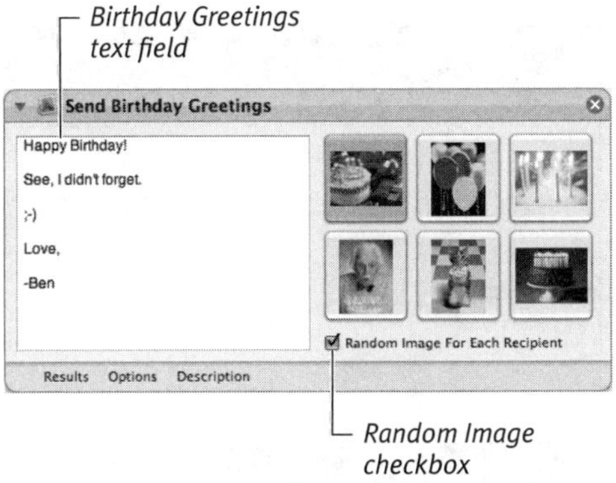

Figure 2.16 The Send Birthday Greetings action's interface with its settings configured.

4. Type a birthday greeting into the text field in the action's interface (**Figure 2.16**).

5. Click the Random Image For Each Recipient checkbox in the action's interface (Figure 2.16).

It's that simple! The workflow is complete and ready to be run (**Figure 2.17**).

✔ Tips

- If you accidentally drop the Send Birthday Greetings action into the workflow window before Find People with Birthdays, simply select the action's interface in the workflow area and drag it below the Find People with Birthdays action's interface.
- Because this workflow uses Mail to send the birthday greetings, you must have an account configured in Mail to run this workflow.
- Because this workflow searches the Birthday field in Address Book, you must have dates entered there for the workflow to run successfully (**Figure 2.18**).

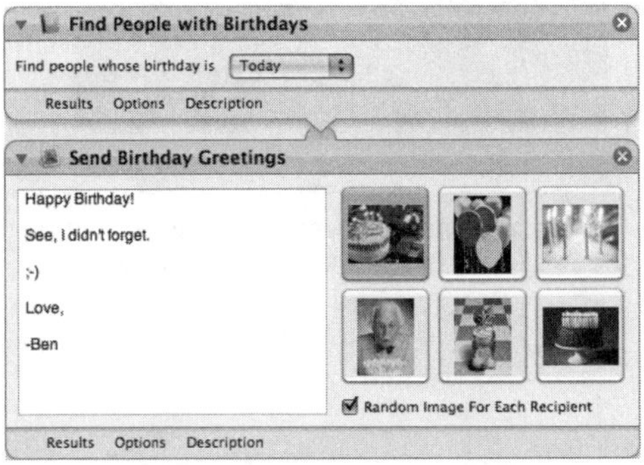

Figure 2.17 The completed Email Daily Birthday Greetings workflow.

Figure 2.18 An Address Book entry with a birthday specified.

To run the workflow:

Click the Run button in Automator's toolbar at the top of the workflow (**Figure 2.19**).

Figure 2.19 The Run button in Automator's toolbar.

Automator begins running the actions in your workflow. You can monitor its progress in the status area, located at the bottom of the workflow area (**Figure 2.20**).

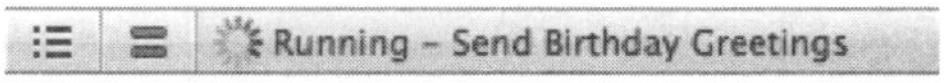

Figure 2.20 The status of the workflow, as it runs.

As the workflow runs, it:

1. Opens Address Book.
2. Searches for and identifies any people with a birthday on the current day.
3. Creates a new birthday greeting email in Mail for any people found to have a birthday.
4. Personalizes each email with the first name of the person receiving the greeting (assuming it is entered in Address Book) and inserts your username into the subject of the email (**Figure 2.21**).

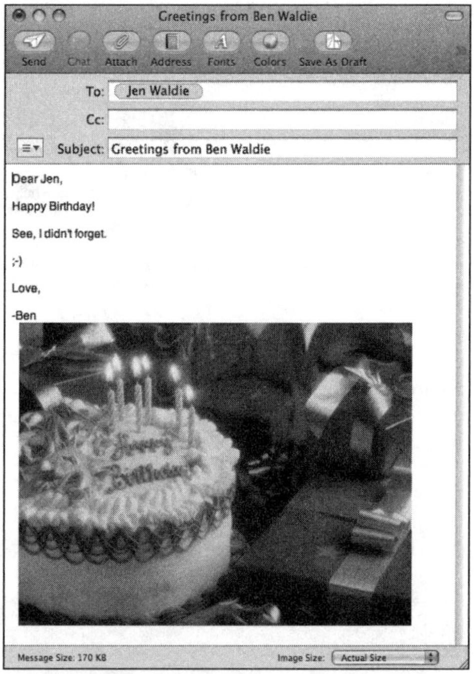

Figure 2.21 A birthday greeting email generated by the Email Daily Birthday Greetings workflow.

Add Spotlight Comments to Photos

In Mac OS X, Spotlight makes searching for files a breeze—as long as they contain searchable text or descriptive names. If they don't, locating them can be a bit more difficult. Take digital photos, for example. Digital cameras typically assign nondescript unique numeric names, such as IMG_1234.JPG, to your photos. How can you quickly locate specific photos from a list of names like that?

Automator makes it easy. Adding meaningful comments to these files can help you find them later, and with Automator, you can create a workflow that assigns Spotlight comments to your photos.

Actions used:

- Ask for Finder Items
- Get Folder Contents
- Set Spotlight Comments for Finder Items

✔ Tip

- Automator also includes a useful Spotlight action, which performs Spotlight searches and passes items it finds to later actions in a workflow for further processing.

To build the workflow:

1. Choose File > New.

   or

   Press ⌘N.

   A new workflow window and Starting Points panel appear.

2. Click the Files & Folders button in the Starting Points panel to create a Files & Folders workflow (**Figure 2.22**).

   Automator displays options that enable you to specify the location of the files and folders to process.

3. Ensure that the first pop-up menu in the Starting Points panel is set to get content from "my Mac" (**Figure 2.23**).

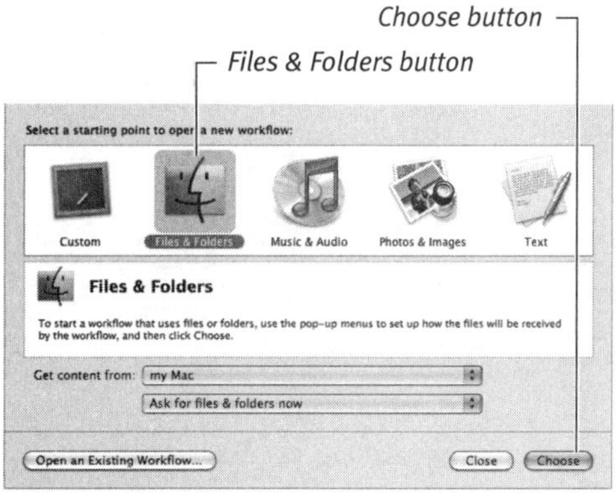

Figure 2.22 Creating a Files & Folders workflow using Starting Points.

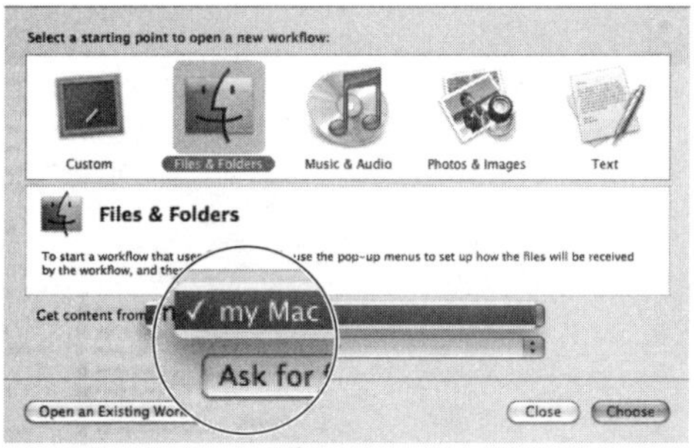

Figure 2.23 Configuring the workflow to get content from "my Mac."

Figure 2.24 Configuring the workflow to "Ask for files & folders when my workflow runs."

4. Choose "Ask for files & folders when my workflow runs" from the second pop-up menu in the Starting Points panel (**Figure 2.24**).
5. Click the Choose button in the Starting Points panel.

   Automator creates a workflow window prefilled with the Ask for Finder Items action (**Figures 2.25** and **2.26**).

✔ Tip

- As its name indicates, Starting Points gets you started by automatically inserting one or more actions into your workflow. You then complete the workflow by finding and inserting any additional actions that are necessary.

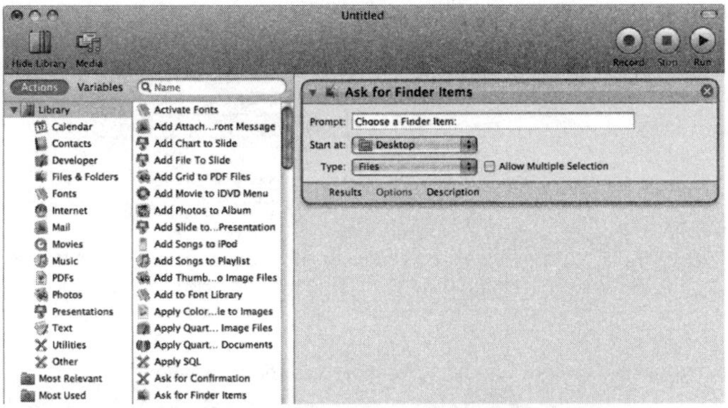

Figure 2.25 The Ask for Finder Items action, in a new workflow.

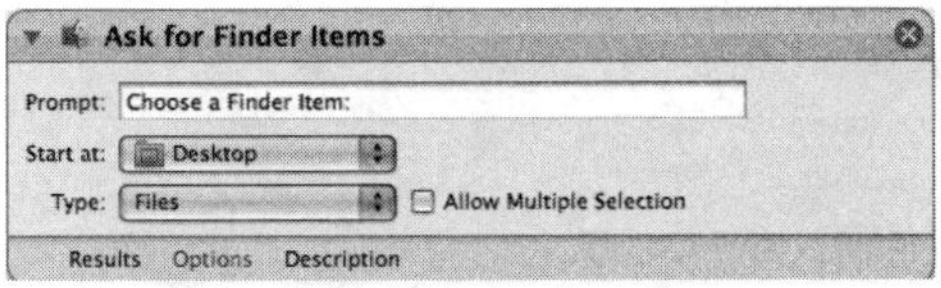

Figure 2.26 The Ask for Finder Items action requires you to make three choices: what the user sees when the workflow is run, where the user starts looking for items, and which kind of items the user can choose.

To prepare the Ask for Finder Items action:

1. Enter `Choose a folder of items to apply Spotlight comments to:` into the Prompt text field of the Ask for Finder Items action (**Figure 2.27**).

   The text you type here will appear in a dialog when the workflow is run.

2. Choose the Desktop option from the "Start at" pop-up menu within the action's interface (**Figures 2.28** and **2.30**).

3. Select the Folders option from the Type pop-up menu (**Figures 2.29** and 2.30) to ensure that you are prompted for folders only when the workflow is run.

4. Verify that the Allow Multiple Selection checkbox is not selected on the action's interface, to ensure that you're only prompted to choose a single folder (Figure 2.30).

✔ Tip

- When configuring the Ask for Finder Items action you can choose any folder that's convenient for you as the default.

Figure 2.27 Specifying a prompt for the Ask Finder Items action to display in a dialog when the workflow is run.

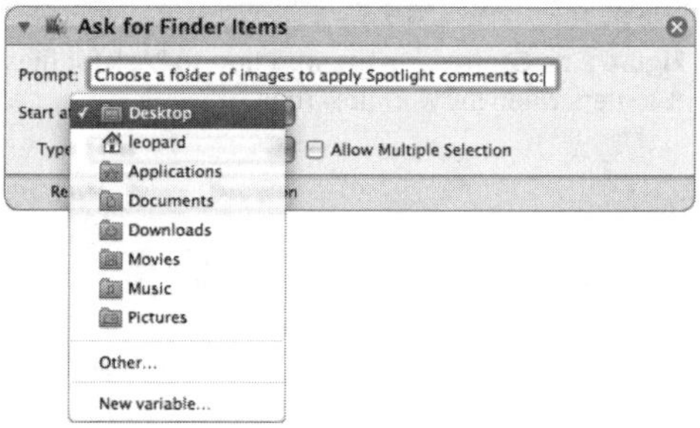

Figure 2.28 Selecting the default folder for the Ask for Finder Items action.

Figure 2.29 Selecting the type of Finder items to ask for in the Ask for Finder Items action.

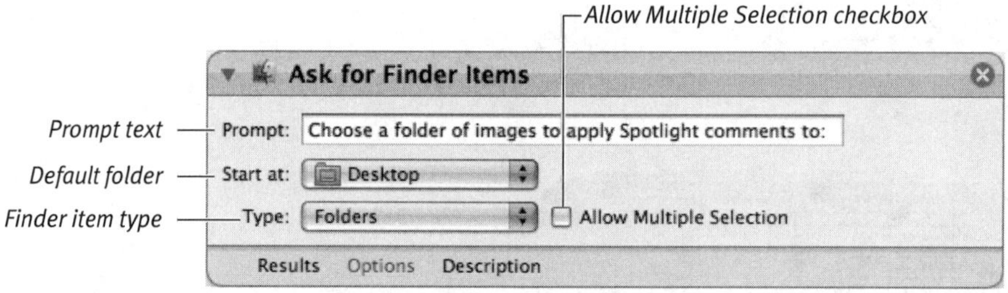

Figure 2.30 The configured Ask for Finder Items action.

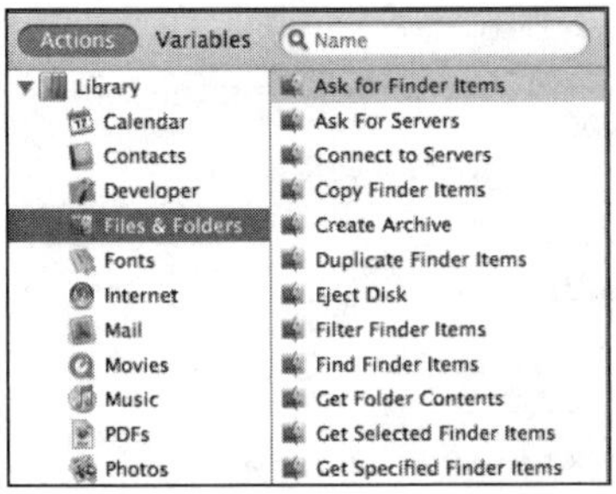

Figure 2.31 Selecting the Files & Folders category in the Library list.

Figure 2.32 Selecting the Get Folder Contents action in the Library list.

To add the Get Folder Contents action:

1. Click the Files & Folders category in the left column of the Library list (**Figure 2.31**) to see the related list of actions in the right column.
2. Select the Get Folder Contents action in the right column of the Library list (**Figure 2.32**), and drag it into the workflow area (**Figure 2.33**).
3. Click the "Repeat for each subfolder found" checkbox on the action's interface (**Figure 2.34**).

   With this option checked, when you choose a folder containing other folders, the workflow processes the contents of those subfolders as well.

✔ Tip

- Why do you need to get the contents of the specified folder? If you don't first get the folder's contents, then the next action adds Spotlight comments to just the folder itself.

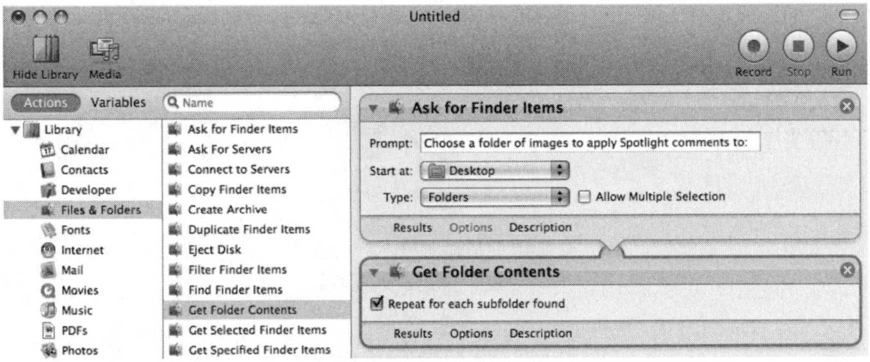

Figure 2.33 The Get Folder Contents action, once added into the workflow area.

Figure 2.34 The Get Folder Contents action's interface, once its settings have been configured.

To add the Set Spotlight Comments for Finder Items action:

1. Drag the Set Spotlight Comments for Finder Items action from the right column of the Library list (in the Files & Folders category, which should still be selected) into the workflow area (**Figure 2.35**).
2. Verify that the "Append to existing comments" checkbox is selected in the action (Figure 2.35). If it is not, existing Spotlight comments will be overwritten!
3. Click the Options button at the bottom of the action.

   The action expands to display additional options (**Figure 2.36**).
4. Click the "Show this action when the workflow runs" checkbox at the bottom of the action (Figure 2.36) to instruct the action to prompt you to enter the desired Spotlight comments when the workflow is run.

The workflow is now complete and ready to be run (**Figure 2.37**).

✔ Tip

- If you'd rather replace existing Spotlight comments, then deselect the "Append to existing comments" checkbox.

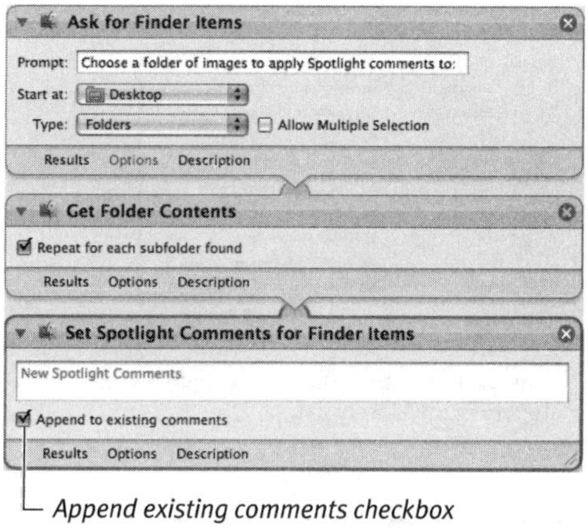

Figure 2.35 The Set Spotlight Comments for Finder Items action, once added into the workflow area.

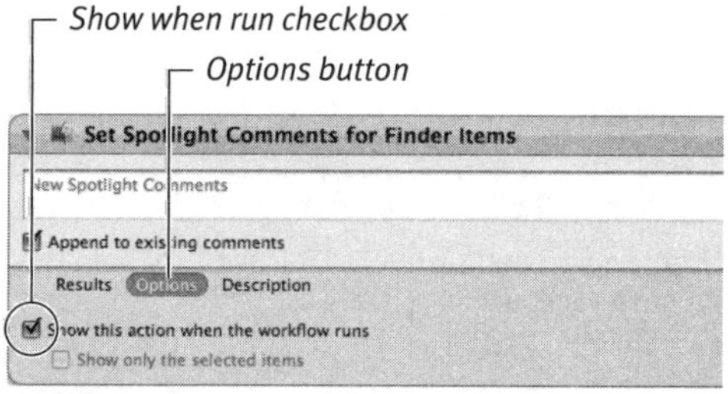

Figure 2.36 Configuring the Set Spotlight Comments for Finder Items action to "Show this action when the workflow runs."

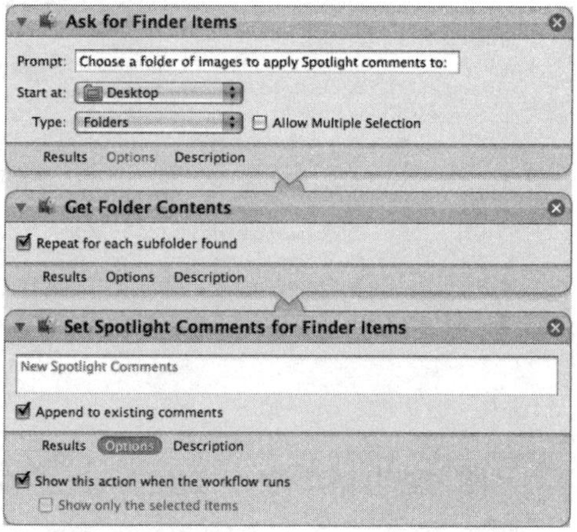

Figure 2.37 The completed Add Spotlight Comments to Photos workflow.

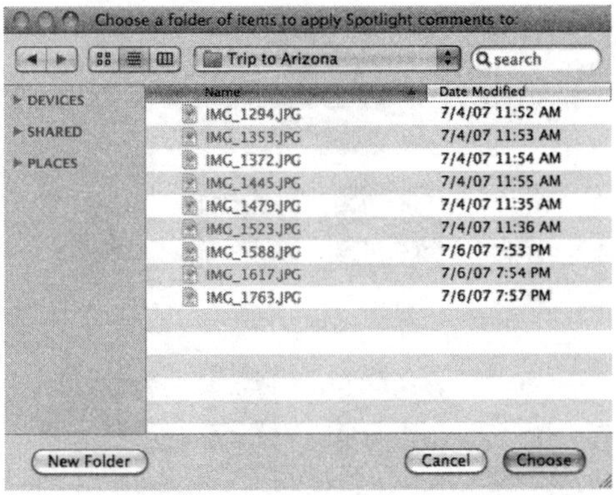

Figure 2.38 Choosing a folder of items to receive Spotlight comments.

Figure 2.39 Entering Spotlight comments to be applied to the items in the specified folder.

To run the workflow:

1. Click the Run button in Automator's toolbar at the top of the workflow.

   The Ask for Finder Items action runs first and prompts you to choose a folder of items.

2. Navigate to and select a folder of items. For example, I chose a folder of images from an Arizona vacation (**Figure 2.38**).

   Ask for Finder Items then passes the chosen folder to the next action.

   The Get Folder Contents action retrieves a list of the items in the specified folder (received as input) and passes those items to the next action.

   The Set Spotlight Comments for Finder Items action runs next, and the action's window prompts you to enter some Spotlight comments.

3. Enter the desired comments. For example, I entered Grand Canyon and Sedona (**Figure 2.39**).

   The action now applies these comments to the items received from the previous action.

To verify that the workflow was successful:

1. Press [⌘ ⌘][F] in the Finder to perform a Spotlight search.

   A search window is displayed.

2. In the window's search field, enter the Spotlight comments that you typed when the workflow ran (**Figure 2.40**).

   Spotlight locates the items in the folder you chose while running the workflow (Figure 2.40).

✔ Tip

- You can also perform a Spotlight search from the search field in the upper-right corner of the Mac OS X menu bar (**Figure 2.41**).

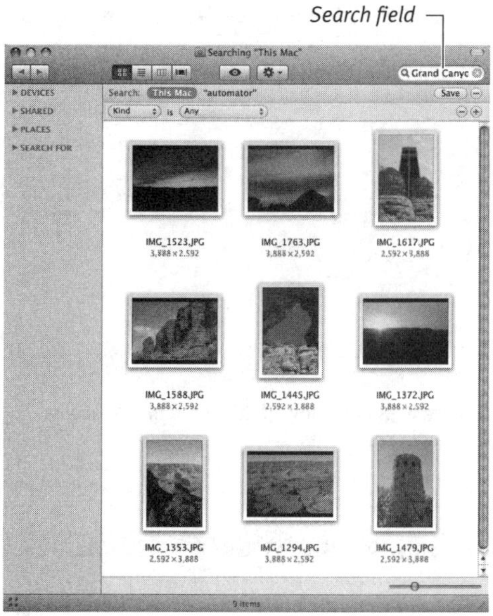

Figure 2.40 Locating commented items using Spotlight.

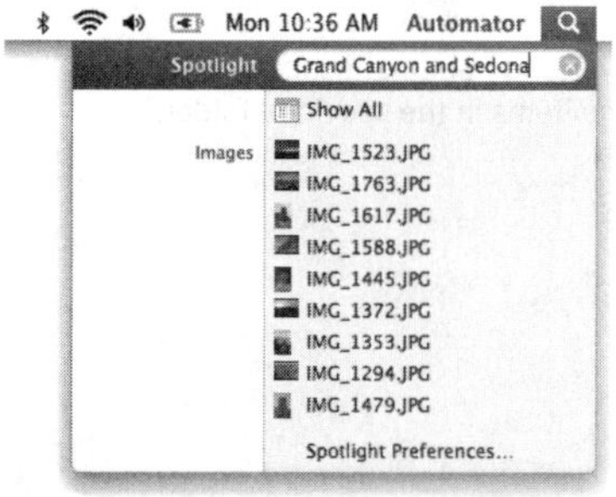

Figure 2.41 Performing a Spotlight search from the menu bar.

Email Photo Thumbnails

Want a quick way to email thumbnail versions of your latest and greatest digital photos to friends? Sure, you can do this from within iPhoto. But, if you don't have or use iPhoto, you can also do it with an Automator workflow.

Actions used:

- Ask for Photos
- Create Thumbnail Images
- Move Finder Items
- New Mail Message

To build the workflow:

1. Choose File > New.

   or

   Press [⌘][N].

   A new workflow window and Starting Points panel appear.

2. Click the Photos & Images button in the Starting Points panel (**Figure 2.42**).

   Automator displays additional options that enable you to specify the location of the photos and images to be processed.

continues on next page

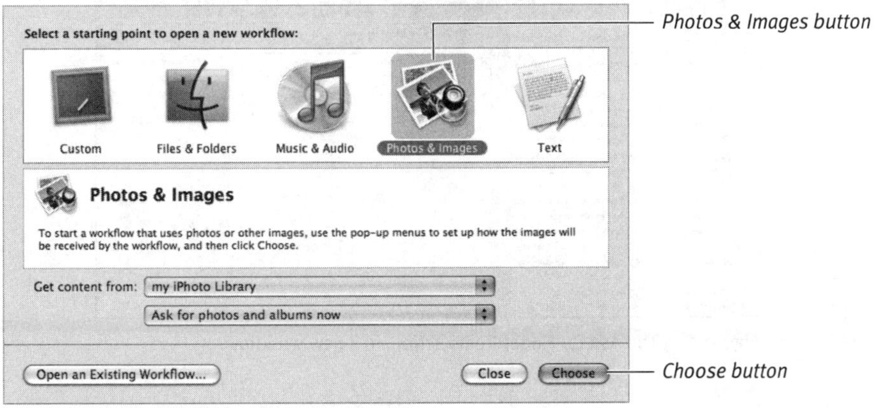

Figure 2.42 Creating a Photos & Images workflow using Starting Points.

3. Confirm that the Starting Points panel's "Get content from" pop-up is set to the default of "my iPhoto Library" (**Figure 2.43**).
4. Choose "Ask for photos and albums when my workflow runs" from the second pop-up menu in the Starting Points panel (**Figure 2.44**). This way, when the workflow is run, you'll be prompted to locate the photos to process.
5. Click the Choose button in the Starting Points panel.

   Automator opens a workflow window, prefilled with an Ask for Photos action in the workflow area (**Figure 2.45**).

✔ Tip

- If you don't have iPhoto installed, you can still create this workflow. Configure the Starting Points panel's "Get content from" pop-up menu to "my Mac" and the second pop-up menu to "Ask for files & folders when my workflow runs." As you follow along, just be aware that some of the steps below will differ slightly. For example, step 5 will open a workflow window prefilled with the Ask for Finder Items action.

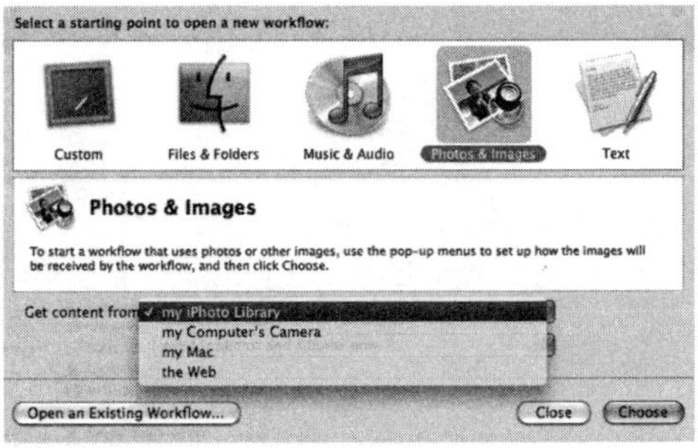

Figure 2.43 Configuring the workflow to get content from "my iPhoto library."

Figure 2.44 Configuring the workflow to "Ask for photos when my workflow runs."

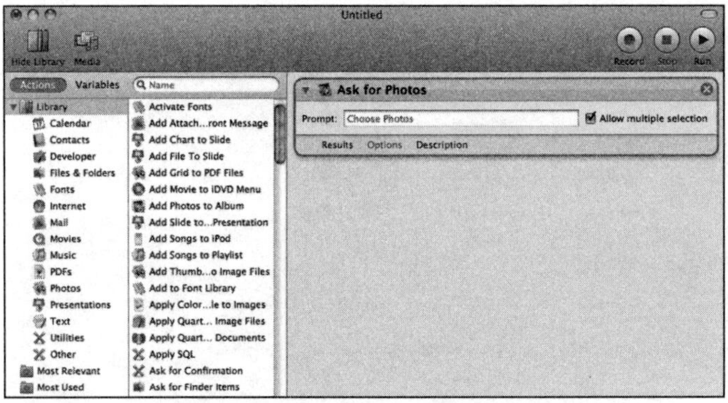

Figure 2.45 The Ask for Finder Items action, in a new workflow.

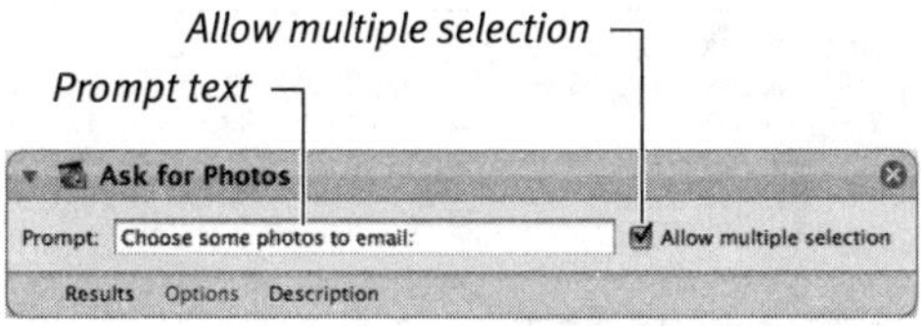

Figure 2.46 The configured Ask for Photos action.

To prepare the Ask for Photos action:

1. Type `Choose some photos to email:` in the Prompt text field of the Ask for Photos action (**Figure 2.46**).

   When the workflow is run, this text will be displayed at the top of the window that asks you to choose photos.

2. Verify that the "Allow multiple selection" checkbox is selected on the action's interface (Figure 2.46). Otherwise, you'd be able to select a single photo only!

To add the Create Thumbnail Images action:

1. Click the Photos category in the left column of the Library list to display that category's actions in the right column.

2. Select the Create Thumbnail Images action in the right column of the Library list, and drag it into the workflow area (**Figure 2.47**). You'll use the default settings for this action, so you don't need to change anything.

Figure 2.47 Locating the Create Thumbnail Images action, and adding it to the workflow area.

To add the Move Finder Items action:

1. Click the Files & Folders category in the left column of the Library list to display its actions in the right column (**Figure 2.48**).
2. Drag the Move Finder Items action from the right column of the Library list into the workflow area.

   The action is displayed within the workflow area (**Figure 2.49**) and by default is configured to move items to the Desktop, with the "Replacing existing files" checkbox not selected. No changes are necessary.

✔ Tip

- The photos that you choose to process most likely reside within your iPhoto library folder, but you probably don't want to leave the thumbnails in your iPhoto library folder. The Move Finder Items action moves the thumbnails to your Desktop.

Figure 2.48 The Files & Folders category of actions, displayed in the Library list.

Figure 2.49 The Move Finder Items action, once added into the workflow area.

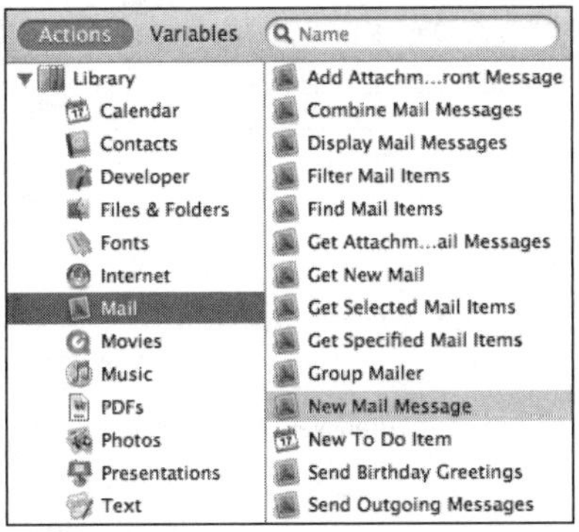

Figure 2.50 Mail-related actions, displayed within the Library list.

To add the New Mail Message action:

1. Click the Mail category in the left column of the Library list to display that category's actions (**Figure 2.50**).
2. Click the New Mail Message action in the right column, and drag it into the workflow area.

   The action displays within the workflow area (**Figure 2.51**).

continues on next page

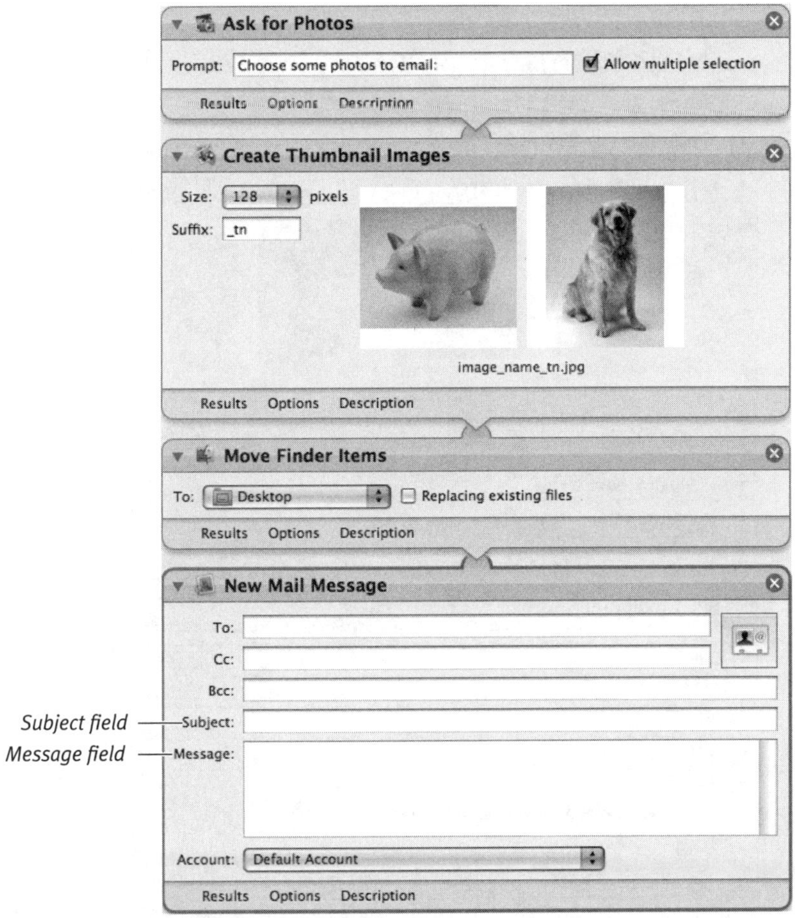

Figure 2.51 The New Mail Message action, once added into the workflow area.

3. Enter the desired text into the Subject and Message text fields in the action's interface (**Figure 2.52**).

The workflow is now complete and ready to be run (**Figure 2.53**).

✔ Tip

- Because this workflow uses Mail to send the thumbnail images, you need an account configured in Mail to run the workflow.

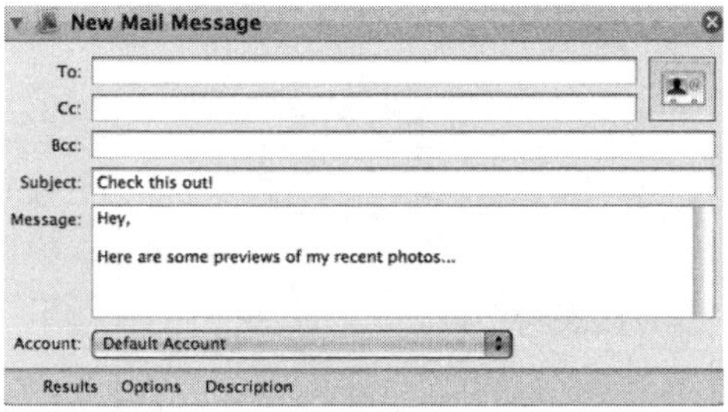

Figure 2.52 The configured New Mail Message action.

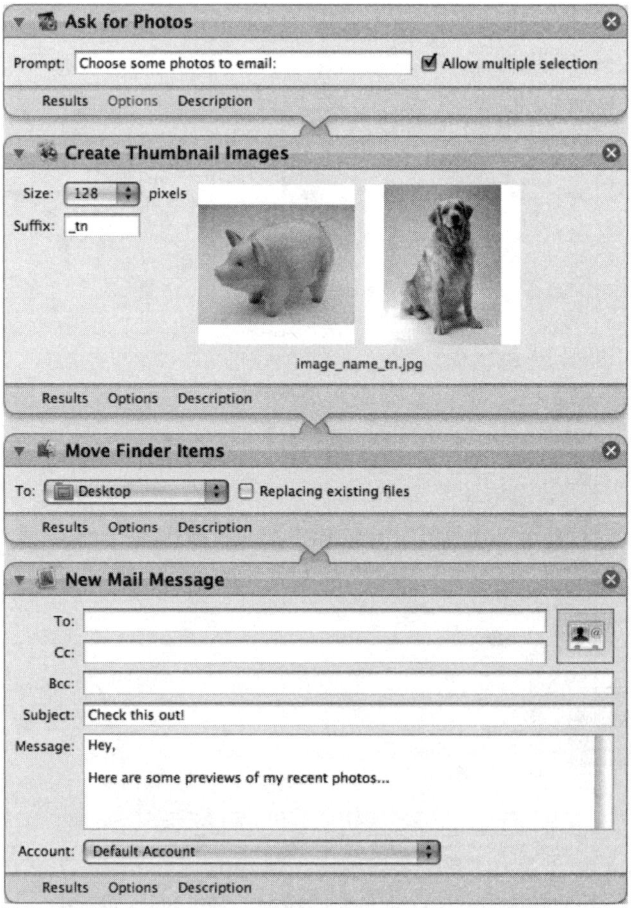

Figure 2.53 The completed Email Photo Thumbnails workflow.

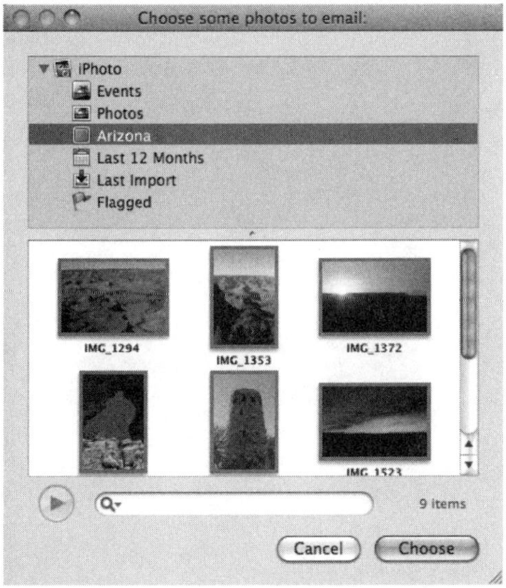

Figure 2.54 Choosing iPhoto photos for processing by the workflow.

To run the workflow:

1. Click the Run button in Automator's toolbar at the top of the workflow.

   The workflow begins to run, and the Ask for Photos action prompts you to choose some photos from your iPhoto library.

2. Choose the desired photos (**Figure 2.54**).

3. The Create Thumbnail Images action runs next. It may take a few seconds, as it generates thumbnail versions of the images that you chose.

4. The Move Finder Items action moves the thumbnail images to the Desktop.

5. Finally, the workflow creates a new message in Mail that contains the subject and body that you specified in the New Mail Message action. Thumbnail versions of the specified images are attached (**Figure 2.55**).

✔ Tip

- If you don't have iPhoto installed and your workflow contains a Get Specified Finder Items action instead, you are prompted to locate image files now.

Figure 2.55 An email generated by the Email Photo Thumbnails workflow, with thumbnail images attached.

3

Workflow Creation Basics

So far, you've created a few simple Automator workflows. Now, it's time to get some more serious work done.

Need to build a workflow that resizes and crops photos from your iPhoto library? How about one that downloads audio files from a webpage and imports them into iTunes? Perhaps you regularly need to extract content from TextEdit documents to email to friends or coworkers.

In this chapter, you'll explore how Starting Points can help you create workflows like these. In addition, you'll learn to create Automator workflows directly from the Finder and add audio, photos, or movies to your workflow from Automator's Media Browser.

Planning a Workflow

Before creating a workflow, take time to plan out what you want it to do. For simple workflows, thinking about the overall job you want to accomplish is often enough. For complex workflows, however, writing an outline may be more helpful. Guiding you through a workflow's creation, an outline helps to ensure that you aren't leaving out any steps along the way and that things are in the proper order.

To outline a workflow:

1. Think about the entire job you want to perform.
2. Break the job into individual tasks, and make a list of these: create a folder, rename the folder, move the folder, and so on.
3. Translate each task to an Automator action. To make this step easier, try to narrow down the list of actions by entering some keywords into the search field in Automator's Library list.

✔ Tip

- If you're unsure of the exact tasks within a complicated workflow, go through the process manually and list the steps as you perform them.

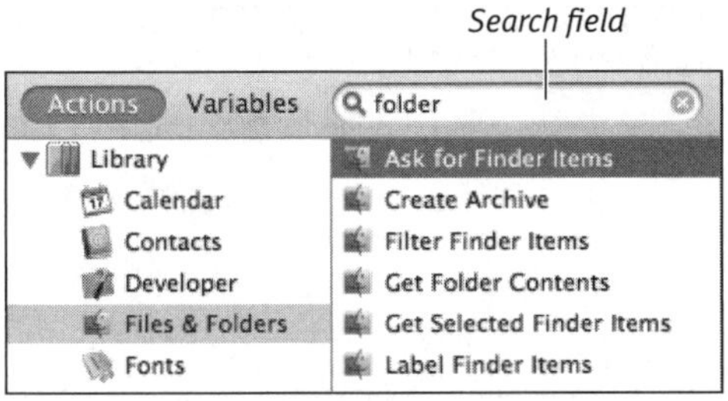

Figure 3.1 To quickly locate an action, enter keywords into Automator's search field. Typing `folder` helps find the Ask for Finder Items action.

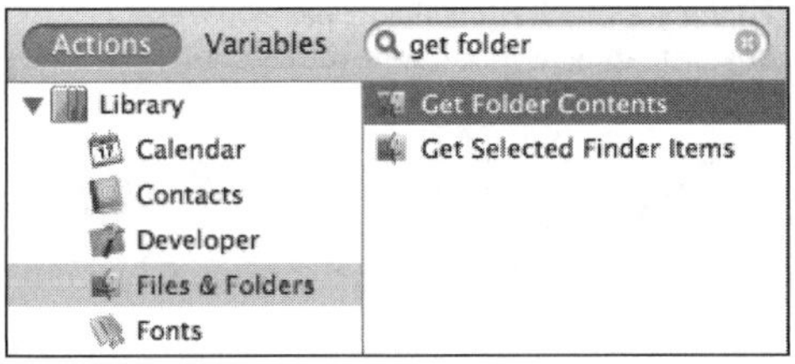

Figure 3.2 The keywords `get` and `folder` take you right to the Get Folder Contents action.

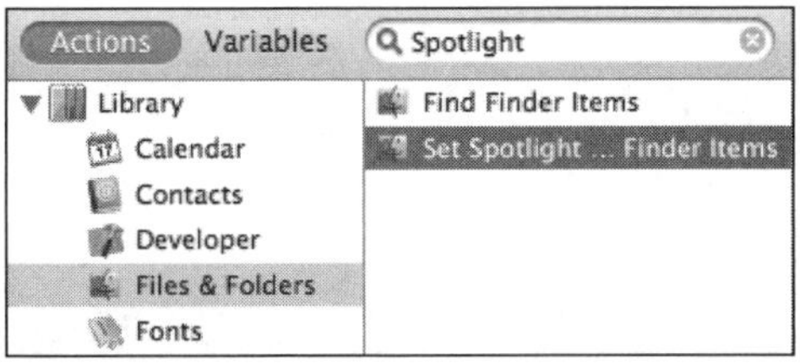

Figure 3.3 The `Spotlight` keyword displays a list of Spotlight-related actions.

Outlining an Example Workflow

Suppose you want to create a workflow that adds Spotlight comments to some photos. An outline for this task might consist of three steps:

1. Locate a folder of photos.
2. Get a list of photos inside the folder.
3. Add Spotlight comments to the photos.

When you're ready to build the workflow, you must find Automator actions for the steps you've outlined.

Step 1: Locate the folder:

1. Select the Files & Folders category in the Library list.

   Automator displays list of actions related to files and folders.
2. Enter a keyword, such as `folder`, into the search field to narrow the list of action.
3. Look for an action that does what you need. In this case, Ask for Finder Items should do the trick (**Figure 3.1**).

Step 2: Get the photos:

Type the keywords `get folder` into the search field.

The Get Folder Contents action appears, which looks like just what you need (**Figure 3.2**).

Step 3: Add Spotlight comments:

Enter `Spotlight` as a keyword, and the Set Spotlight Comments for Finder Items action appears (**Figure 3.3**).

✔ Tips

- Locating actions to do what you want may sound simple, but it's often easier said than done. It becomes easier, however, with practice.
- If you can't find an action within Automator that performs a specific task, check the Automator section of Apple's Mac OS X Downloads page at www.apple.com/downloads/macosx/automator for third-party actions.

Creating a Workflow Using Starting Points

When you launch Automator, or attempt to create a new workflow, the program displays the Starting Points panel (**Figure 3.4**), which serves as a guide and asks a few simple questions to help get your workflow started.

It begins by asking what type of workflow you want to create. Starting Points allows you to create a Files & Folders workflow, a Music & Audio workflow, a Photos & Images workflow, or a Text workflow. The one you choose depends on the task you want to perform. If none of these workflow types meet your needs, you can choose to create a custom workflow instead.

Next, Starting Points asks what type of content you want to process with the workflow. If your workflow processes music and audio content, for example, you tell Starting Points where to find the music and audio content.

Finally, Starting Points opens a new workflow window that's prefilled with actions to get you started.

✔ Tips

- You can open a saved Automator workflow from the Starting Points panel. To do so, simply click the "Open an Existing Workflow" button.
- Clicking the Close button in Starting Points dismisses the Starting Points panel and closes the workflow. Starting Points can also be disabled, if you prefer. See "Creating a Workflow Without Starting Points," later in this chapter.

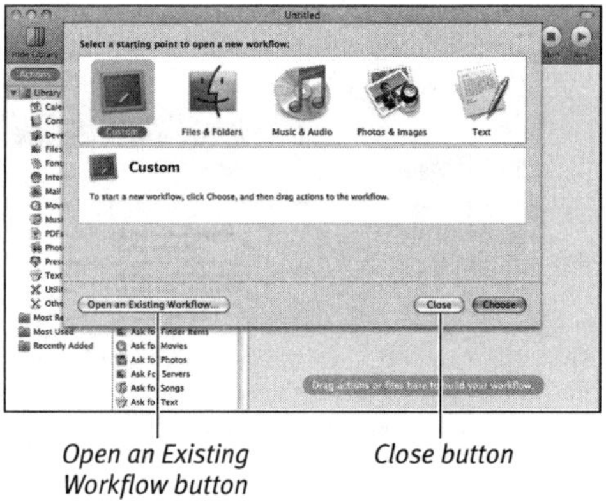

Figure 3.4 The Starting Points panel makes it easy to begin creating a workflow in Automator.

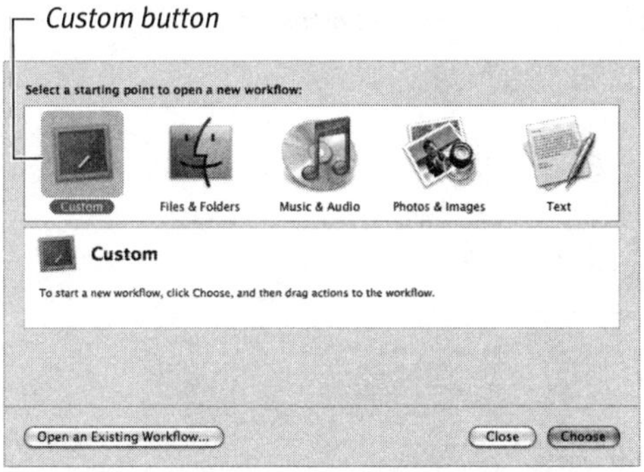

Figure 3.5 To create a custom Automator workflow, click the Custom button in Starting Points.

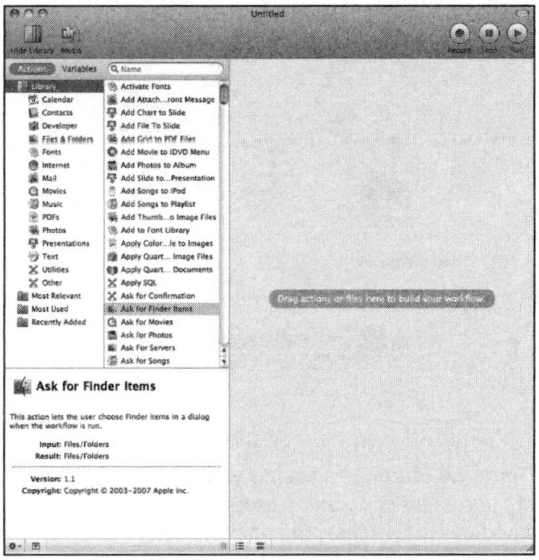

Figure 3.6 A custom workflow is nothing more than an empty workflow, ready for you to begin adding actions.

Creating a Custom Workflow

Although Starting Points is a great way to get started, occasionally you may need something that doesn't fall into a specific, prefilled Starting Points workflow. For these situations, choose Custom from the panel. Because they are not prefilled with any actions, Custom workflows offer the most flexibility. You can create any kind of workflow from scratch—Files & Folders, Music & Audio, or something unique.

To create a custom workflow:

1. Choose File > New

   or

   Press [⌘][N].

   Automator opens a new workflow window with the Starting Points panel attached.
2. In the Starting Points panel, click the Custom button (**Figure 3.5**).
3. Click the Choose button to create an empty workflow (**Figure 3.6**). Now, locate the desired actions, and drag them into the workflow area. Use the outline you created as your guide.

Creating a Files & Folders Workflow

Some of the most common tasks on any system involve processing files or folders. Starting Points provides several ways to begin creating a workflow of this nature. For example, you can specify the files and folders to be processed up front, or you can tell Starting Points that you want the files and folders to be located when the workflow runs.

To create a Files & Folders workflow:

1. Choose File > New

   or

   Press ⌘N.

   Automator opens a new workflow window with the Starting Points panel attached.

2. In the Starting Points panel, click the Files & Folders button (**Figure 3.7**).

3. From the "Get content from" pop-up menu in the Starting Points panel, choose the location of the content you want to process (**Figure 3.8**).

4. From the second pop-up menu, choose how you'd like to locate the files for processing (**Figure 3.9**). You can locate them now or tell Starting Points to locate them when you run the workflow.

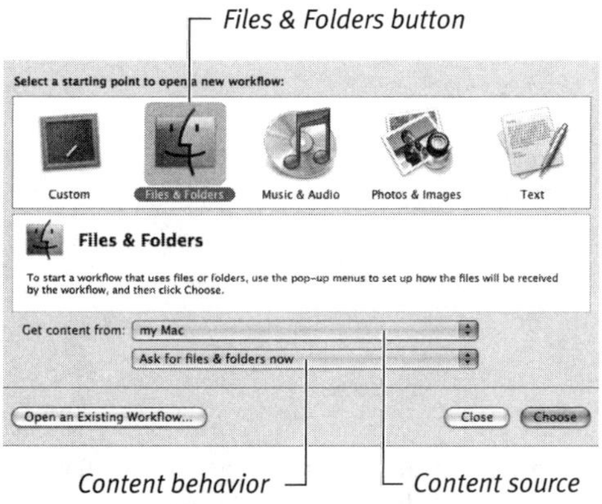

Figure 3.7 To create a workflow that processes files and folders, click the Files & Folders button in Starting Points.

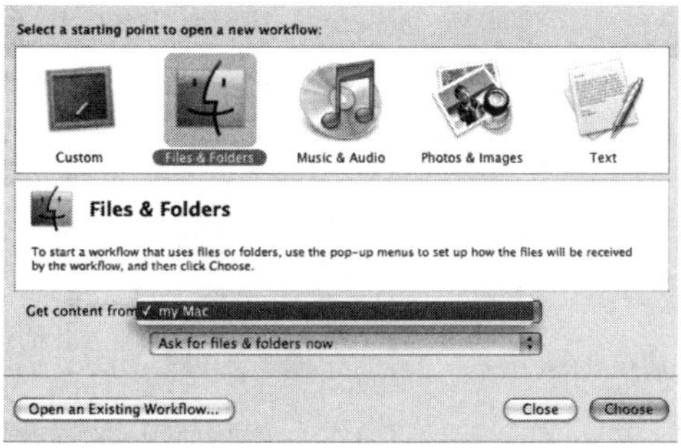

Figure 3.8 Starting Points lets you specify the location of the content you want to process for a Files & Folders workflow. In this case, the only choice available is "my Mac."

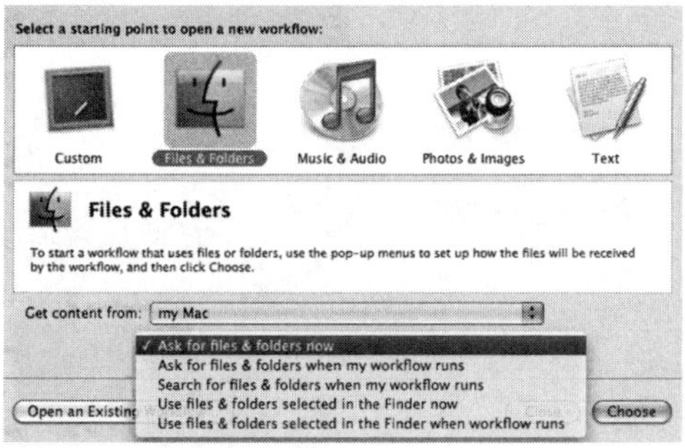

Figure 3.9 Starting Points allows you to choose files and folders to process immediately or to locate them when your workflow is run.

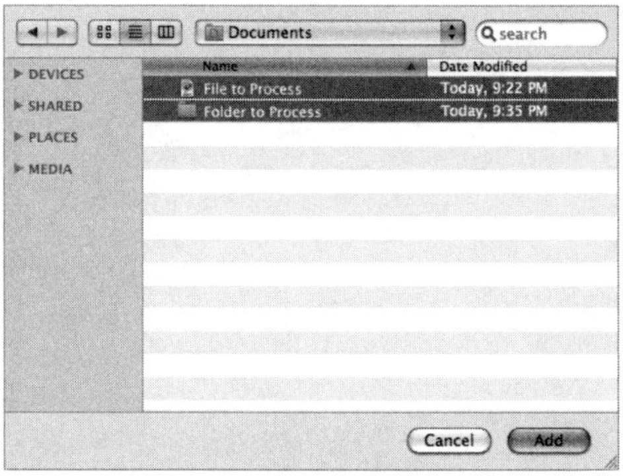

Figure 3.10 Choosing the files and folders you want to process.

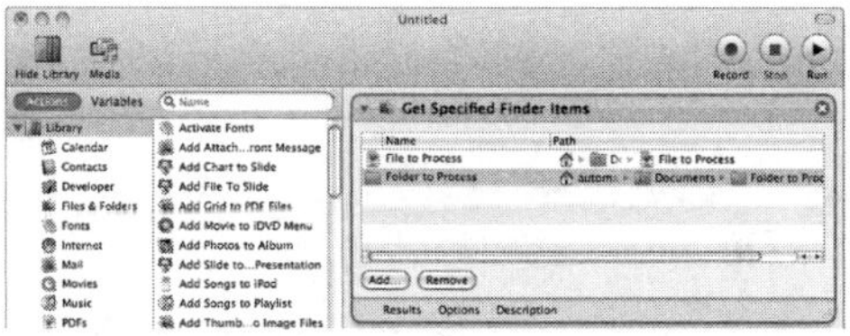

Figure 3.11 A Files & Folders workflow, prefilled with specified files and folders.

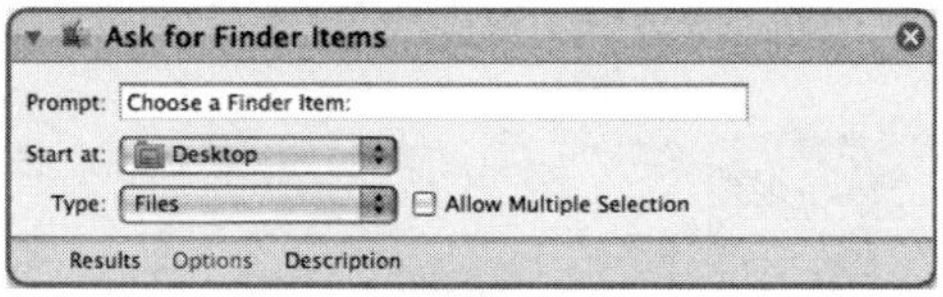

Figure 3.12 A Files & Folders workflow that is prefilled with the Ask for Finder Items action allows you to choose the files and folders you want to process when the workflow runs.

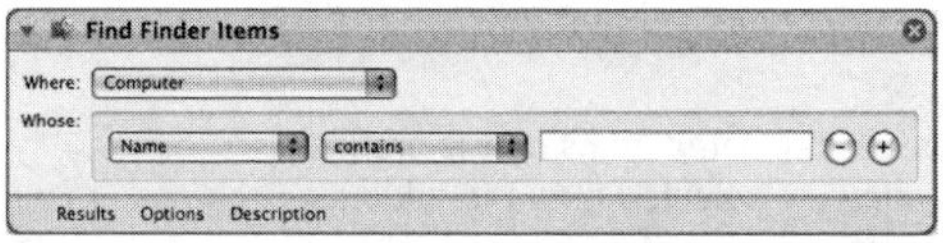

Figure 3.13 A Files & Folders workflow, prefilled with a Find Finder Items action, searches for files and folders to process when the workflow runs.

5. Click the Choose button to begin creating the workflow. Based on the choices you made, one of several things happens next.
   - ▲ If you told Starting Points to "Ask for files & folders now," you are prompted to choose the files and folders you want to process in your workflow. Locate the desired items, and click Add (**Figure 3.10**).

     Starting Points creates a new workflow window, prefilled with a Get Specified Finder Items action containing the chosen files and folders (**Figure 3.11**).
   - ▲ If you set Starting Points to "Ask for files & folders when my workflow runs," Automator opens a new workflow window containing a Ask for Finder Items action (**Figure 3.12**). This makes your workflow more flexible. Rather than using predefined files and folders, you can now choose different ones every time you run the workflow.
   - ▲ If you set Starting Points to "Search for files & folders when my workflow runs," then Automator opens a new workflow window containing a Find Finder Items action (**Figure 3.13**). Here, you can specify any desired search criteria. For example, you could set the action to search your computer for every file whose extension is .jpg. This way, when the workflow runs, any .jpg images would be processed.

continues on next page

- If you specified "Use files & folders selected in the Finder now," Starting Points opens a new workflow window that's prefilled with a Get Specified Finder Items action. This action contains a list of files and folders that are currently selected in the Finder (**Figure 3.14**).
- If you chose "Use files & folders selected in the Finder when workflow runs," Starting Points opens a workflow window containing a Get Selected Finder Items action (**Figure 3.15**). When you run the workflow, Automator retrieves any files and folders that are selected in the Finder at that time and processes them.

This is as far as Starting Points takes you. You must now continue building the workflow by dragging additional actions from the Library list into the workflow area. The actions you insert depend on the job you want to perform. Now is a good time to refer to your workflow outline.

✔ Tip

- Processing selected files and folders gets even easier. Learn how in "Creating a Workflow from Finder Items," later in this chapter.

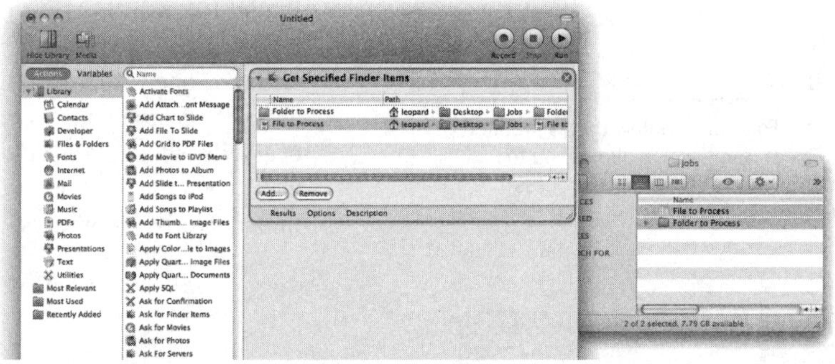

Figure 3.14 A Files & Folders workflow set to process selected items now is prefilled with a Get Specified Finder Items action, containing the selected files and folders.

Figure 3.15 A Files & Folders workflow, prefilled with the Get Selected Finder Items action, retrieves the selected files and folders when you run the workflow.

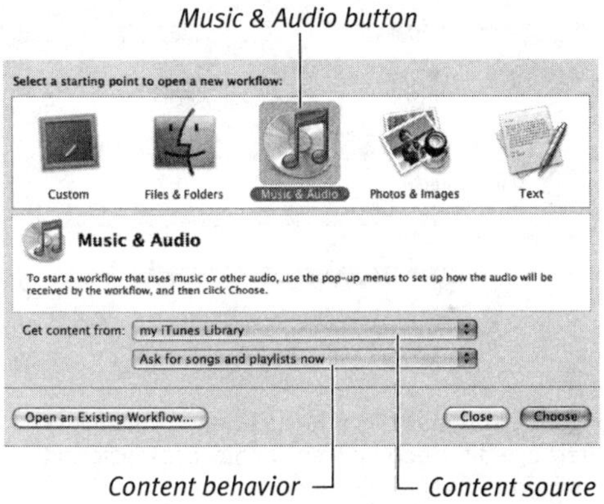

Figure 3.16 To create a workflow that processes music and audio, click the Music & Audio button in Starting Points.

Creating a Music & Audio Workflow

Automator isn't just for files and folders. It can also work with music and audio, whether in your iTunes library, on your Mac, or on the Web, and again, Starting Points can help. It lets you choose the location of the music and audio content that you want to process, then it inserts the appropriate actions in a workflow to retrieve that content.

To begin a Music & Audio workflow:

1. Choose File > New

   or

   Press [⌘][N] to open a new workflow window with Starting Points attached.

2. Click the Music & Audio button to get started (**Figure 3.16**).

To create a Music & Audio workflow using content from your iTunes Library:

1. In the "Get content from" pop-up menu, choose "my iTunes Library" (**Figure 3.17**).
2. From the second pop-up menu, choose how and when you'd like to locate the iTunes content. You can find it now or when the workflow runs (**Figure 3.18**).

   (For this example, your specific choice doesn't matter. The next step examines the results of each option.)
3. Click Choose to begin creating the workflow.

   Depending on which option you chose for the second pop-up menu, Starting Points now asks you to choose the music and audio you want to process, or it adds an action to retrieve the music and audio when the workflow runs.

   - ▲ If you selected "Ask for songs and playlists now," Starting Points displays a list of music and audio from your iTunes library. Choose the songs and playlists you want the workflow to process (**Figure 3.19**).

     After you choose the desired songs and playlists, Starting Points opens a new workflow window prefilled with a Get Specified iTunes Items action that contains the chosen songs and playlists (**Figure 3.20**).
   - ▲ If you chose "Ask for songs and playlists when my workflow runs," Starting Points opens a new workflow window containing an Ask for Songs action (**Figure 3.21**). Now, when you run the workflow, it prompts you to locate songs and playlists to process.

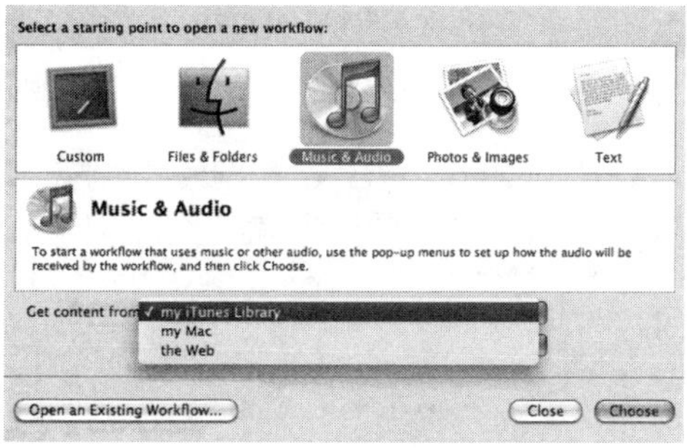

Figure 3.17 Choose "my iTunes Library" from the first Starting Points pop-up menu to process music and audio from iTunes.

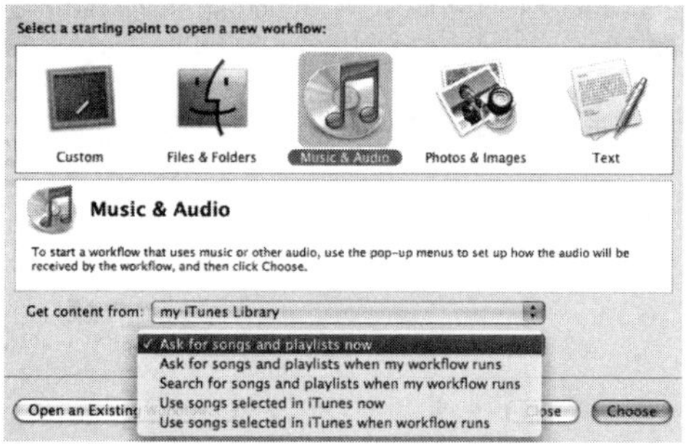

Figure 3.18 Starting Points allows you to locate music and audio from iTunes up front, or when your workflow runs.

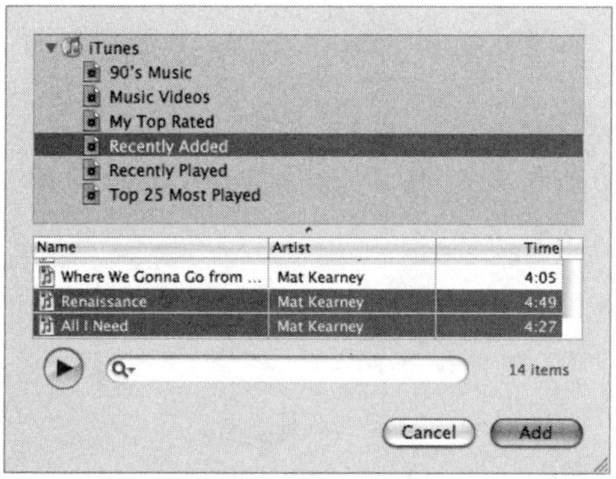

Figure 3.19 Starting Points enables you to choose songs and playlists from iTunes for processing before the workflow runs.

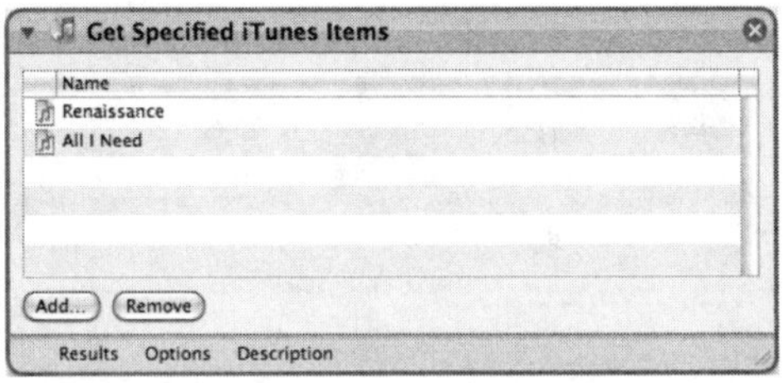

Figure 3.20 When choosing music and audio up front, Starting Points automatically inserts a Get Specified iTunes Items action, containing the chosen songs and playlists.

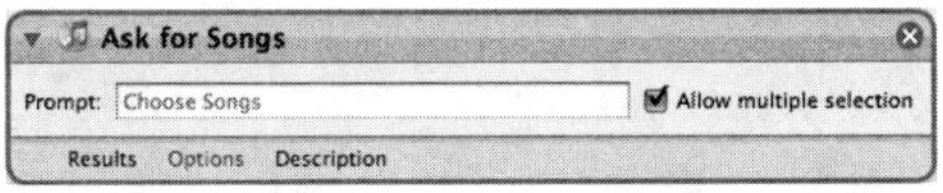

Figure 3.21 The Ask for Songs action prompts you for songs and playlists when the workflow runs.

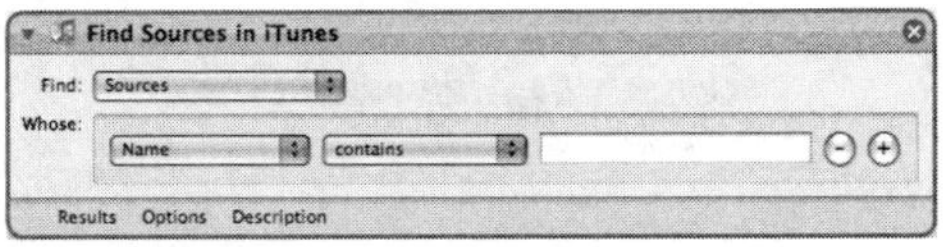

Figure 3.22 The Find iTunes Items action searches for music sources, songs, or playlists when a workflow runs.

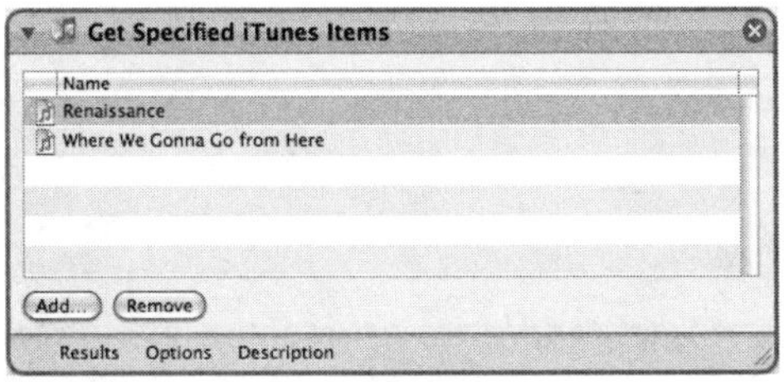

Figure 3.23 Starting Points can fetch songs currently selected in iTunes and add them to your workflow within a Get Specified iTunes Items action.

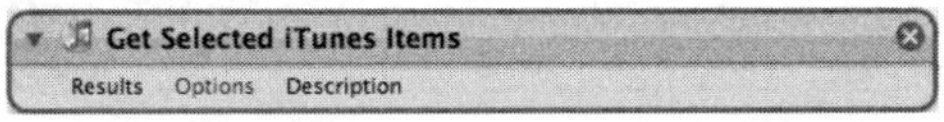

Figure 3.24 The Get Selected iTunes Items retrieves any currently selected songs from iTunes when you run the workflow.

- ▲ If you specified "Search for songs and playlists when my workflow runs," Starting Points opens a new workflow window containing a Find iTunes Items action (**Figure 3.22**). You now enter the desired search criteria, such as songs with a five-star rating. When you run the workflow, Automator searches for music sources, songs, or playlists matching the criteria you specified.
- ▲ If you chose "Use songs selected in iTunes now," Starting Points opens a new workflow window that's prefilled with a Get Specified iTunes Items action. This action contains a list of songs currently selected in iTunes (**Figure 3.23**).
- ▲ If you specified "Use songs selected in iTunes when workflow runs," Starting Points opens a new workflow window containing a Get Selected iTunes Items action (**Figure 3.24**). This time, when you run the workflow, Automator processes any songs selected in iTunes at that time.

From this point, you can continue building onto the started workflow by dragging additional actions from the Library list into the workflow area. For example, if you want to upload the music and audio to your iPod, try inserting the Add Songs to iPod action.

✔ Tip

- When the Find iTunes Items action is added to a workflow, its title changes to reflect the item being searched for, such as Find Sources in iTunes, Find Playlists in iTunes, Find Songs in iTunes. You may see this behavior in other actions, as well.

To create a Music & Audio workflow using content from your Mac:

1. From the "Get content from" pop-up menu in Starting Points, choose "my Mac" (**Figure 3.25**).
2. From the second pop-up menu, choose how and when you'd like the workflow to locate the content to be processed (**Figure 3.26**). As in the previous workflow, you can locate content now or when your workflow runs.
3. Click Choose to begin creating your workflow. Starting Points now asks you to locate the desired audio files, or it configures the workflow to locate them when it is run.
   - ▲ If you set "Ask for audio files now," Starting Points prompts you to choose the audio files that you want to process with the workflow (**Figure 3.27**).

     After you pick your audio files, Starting Points opens a new workflow window prefilled with a Get Specified Finder Items action that contains the files (**Figure 3.28**).

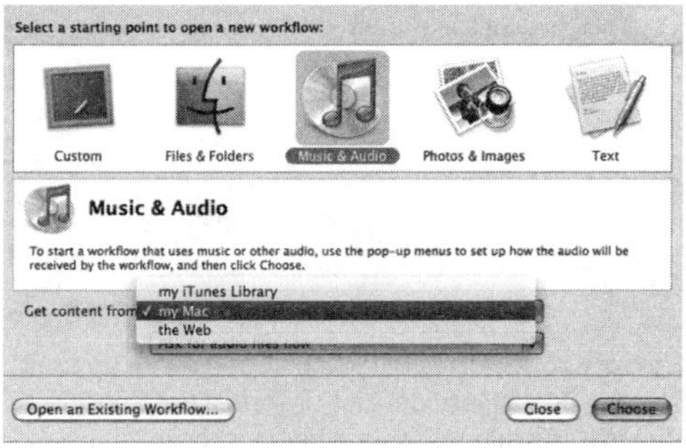

Figure 3.25 Music and audio content doesn't just come from iTunes. You can also get it from your Mac.

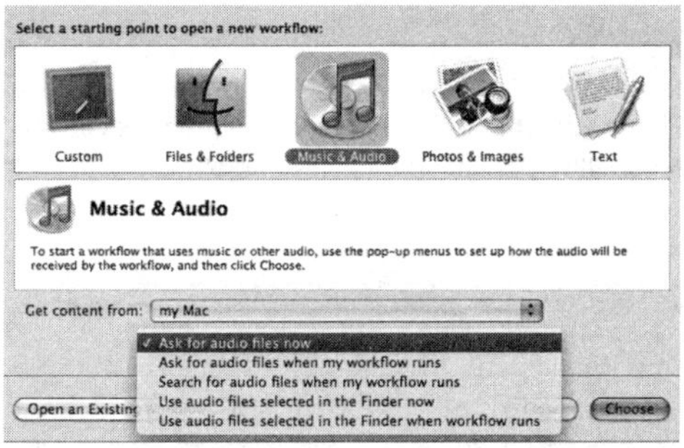

Figure 3.26 Starting Points lets you locate music and audio now or retrieve it when your workflow runs.

Figure 3.27 Choosing the audio files you want to process with the workflow.

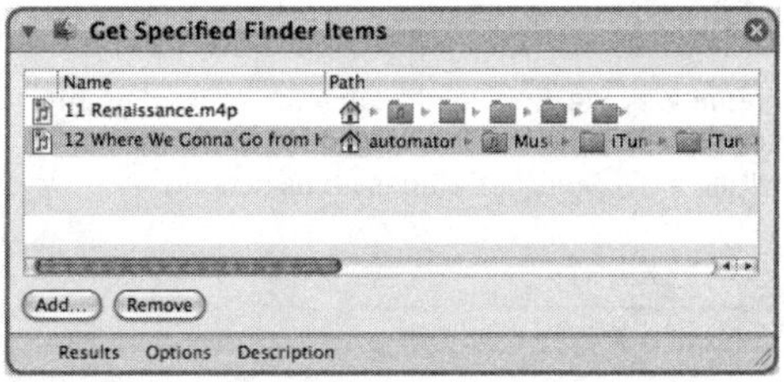

Figure 3.28 The Get Specified Finder Items action contains your specified audio files to be processed when the workflow is run.

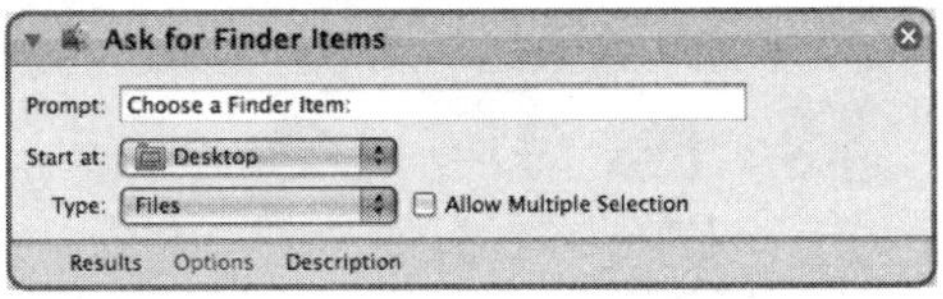

Figure 3.29 A Music & Audio workflow, prefilled with the Ask for Finder Items action, asks for audio files when you run the workflow.

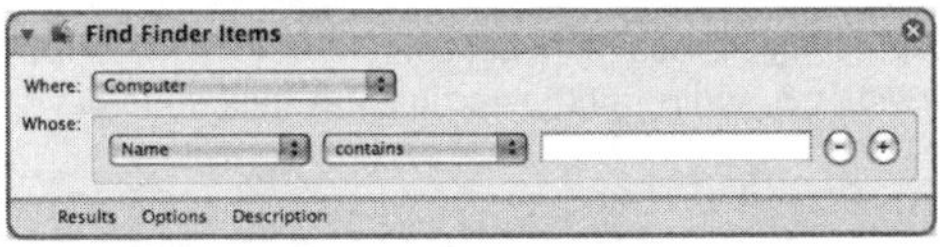

Figure 3.30 A Music & Audio workflow, prefilled with a Find Finder Items action, searches for audio files when you run the workflow.

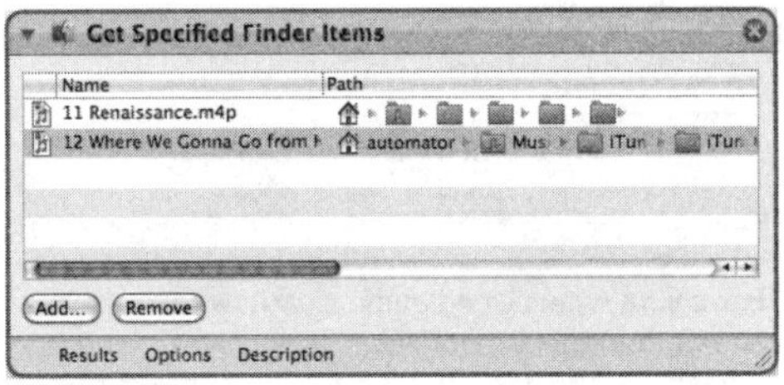

Figure 3.31 In a Music & Audio workflow, the Get Specified Finder Items action is used to process audio files that are currently selected in the Finder.

Figure 3.32 The Get Selected Finder Items action processes selected audio files when your run a workflow.

- ▲ If you selected "Ask for audio files when my workflow runs," Starting Points opens a new workflow window that contains an Ask for Finder Items action (**Figure 3.29**). Now, you'll be asked to choose audio files when you run the workflow.
- ▲ If you chose "Search for audio files when my workflow runs," Starting Points opens a new workflow window containing a Find Finder Items action (**Figure 3.30**). In this action, you then enter the desired search criteria, such as files with an .mp3 extension. When you run your workflow, Automator searches for and processes the specified items.
- ▲ If you selected "Use audio files selected in the Finder now," Starting Points opens a new workflow window prefilled with a Get Specified Finder Items action containing a list of the audio files currently selected in the Finder (**Figure 3.31**).
- ▲ If you specified "Use audio files selected in the Finder when workflow runs," Starting Points opens a new workflow window containing a Get Selected Finder Items action (**Figure 3.32**). When you run the workflow, Automator processes the audio files selected in the Finder at that time.

You can continue building onto this workflow by dragging additional actions from the Library list into the workflow area. For example, try adding the Import Files into iTunes action.

✔ Tip

- ■ If you plan to choose "Use audio files selected in the Finder now," be sure that you select audio files prior to creating the workflow. If not, simply close the workflow, select the audio files, and start again.

To create a Music & Audio workflow using content from the Web:

1. From the "Get content from" pop-up menu in Starting Points, choose "the Web" (**Figure 3.33**).
2. From the second pop-up menu, choose how and when to locate the content for the workflow (**Figure 3.34**). You can specify the URLs containing the audio content now, or you can specify them when you run the workflow.
3. Click Choose to begin creating the workflow. As always, Starting Points helps you in one of several ways.
   - ▲ If you specified "Ask for URLs now," Starting Points opens a new workflow window containing a Get Specified URLs action (**Figure 3.35**). You must now add the desired URLs to the action; just be sure they contain audio content. For example, you might add URLs that point directly to audio files themselves. If the URL you've specified contains links to audio files, then it would be a good idea to insert a Get Link URLs from Webpages action.

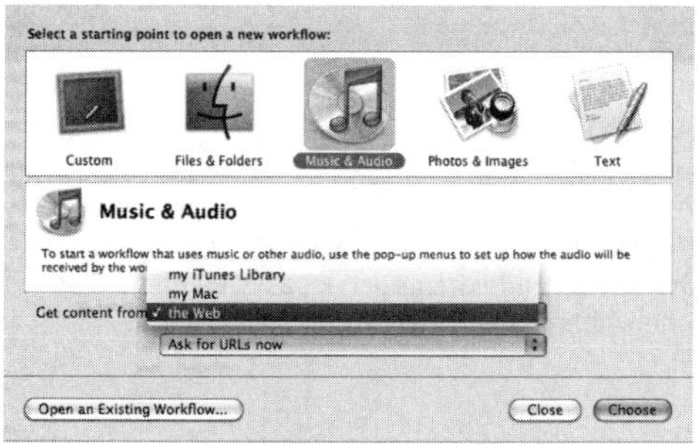

Figure 3.33 Choosing to get content from the Web for a Music & Audio workflow using Starting Points.

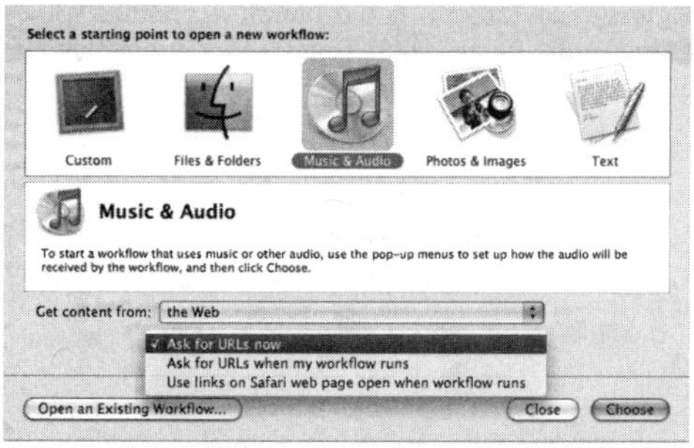

Figure 3.34 A music and audio workflow can get content from URLs specified now when you create it or when you run it. It can also get content from the current webpage in Safari.

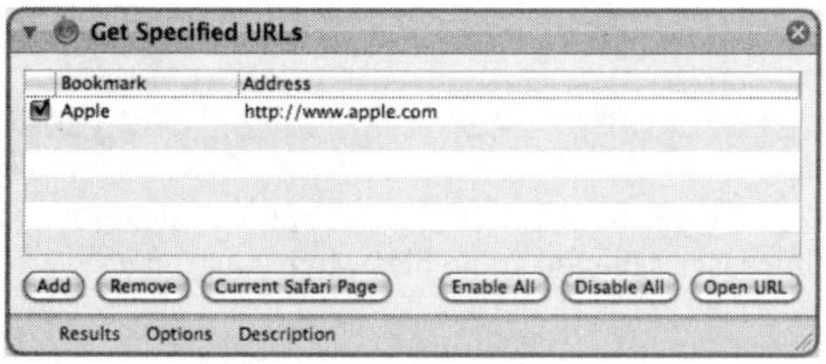

Figure 3.35 The Get Specified URLs action allows you to specify the location of web-based audio content.

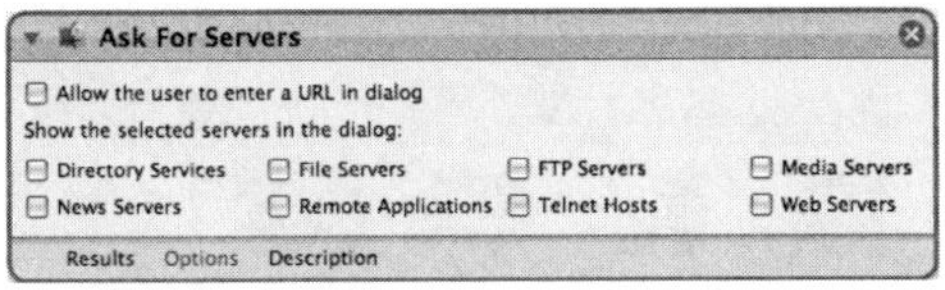

Figure 3.36 A Music & Audio workflow, prefilled with an Ask for Servers action, prompts you to enter a URL when you run the workflow.

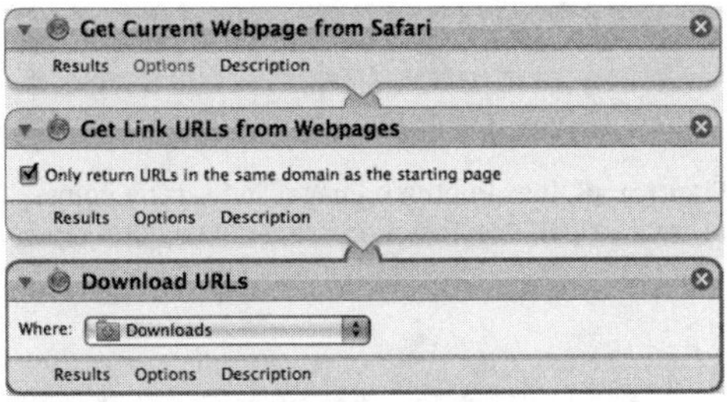

Figure 3.37 A Music & Audio workflow, prefilled with the Get Current Webpage from Safari, Get Link URLs from Webpages, and Download URLs actions, processes music using links on the current Safari web page.

- ▲ If you chose "Ask for URLs when my workflow runs," Starting Points opens a workflow window and prefills it with an Ask for Servers action (**Figure 3.36**). This time, when you run the workflow, you're asked to specify a URL to process. Again, make sure it contains audio content.
- ▲ If you specified "Use links on Safari web page open when workflow runs," Starting Points opens a workflow window that contains three actions: Get Current Webpage from Safari, Get Link URLs from Webpages, and Download URLs (**Figure 3.37**). This is really a good start!

You can continue building onto your workflow by dragging additional actions from the library list into the workflow area. For example, you may want to import that music into your iTunes library, upload it to your iDisk, or compress it into an archive.

✔ Tip

- ■ In a Music & Audio workflow, make very sure that the URLs your workflow processes are actually audio files. To do this, use the Filter URLs action to look for URLs ending with a specific file extension, such as .aif or .mp3. Consider using this action in all of your music and audio workflows.

Creating a Photos & Images Workflow

The age of the digital camera has brought with it the daunting task of maintaining countless digital photos. Applications such as iPhoto can help, but they can't do everything. Automator gives you control. Whether you need to organize a stack of personal photos or prepare your images for a graphic design project, dozens of image-related actions are at the ready.

Use these actions to automate time consuming, repetitive image-related tasks, including resizing, rotating, and cropping. Additional actions installed with iPhoto or available from third-party developers expand your possibilities, enabling you to import photos into an iPhoto album, create a Photoshop workflow to manipulate your photos, and more.

To begin creating a Photos & Images workflow:

1. Choose File > New

   or

   Press ⌘N to create a new workflow window with Starting Points attached.

2. Click Photos & Images (**Figure 3.38**) to get started.

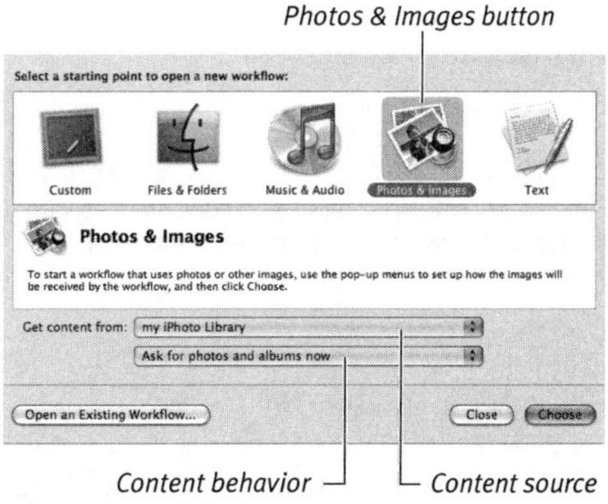

Figure 3.38 Click Photos & Images in Starting Points to create a workflow that processes your digital images.

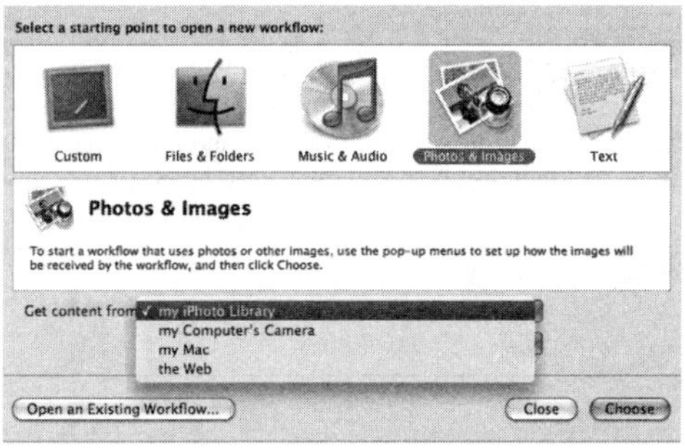

Figure 3.39 Choosing to get content from your iPhoto Library for a Photos & Images workflow using Starting Points.

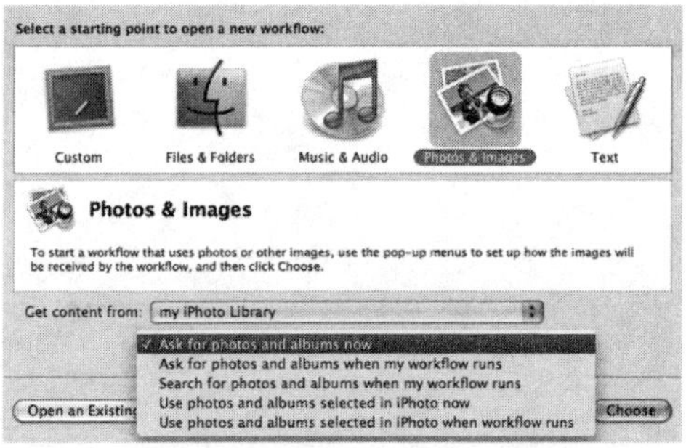

Figure 3.40 Specifying how to locate iPhoto content for a Photos & Images workflow using Starting Points.

Figure 3.41 Starting Points lets you choose the photos and albums you want to process with your workflow.

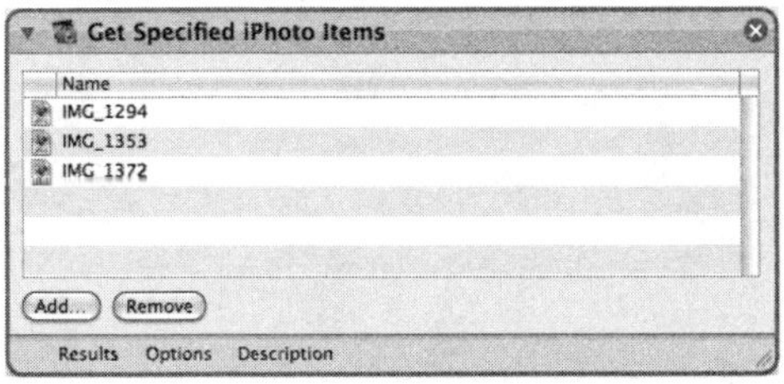

Figure 3.42 A Photos & Images workflow, prefilled with the Get Specified iPhoto Items action that lists specified photos.

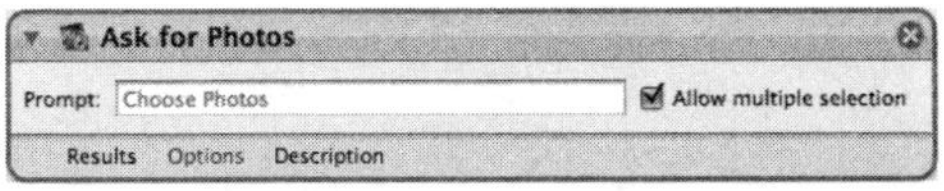

Figure 3.43 The Ask for Photos action prompts you for photos and albums when you run the workflow.

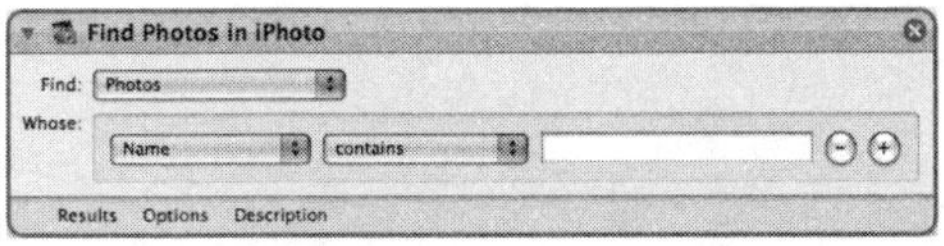

Figure 3.44 A Photos & Images workflow can search for photos or albums when you run the workflow.

To create a Photos & Images workflow using content from your iPhoto Library:

1. From the "Get Content from" pop-up button in the Starting Points panel, choose "my iPhoto Library" (**Figure 3.39**).
2. From the second pop-up menu, choose how and when you'd like to locate the iPhoto content for processing (**Figure 3.40**).
3. Click Choose to proceed. What happens next depends on the choices you made in Starting Points.
   - ▲ If you chose "Ask for photos and albums now," Starting Points prompts you to choose the photos and albums that you want to process with the workflow (**Figure 3.41**). Browse through your iPhoto library, pick out some items, and click Add.

     Next, Starting Points opens a workflow window containing a Get Specified iPhoto Items action, which lists the selected photos and albums (**Figure 3.42**).
   - ▲ If you specify "Ask for photos and albums when my workflow runs," Starting Points opens a workflow window containing an Ask for Photos action (**Figure 3.43**). Now, when you run the workflow it asks you to locate photos and albums to process.
   - ▲ If you selected "Search for photos and albums when my workflow runs," Starting Points opens a workflow window containing a Find iPhoto Items action (**Figure 3.44**). You can now specify the desired search criteria, such as any photo containing `Vacation` in its title. When you run the workflow, Automator searches for photos that match your criteria.

continues on next page

- If you selected "Use photos and albums selected in iPhoto now," Starting Points opens a workflow window that includes a Get Specified iPhoto Items action containing a list of the photos and albums currently selected in iPhoto (**Figure 3.45**).
- If you chose "Use photos and albums selected in iPhoto when workflow runs," Starting Points opens a workflow window containing a Get Selected iPhoto Items action (**Figure 3.46**). Now, Automator processes photos and albums selected in iPhoto at runtime.

You can continue building this workflow by dragging additional actions from the Library list into the workflow area. For example, you may wish to add actions that resize your photos, crop them, or copy them to your iDisk.

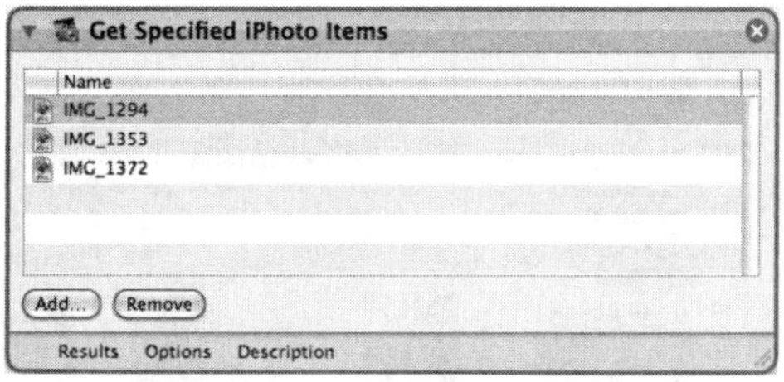

Figure 3.45 A Photos & Images workflow, prefilled with the Get Specified iPhoto Items action, lists selected photos.

Figure 3.46 The Get Selected iPhoto Items action retrieves selected photos when you run the workflow.

✔ Tips

- If you don't have iPhoto installed, then you won't see the option to build this type of workflow in Starting Points.
- If your Photos & Images workflow manipulates images, be careful not to overwrite your originals. To ensure that they're safe, use the Copy Finder Items action to duplicate them to another folder before processing them.

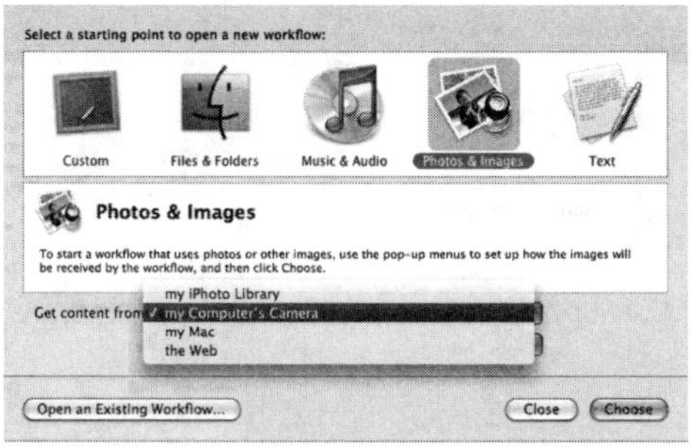

Figure 3.47 If you have a camera, such as an iSight, connected to your Mac, you can retrieve content from it to process.

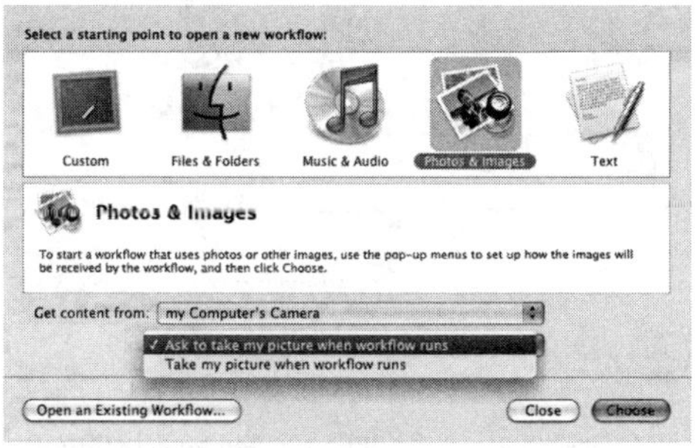

Figure 3.48 Specifying how to locate camera content to process for a Photos & Images workflow.

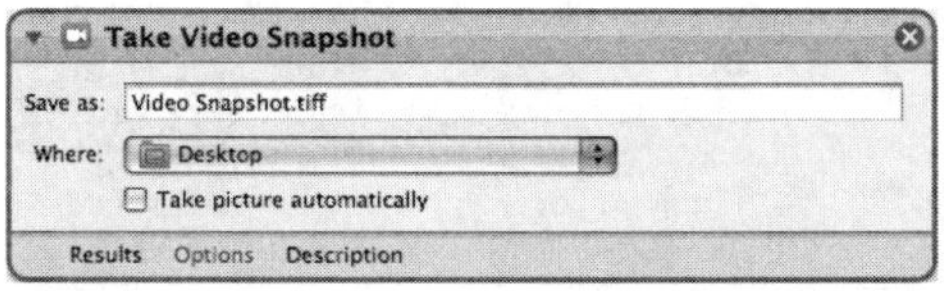

Figure 3.49 A Photos & Images workflow can be configured to ask to take your picture when you run the workflow.

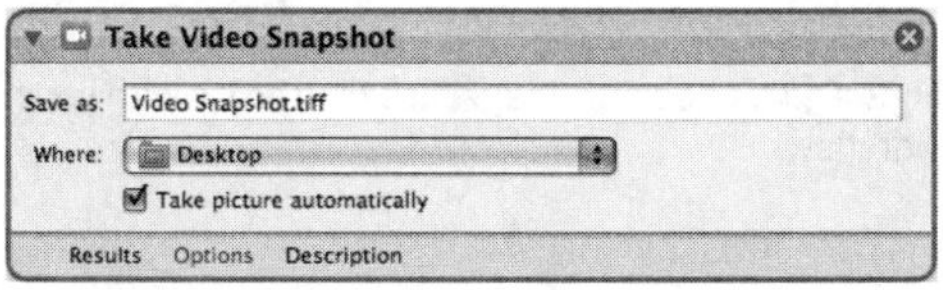

Figure 3.50 A Photos & Images workflow can also take your picture automatically when you run the workflow.

To create a Photos & Images workflow using content from your computer's camera:

1. From the "Get content from" pop-up menu in Starting Points, choose "my Computer's Camera" (**Figure 3.47**).
2. From the second pop-up menu, choose when and how you'd like to locate the camera content for processing (**Figure 3.48**). Your workflow can take your picture automatically, or it will wait for you to pose and click a button when you're ready.
3. Click Choose. What happens next depends on your choices in the Starting Points panel.
   - ▲ If you chose "Ask to take my picture when workflow runs," Starting Points opens a workflow that contains a Take Video Snapshot action (**Figure 3.49**). Note that the "Take picture automatically" checkbox in the action's interface is not selected. When you run the workflow, it displays a window, giving you time to pose and allowing you to snap the picture once you're ready.
   - ▲ If you specified "Take my picture when workflow runs," Starting Points again opens a workflow with a Take Video Snapshot action (**Figure 3.50**). This time, the "Take picture automatically" checkbox is selected. When you run the workflow, there's no time to strike a pose. It takes a snapshot right away.

From here, you can continue building onto the workflow. Try adding the New Mail Message action to send your snapshot to a friend.

To create a Photos & Images workflow using content from your Mac:

1. From the "Get content from" pop-up menu in Starting Points, choose "my Mac" (**Figure 3.51**).
2. Choose when and how you'd like to locate images to be processed (**Figure 3.52**).
3. Click Choose.
   - ▲ If you selected "Ask for image files now," Starting Points opens a file selection window. Locate the image files that you want to process with the workflow, and click Add (**Figure 3.53**).

     A new workflow window appears, prefilled with a Get Specified Finder Items action. This action contains the specified image files (**Figure 3.54**).
   - ▲ If you chose "Ask for image files when my workflow runs," Starting Points opens a workflow window, containing an Ask for Finder Items action (**Figure 3.55**). You'll locate the desired image files when you run the workflow.
   - ▲ If you specified "Search for image files when my workflow runs," Starting Points opens a new workflow window containing a Find Finder Items action (**Figure 3.56**). You may now enter the desired search criteria. When you run the workflow, Automator searches for image files, based on the criteria you specified.

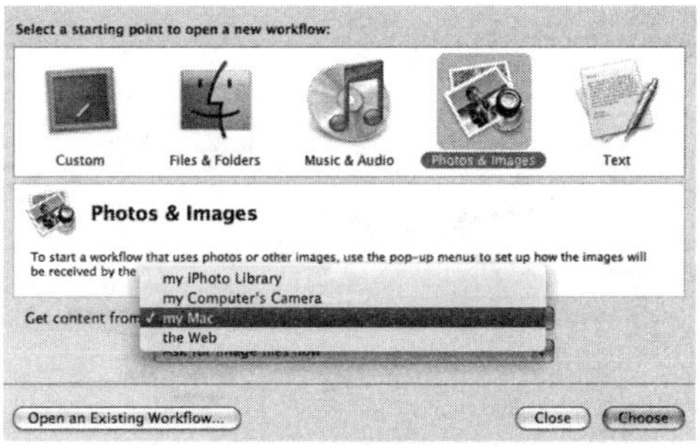

Figure 3.51 You can use Starting Points to get content from your Mac for a Photos & Images workflow.

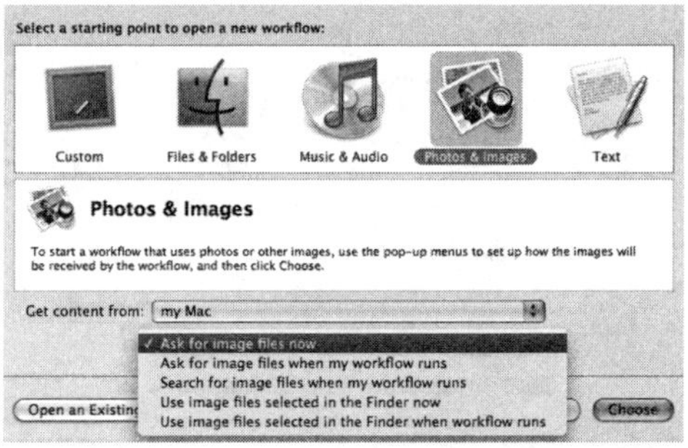

Figure 3.52 In Starting Points you can specify how to locate content for a Photos & Images workflow.

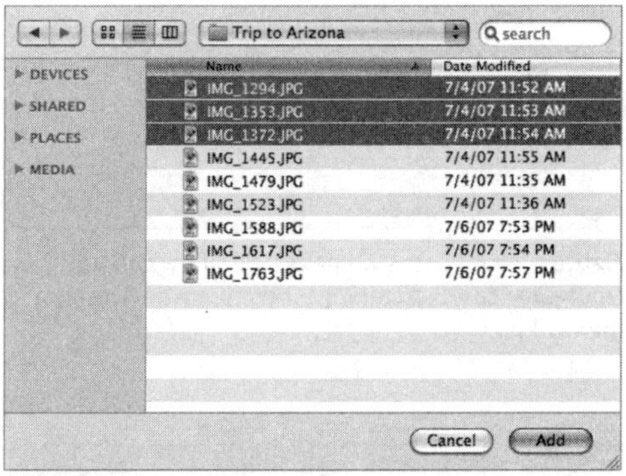

Figure 3.53 Choosing image files to process with your workflow.

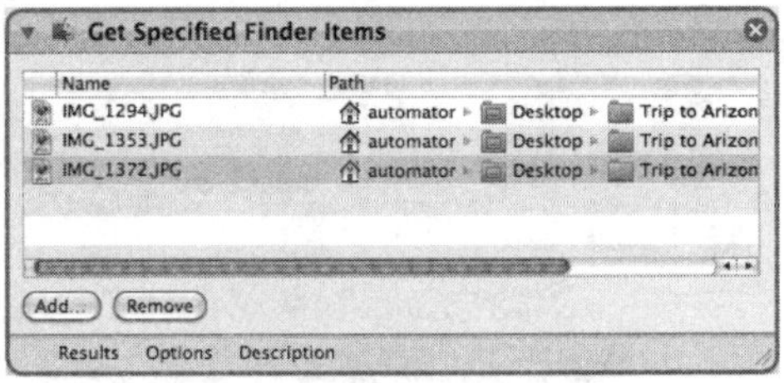

Figure 3.54 The Get Specified Finder Items action containing specified image files.

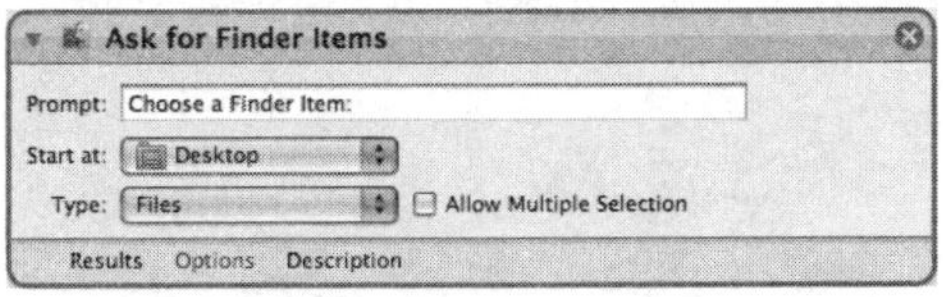

Figure 3.55 The Ask for Finder Items action asks for image files when you run the workflow.

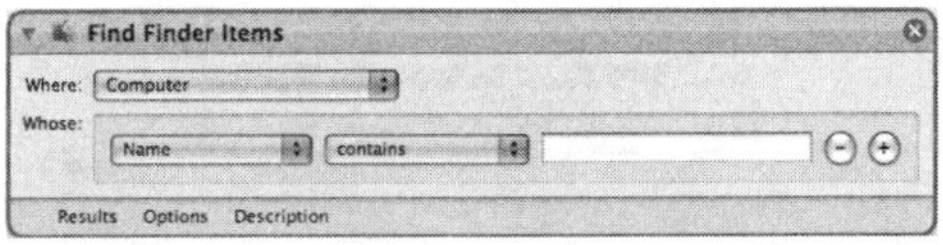

Figure 3.56 The Find Finder Items action searches for image files when you run a workflow.

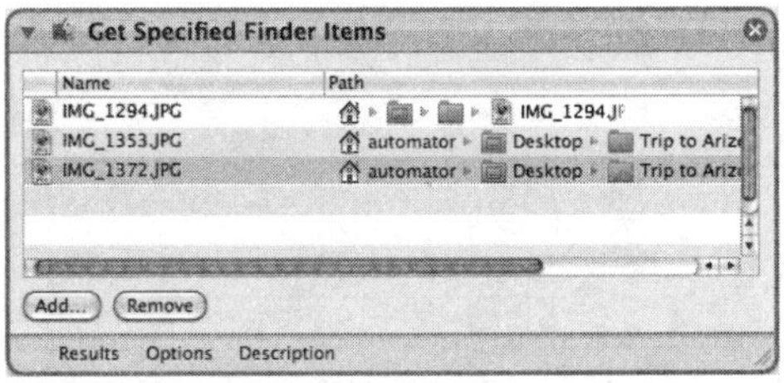

Figure 3.57 A Photos & Images workflow, prefilled with the Get Specified Finder Items action that lists selected image files.

Figure 3.58 The Get Selected Finder Items action is used to processes selected image files when you run your workflow.

- If you chose "Use image files selected in the Finder now," Starting Points opens a workflow window prefilled with a Get Specified Finder Items action that lists image files currently selected in the Finder (**Figure 3.57**).
- If you chose "Use image files selected in the Finder when workflow runs," Starting Points opens a workflow window containing a Get Selected Finder Items action (**Figure 3.58**). This action gets any selected image files at the time you run the workflow.

You can continue building onto the started workflow.

✔ Tip

- To ensure that invalid Finder items are not processed by your Photos & Images workflow, insert a Filter Finder Items action and configure it to look for only image files. To be safe, it's a good idea to include this in all of your workflows that process image files.

To create a Photos & Images workflow using content from the Web:

1. From the "Get content from" pop-up menu in Starting Points, choose "the Web" (**Figure 3.59**).
2. From the second pop-up menu, choose how and when you'd like to locate the images to be processed (**Figure 3.60**).
3. Click Choose. What happens next depends on the options you chose in Starting Points.
   - ▲ If you selected "Ask for URLs now," Starting Points opens a workflow window with a Get Specified URLs action (**Figure 3.61**). You can now add the desired URLs.
   - ▲ If you chose "Ask for URLs when my workflow runs," Starting Points opens a workflow window containing an Ask for Servers action (**Figure 3.62**). When you run your workflow, it prompts you to choose a URL for processing.
   - ▲ If you specified "Use links on Safari web page open when workflow runs," Starting Points opens a workflow window containing three actions: Get Current Webpage from Safari, Get Link URLs from Webpages, and Download URLs (**Figure 3.63**).

You can continue building onto the workflow by dragging additional actions from the Library list into the workflow area.

✔ Tip

- To ensure that invalid URLs aren't processed by your Photos & Images workflow, insert a Filter URLs action to filter for URLs ending with a specific file extension, such as .jpg or .gif.

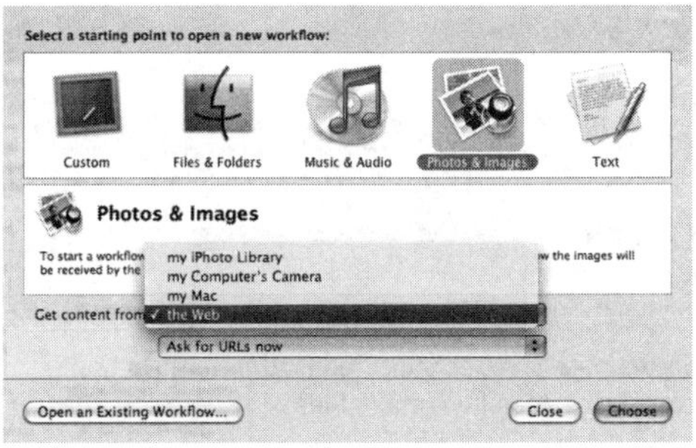

Figure 3.59 Choosing to get content from the Web for a Photos & Images workflow using Starting Points.

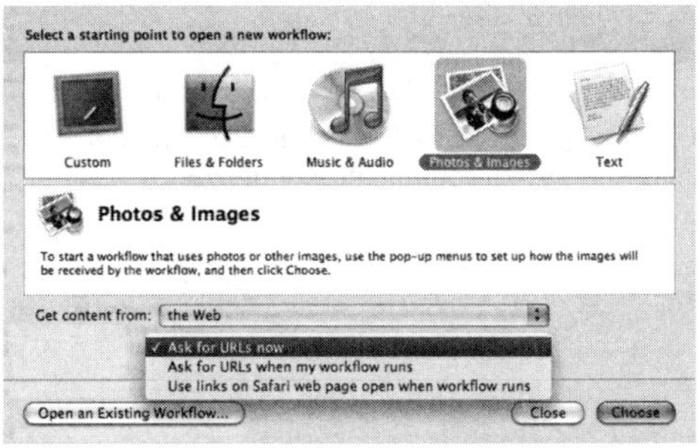

Figure 3.60 Specifying how to locate the content you want to process for a Photos & Images workflow using Starting Points.

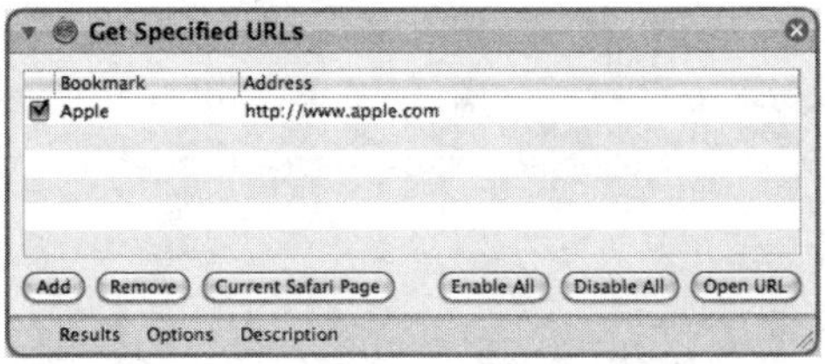

Figure 3.61 The Get Specified URLs action allows you to specify a webpage from which to process photos and images.

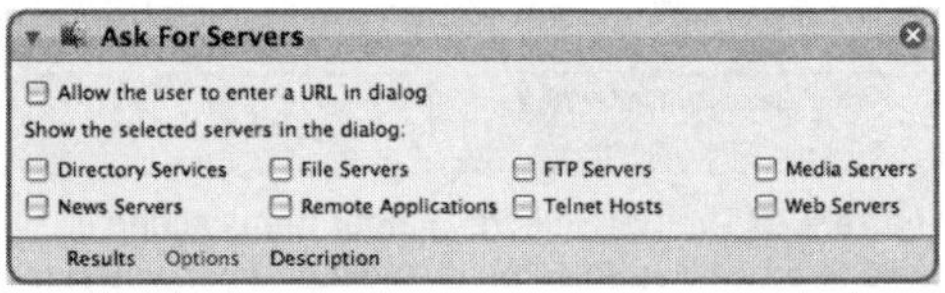

Figure 3.62 The Ask for Servers action prompts you for a URL when you run a workflow.

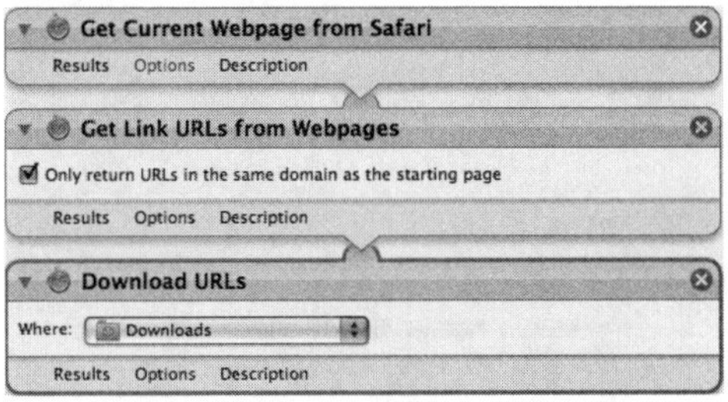

Figure 3.63 A Photos & Images workflow, prefilled with the Get Current Webpage from Safari, Get Link URLs from Webpages, and Download URLs actions, prepared to process photos using links on the current Safari webpage.

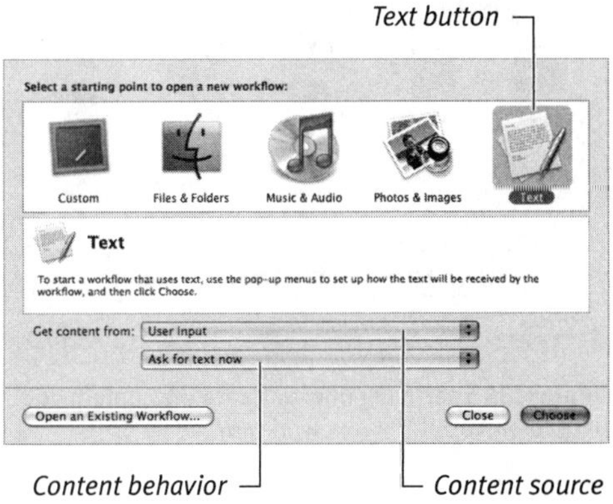

Figure 3.64 Starting Points helps you create text-based workflows.

Creating a Text-Based Workflow

Automator isn't just for processing music, audio, files, and folders. It can also perform text-based functions, such as getting text from a TextEdit document and inserting it into an email message, or creating an iPod note.

To begin creating a text-based workflow:

1. Choose File > New

   or

   Press [⌘][N].

   Automator creates a new workflow window with the Starting Points panel attached.

2. In the Starting Points panel, click the Text button (**Figure 3.64**).

To create a text-based workflow using user input:

1. From the "Get content from" pop-up menu choose User Input (**Figure 3.65**) to instruct Automator to prompt you to enter text either now or when your workflow runs.
2. From the second pop-up menu in the Starting Points panel, choose how you'd like to specify the text to be processed (**Figure 3.66**).
3. Click Choose. What happens next depends on what you selected in the second pop-up menu.
   - ▲ If you chose "Ask for text now," Starting Points opens a workflow window with a Get Specified Text action (**Figure 3.67**). You can now enter the text you the workflow to process.
   - ▲ If you selected "Ask for text when my workflow runs," Starting Points opens a workflow window containing an Ask for Text action (**Figure 3.68**), which instructs Automator to ask you for text input when you run your workflow.

You can continue building onto the workflow by dragging additional actions from the Library list into the workflow area. For example, you could insert the New To Do Item action to create a to do item in iCal.

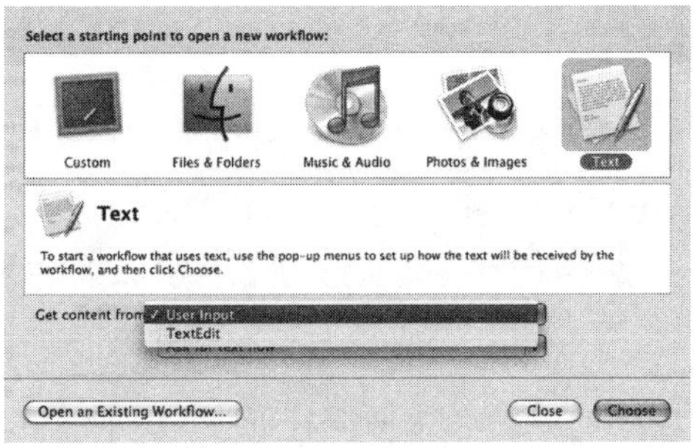

Figure 3.65 A text-based workflow can be configured to ask you for the text to process.

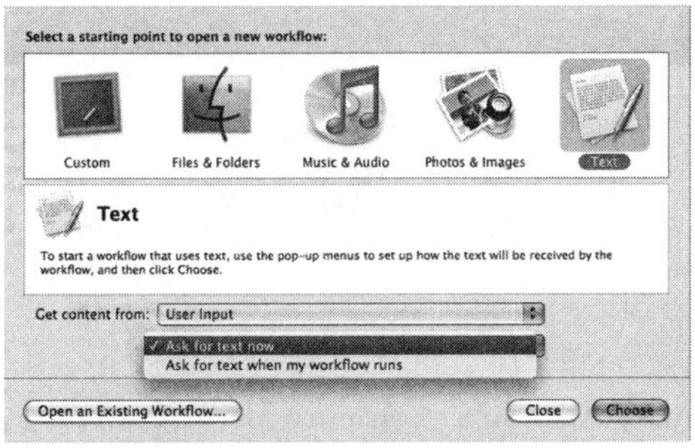

Figure 3.66 Specifying how to locate the content you want to process for a Text workflow.

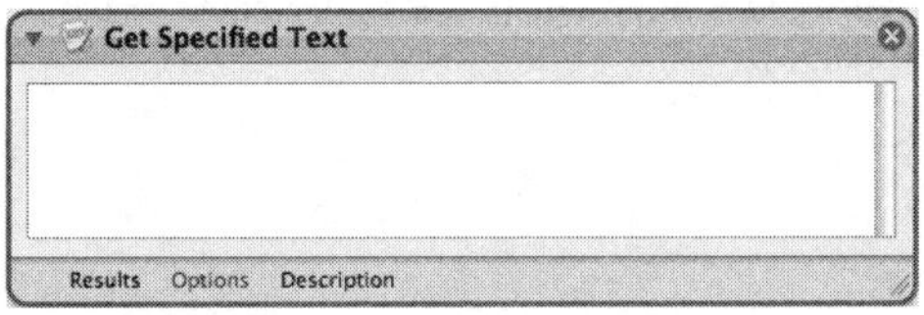

Figure 3.67 The Get Specified Text action enables you to enter some text for the workflow to process.

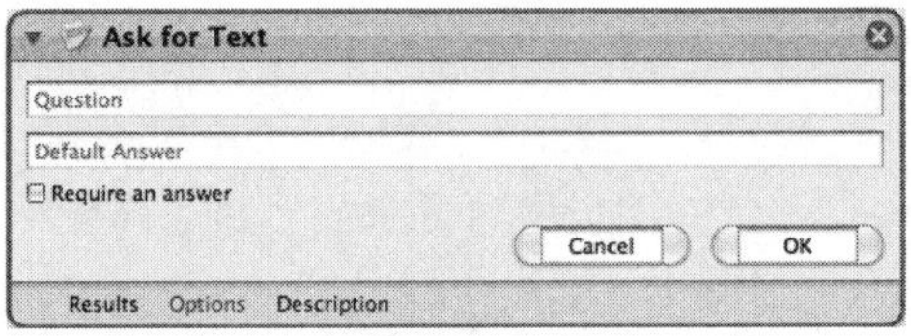

Figure 3.68 The Ask for Text action asks you to enter text while you run the workflow.

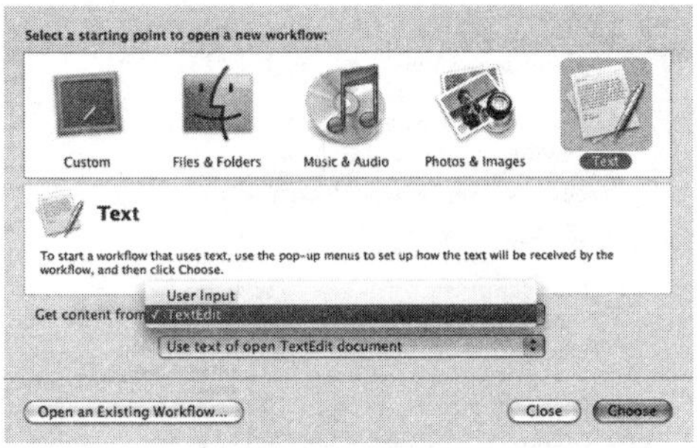

Figure 3.69 Select TextEdit from the "Get content from" pop-up menu to begin creating a text-based workflow.

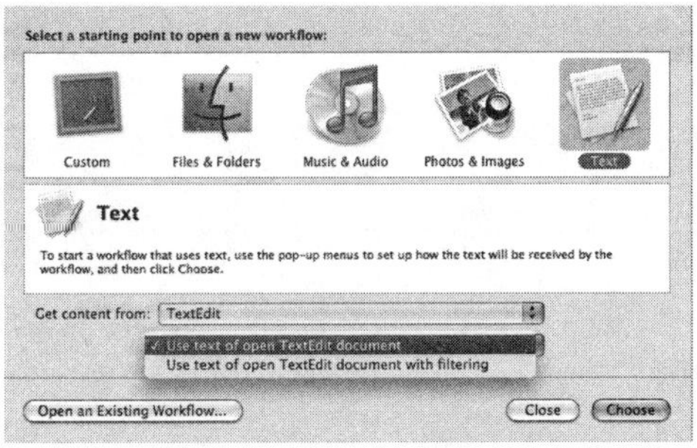

Figure 3.70 Starting Points allows you to retrieve all text from a TextEdit document or filter for specific text.

Figure 3.71 The Get Contents of TextEdit Document action gets all the text in the open TextEdit document.

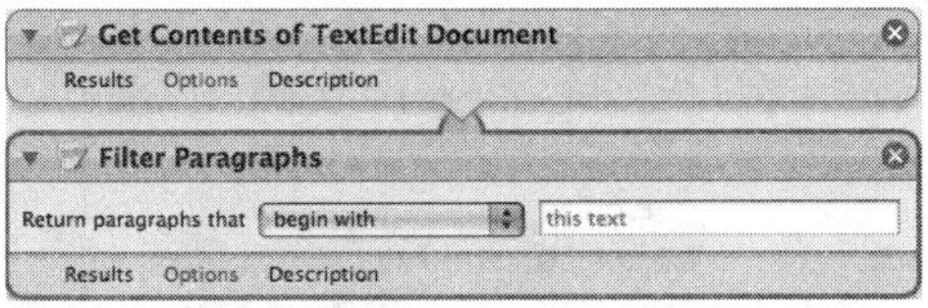

Figure 3.72 A Text workflow, prefilled with the Get Contents of TextEdit Document and Filter Paragraphs actions. This workflow processes paragraphs matching your specified criteria only.

To create a text-based workflow using content from TextEdit:

1. From the "Get content from" pop-up menu in Starting Points, choose TextEdit (**Figure 3.69**).
2. From the second pop-up menu, specify whether you'd like to filter the TextEdit content (**Figure 3.70**). You can get all of the text from an open TextEdit document, or you can filter for specific text. For example, you may want only paragraphs that aren't empty.
3. Click Choose.
   - ▲ If you selected "Use text of open TextEdit document," Starting Points opens a workflow window containing a Get Contents of TextEdit Document action (**Figure 3.71**). When you run the workflow, all text in the frontmost open TextEdit document gets processed.
   - ▲ If you selected "Use text of open TextEdit document with filtering," Starting Points opens a workflow window containing a Get Contents of TextEdit Document action and a Filter Paragraphs action (**Figure 3.72**). You can now configure the Filter Paragraphs action to filter for only specific paragraphs. When you run the workflow, the first action retrieves text from the frontmost open TextEdit document and passes it to the Filter Paragraphs action for filtering. Only paragraphs matching your specified criteria are passed down from here for further processing.

You can continue building onto the workflow by dragging additional actions from the Library list into the workflow area.

Creating a Workflow Without Starting Points

Starting Points can be a big help, but if you find yourself creating mainly custom workflows, it may be less useful. If this is the case, you can disable it, so it doesn't appear whenever you create a new workflow.

To disable Starting Points:

Choose Automator > Disable Starting Points. (**Figure 3.73**).

Now, whenever you create a new workflow, it is automatically empty and ready for you to customize (**Figure 3.74**).

To enable Starting Points:

Choose Automator > Enable Starting Points (**Figure 3.75**).

Figure 3.73 Choose Disable Starting Points from the Automator menu to turn off Starting Points.

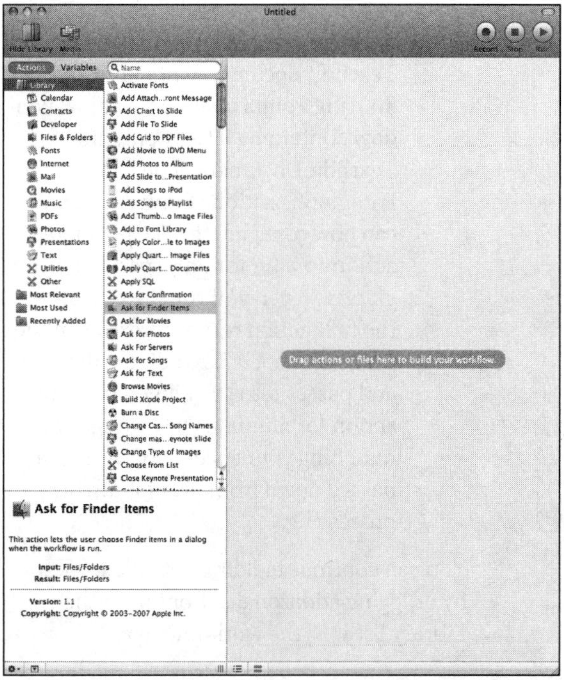

Figure 3.74 A new workflow window, without Starting Points attached.

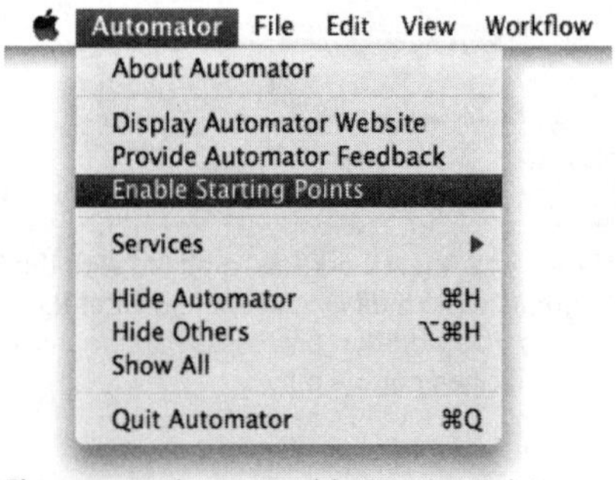

Figure 3.75 Choose Enable Starting Points from the Automator menu to turn Starting Points back on.

Creating a Workflow from Finder Items

It doesn't get much easier than using Starting Points to create a workflow that processes files and folders... or does it? In Mac OS X, you can quickly create a files and folders workflow from right within the Finder!

To create a files and folders workflow from the Finder:

1. Select the files and folders you want to process in the Finder.
2. Hold down the Control key, and click the selected files and folders.

   The Finder's contextual menu appears.
3. Choose More > Automator > Create Workflow from the contextual menu (**Figure 3.76**).

Automator creates a new workflow window containing a Get Specified Finder Items action and fills it with the selected files and folders (**Figure 3.77**).

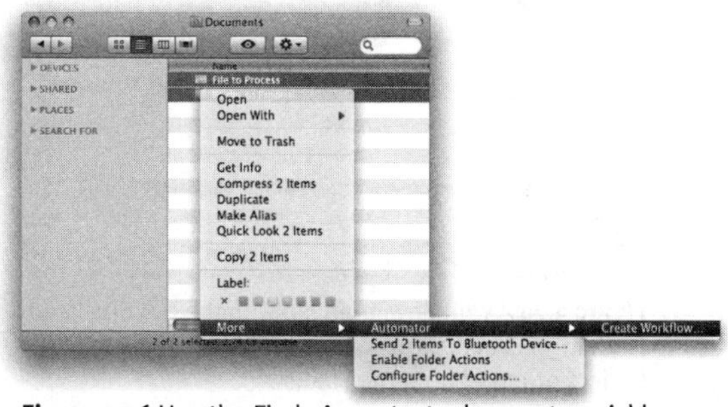

Figure 3.76 Use the Finder's contextual menu to quickly create an Automator workflow to process selected items.

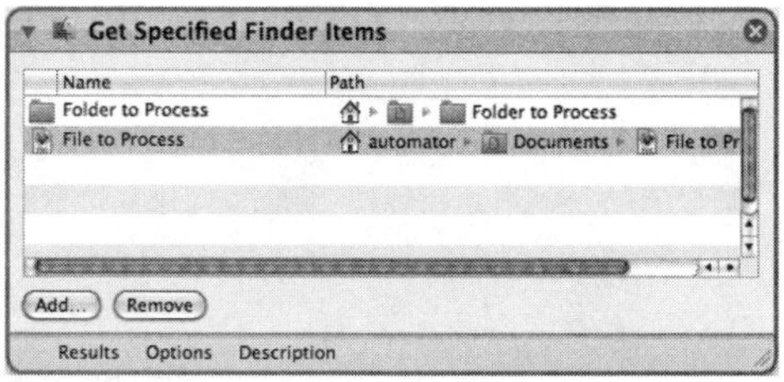

Figure 3.77 A newly created workflow, prefilled with the Get Specified Finder Items action, prepared with selected files and folders in the Finder.

Adding Finder Items to a Workflow

You now know how to create a new workflow to process files and folders, but what if you need to insert files and folders into an existing workflow? This is easy, too.

To quickly add Finder items to an opened workflow:

1. Select the Finder items you want to insert into your workflow.
2. Drag the selected items into your workflow window (**Figure 3.78**).

   Automator inserts a Get Specified Finder Items action containing the dropped files and folders (**Figure 3.79**).

✔ Tips

- If your opened workflow contains other actions, drag the files and folders to the desired location within the workflow. The Get Specified Finder Items action is inserted wherever you drop the files and folders.
- Drop your files in the wrong location? No problem. Simply drag the resulting Get Specified Finder Items action to the correct spot in your workflow.

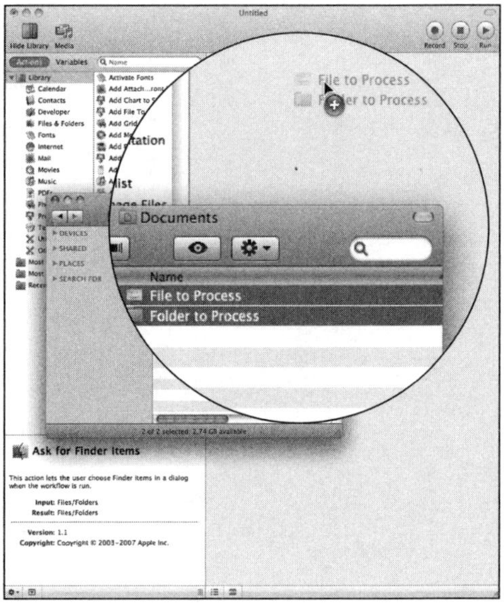

Figure 3.78 Drag Finder items to add them to an Automator workflow in a Get Specified Finder Items action.

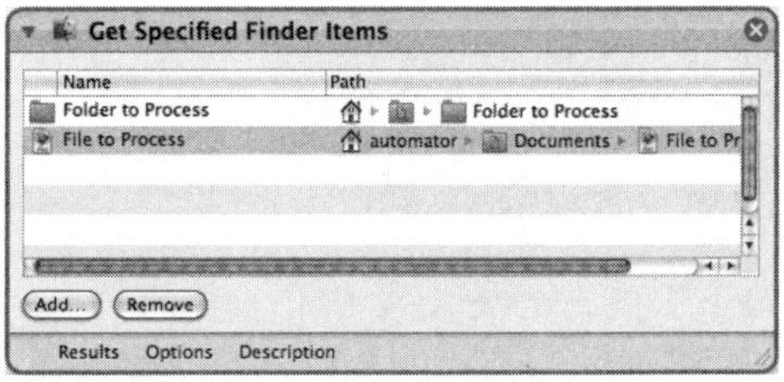

Figure 3.79 A workflow, prefilled with the Get Specified Finder Items action, prepared to process files and folders dropped from the Finder.

Figure 3.80 Click the Media button in a workflow window's toolbar to display Automator's Media Browser.

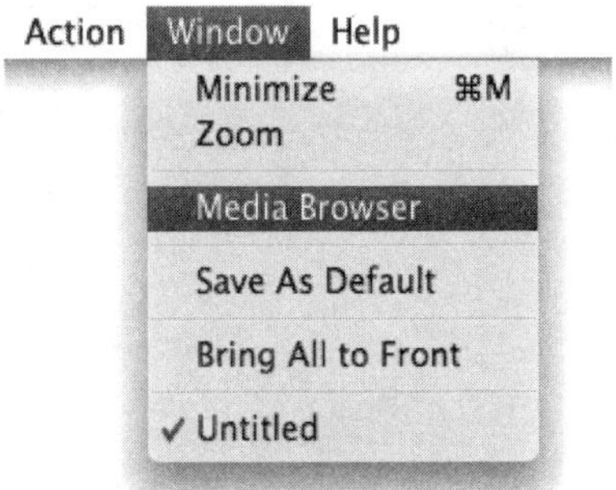

Figure 3.81 If you prefer, display the Media Browser from the menu bar.

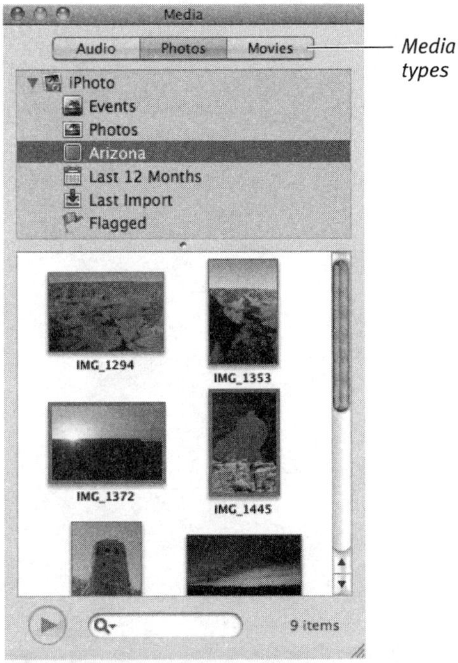

Figure 3.82 The Media Browser allows you to pick and choose the photos, audio, and movies you want to process.

Adding Audio, Photos, or Movies to a Workflow

It's never been easier to create a workflow to process your media content. Automator's Media Browser finds and displays a list of all your audio, photos, and movies. Here, you can preview the media, such as listen to a song or view a photo or movie, and insert it into your workflow.

To add audio, photos, or movies to a workflow:

1. Display Automator's Media Browser. Click the Media button in the toolbar of your workflow window (**Figure 3.80**).

   or

   Choose Window > Media Browser (**Figure 3.81**).
2. Click the Audio, Photos, or Movies tab at the top of the Media Browser window to choose the type of content you want to add (**Figure 3.82**).
3. Select the desired audio, photos, or movies, and drag them to your workflow. Based on the type of content chosen, Automator adds a Get Specified Finder Items action, Get Specified iPhoto Items action, Get Specified iTunes Items action, or Get Specified Movies action to your work-flow. In all cases, the action contains the dropped media content (**Figure 3.83**).

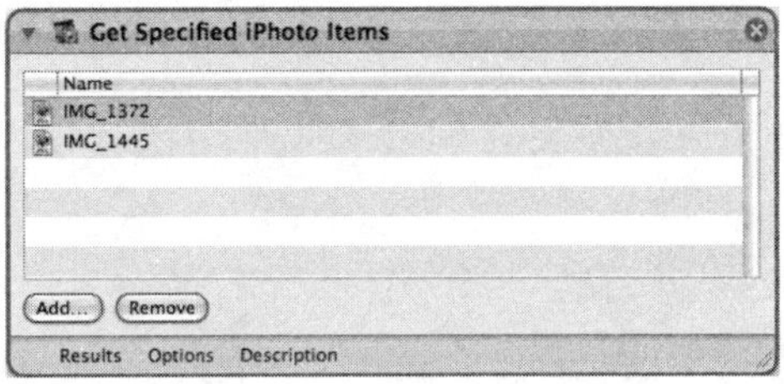

Figure 3.83 Automator inserts a Get Specified iPhoto Items action when you drag iPhoto images from the Media Browser to your workflow.

4

Working with Actions

By now you should be comfortable creating workflows with Starting Points, which will automatically insert actions into your workflow to get you going. There's a lot more to Automator, however, than these simple beginnings. To do anything truly useful, you need to add more actions to your workflow than Starting Points provides, and you need to configure those actions to do what you want. This chapter helps you get to this next level by showing you how to:

- Find an action that's right for your workflow
- Add actions to your workflow and understand warning messages that may be displayed
- Configure an action's settings and options so the action will do what you want
- Adjust your workflow by renaming, deleting, and disabling actions
- Use action input and output values properly so that your actions work together when you run the workflow

The techniques you learn in this chapter will apply to working with virtually any action within an Automator workflow.

Locating Actions to Do What You Want

Automator comes with hundreds of actions, and that list grows every time you add new Automator-ready applications or third-party actions to your machine. With so many actions, locating the one to do what you want is no small feat. However, there are some practical ways to find them.

Picking the Right Action for a Task

In Chapter 3 (see "Planning a Workflow"), you learned that it's a good idea to think through the job of a workflow before creating it. Break it into individual tasks, then translate those tasks to actions.

But how do you pick the right action for a task? Think about the task. What does it do? For example, does it create a folder on the Desktop? What is its result? The newly created folder? What application or process does it target? The Finder? Use the words from these questions and answers as keywords, and type them into Automator's search field to help find an appropriate action.

✔ Tip

- Be sure to check action descriptions frequently, too, as they often contain important information. See "Viewing an Action's Description" later in this chapter.

Five Useful File & Folder Actions

1. **Find Finder Items.** Helps you locate specific files and folders on your Mac when your workflow runs.
2. **Filter Finder Items.** Allows you to filter a list of files for ones matching a specific criteria. For example, you could use this action to filter for only image files.
3. **Sort Finder Items.** Use this action to sort Finder items into the order you want to process them. This can be especially useful if you want to process files sequentially or in the order they were last modified.
4. **Connect to Servers.** Does your workflow process files and folders on a server volume? Use this action to make sure that server volume is connected when your workflow runs.
5. **Set Spotlight.** Comments for Finder Items. Spotlight searching makes locating files a breeze. Use this action to ensure that files without descriptive names, such as your digital photos, are found when you perform a search.

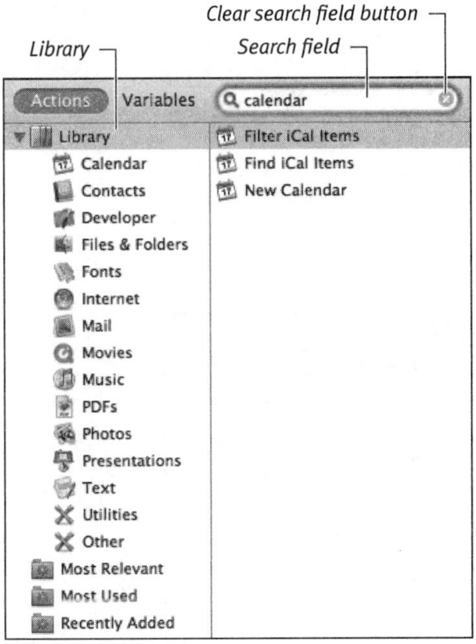

Figure 4.1 Searching for calendar actions using a keyword.

To locate an action by application name, action name, or keyword:

1. In your workflow window, click Library in the left column of the Library list to display a list of all available actions (**Figure 4.1**).
2. In the search field at the top of the Library list, type a search term, such as an application name, action name, or a keyword. For example, to find an action that creates a new calendar in iCal, you might enter `iCal` or `calendar`.

   Automator lists any actions that match the specified criteria (Figure 4.1).
3. Scan through the list of found actions and look for one that does what you need. Then, drag it into your workflow.

✔ Tips

- If you're having trouble locating an action using one keyword, try a synonym. For example, if you want to locate an action that will search for something, try the keywords `search` and `find`.
- If no actions are found by your search, verify that you have clicked Library at the top of the left column in the Library list.
- Click the X button on the right side of the search field to clear the search and display other actions again (Figure 4.1).
- If you've tried and tried, but are unable to locate an action, see if a third-party developer has created one. Search Apple's Mac OS X Automator action download site at www.apple.com/downloads/macosx/automator/.

To locate all actions within a category:

1. Ensure that Automator's Library list is arranged by category. If it's not, then choose View > Arrange Actions By > Category (**Figure 4.2**).
2. Click the desired category name within the Library list.

   Automator displays the actions within that specific category (**Figure 4.3**).

   Now, you can scan through the list of actions within the category for the desired action or actions. Once you find what you're looking for, drag it into your workflow.

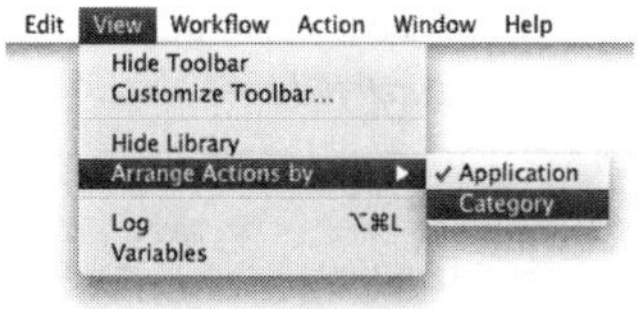

Figure 4.2 Configuring Automator's Library list to arrange actions by category.

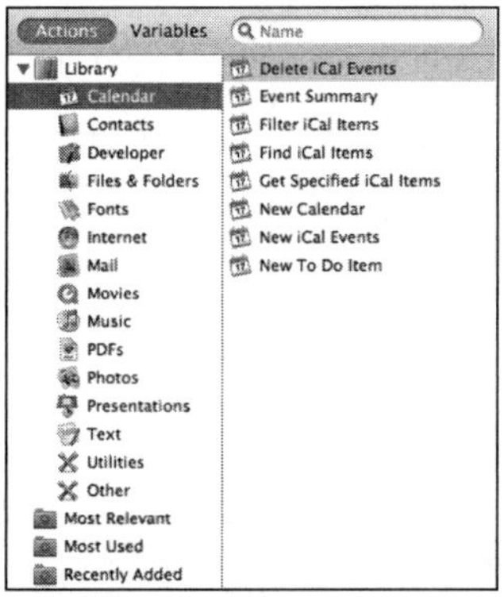

Figure 4.3 Selecting a category of actions.

✔ Tip

- If actions don't fit into a specific category, they'll be in the category Other. Check in that category if you can't find the action you want. If you don't see the Other category, then all of your actions fit into Automator's built-in categories.

To locate all actions for a given application:

1. You may find it easier to locate actions by application, rather than by category. To do this, first ensure that the Library list is arranged by application. If it's not, choose View > Arrange Actions By > Application (**Figure 4.4**).
2. Click the appropriate application name within the Library list to display the actions that pertain to that specific application (**Figure 4.5**). For example, to see all iCal-related actions, click iCal.
3. Scan through the list of application actions for one that does what you need, and insert it into your workflow.

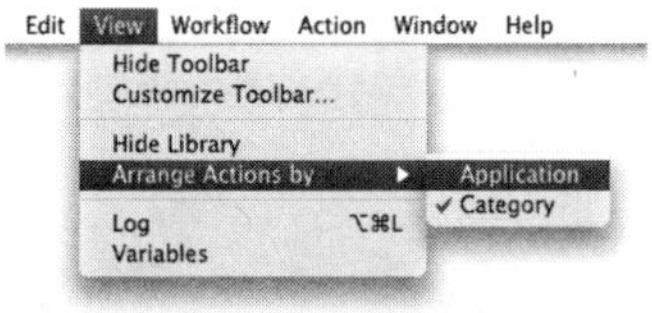

Figure 4.4 Configuring Automator's Library list to arrange actions by application.

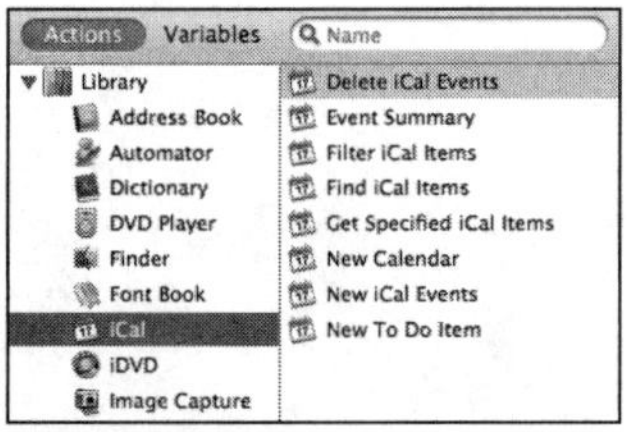

Figure 4.5 Selecting an application, to display all actions for that application.

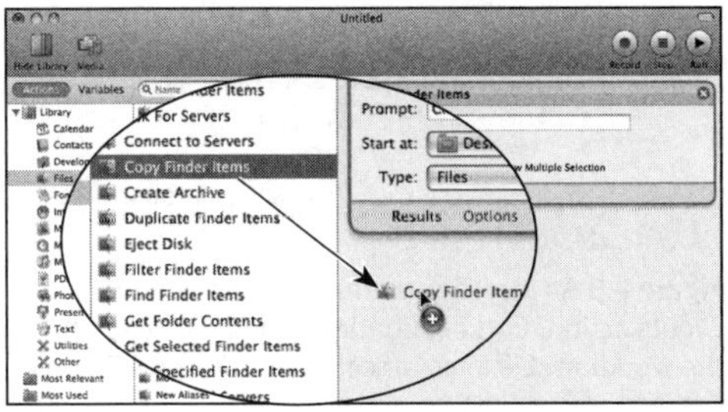

Figure 4.6 Dragging an action into a workflow.

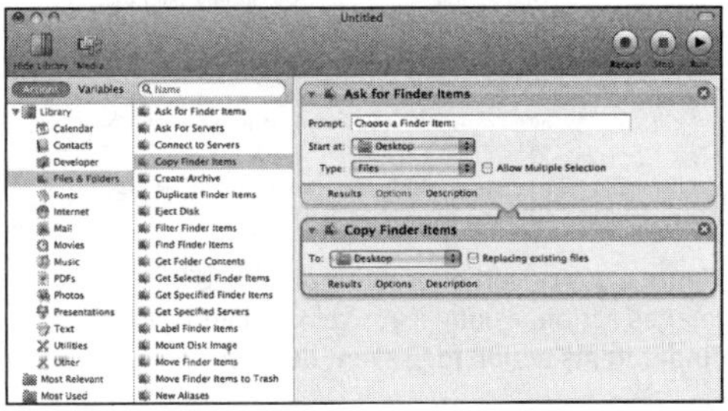

Figure 4.7 An action's interface, once added to a workflow.

Inserting Actions into a Workflow

You already know that you can add an action to your workflow by selecting it in the Library list and dragging it to the desired spot in your workflow. You can also insert an action at the end of your workflow by double-clicking it in the Library list (**Figures 4.6** and **4.7**).

✔ Tip

- If you've accidentally added an action to the wrong place in a workflow, simply select it and drag it to the correct location.

Four Useful Actions for Advanced Automator Users

1. **Run AppleScript.** Automator's a great tool, but as discussed in the Introduction, it does have some limitations that can be overcome with AppleScript functions. This action allows you to paste in AppleScript code, so that it runs as part of your workflow.
2. **Run Shell Script.** This action provides even greater possibilities for creating robust workflows by providing access to the UNIX underpinnings of Mac OS X. Just paste in the desired shell commands to incorporate them into your workflow.
3. **Loop.** Need to create a workflow that runs over and over again? As you'll learn in Chapter 10, "Workflow Looping," this action allows you to do just that.
4. **Set/Get Value of Variable.** Does your workflow include actions in different locations that need to share information? As you'll learn in Chapter 11, "Using Variables," this pair of actions allows you to store the output of an action in memory and then refer back to it later in your workflow.

Understanding Action Insertion Warnings

Sometimes when you drag an action into a workflow, Automator displays an alert panel. This generally occurs when the action you're adding will modify files, folders, or other data in some irreversible way. The type of warning displayed determines how you handle it.

- Some warnings simply alert you to something important. In these cases, you can usually choose to continue adding the action to the workflow, or you can cancel and not add the action (**Figure 4.8**).
- Other warnings provide a message and ask if you'd like to insert another suggested action first, in order to perform some function before the action in question, which is usually to prevent data loss. In these cases, you can choose to cancel, add the suggested action in addition to the action you've dragged into the workflow, or insert only the action you've dragged into the workflow (**Figure 4.9**).

  If you click Add, Automator inserts the suggested action immediately before the action you dragged into the workflow (**Figure 4.10**).

  If you click Don't Add, Automator adds only the action you dragged into the workflow.

  If you click Cancel, the workflow remains unchanged.

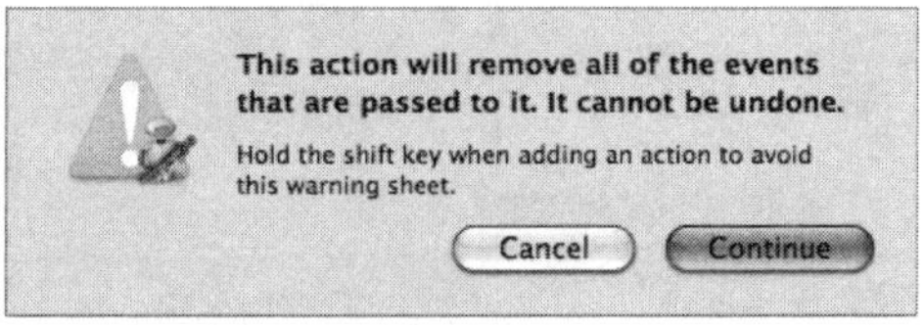
This action will remove all of the events that are passed to it. It cannot be undone.
Hold the shift key when adding an action to avoid this warning sheet.
Cancel
Continue

Figure 4.8 An insertion warning for the Delete iCal Events action. Clicking Continue adds the action to the workflow. Clicking Cancel leaves the workflow as it is.

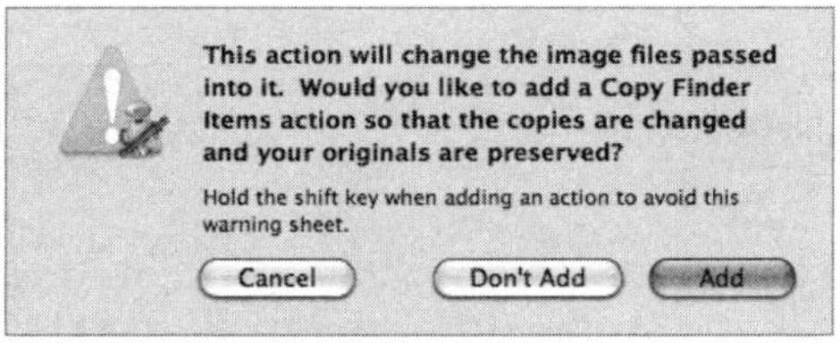
This action will change the image files passed into it. Would you like to add a Copy Finder Items action so that the copies are changed and your originals are preserved?
Hold the shift key when adding an action to avoid this warning sheet.
Cancel
Don't Add
Add

Figure 4.9 An insertion warning displayed by the Scale Images action, asking if you'd like to add a Copy Finder Items action to prevent data loss.

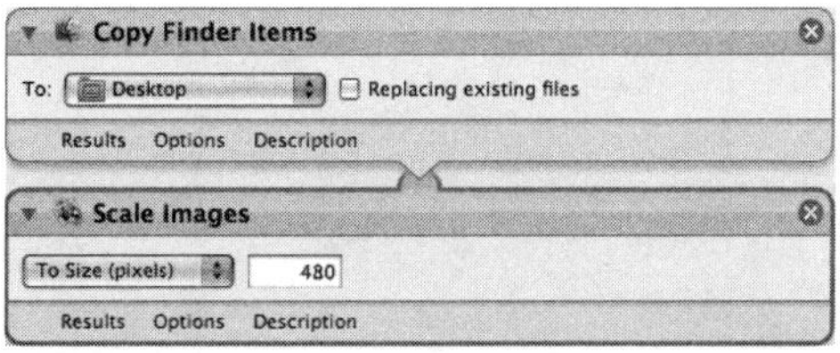
Copy Finder Items
To:
Desktop
Replacing existing files
Results
Options
Description
Scale Images
To Size (pixels)
480
Results
Options
Description

Figure 4.10 An auto-inserted Copy Finder Items action, preceding the Scale Images action, to prevent data loss.

✔ Tips

- Don't be afraid to add a suggested action to your workflow. You can always remove it if you decide later that you don't need it.
- To insert an action into a workflow without displaying its action insertion warning, hold Shift while dragging the action into the workflow area.

Insertion Warnings and the Actions That Cause Them

Two common types of actions that cause insertion warnings are:

- **Deletion Actions.** Most actions that permanently delete something display a warning of some type when inserted into a workflow. For example, the Remove Empty Playlists action lets you know that once you run it, there's no way to get those playlists back.
- **Image Manipulation Actions.** Most actions that modify image files display a warning letting you know that those modifications can't be undone. If you want to retain your originals, consider adding an action, such as a Copy Finder Items or Create Archive action, to back up your image files prior to modifying them.

Viewing an Action's Description

Each Automator action has a description that provides an overview of the action, the types of input the action accepts, the types of output the action produces, and more—a treasure trove of information for any Automator user. You can view an action's description in the Library list or in the workflow area.

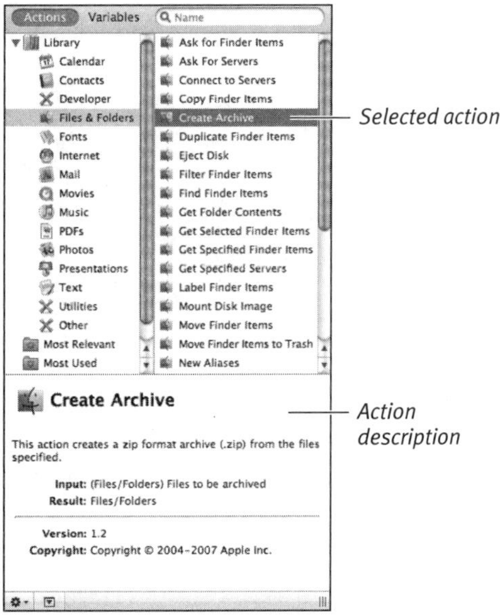

Figure 4.11 Viewing the description of the Create Archive action in the Library list.

To view the description of an action in the Library list:

- In the Library list, select the action you want to view to see its description in the workflow window's lower-left corner (**Figure 4.11**).

✔ Tips

- If you're unsure of an action's function or one of its settings, check its description.
- If the description area is not visible in the lower left of the workflow window, click the icon at the bottom of the window to display it.

To view the description of an action in the workflow area:

- Click the Description button at the bottom of the action's interface. The action's interface expands to show its description (**Figure 4.12**). To hide the description, click the Description button again.

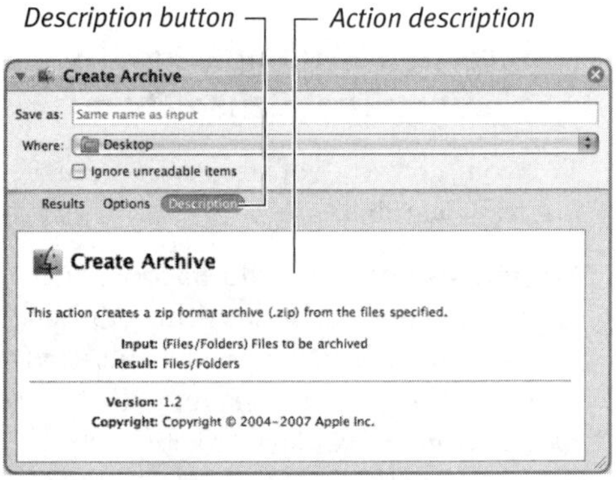

Figure 4.12 Viewing the description of an action in the workflow area.

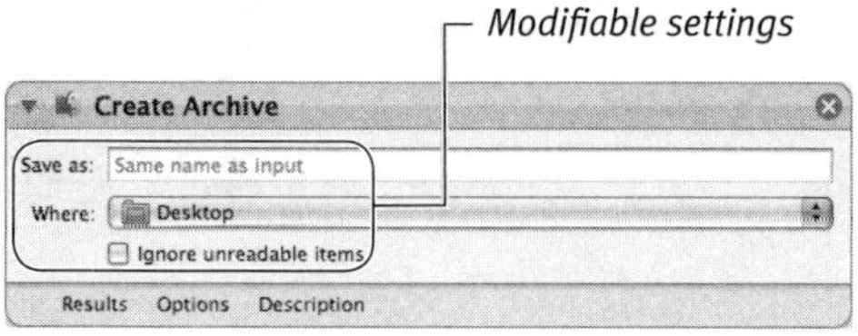

Figure 4.13 Modifiable settings for the Create Archive action.

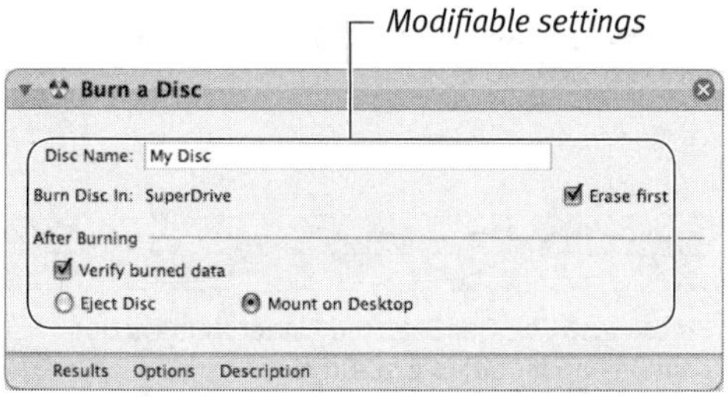

Figure 4.14 Modifiable settings for the Burn a Disc action.

Action Settings

Many actions have settings you can change to control the action's behavior when you run the workflow. Take the New iCal Events action, for example. This action allows you to specify a calendar and title for the event, along with a start and end time, an alarm, and more. When run within a workflow, this action behaves according to the settings you've specified.

Whenever you add an action to a workflow, you should check to see whether the action contains any modifiable settings, and if so, adjust them accordingly.

Actions with Settings

It's difficult to talk about individual action settings. Because every action performs a different task, each action's settings are different. When you begin working with a new action, you need to become familiar with its settings so you can make it do what you want.

To understand how modifying the settings on an action affects how it behaves when run, experiment with some examples:

- The Create Archive action's settings allow you to specify the name and location of the archive and whether any unreadable items should be ignored (**Figure 4.13**).
- The Burn a Disc action's settings enable you to specify the name of the disc, whether it should be erased first, and whether it should be verified, ejected, or mounted on the Desktop after burning (**Figure 4.14**).

continues on next page

- The New Mail Message action's settings allow you to specify the To, Cc, and Bcc recipients, the subject, the message content, and the account for the message (**Figure 4.15**).

✔ Tip

- Don't be afraid to try new things. If you're unsure of what an action setting does, try running the action in a test workflow to find out. Just be careful. If the action deletes or changes something, make sure you test it with data you don't mind deleting or changing.

Actions Without Settings

Some actions don't have modifiable settings. The interface for such an action is simply a title bar and a footer area—rather plain, as you can see (**Figure 4.16**).

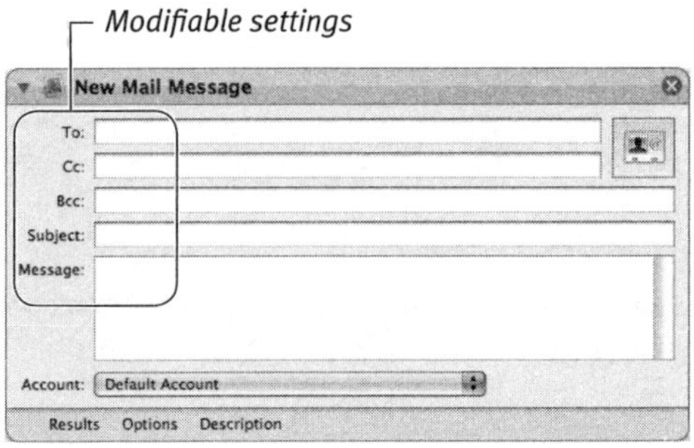

Figure 4.15 Modifiable settings for the New Mail Message action.

Figure 4.16 The Get Selected Finder Items action contains no modifiable settings.

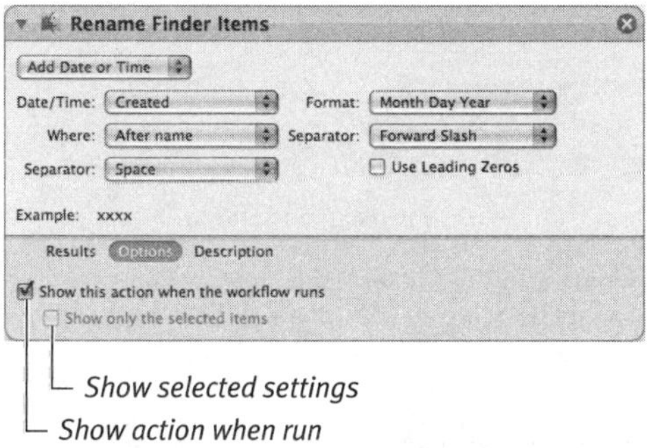

Figure 4.17 Configuring the Rename Finder Items action to allow its settings to be adjusted when run within a workflow.

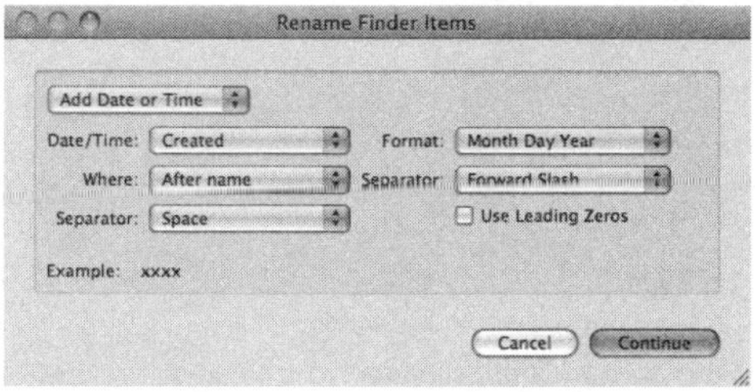

Figure 4.18 The Rename Finder Items action's interface, as displayed when run within a workflow, allowing its settings to be adjusted.

Action Options

Configuring an action's settings in advance can be helpful, but for some situations you may need to change the action's settings when the workflow runs. For example, suppose you're creating a workflow that creates a new email message in Mail. Rather than using the same settings every time, you may want to change the subject, message content, and more each time the workflow runs.

Allowing an action's settings to be adjusted when the workflow runs is also extremely helpful in a workflow that you're giving to other people. Users then can modify the workflow's behavior to meet their own unique needs.

Many Automator actions can be set to show their settings when run, and this can often make your workflow more flexible.

To configure an action to allow all of its settings to be modified when run:

1. Click the Options button.
   The action's interface expands to display some additional configuration options.
2. Select the "Show this action when the workflow runs" checkbox (**Figure 4.17**).

Now, when the workflow is run, the interface for the action is displayed, allowing the action's settings to be adjusted as needed (**Figure 4.18**).

Some actions allow you to be a bit more selective with regard to which of the action's settings may be modified. Rather than allowing all of the action's settings to be adjusted when the workflow is run, you can pick and choose the ones that you'd like to be modifiable.

continues on next page

✔ Tips

- If an action is configured to allow its settings to be modified when the workflow runs, then any preconfigured settings serve as the default settings for the action.
- Even if you've configured an action with modifiable settings, it's still a good idea to enter some defaults. Enter the settings that you expect to be used most often when the action is run.
- If an action's Options button is disabled, then the action cannot be configured to allow settings modification at runtime (**Figure 4.19**).

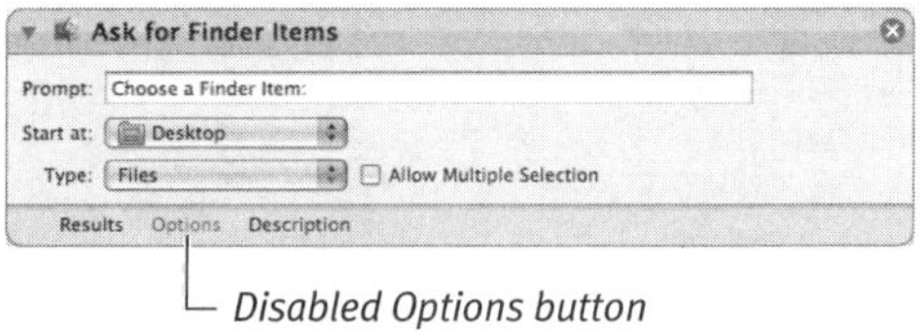

Figure 4.19 The Ask for Finder Items action's settings cannot be adjusted when the workflow is run.

To configure an action to allow only specified settings to be modified when run:

1. Select the "Show this action when the workflow runs" checkbox in the Options area.
2. Click the "Show only the selected items" checkbox in the Options area.

   The settings within the action's interface become highlighted, with checkboxes displayed next to them (**Figure 4.20**).
3. Select the checkboxes next to any settings that you'd like to be adjustable (Figure 4.20).

   Now, when the workflow is run, only the settings you checked are displayed, allowing users to adjust only these as needed (**Figure 4.21**).

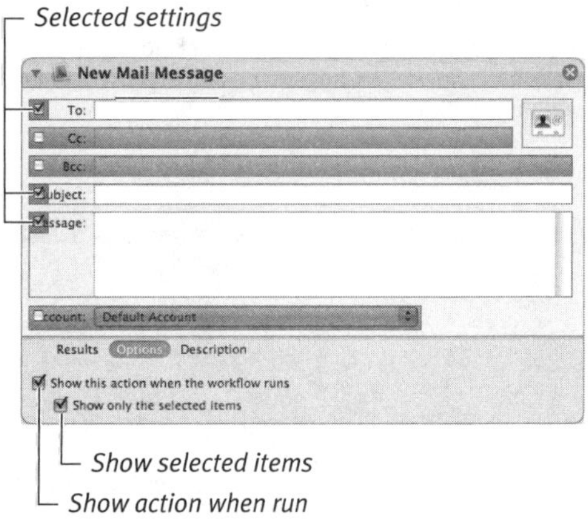

Figure 4.20 Configuring the New Mail Message action to allow only specified settings to be adjusted when run within a workflow.

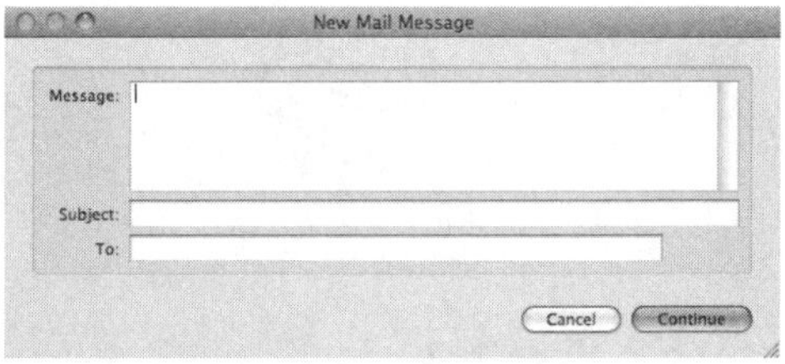

Figure 4.21 Specified adjustable settings for the New Mail Message action's interface, as displayed when run within a workflow.

✔ Tip

- If an action does not allow for this type of configuration, then the "Show only the selected items" checkbox in the Options area is disabled (Figure 4.17).

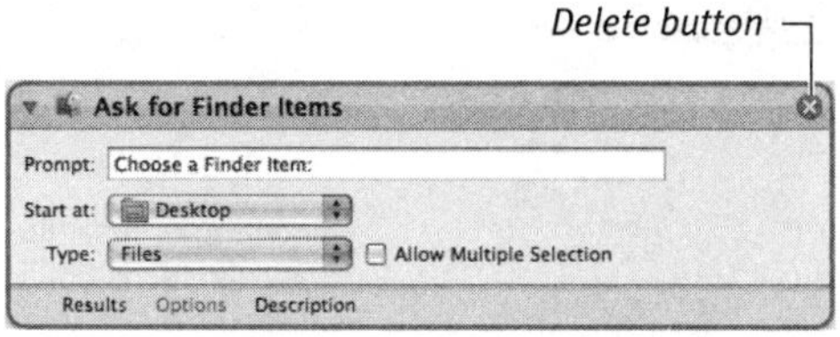

Figure 4.22 Deleting an action from a workflow.

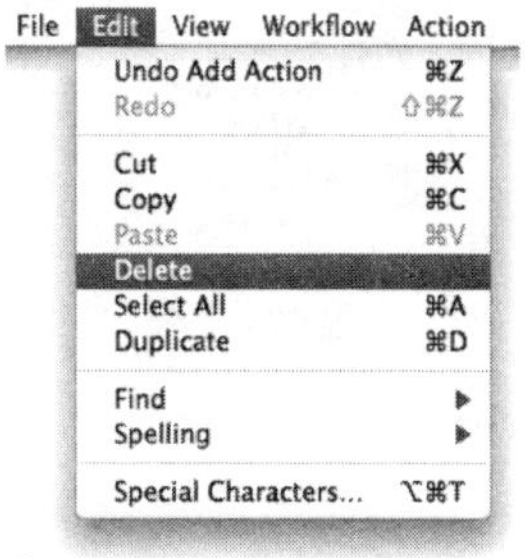

Figure 4.23 Deleting the selected action in a workflow.

Deleting Actions

As you build a workflow, you may place the wrong action or change your mind about whether to include a certain action—hey, it happens. Don't worry; you can delete the undesirable action.

To delete an action from a workflow:

1. Select the action in the workflow area.
2. Press the Delete key.

   or

   Click the X button on the right side of the action's title bar (**Figure 4.22**).

   or

   Choose Edit > Delete (**Figure 4.23**).

   The action disappears from the workflow. If any actions were below it, they move up to fill in the gap.

✔ Tip

- A note of warning: When you delete an action from a workflow, you will not be prompted to confirm your intent. Rather, Automator deletes the action immediately, settings and all. So, before you choose to delete an action, make sure that you really want to delete it. If you're unsure, try disabling it instead (see the next section).

Disabling Actions

Instead of completely deleting an action from a workflow, you way want to disable it. This can be useful for testing purposes, because disabling the action allows you to see how your workflow behaves without the action. If the workflow works okay, you can then delete the action. One extremely helpful benefit of disabling an action is that, if you do change your mind, you can always enable the action and you won't lose any of the settings that you may have configured.

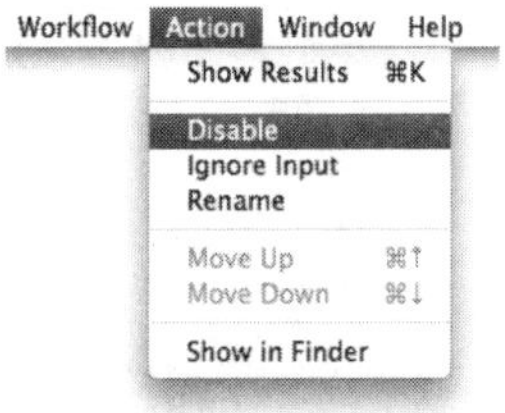

Figure 4.24 Disabling the selected action in a workflow.

To disable an action in a workflow:

1. Select the action in the workflow area.
2. Choose Action > Disable (**Figure 4.24**).

   or

   While holding down the Control key, click the action's title bar to display the contextual menu and choose Disable (**Figure 4.25**).

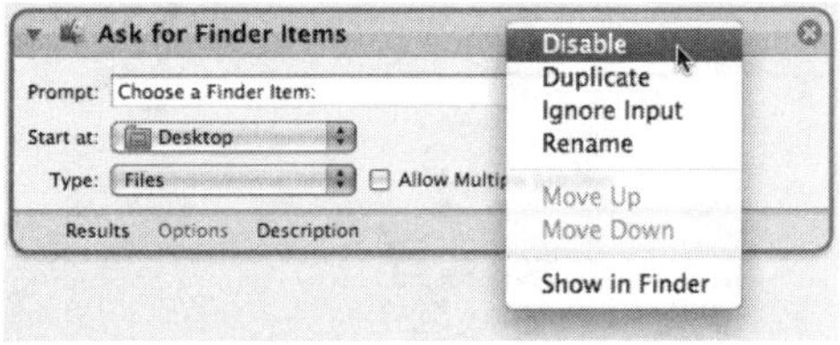

Figure 4.25 Disabling an action within a workflow, from the action's contextual menu.

After you disable an action, it appears dimmed within the workflow (**Figure 4.26**). When you run your workflow, it simply ignores the action.

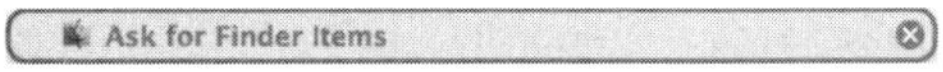

Figure 4.26 A disabled action.

To enable a disabled action:

1. Select the disabled action.
2. Choose Action > Enable (**Figure 4.27**).

   or

   While holding down the Control key, click the action's title bar to display the contextual menu and choose Enable (**Figure 4.28**).

   The action regains its normal appearance and runs as part of your workflow again.

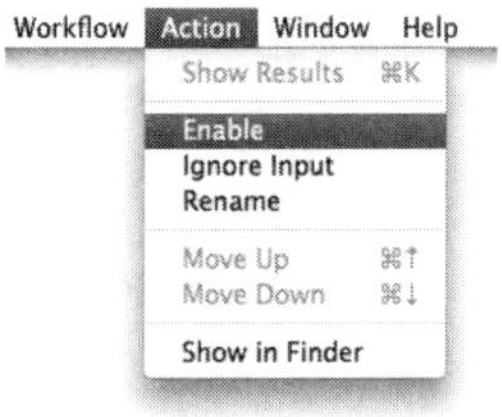

Figure 4.27 Enabling the selected disabled action in a workflow.

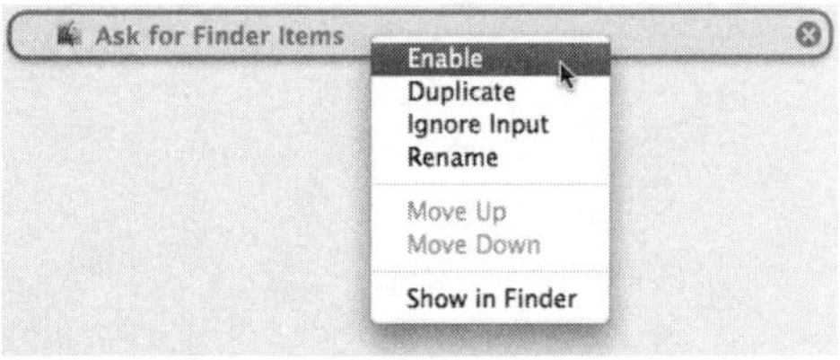

Figure 4.28 Enabling a disabled action within a workflow.

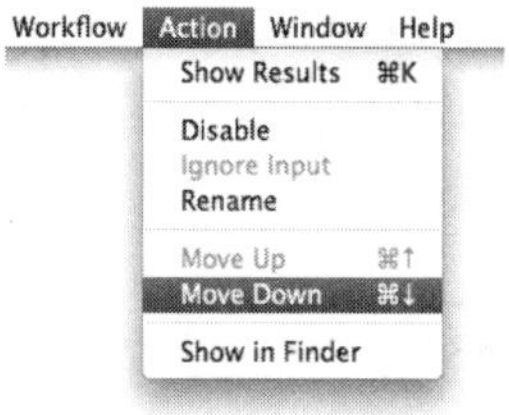

Figure 4.29 Moving the selected action down in a workflow.

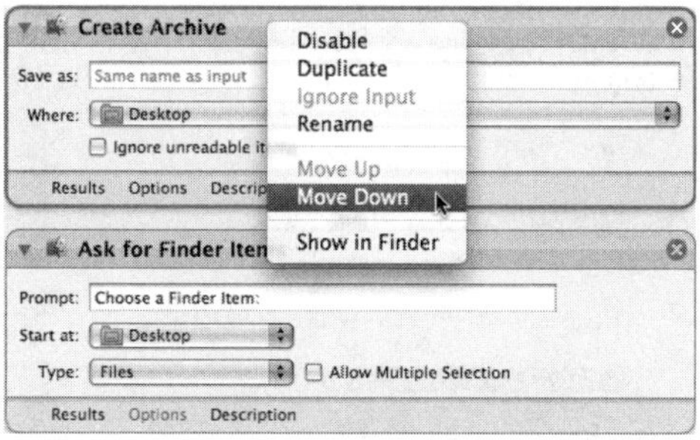

Figure 4.30 Moving an action down in a workflow, using the action's contextual menu.

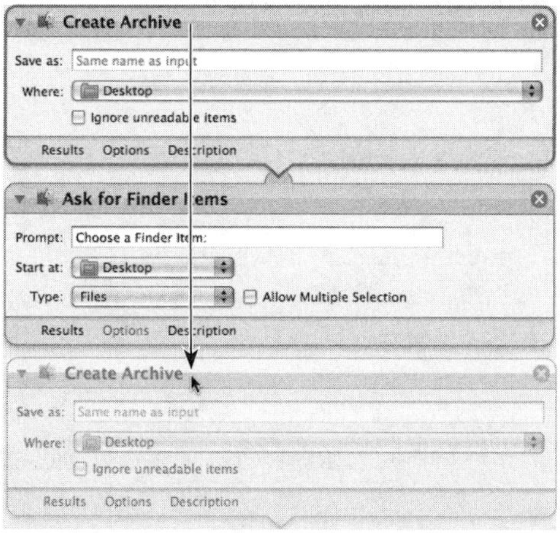

Figure 4.31 Dragging an action to a new location in a workflow.

Moving Actions

As your workflow takes shape you may have to move actions to new locations in the workflow. Automator makes this easy.

To move an action up or down in a workflow:

1. Select the action.
2. Press ⌘ ↑ to move the selected action up one step, or press ⌘ ↓ to move it down one step.

   or

   Choose Action > Move Up to move the selected action up one step or Action > Move Down to move down one (**Figure 4.29**).

   or

   While holding down the Control key, click the title bar of the action to display the contextual menu and choose Move Up to move the action up or Move Down to go the opposite way (**Figure 4.30**).

To move an action into a specific location within a workflow:

1. Select the action in the workflow area.
2. Click the action's title bar, and drag it to the desired location within the workflow (**Figure 4.31**).

✔ Tip

- Dragging an action to a new location is the fastest way to move an action to the right spot in a long workflow.

Copying Actions

Sometimes you want an action to stay put but you need another copy of it elsewhere. You can do this by copying the action and then placing it at the desired location in your workflow or even in a different workflow entirely.

Copying and relocating actions, method 1:

1. Select the action in the workflow area and choose Edit > Copy to copy the action to the clipboard (**Figure 4.32**).

   or

   Press ⌘ C.
2. Select the workflow in which you want to insert the copied action. You can use the same workflow or a different one.
3. Choose Edit > Paste (**Figure 4.33**).

   or

   Press ⌘ V.

   Automator pastes the action at the end of the workflow. If you pasted into the same workflow, the action now resides in two places.

Copying and relocating actions, method 2:

1. Select the action in the workflow area.
2. While holding down the Option key, drag the action to the desired location.

   Automator copies the action to that location (**Figure 4.34**).

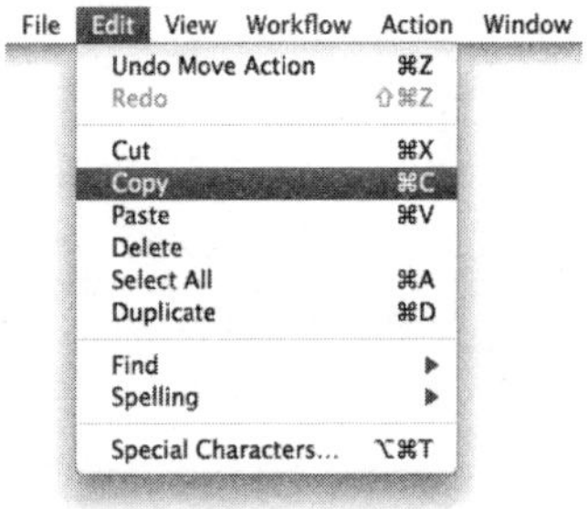

Figure 4.32 Copying a selected action to the clipboard.

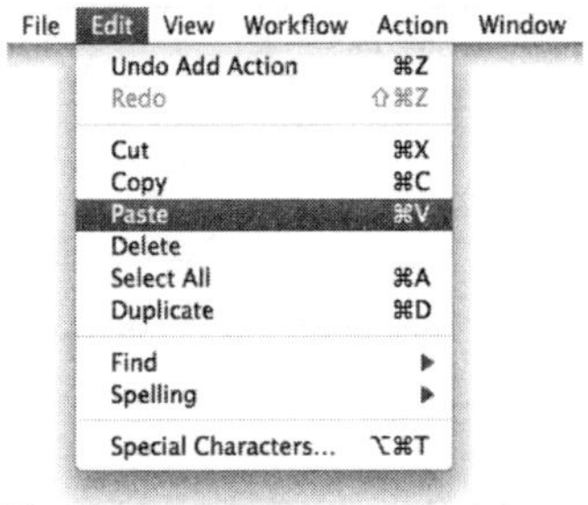

Figure 4.33 Pasting an action into the currently selected workflow.

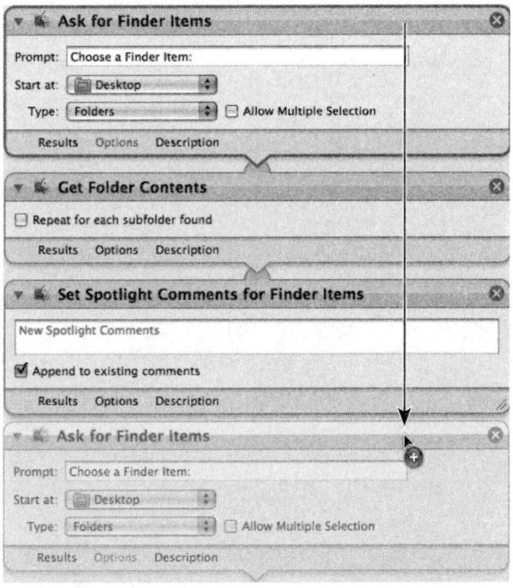

Figure 4.34 Copying an action from one location to another.

Copying and relocating actions, method 3:

1. Select the action in the workflow area.
2. Drag the action from the current workflow into the desired location in a different workflow (**Figure 4.35**).

   Automator copies the action to the other workflow.

✔ Tip

- When you copy an action, Automator retains the settings you configured for the original action in the pasted action.

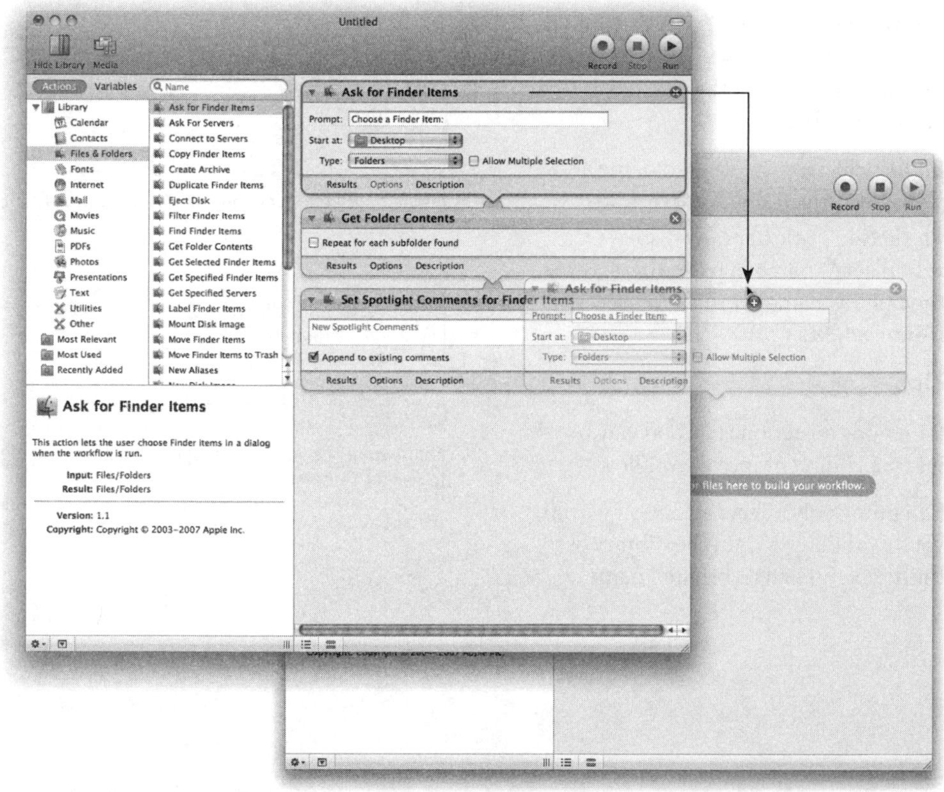

Figure 4.35 Copying an action from one workflow to another.

Renaming Actions

When building a workflow, there may be times that you'd like an action's name to be a bit more descriptive than the default name. Take the Connect to Servers action, for example. Renaming this action to include the name of the server volume to which it connects would be helpful. You can rename a workflow's action in two steps.

To rename an action:

1. Select the action in the workflow area and choose Action > Rename (**Figure 4.36**).

   or

   While holding down the Control key, click the action's title bar to open the contextual menu and choose Rename (**Figure 4.37**).

   The action's name in the title bar becomes editable.

2. In the field, type the desired name and press the Return key (**Figure 4.38**).

   The action's title bar now displays the action's new name in parentheses after the original name for the action (**Figure 4.39**).

✔ Tips

- Renaming an action is a good way to insert a comment into a workflow.
- Renaming only affects an action within your workflow. Within the Library list, the action retains its original name.

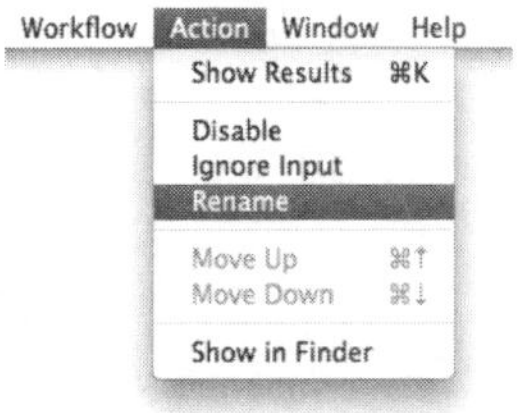

Figure 4.36 Renaming the selected action in a workflow.

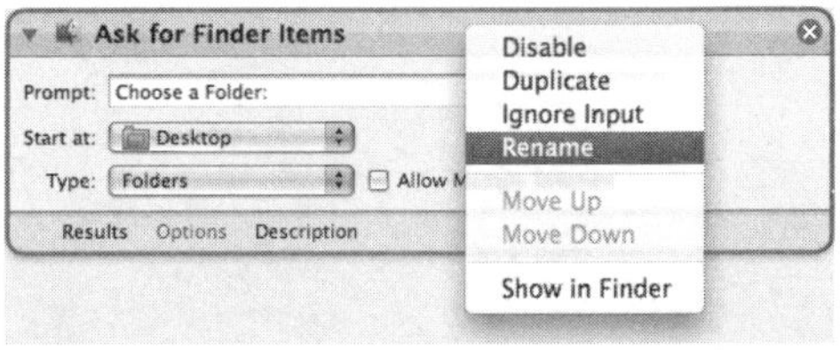

Figure 4.37 Renaming an action within a workflow, from the action's contextual menu.

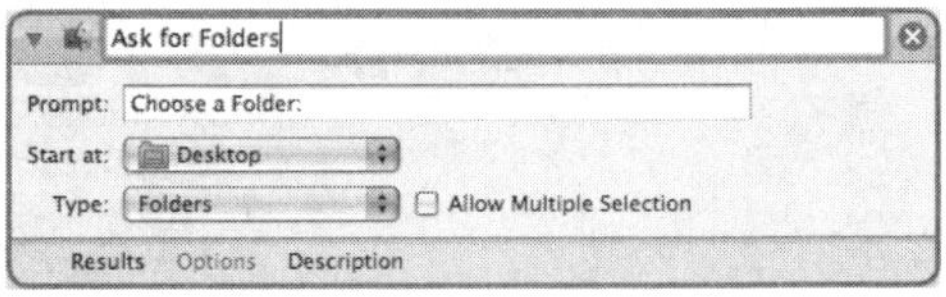

Figure 4.38 Renaming the Ask for Finder Items action.

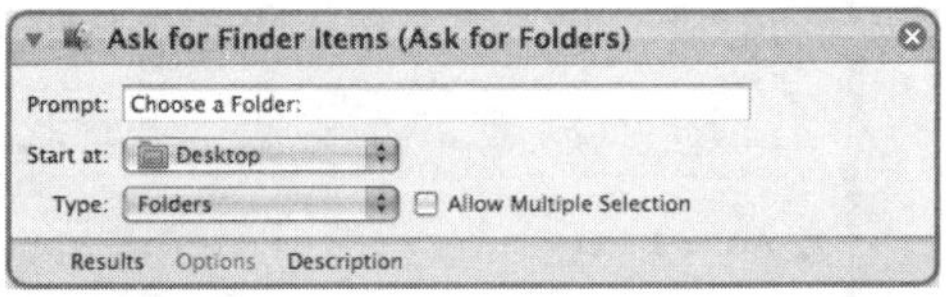

Figure 4.39 The Ask for Finder Items action, renamed to Ask for Folders.

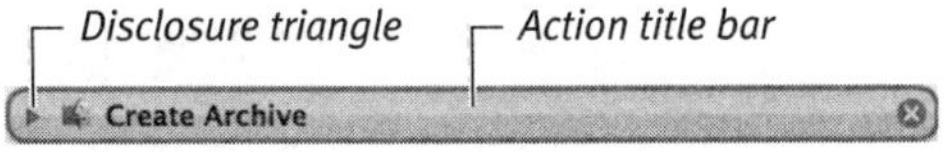

Figure 4.40 A collapsed action in the workflow area.

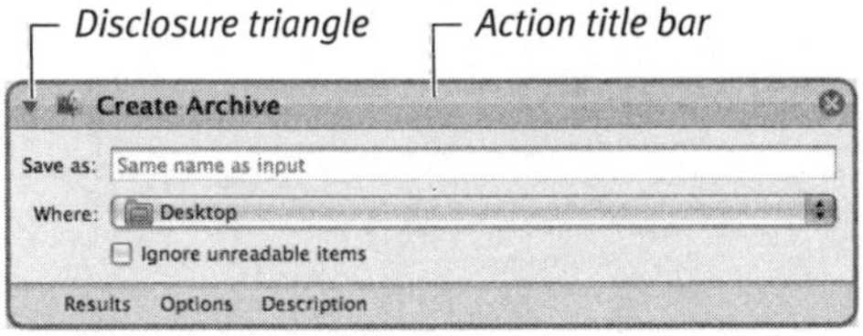

Figure 4.41 An expanded action in the workflow area.

Collapsing Actions

As your begin creating longer workflows, you may find yourself scrolling a lot to reach an action. There is a solution, however. Automator makes it easy to collapse individual actions, enabling you to view more of your workflow at a time, which means less scrolling. Collapsing an action condenses the action's interface down to a single title bar, hiding the action's settings, options, description, and so on.

To collapse an action in the workflow area:

◆ Double-click the action's title bar (**Figure 4.40**).

or

Click the small disclosure triangle to the left of the action's name in the title bar.

To expand a collapsed action in the workflow area:

◆ Double-click the title bar of the action (**Figure 4.41**).

or

Click the small disclosure triangle to the left of the action's name in the title bar again.

Working with Input and Output Values

Actions can talk to each other. As you learned in Chapter 1, "Getting Started," most actions can receive information (called *input*) from a previous action, and they can pass information (called *output*) to the next action in a workflow sequence. This process allows actions to work together like an assembly line, passing information along from one action to the next.

Matching Action Input and Output Values

Some actions can receive any kind of input and can live anywhere in a workflow. Many actions, however, need a specific kind of input to work properly. These actions must be placed into a workflow immediately following an action that gives the right kind of output. For example, an action that takes files and folders as input must come after an action that gives files and folders as output.

An action's description tells the kind of input it needs as well as the kind of output (result) it gives (**Figure 4.42**).

When actions are placed together in a workflow, Automator checks if their input and output information matches. If it does, Automator links the actions visually (**Figure 4.43**). If the actions don't match, then they appear to be separated (**Figure 4.44**). These visual clues can help you to determine whether information will pass through your workflow as expected.

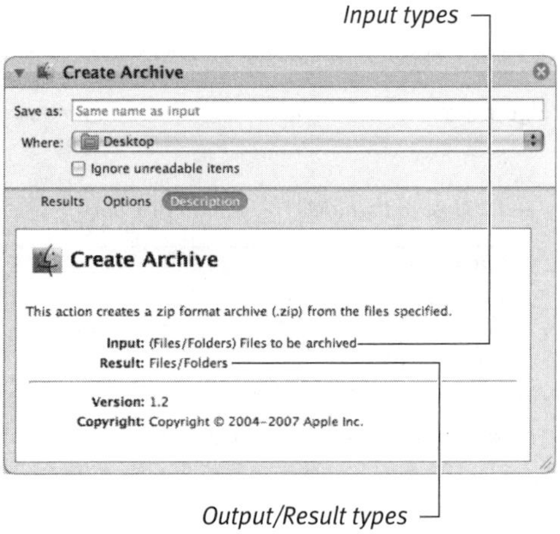

Figure 4.42 Viewing the input and result types for the Create Archive action.

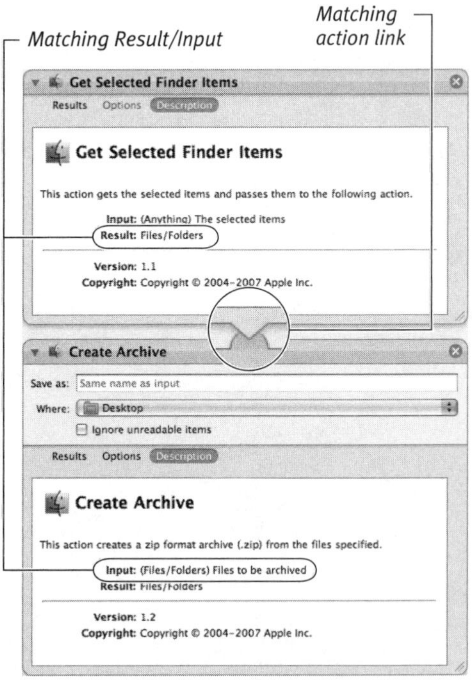

Figure 4.43 Two properly matched actions within a workflow, passing Files/Folders between one another.

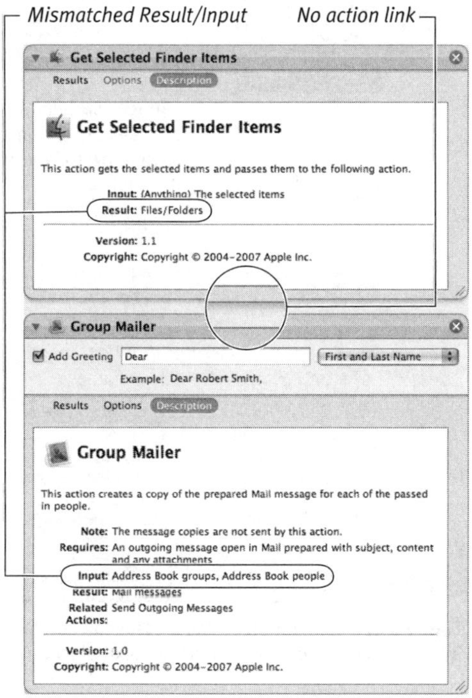

Figure 4.44 Two improperly matched actions within a workflow.

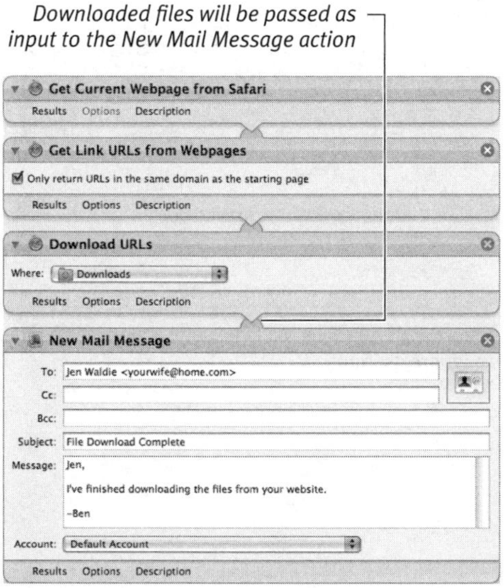

Figure 4.45 An example workflow, which downloads URLs from the current webpage in Safari and sends out an email notice when complete.

✔ Tip

- Mismatched actions don't always cause a problem. Whenever a mismatch occurs, Automator converts the input and output values of the actions to matching types using a conversion action. For more on conversion actions, see the sidebar in the "About Actions" section of Chapter 1.

Ignoring an Action's Input

There may be times when you don't want an action to do anything with the input it receives. For example, **Figure 4.45** shows a workflow that retrieves URLs from a current webpage in Safari, downloads those URLs, and then sends out an email notice. This workflow consists of four actions:

- Get Current Webpage from Safari
- Get Link URLs from Webpages
- Download URLs
- New Mail Message

In this workflow, the Download URLs action passes downloaded files as input to the New Mail Message action. The New Mail Message action then adds those files as attachments to the Mail message that it creates. Although that's a nice feature, you may just want to send a notice that the files have been downloaded without actually attaching the downloaded files. To do this, you can tell the New Mail Message action to ignore its input.

To tell an action to ignore its input:

- In the workflow area, select the action whose input you'd like to ignore and choose Action > Ignore Input (**Figure 4.46**).

  or

  While holding down the Control key, click the action's title bar to display the contextual menu and choose Ignore Input (**Figure 4.47**).

  The action becomes visually separated from the preceding action in the workflow, indicating that the action no longer accepts input (**Figure 4.48**).

After you disable an action's input, you can turn it back on again, should the need arise.

✔ Tip

- Not all actions can be told to ignore their input. If an action won't let you do this, then the Ignore Input option is disabled in the Action menu, as well as in the action's contextual menu. Download URLs is one such action.

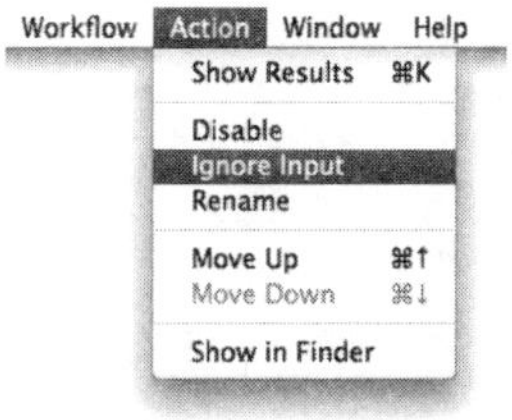

Figure 4.46 Telling the selected action in a workflow to ignore its input.

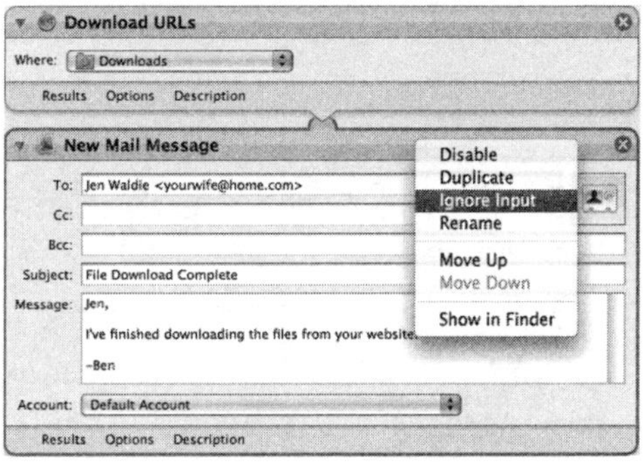

Figure 4.47 Telling the New Mail Message action to ignore its input, from the action's contextual menu.

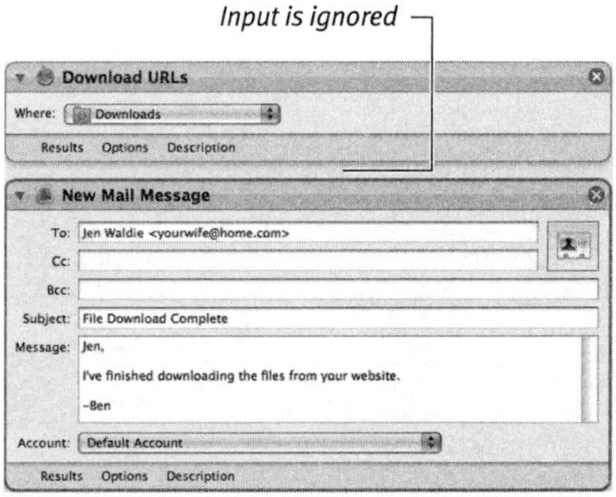

Figure 4.48 The New Mail Message action, configured to ignore its input.

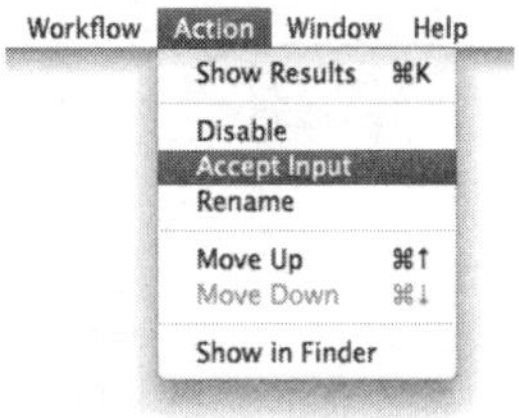

Figure 4.49 Telling the selected action in a workflow to accept its input.

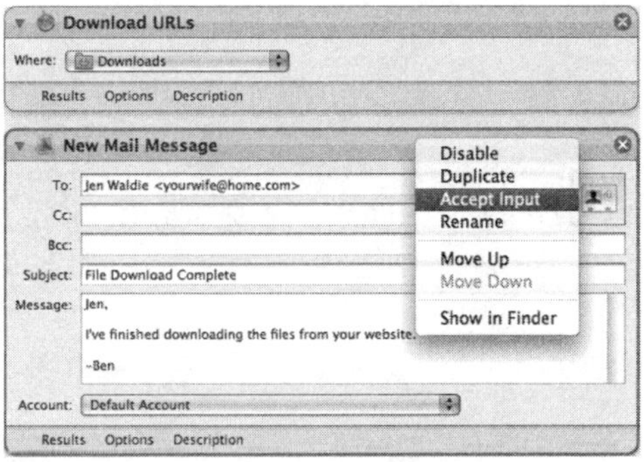

Figure 4.50 Telling the New Mail Message action to accept its input, from the action's contextual menu.

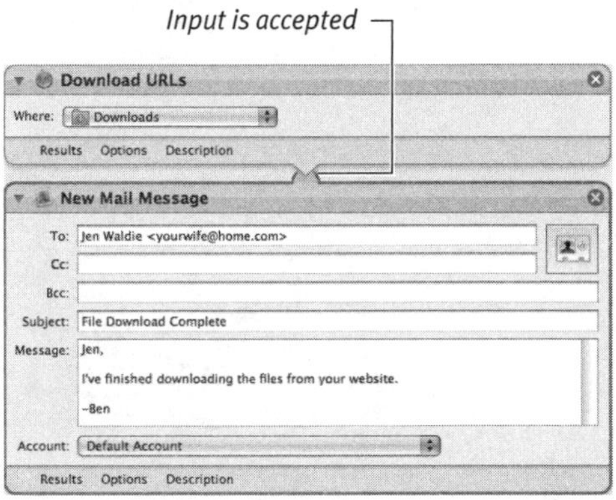

Figure 4.51 The New Mail Message action, configured to accept its input.

To tell an action to accept its input:

- Select the action in the workflow area and choose Action > Accept Input (**Figure 4.49**).

  or

  While holding down the Control key, click the action's title bar to display the contextual menu and choose Accept Input (**Figure 4.50**).

Automator links the action to the preceding action in the workflow again, visually indicating that it now accepts input again (**Figure 4.51**).

Three Action Gems

Automator includes dozens of great actions that are sure to benefit the workflows of many. Here are a few really useful ones:

1. **Spotlight.** Need to find files to process when your workflow runs? Check out this action. It performs a Spotlight search for the specified criteria and passes the results down to the next action for further processing.
2. **Burn a Disc.** This great action burns files and folders directly to a CD or DVD. Consider using this action to create a workflow that backs up your modified files to DVD once per week.
3. **Text to Audio File.** This action can actually convert input text to audio format. In a hurry, and don't have time to read your email at your desk? Why not process it with this action, and listen to it on your iPod?

5

Recording Manual Events

Automator's most useful feature may be its ability to record what you do and then play that back as part of a workflow. This means that even if Automator actions aren't available for a particular application, you may still be able to automate it by recording tasks and playing them back.

When you record manual tasks, Automator watches your key presses, mouse movements, and clicks, and then saves these events as an action, so you can play them back as part of the workflow in which you recorded them. So, essentially, any individual task you perform with your keyboard or mouse is considered to be an event.

The ability to record means that Automator can automate almost any task you can perform manually on your Mac. This chapter covers what you need to know about recording and playing back manual tasks within a workflow.

Enabling Recording

Before you can record manual events with Automator, you must enable Accessibility. Accessibility is a Mac OS X feature that allows applications and processes to watch your mouse clicks, text typing, and so on. Without Accessibility enabled, Automator can't watch you do things and thus can't record them in your workflow.

✔ Tip

- Recording with Automator is not possible in Tiger (Mac OS X v10.4).

To enable Accessibility:

1. From the Apple menu, choose System Preferences.

   The System Preferences application launches and displays the System Preferences window.

2. In the lower-right corner of Preferences, click the Universal Access icon (**Figure 5.1**).

   The system displays your current Universal Access preferences.

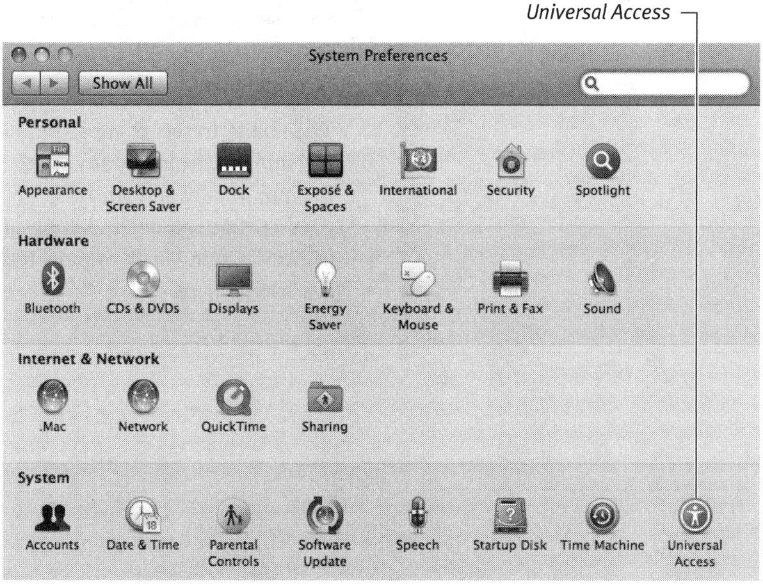

Figure 5.1 Locating the Universal Access system preference.

3. Check the "Enable access for assistive devices" checkbox to enable Accessibility (**Figure 5.2**).

✔ Tips

- You need administrator access to turn on Accessibility.
- If you forget to enable Accessibility, don't worry. If you try to start recording without it, Automator will remind you to turn it on.

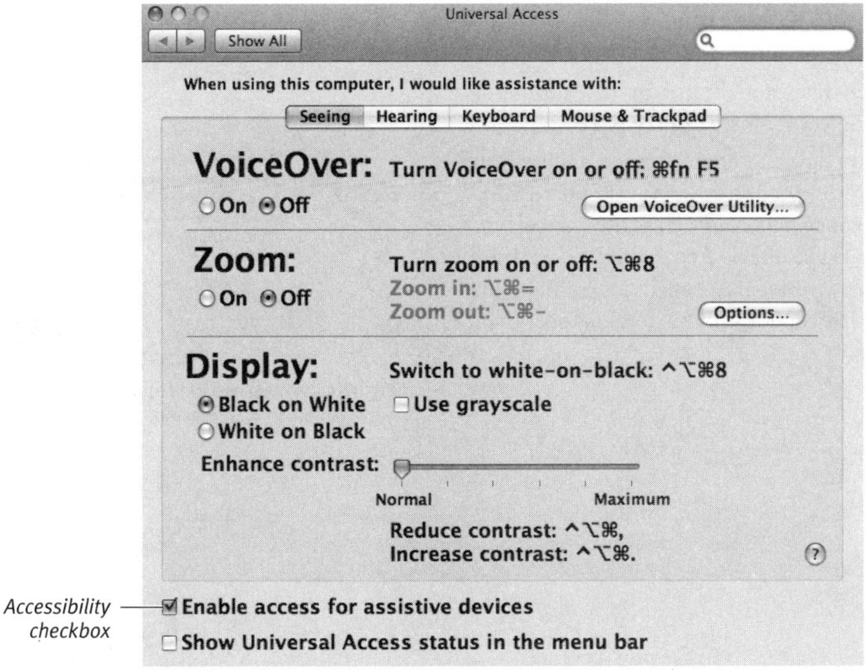

Figure 5.2 Enabling Accessibility from System Preferences.

Recording Manual Tasks

You can record manual events in an empty Automator workflow or in a workflow that contains existing actions. There's no need to insert an action; Automator takes care of this for you automatically when you stop recording.

To record manual events:

1. Create a new workflow or open a saved one.
2. Choose Workflow > Record (**Figure 5.3**).

   or

   Press [⌘ Option R].

   or

   Click the Record button in the Automator workflow toolbar (**Figure 5.4**).

   If you have not enabled Accessibility, you are prompted to do so now (**Figure 5.5**). To cancel recording, click the Cancel button. Or, to enable Accessibility, click the Open Universal Access button and follow the instructions in the previous section.

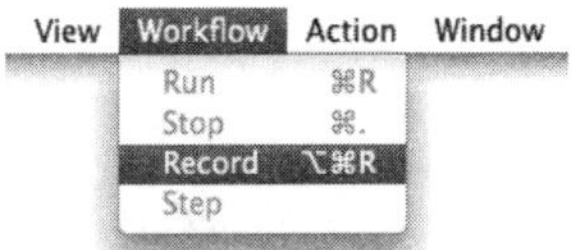

Figure 5.3 The menu method of beginning to record an Automator workflow.

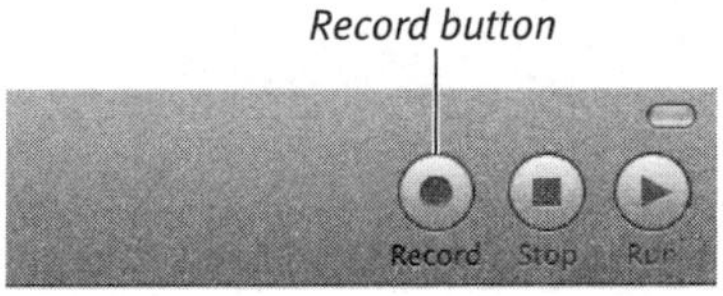

Figure 5.4 The icon method of beginning to record an Automator workflow.

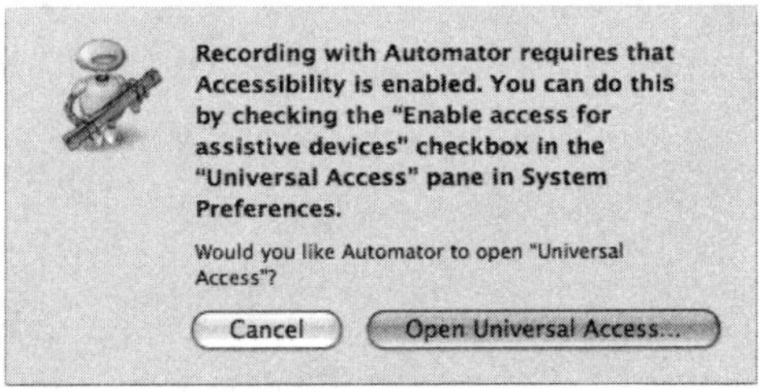

Figure 5.5 A message indicating that Accessibility is not enabled on your machine.

Preparing for Recording

Think things through first! Anticipate what you want to record, and prepare for it. For example, if you expect a document to exist when you play your recorded events, make sure that document exists before you begin recording. If you don't, your action might not work.

Figure 5.6 Automator, in recording mode.

When you begin recording, Automator hides your workflow window and displays a small recording mode indicator (**Figure 5.6**). You may now bring the desired application to the front, and begin doing things. Automator watches you, and keeps track of your key presses and mouse clicks.

✔ Tips

- For you to record manual events within an application, that application must support accessibility.
- Automator may not record absolutely every single thing you do. You may encounter certain tasks that are simply not recordable.
- Automator may sometimes record events that you don't want or need in your workflow. If this happens, don't worry. You can remove unwanted events when you're done recording.
- When recording, go slowly. It may take Automator a second or two to recognize what you've clicked or typed. Giving it time to keep up is always a good idea.

Once you've finished your manual tasks, you're ready to stop recording and return to your workflow.

Know When to Record

Look for existing actions first. Before recording a manual task, see if an Automator action exists for that task. If it does, use it. It will probably run faster in your workflow, work more reliably, and give you more control over the task being performed.

To stop recording:

1. Select the Automator recording window.
2. Click the Stop button in the Automator recording window (**Figure 5.7**).

   or

   Choose Workflow > Stop (**Figure 5.8**).

   or

   Press [⌘][.].

   Automator closes the recording window, and your workflow becomes visible, prefilled with a new Watch Me Do action at the end of the workflow. This action includes a list of all of the manual events that were recorded. You can view additional information about an event, such as the application it targets, by clicking it (**Figure 5.9**).

Figure 5.7 The icon method of stopping Automator from recording.

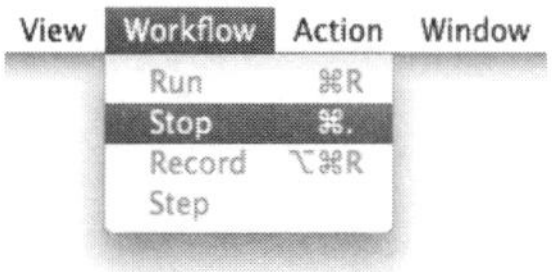

Figure 5.8 The menu method of stopping Automator from recording.

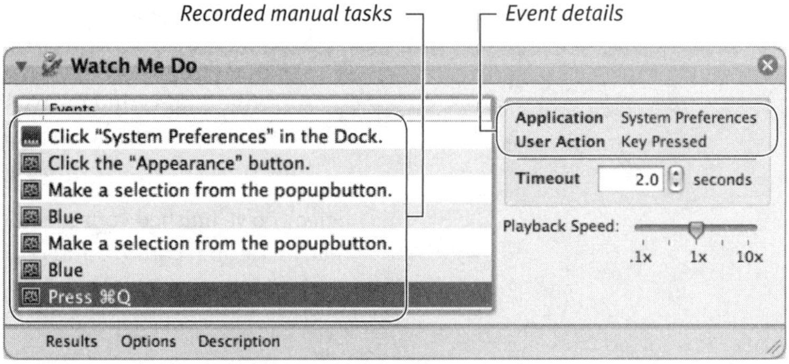

Figure 5.9 Viewing the details for a recorded event.

✔ Tips

- After stopping recording, if you realize that you need to record some more, don't panic. Simply begin recording again. Automator will record the additional events and insert a second Watch Me Do action into your workflow.
- Recording may not always work as anticipated. When you're finished recording, it's always a good idea to play the recorded events. If they don't do exactly what you expect, then try recording them again. If they still don't work, then try doing them in a different way. For example, if creating a new document in an application is giving you trouble, instead of choosing File > New, try pressing [⌘][N].

Removing Recorded Events

When recording manual tasks, keep in mind that Automator records what you do. This may not, however, always be what you want the workflow to do when run. Sometimes extra steps are recorded, or you may decide that a step is no longer necessary. In these cases you can delete individual recorded events, leaving only the ones you need.

To remove a recorded event:

1. Select the events that you want to delete in the list of events on the left side of the Watch Me Do action (**Figure 5.10**).
2. Press Delete.

   Automator removes the selected events from the action (**Figure 5.11**).

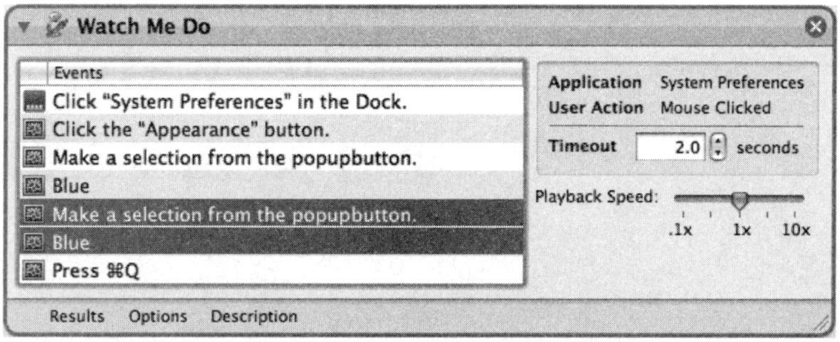

Figure 5.10 Selecting recorded events in the Watch Me Do action.

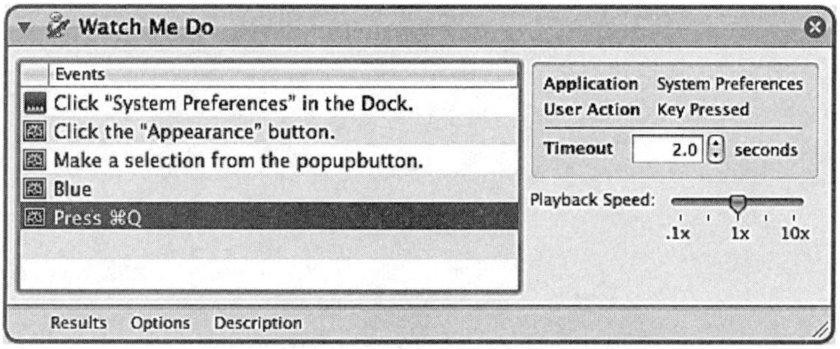

Figure 5.11 The Watch Me Do action, after deleting some events.

Preparing to Play Recorded Events

Recorded events are played when your workflow is run. Before this, however, you may wish to make some adjustments to their behavior.

Event Playback Timeouts

When an individual event plays, Automator gives it a limited amount of time to finish; this is called a *timeout*. For example, you wouldn't want Automator to try clicking a checkbox in a window before that window has fully opened. By default, timeouts are two seconds. In rare circumstances, however, this may not be enough. The Watch Me Do action allows you to adjust the timeouts for individual events, if needed.

To increase an event's playback timeout:

1. In your workflow, select the desired event within the Watch Me Do action.
2. In the Timeout field, enter the maximum number of seconds you'd like Automator to allow for the event to complete (**Figure 5.12**).

   When your workflow is run, Automator will now allow the specified number of seconds for the event to execute.

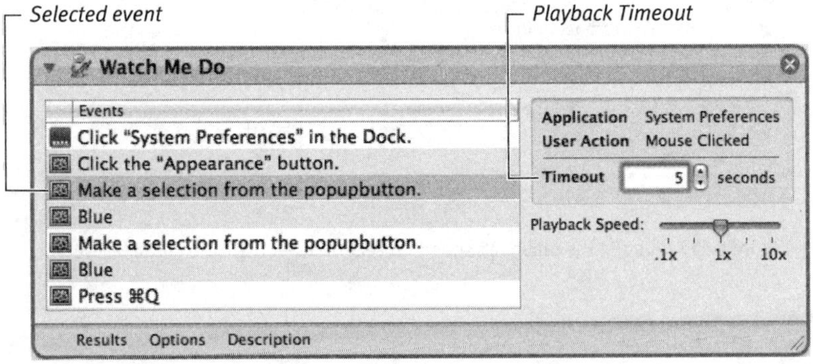

Figure 5.12 Adjusting the playback timeout for a recorded event.

Playback Speed

By default, Automator plays back recorded events at the speed you recorded them. When you need to get a job done quicker, however, you can increase the playback speed of the Watch Me Do action. This affects the speed of the events as a whole, not the speed of an individual event. You can also play events more slowly should the rare need arise.

To adjust the playback speed of recorded events:

Set the Playback Speed slider in the Watch Me Do action within your workflow to the desired speed. To decrease playback speed, move the slider to the left. To increase playback speed, move the slider to the right (**Figure 5.13**).

✔ Tip

- Don't move a muscle. When playing recorded tasks, avoid moving the mouse or pressing keys. Doing so can interfere with the events being played, and in some cases, may cause them to produce an error.

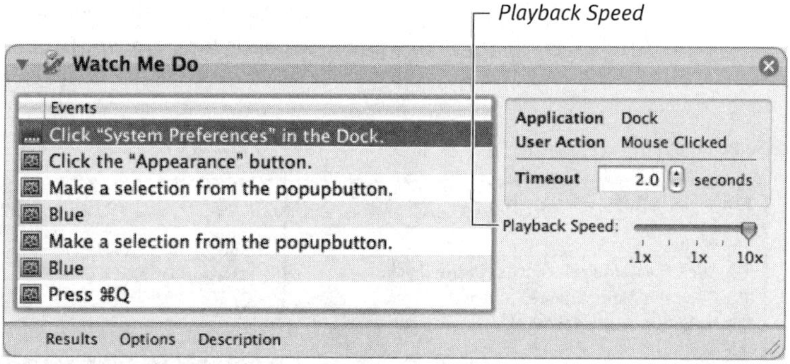

Figure 5.13 Adjusting the playback speed for recorded events to 10x normal speed.

Running, Saving, and Opening Workflows

6

You know the basics of Automator. By now you can create a workflow, add actions to a workflow, modify action settings, and more. In this chapter, you'll move up to running, saving, opening, and closing workflow files and applications.

What's the big deal? Well, workflows can be saved as workflow files, applications, or plug-ins—they're pretty versatile. Think of a workflow file like a document file, such as a Word document. Once saved, you can open a workflow file in Automator, make changes to it, resave it, and close it. You can also run it within Automator. Workflows saved as applications are a bit different, though. They work like other applications on your Mac. You launch them, and they run by themselves; Automator doesn't even need to be launched. As Chapter 9, "Saving Workflow Plug-Ins," discusses, workflows can also be saved as plug-ins, allowing them be run from other applications and processes—a great way to add custom functions to other applications.

For this chapter's examples, I've used the Add Spotlight Comments to Photos workflow from Chapter 2, "Building Simple Workflows." To follow along, create this workflow. Or, if you're feeling brave, create a new workflow of your own and jump right in.

Running a Workflow Within Automator

When you complete a workflow, always run it within Automator first. Testing this way gives you quick access to valuable troubleshooting tools, such as Automator's log, and enables you to adjust the workflow by changing an action's settings, inserting a new action, or whatever else might be necessary. Once it's running properly, you'll probably want to save the workflow for quick access as an application or plug-in, but we'll get to that in a minute.

✔ Tip

- For more advice on troubleshooting workflows, see Chapter 7, "Troubleshooting."

To run a workflow:

- Choose Workflow > Run (**Figure 6.1**).

  or

  Click the Run button in the workflow window toolbar (**Figure 6.2**).

  or

  Press ⌘R.

  The workflow begins to run.

Figure 6.1 Choosing Run from the Workflow menu to run the current workflow.

Figure 6.2 Running a workflow by clicking the Run button in the Automator workflow window toolbar.

Figure 6.3 The workflow window toolbar buttons change while a workflow is running. Record is disabled, Stop is enabled, and Run changes to Pause.

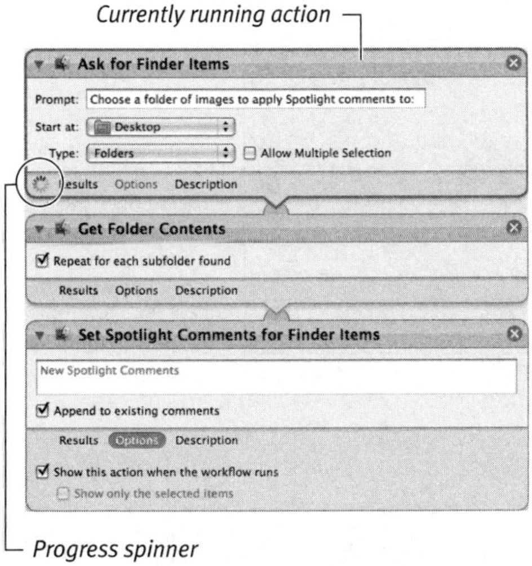

Figure 6.4 As a workflow runs within Automator, a spinner displays in the lower-left corner of the currently running action.

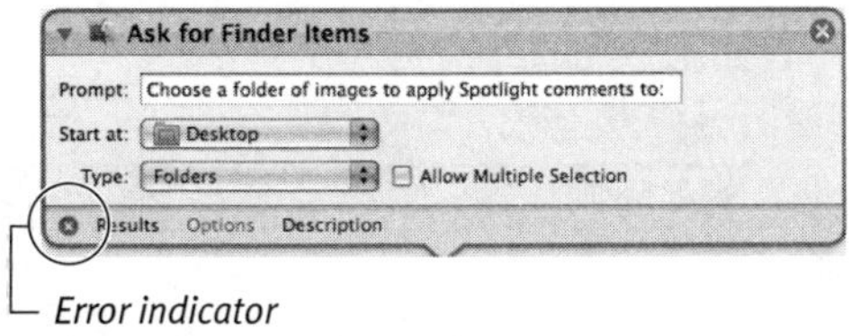

Figure 6.5 If an action generates an error while a workflow runs, a red X appears in the lower-left corner of that action.

What You See as a Workflow Runs

As a workflow runs within Automator, you'll notice several things:

- The buttons in the workflow window's toolbar change. The Record button is disabled, the Stop button is enabled, and the Run button changes to Pause (**Figure 6.3**).
- The currently running action displays a progress spinner in its lower-left corner (**Figure 6.4**).
- If an action produces an error, Automator displays a red X in the lower-left corner of the action (**Figure 6.5**). The workflow then stops running.
- After an action runs successfully, Automator displays a green checkmark in its lower-left corner (**Figure 6.6**) and proceeds to run the next action in the workflow.

continues on next page

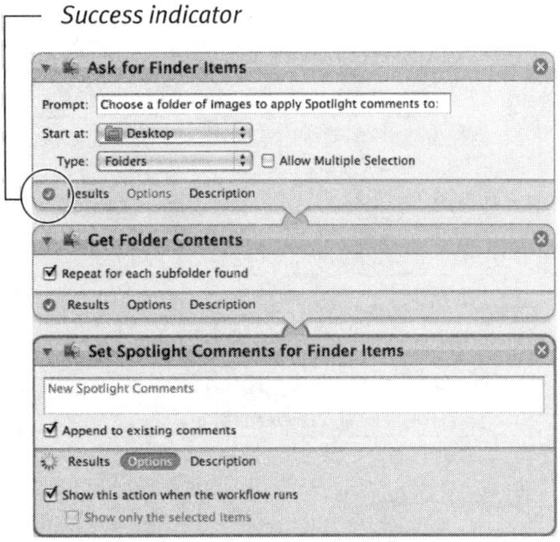

Figure 6.6 A green checkmark displays in the lower-left corner of an action that runs successfully.

- The bottom of the workflow window reports the overall status of your workflow, displaying the name of the currently running action, errors, or successful completion (**Figures 6.7, 6.8,** and **6.9**).

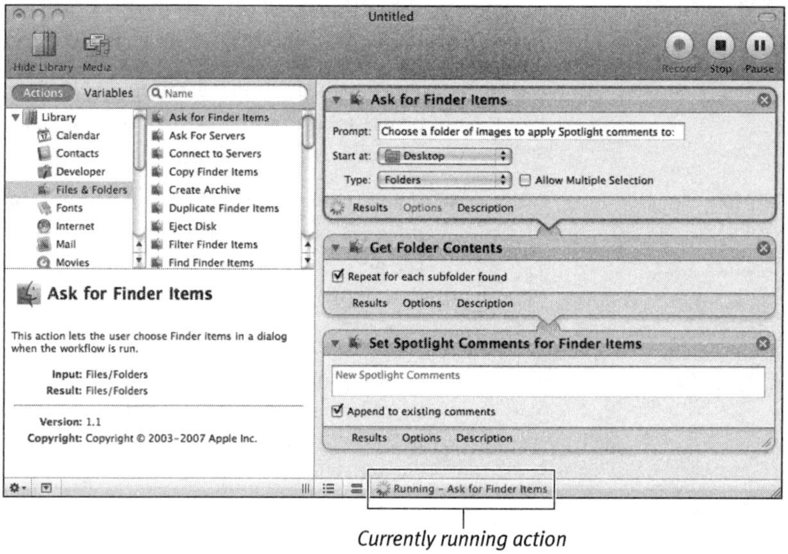

Figure 6.7 As a workflow runs, the bottom of the workflow window lists the currently running action.

Figure 6.8 The bottom of the workflow window indicates when an error occurs.

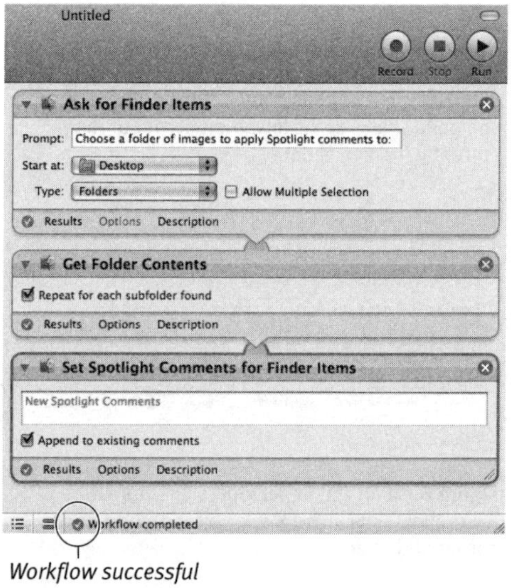

Figure 6.9 The bottom of the workflow window indicates when the workflow runs successfully.

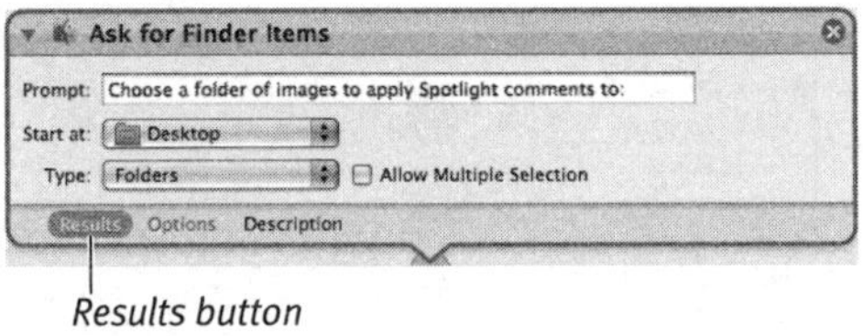

Figure 6.10 Click the Results button at the bottom of an action to display the action's results when the workflow runs.

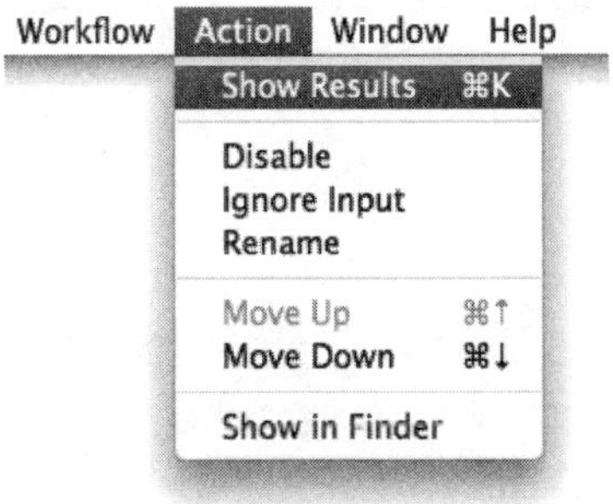

Figure 6.11 Choosing Show Results from the Action menu displays the selected action's results when the workflow runs.

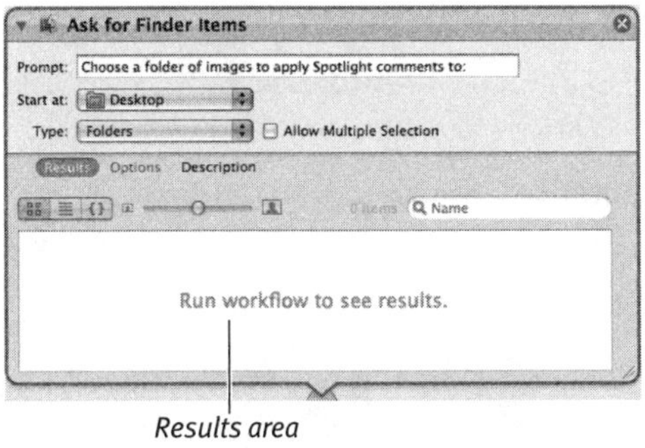

Figure 6.12 The results area of an expanded action, ready to show its results when the workflow runs.

Viewing Action Results as a Workflow Runs

As a workflow runs within Automator, you may want to monitor the results of each action. Doing so lets you make sure that the correct information passes from action to action. As Chapter 7 explains, this can be a valuable way to determine the cause of any problems you may encounter.

To view an action's result:

1. Select an action within the workflow.
2. Click the Results button at the bottom of the action (**Figure 6.10**).

   or

   Choose Action > Show Results (**Figure 6.11**).

   or

   Press ⌘K.

   The action expands to display a results area (**Figure 6.12**).

continues on next page

3. Run the workflow.

   As the workflow runs, the results area displays the results of the action (**Figure 6.13**).

By default, action results are displayed as icons. You can, however, view action results as a table or list. To change the view, click one of the view icons above the result area (**Figures 6.13, 6.14,** and **6.15**).

✔ Tip

- Not all actions can display their results as icons. If you don't see anything listed when viewing an action's results as icons, try selecting another view instead.

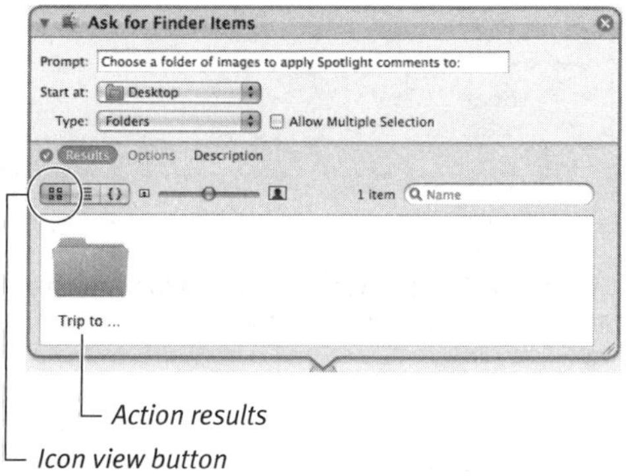

Figure 6.13 By default, action results are displayed as icons.

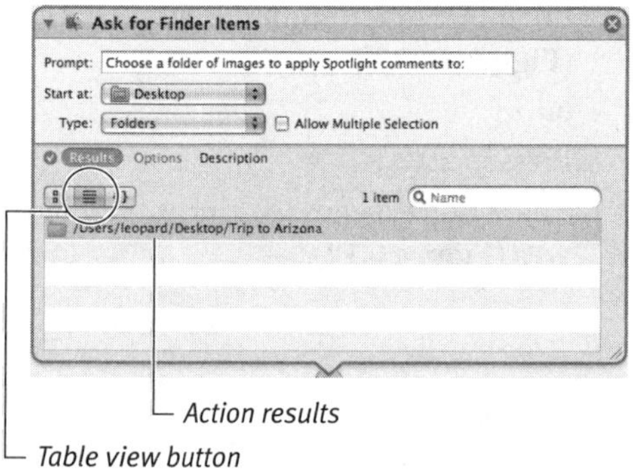

Figure 6.14 Choosing to view an action's results as a table.

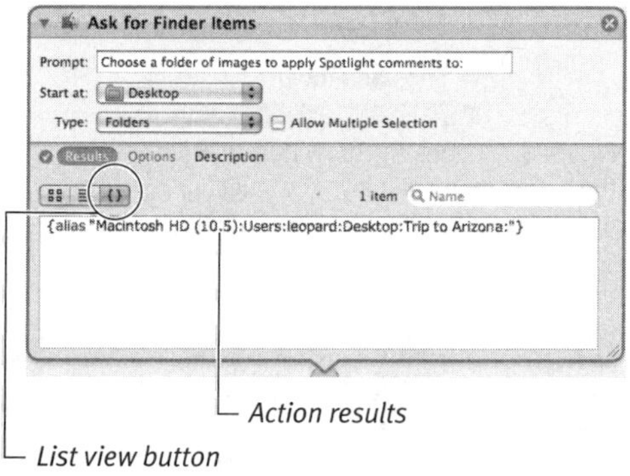

Figure 6.15 Choosing to view an action's results as a list.

Interpreting Action Results

Results vary from action to action. Some results, such as files and folders, iPhoto items, and iTunes songs, may be easy to interpret. Others, however, may be more difficult. Take your time, and do your best to make sense of them.

Start by viewing action results as icons. In many cases, you'll see previews, such as iPhoto image thumbnails. If no icons are displayed or if they all look the same, then try list view. Here, you may find a bit more information, such as the full paths of files and folders.

View the results in list view as a last resort, however. Often, list view will display results as AppleScript code, which may not make a whole lot of sense if you don't know AppleScript.

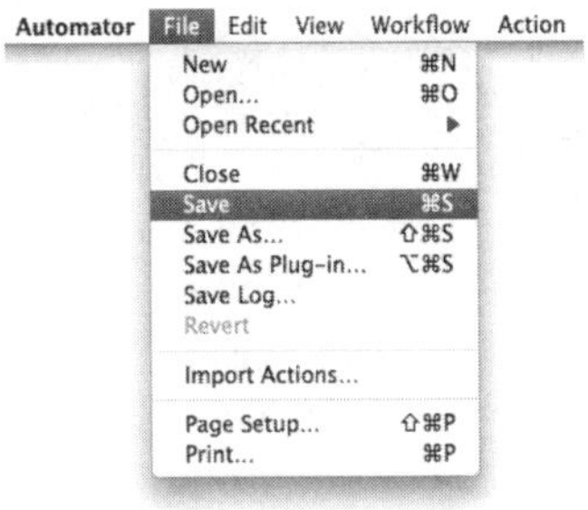

Figure 6.16 Save a new workflow as a workflow file by choosing File > Save.

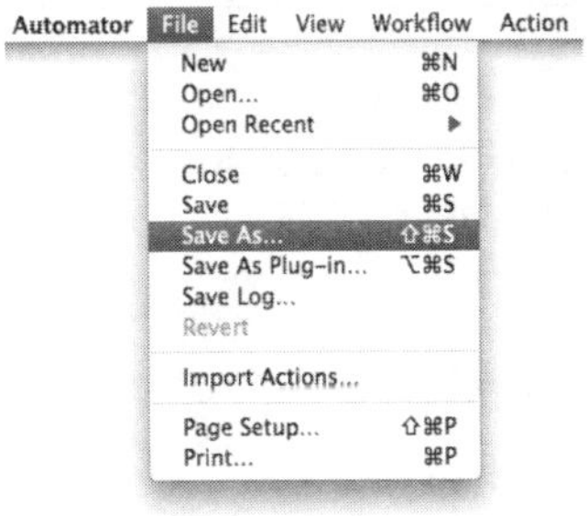

Figure 6.17 Save an existing workflow as a workflow file by choosing File > Save As.

Saving and Opening a Workflow File

Once you've created and tested a workflow, you're ready to save it.

To save a workflow file:

1. If your workflow is a new workflow, choose File > Save (**Figure 6.16**) or press ⌘S.

   or

   If your workflow is an existing workflow, choose File > Save As (**Figure 6.17**) or press Shift⌘S. Do this so you don't overwrite your existing workflow.

   Automator displays the Save panel attached to the front workflow window (**Figure 6.18**).

continues on next page

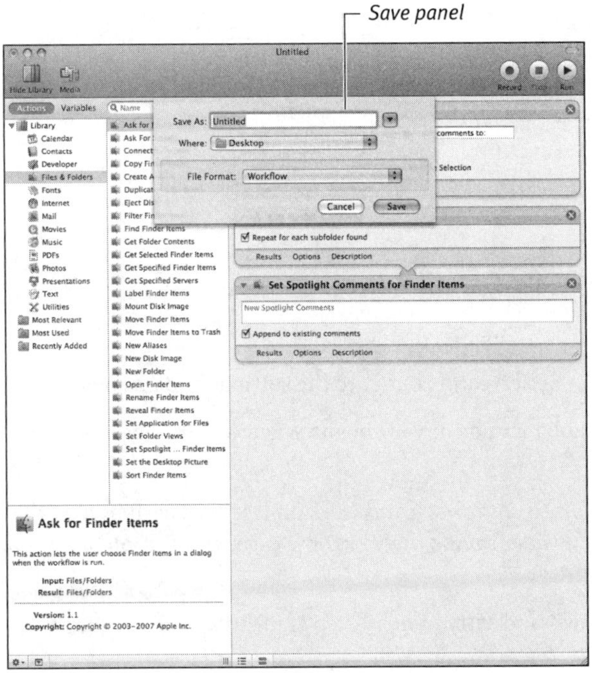

Figure 6.18 When you save a workflow as a workflow file, Automator displays the Save panel.

2. In the panel's Save As text field, type a name for your workflow (**Figure 6.19**).
3. From the Where pop-up menu, choose where you want to save the workflow (**Figure 6.20**).
4. From the File Format pop-up menu, choose Workflow (**Figure 6.21**).
5. Click Save.

   Automator saves the workflow as a workflow file (**Figure 6.22**). You can now file it somewhere on your Mac for later use or send it to a friend.

✔ Tip

- Press [⌘][D] to quickly choose the Desktop as the desired location.

Figure 6.19 Enter a name for the workflow file into the Save As field within the Save panel.

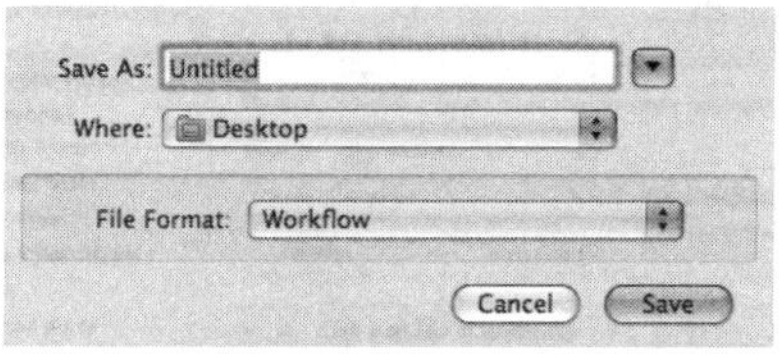

Figure 6.20 Choose the desired location for the workflow file from the Save panel's Where pop-up menu.

Figure 6.21 Choose Workflow from the Save panel's File Format pop-up menu to save a workflow file.

Figure 6.22 A saved workflow file.

Automator Workflow Creation in a Nutshell

Think of creating Automator workflows as a three-step process:

- **Step 1.** Create the workflow. Add the actions and configure the settings and options.
- **Step 2.** Test the workflow, troubleshoot, and fix any problems. Make sure things are running smoothly.
- **Step 3.** Save the workflow. If you want to come back and work on it later, save it as a workflow file. If you plan to run it often, consider saving the workflow as an application or a plug-in for quick access.

Be sure to check out Appendix A for a down-and-dirty, step-by-step guide to workflow creation.

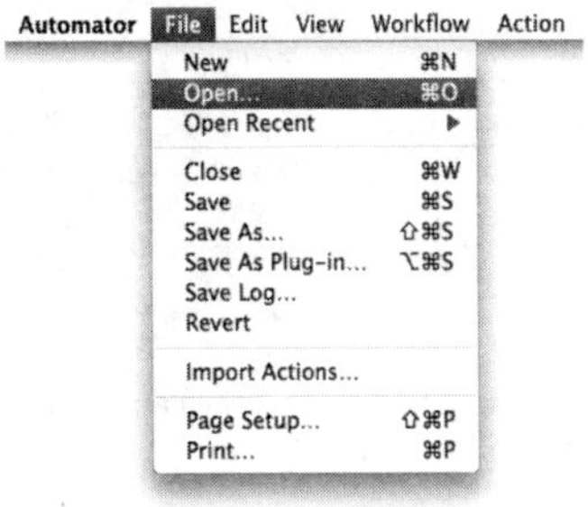

Figure 6.23 Open a workflow by choosing File > Open.

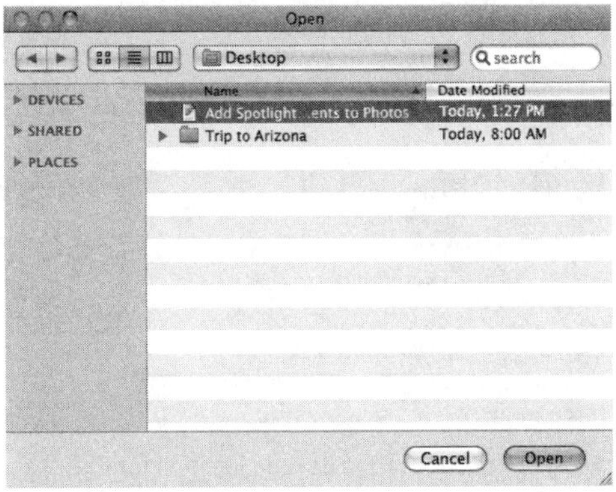

Figure 6.24 When the Open dialog appears, locate the workflow file you want to open, and click Open.

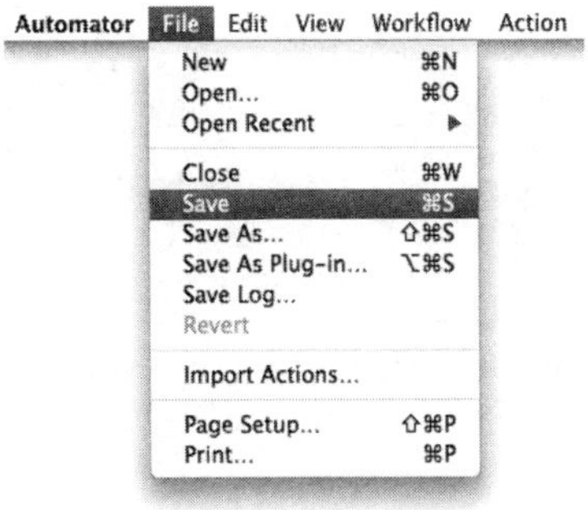

Figure 6.25 Save a modified workflow file by choosing File > Save.

To open a workflow file:

1. Choose File > Open (**Figure 6.23**).

   or

   Press [⌘ ⌘][O].

   The Open dialog appears.

2. In the Open dialog, locate the workflow file and click Open (**Figure 6.24**).

   The workflow file opens in Automator. You can now modify the workflow, if desired, by inserting new actions, removing actions, or modifying action settings.

✔ Tip

- You can also open a workflow file by double-clicking it or dragging it onto the Automator icon in your Dock.

To save a modified workflow file:

- Choose File > Save (**Figure 6.25**).

  or

  Press [⌘ ⌘][S].

The modified workflow file is saved.

Saving and Opening a Workflow Application

Saving a workflow as an application lets you run the workflow any time you want without launching Automator.

To save a workflow application:

1. If your workflow is a new workflow, choose File > Save or press [⌘][S].

   or

   If your workflow is an existing workflow, choose File > Save As or press [⇧Shift][⌘][S].

   A Save panel is displayed, attached to the front workflow window.

2. In the Save As text field, type your workflow's name (**Figure 6.26**).
3. From the Where pop-up menu, choose the desired location (**Figure 6.27**).
4. From the File Format pop-up menu, choose Application (**Figure 6.28**).
5. Click Save.

   Automator saves the workflow as a workflow application (**Figure 6.29**). You can now run the workflow, send it to a friend, or file it on your Mac for later use.

✔ Tip

- You can run workflow applications by double-clicking them or dropping files and folders onto them. Learn how in the next section of this chapter, "Running a Workflow Application."

Figure 6.26 Enter a name for the workflow application into the Save panel's Save As field.

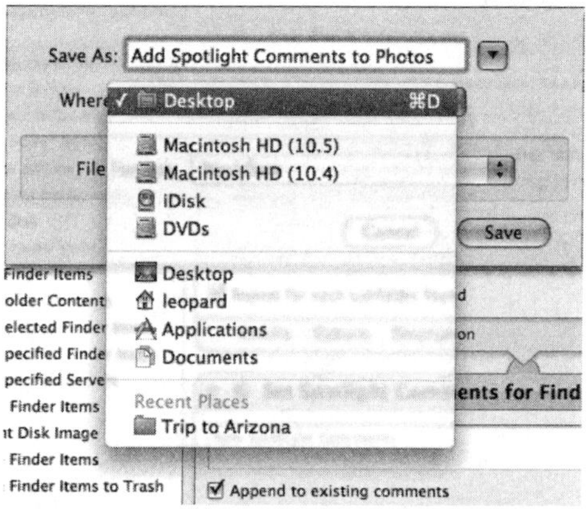

Figure 6.27 Choose the desired location for the workflow application from the Save panel's Where pop-up menu.

Figure 6.28 Choose Application from the Save panel's File Format pop-up menu to save a workflow application.

Figure 6.29 A saved workflow application.

To open a workflow application:

1. Choose File > Open.

   or

   Press ⌘O.

   The Open dialog appears.

2. In the Open dialog, find your workflow application and click Open.

   The workflow application opens in Automator. You can now modify the workflow, if desired.

✔ Tip

■ You can also open a workflow application by dragging it onto the Automator icon in your Dock.

To save a modified workflow application:

◆ Choose File > Save.

  or

  Press ⌘S.

  The modified workflow application is saved.

Running a Workflow Application

A workflow application behaves like any other Mac OS X application, and Automator doesn't need to be running to use it. You can move a workflow application to, and run it from, anywhere on your Mac, such as the Applications or Documents folder (**Figure 6.30**).

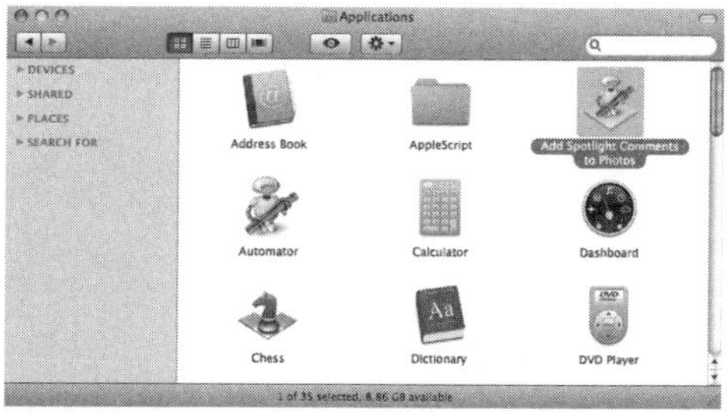

Figure 6.30 You can run Automator workflow applications from anywhere on your Mac, including the Applications folder.

To run a workflow application:

- Double-click the workflow application.

  The workflow launches and runs.

What you see when a workflow application runs:

- As a workflow application runs, the menu bar displays status messages, along with a Stop button. These status messages indicate the currently running action.
- To stop the workflow application from running, click the Stop button (**Figure 6.31**).

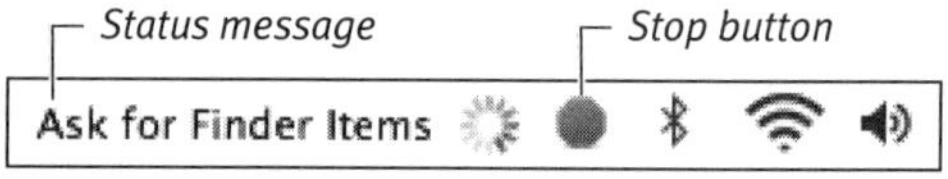

Figure 6.31 When a workflow application runs outside of Automator, the menu bar displays status messages. It also displays a Stop button, which you can click to stop the workflow from running.

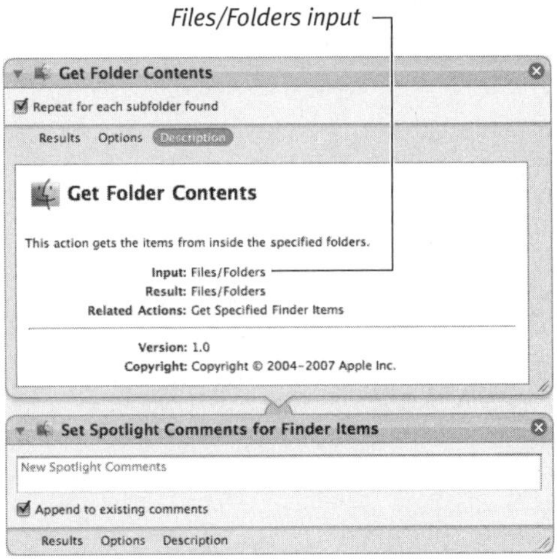

Figure 6.32 The first action in this workflow, Get Folder Contents, accepts files and folders as input.

Processing Files and Folders with a Workflow Application

One of the best things about workflow applications is that they are automatically saved as drag-and-drop applications, making it super easy to process files and folders. Simply drop some files or folders onto your workflow, and they automatically get passed as input to the first action for processing.

Prepare your workflow:

The first action in the example Add Spotlight Comments to Finder Items workflow asks you to choose a folder of images to process. Because you've saved the workflow as an application, however, you can now drag a folder onto the workflow to begin processing. The Ask for Finder Items action is therefore no longer necessary.

With the workflow opened in Automator, select the Ask for Finder Items action and remove it (press Delete). The workflow should now contain only two actions: Get Folder Contents and Set Spotlight Comments for Finder Items. Save the modified workflow (press ⌘S).

Always be sure to check the description area of the first action in a workflow application to make sure it accepts files and folders as input. Otherwise, the workflow won't be able to process dropped files and folders. In the Add Spotlight Comments to Finder Items workflow, the Get Folder Contents action does accept files and folders, so you should be good to go (**Figure 6.32**).

To process files or folders:

- Simply drag and drop the files and folders you want to process onto the workflow application to begin processing. For the example workflow, the Get Folder Contents action needs a folder, so be sure you drop a folder (**Figure 6.33**).

  Any dropped files and folders are passed as input to the first action in the workflow application. If the first action accepts files and folders, the items you drop will be processed, and you're off and rolling.

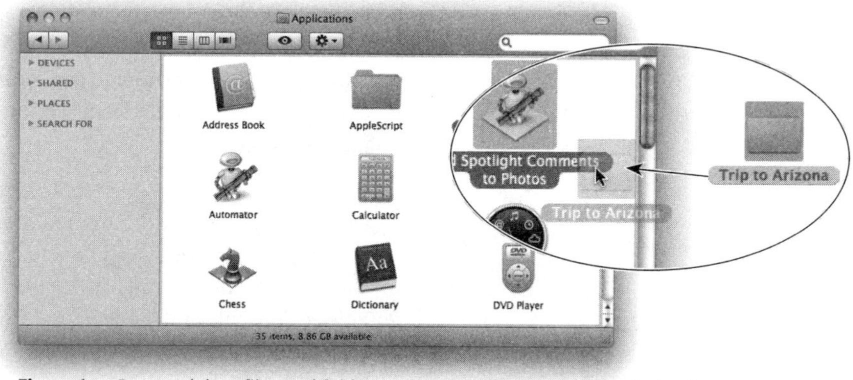

Figure 6.33 Drag and drop files and folders onto a workflow application to begin processing them.

7

TROUBLESHOOTING

Automator workflows are huge time-savers when they run properly; however, getting them to that point is sometimes easier said than done. Whether you're trying to run an existing workflow or create a new one, at some point you're likely to encounter a problem.

Most problems occur when running workflows, and you usually can resolve them by adjusting action settings. Occasionally, though, you'll encounter problems when opening workflows or even with the Automator application itself.

Finding and fixing a problem can be a challenge, but this chapter identifies some common problems and walks you through practical steps to help resolve them.

Problems Running Workflows

In general, creating Automator workflows involves a lot of trial and error: configure actions one way, see if the workflow runs, make adjustments, and try the workflow again. Along the way, problems sometimes occur, but when they do, you don't need to panic. Work through each issue slowly, and gradually you'll get the workflow to do what you want.

Step Through Your Workflow

New in Leopard is the ability to step through your workflow one action at a time. In other words, Automator runs an action, and then pauses. While it waits, you are free to check the result of the action, view Automator's log, and more. When you're ready to proceed, Automator runs the next action, and then pauses again.

This is a *huge* breakthrough for troubleshooting workflow problems! Using this technique, you can move slowly through your workflow, one action at a time, and make sure everything works properly at each step. If you find a problem, stop, fix it, and try again. After you identify and resolve any problems, run the workflow as a whole. If you proceed in this manner, your workflows have a much higher likelihood of running successfully and reliably.

Help for Tiger Users

If you're still using Mac OS X 10.4 (Tiger), you can't step through your workflows like a Leopard (10.5) user can. You can, however, configure your actions to display when run. Every time an action is displayed, the workflow pauses, allowing you to make sure that the previous action ran successfully.

Figure 7.1 Begin stepping through a workflow by choosing Step from the Workflow menu.

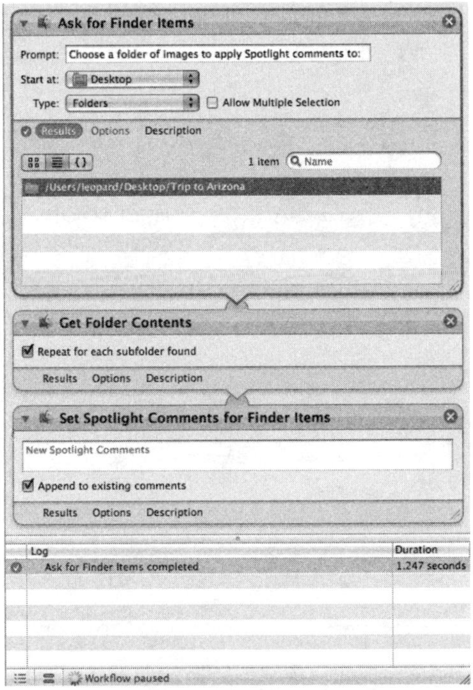

Figure 7.2 When stepping through a workflow, view the current action's results and the log to see if problems occurred.

Figure 7.3 Add a Step button to Automator's toolbar to make stepping through a workflow easier.

To step through your workflow:

1. With a workflow open, choose Workflow > Step (**Figure 7.1**).

   Automator runs the first action in the workflow then pauses. While it's paused, check the results of the action and view the log, to see if any problems occurred (**Figure 7.2**). Make sure the results are correct, and that the action did what it was supposed to do. For example, if the action creates a folder on the Desktop, make sure that the folder was actually created. If the action was successful, then you're ready to proceed to the next action.

2. Choose Workflow > Step.

   Automator runs the next action, and then pauses again. You can stop stepping through a workflow at any time by choosing Workflow > Stop, clicking Stop in the toolbar, or pressing [⌘][.].

✔ Tips

- While a workflow is paused, you can change settings in actions that haven't yet run.
- When stepping through a workflow, you can run all remaining actions by choosing Workflow > Run, clicking Run in the toolbar, or pressing [⌘][R].
- To make stepping through a workflow easier, consider adding a Step button to the toolbar (**Figure 7.3**). To learn how, see Chapter 8, "Customizing Automator."

Troubleshooting a Workflow Problem

A great way to learn to troubleshoot is to walk through a problem workflow. In this section, you'll create a controlled problematic workflow. You'll then learn how to troubleshoot it by checking action results, checking Automator's log, and more. You can apply these same techniques to troubleshooting real-world workflows.

To create a broken workflow for troubleshooting:

1. Launch iTunes, and choose File > New Playlist to create a new music playlist. Name the playlist `My Favorite Songs` (**Figure 7.4**).

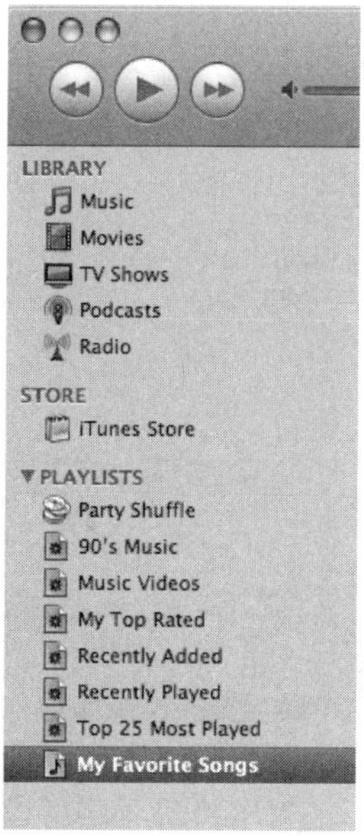

Figure 7.4 Create a playlist named `My Favorite Songs` in iTunes.

2. Bring Automator to the front, and create a new Music & Audio workflow using Starting Points. Set Starting Points to get content from "my iTunes Library" and "Ask for songs and playlists now." Click Choose to proceed (**Figure 7.5**).

   A panel that contains your iTunes songs and playlists appears.

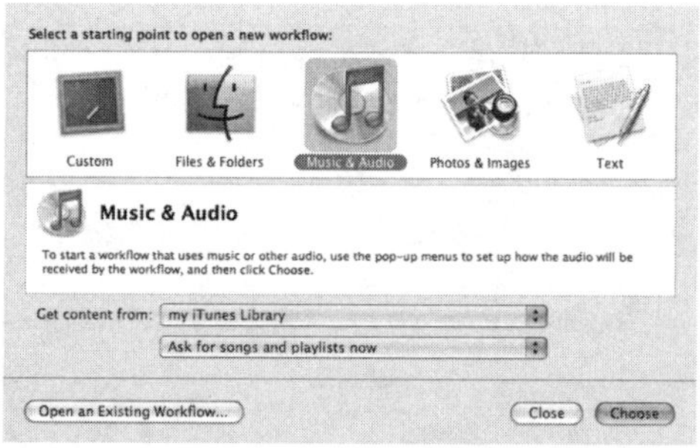

Figure 7.5 Create a Music & Audio workflow. Set Starting Points to get content from "my iTunes Library," and choose "Ask for songs and playlists now."

3. When prompted, select the My Favorite Songs playlist and click Add (**Figure 7.6**).

   Automator creates a workflow and inserts a Get Specified iTunes Items action containing the My Favorite Songs playlist.

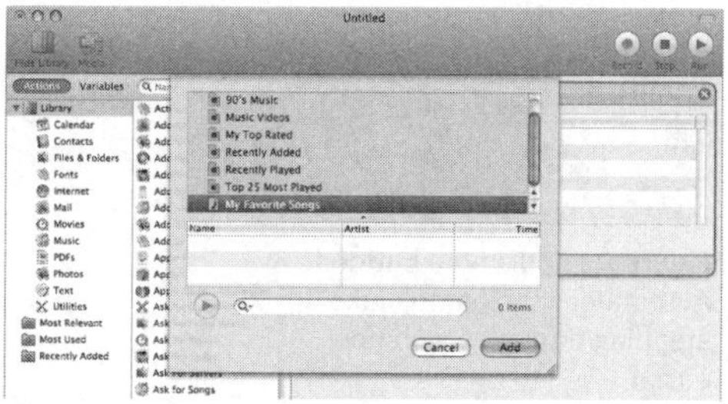

Figure 7.6 Choose the My Favorite Songs playlist when prompted, and click the Add button.

Figure 7.7 A Music & Audio workflow that retrieves a specified playlist from iTunes and plays it.

Figure 7.8 Rename the My Favorite Songs playlist to `My Old Favorite Songs` in iTunes.

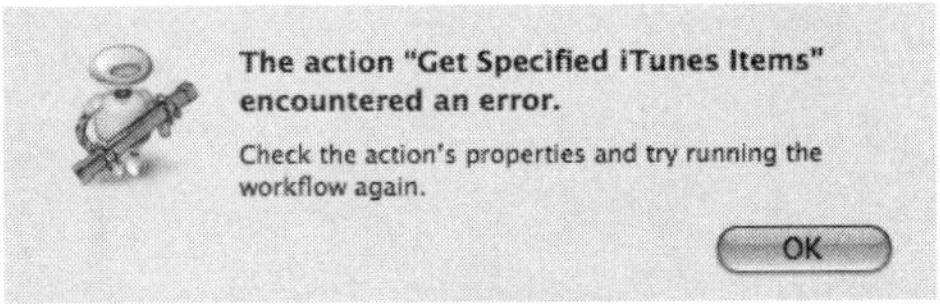

Figure 7.9 Automator displays an error message when an action encounters a problem.

Troubleshooting Workflow Applications

If you encounter a problem with a workflow application, open and run it in Automator. This way, you can step through the workflow, monitor action results, view the log, and more. These capabilities are not available outside of Automator.

4. In the Music category of the Library list, click the Play iTunes Playlist action, and drag it to the end of the workflow.

   You now have a complete workflow that gets the My Favorite Songs playlist from iTunes and plays it (**Figure 7.7**).

   If you run the workflow now, it should run successfully. The purpose of this exercise, however, is to simulate a problem.

5. To create a problem, go back into iTunes, and rename the My Favorite Songs playlist to `My Old Favorite Songs` (**Figure 7.8**).

6. Run the erroneous workflow.

   Automator returns an error. Because the playlist My Favorite Songs was renamed, the Get Specified iTunes Items action can't find it and displays an error message. The message tells you the Get Specified iTunes Items action encountered a problem and suggests checking the action's properties (**Figure 7.9**).

Unfortunately, Automator's error message isn't much help. You, therefore, need to employ some other troubleshooting techniques to find the real source of the problem, specifically:

- Check the workflow status.
- Check the action results.
- Check the workflow log.

✔ Tips

- See Chapter 3, "Workflow Creation Basics," for a refresher on building a Music & Audio workflow.
- When Automator refers to an action's *properties*, it means the action's modifiable settings.

Check the workflow status:

- The first place you should check when troubleshooting a workflow is the status area at the bottom of the workflow window. You won't find much information here, but it will tell you if an error occurred (**Figure 7.10**).

Check the workflow log:

- Perhaps the most useful way to troubleshoot a problem is to consult Automator's log (choose View > Log or press ⌘ Option L). Here, you can find detailed information about any problems that may have occurred. For the example, the log states that iTunes could not locate the My Favorite Songs playlist (**Figure 7.11**).

  To resolve this problem, you can recreate the playlist in iTunes. Or, you can reconfigure the Get Specified iTunes Items action to retrieve a different playlist. Either way, you can get the information you need to solve the problem by looking at the log.

Check action results:

- To view an action's results, click the Results button at the bottom of the action. The results area for an action that encounters an error appears (**Figure 7.12**). If the action accepts input, however, you may find some clues to what went awry by checking the results of the previous action. You want to make sure that the correct information is passed from the previous action to the action that encountered the error. If it isn't, that may be what's causing the error.

  In the example workflow, no actions run before Get Specified iTunes Items, so the results aren't much help.

Figure 7.10 The status bar at the bottom of a workflow window indicates when Automator encounters an error.

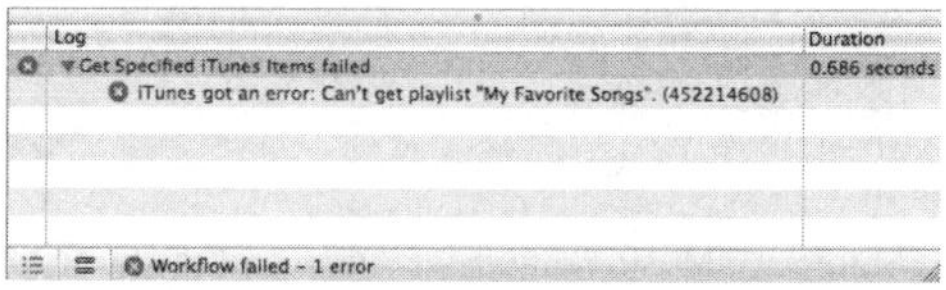

Figure 7.11 The log is an excellent place to find detailed information about workflow problems. Here, the log indicates that iTunes can't locate a playlist named My Favorite Songs.

What's in the Log?

Automator's log provides important information about your workflow, including:

- Actions that have run successfully and their durations
- Actions that have failed with detailed error messages
- Conversion actions that may have run in the background

Refer to the log often, even if you don't receive an error. It may help to shed more light on what's going on as your workflow runs.

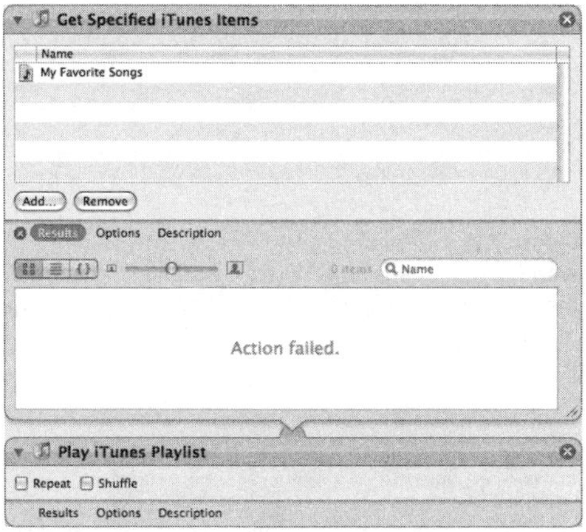

Figure 7.12 Check the results of actions in your workflow to help to identify potential problems. An action that encounters an error will have no results, but checking the results of previous actions may indicate a problem.

Locating the Culprit Action

When a workflow encounters an error, a red X appears at the bottom of the problematic action. Use this clue to identify where the workflow stopped, and start troubleshooting there.

Checking Action Results in Tiger

Tiger users can check action results by using the View Results action, located under Automator in the Library list. Insert this action throughout your workflow to view the results of any action.

Other Troubleshooting Techniques

If you can't solve a workflow problem with the techniques just described, try these:

- **Make action adjustments.** Consider changing the way the action behaves. Sometimes, a simple adjustment to an action's settings may fix the problem. In the example workflow, you might consider configuring the Get Specified iTunes Items action to display when run, allowing you to choose the playlist at runtime.
- **Consider alternate actions.** Some Automator actions do similar things, such as Get Specified iTunes Items and Get Selected iTunes Items. Although these actions may sound very similar, they're actually different. One allows you to specify iTunes items when you build the workflow. The other gets any selected iTunes items when you run the workflow. If you're encountering a problem with one action, try using another that works in a similar way.
- **Disable actions.** Don't forget, you can also disable an action in a workflow. If an action is causing a problem, try disabling it (select the action and choose Action > Disable). See how the workflow runs without the action or with a different action in its place. You can gather some clues from the way the workflow performs at this point. If necessary, you can always enable it again.

Problems Opening Workflows

Not all problems occur when running a workflow; sometimes just opening one can be problematic. These sorts of issues, however, are generally a bit simpler to diagnose. For the most part, Automator tells you what the problem is.

Missing Workflow Actions

To open and run a workflow, you must have all actions used by that workflow installed on your machine. Otherwise, Automator displays an error when the workflow is opened (**Figure 7.13**). You're likely to encounter this problem if you're downloading a lot of workflows or getting them from friends.

When this type of error occurs, you can still open the workflow. Any missing actions, however, are dimmed, and their settings are not visible (**Figure 7.14**). In addition, if you try to run the workflow, Automator displays an error message indicating that some actions were not loaded (**Figure 7.15**).

To troubleshoot this problem:

- Locate and install the missing action. If you downloaded the workflow, see if the action is available for download, too. Or, if you received the workflow from a friend, ask where you can get the action.

  or

- Search the actions you see in Automator's Library list. Perhaps you can locate a similar substitute for the missing one. The workflow might behave slightly differently, but it may still meet your needs.

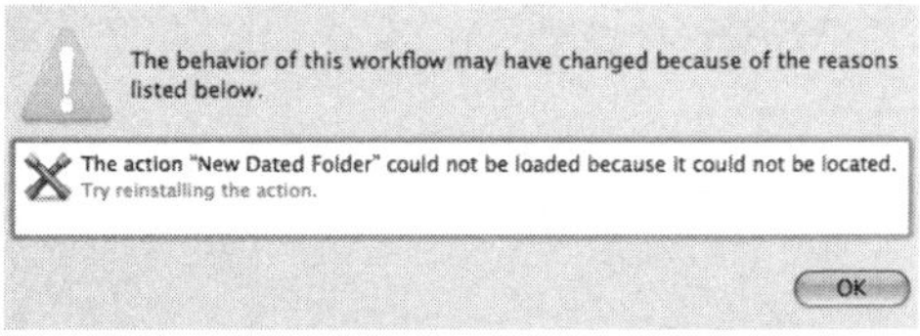
The behavior of this workflow may have changed because of the reasons listed below.
The action "New Dated Folder" could not be loaded because it could not be located.
Try reinstalling the action.
OK

Figure 7.13 Automator notifies you when opening a workflow that uses an action not installed on your machine. For the workflow to run, you must install the missing action.

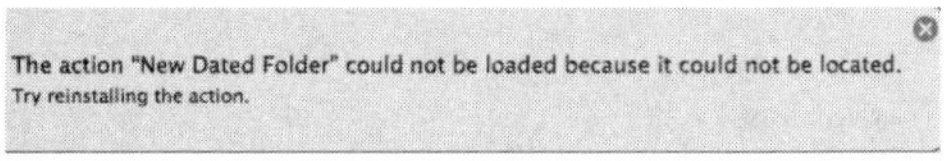
The action "New Dated Folder" could not be loaded because it could not be located.
Try reinstalling the action.

Figure 7.14 A missing workflow action is displayed in Automator, but it's dimmed and its settings are not visible.

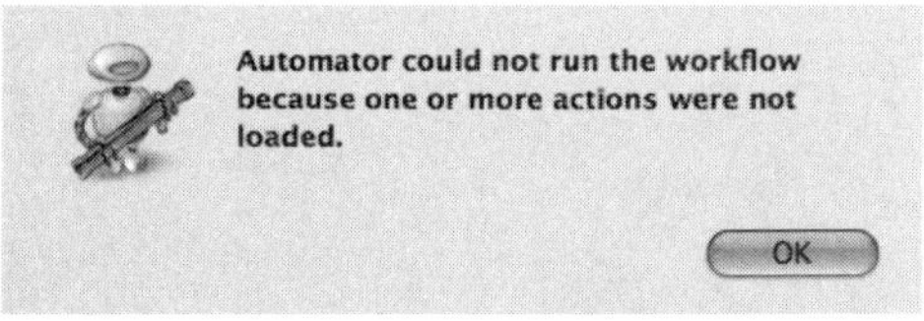
Automator could not run the workflow because one or more actions were not loaded.
OK

Figure 7.15 Automator displays an error message if you try to run a workflow with missing actions.

Action Version Changes

When an action is upgraded—a new version of the action is released—its behavior or settings may change. Because of this, Automator alerts you when opening a workflow that uses an older version of an action that you have installed. You may need to make some changes to the action's settings, so your workflow continues to run successfully (**Figure 7.16**).

When this problem occurs, you can still try running the workflow. In some cases, it may work just fine; in others, however, it may produce an error or not perform as intended. You're likely to encounter this error when opening Tiger workflows in Leopard, as developers upgraded many actions for Leopard.

To troubleshoot this problem:

- Try running the workflow. If it runs successfully, you're home free!
- If the workflow produces an error at runtime, you'll need to configure the action's settings for the newer version. In fact, it's probably best to delete the action from the workflow entirely and insert the new version of the action. This clears any of the action's previously saved settings from the workflow. Once the newer version of the action is inserted, configure it to meet your needs.

continues on next page

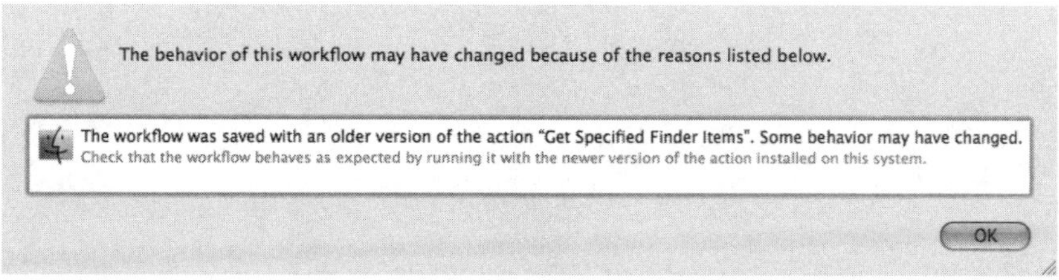
The behavior of this workflow may have changed because of the reasons listed below.
The workflow was saved with an older version of the action "Get Specified Finder Items". Some behavior may have changed.
Check that the workflow behaves as expected by running it with the newer version of the action installed on this system.
OK

Figure 7.16 Automator notifies you when opening a workflow containing an older version of an action. This is your cue to test the workflow to make sure it still runs smoothly.

✔ Tips

- If you're unsure of the latest version available for an action, check the developer's website. If the action has documentation, search it for a version history.
- In Leopard, you can view the version of an action in its description area (**Figure 7.17**). The Finder's information window also displays the version number of an action (**Figure 7.18**). Locate and click the action file in the Finder, and choose File > Get Info.
- In Tiger, some developers include version numbers in the action's description area. For others, you'll need to view the action's information window in the Finder.

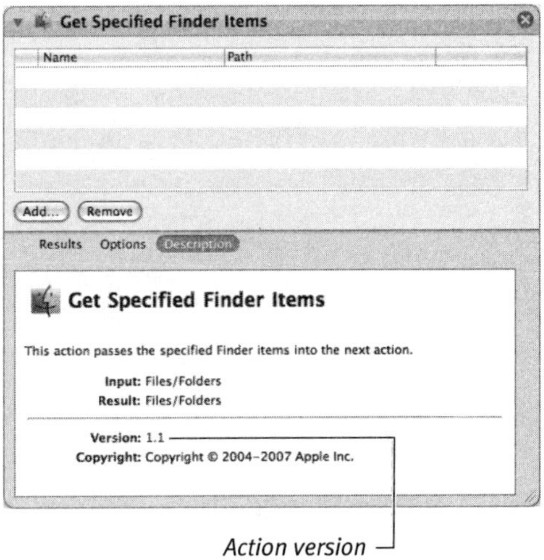

Figure 7.17 In Leopard, an action's version number is shown in its description.

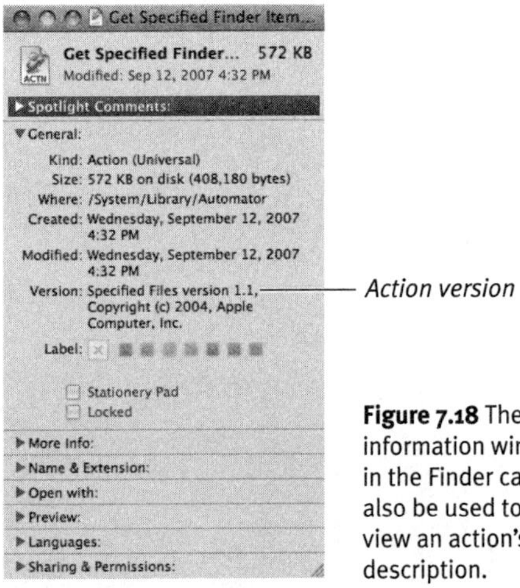

Figure 7.18 The information window in the Finder can also be used to view an action's description.

Figure 7.19 Automator doesn't always display installed actions. Here, the Photos category lists no iPhoto actions, because iPhoto is not installed.

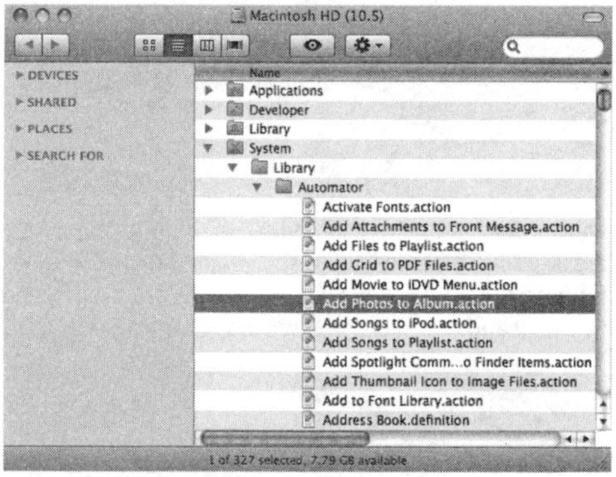

Figure 7.20 The **/System/Library/Automator** folder contains Automator actions for Apple applications. This example shows that the Add Photos to Album iPhoto action is installed.

General Problems

Most Automator problems are likely to involve opening or running workflows. Occasionally, however, you may encounter some general application-level problems.

Missing Actions

Looking for an action in Automator, but just can't seem to find it? Perhaps you saw the action on a friend's machine, but don't see it on yours. There are times when actions may be installed your system, but don't show up in Automator.

Generally, this problem occurs if you're missing an application required for the action to work. For example, although iPhoto actions may be installed on your machine, if iPhoto itself isn't installed, then Automator won't display the actions (**Figure 7.19**).

To troubleshoot this problem:

1. Make sure that any applications required for the action to work are installed. For example, if the action works with iPhoto, make sure iPhoto is installed.
2. Verify that the action itself is installed. To do this, look for the action in one of the following folders:
   - **/System/Library/Automator** This folder contains actions for Apple applications that are installed with Mac OS X (**Figure 7.20**). You probably won't find any other actions here.

continues on next page

Still Not Seeing an Action?

To be visible in Automator, an action sometimes may need a specific version of an application. For example, Automator may not display an action written for Photoshop CS3 if you have Photoshop CS2 installed. Unfortunately, there's no good way to tell which version of an application an action may need. If the action has documentation, check there. If not, try contacting the action's developer.

- **/Library/Automator** This folder may contain third-party actions. Actions here are available to all users on your Mac (**Figure 7.21**).
- **/Users/YourUserName/Library/Automator** This folder may also contain third-party actions. Actions here are available to you only and not to other users of your Mac (**Figure 7.22**).

If the problematic action and its required applications are installed on your Mac, then the action should be listed in Automator (**Figure 7.23**).

✔ Tip

- Need help troubleshooting a problem? Check out Chapter 14, "Automator Resources." Here, you'll find links to Automator websites and mailing lists that can be valuable troubleshooting resources.

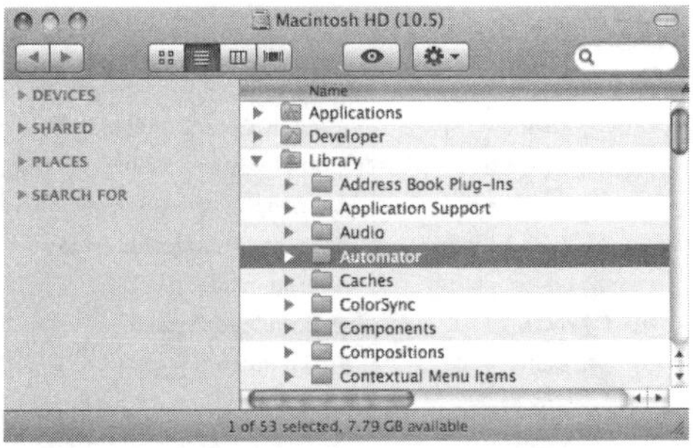

Figure 7.21 Automator actions from third-party developers are sometimes installed in the **/Library/Automator** folder. Actions in this folder are available to all users of your Mac.

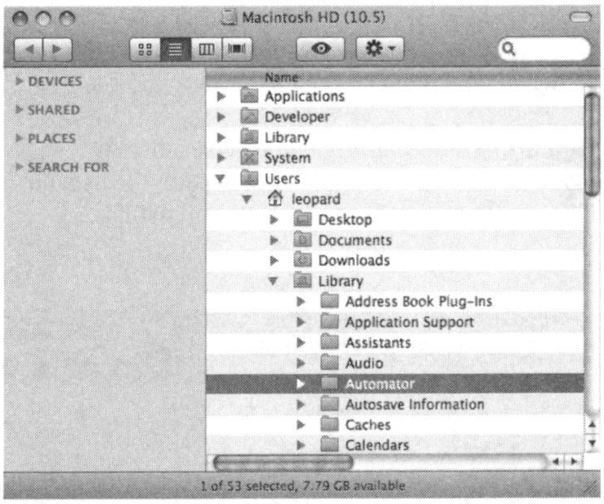

Figure 7.22 Automator actions from third-party developers are also sometimes installed in the **/Users/YourUserName/Library/Automator** folder. These actions are available to you only and not to other users of your machine.

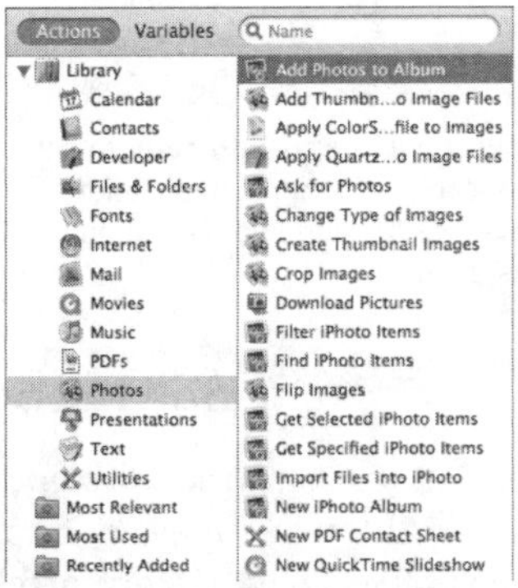

Figure 7.23 If an action and its required applications are installed on your Mac, you should see the action in Automator.

8

CUSTOMIZING AUTOMATOR

Automator is supposed to be easy to use, and as you've seen, most features are easily accessible with a key command or a few clicks of the mouse. By now, you should feel pretty comfortable getting around. You can, however, change things a bit if you prefer.

Like many other Mac OS X applications, Automator's toolbar can be reconfigured. You can reorder or remove the buttons and add new buttons for frequently accessed features. For example, if you regularly step through workflows, you can add a Step button to the toolbar.

Many aspects of the workflow window are also customizable, including the default window size, whether the Library list is visible, and more. You can even create your own groupings of actions and variables. For example, if you frequently use the same actions, you can group them together for quick and easy access, so you don't have to click through different categories to find them.

In this chapter, you'll learn how to adjust Automator's interface to your liking, including adding and removing buttons in the toolbar, resizing the Library list, creating your own custom groups of actions, and more.

Customizing the Toolbar

Even if you're perfectly comfortable using Automator's default toolbar configuration, you may want to consider some customizations. For example, if you regularly print or step through workflows, you can add buttons for these tasks to the toolbar. There's a lot to see in an Automator workflow window; perhaps you'd prefer to reduce the size of the toolbar buttons to gain more screen area to edit your workflows. In this section, you'll learn several ways of customizing Automator's toolbar.

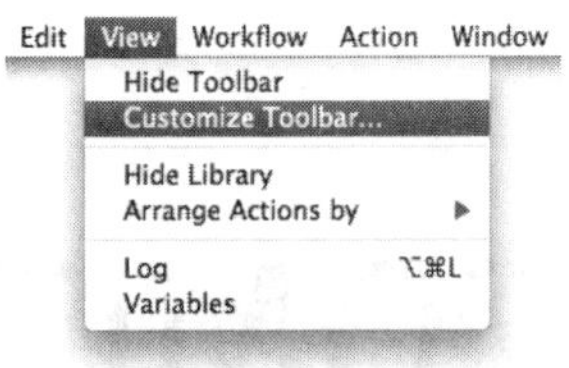

Figure 8.1 Choose View > Customize Toolbar from the menu bar to customize Automator's toolbar.

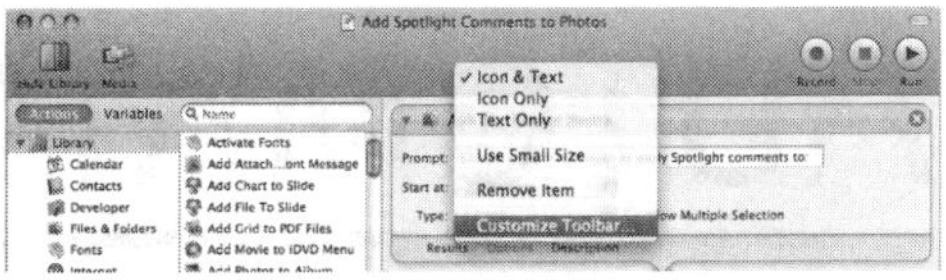

Figure 8.2 You can also customize the toolbar by holding down the Control key, and clicking on the toolbar. Choose Customize Toolbar from the resulting contextual menu.

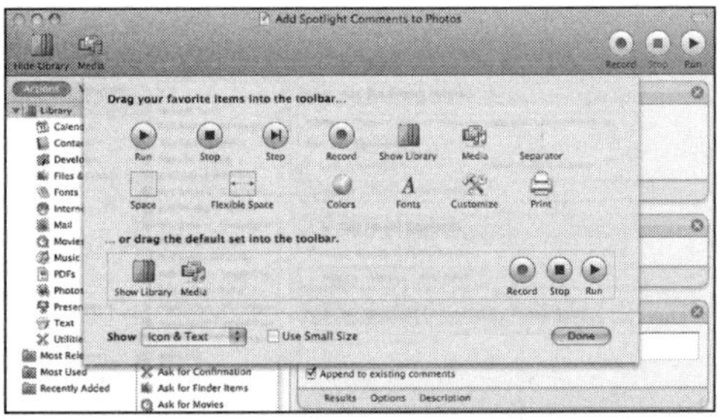

Figure 8.3 When you customize Automator's toolbar, a panel appears, giving you access to new buttons and resizing options.

To customize the toolbar:

1. Open a workflow window.
2. Choose View > Customize Toolbar (**Figure 8.1**),

   or

   While holding down the Control key, click the toolbar to display the contextual menu, then choose Customize Toolbar (**Figure 8.2**).

   A customization panel drops down from the toolbar, containing a variety of options, including new buttons, sizing choices, and more (**Figure 8.3**).
3. Make your desired changes to the toolbar, such as adding or removing a button (see the following page for how to do this).
4. Click Done.

   The customization panel closes.

Automator remembers your toolbar customizations and displays them in workflow windows from now on.

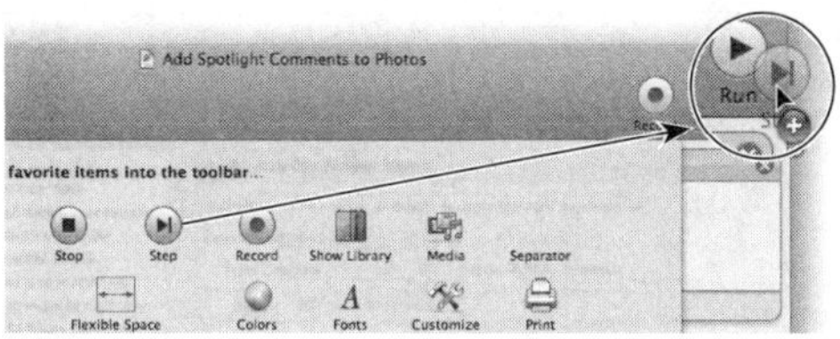

Figure 8.4 To add a button to the toolbar, drag a button from the customization panel to the desired location in the toolbar.

Figure 8.5 When adding a new button to the toolbar, existing buttons move out of the way, if necessary, to make room.

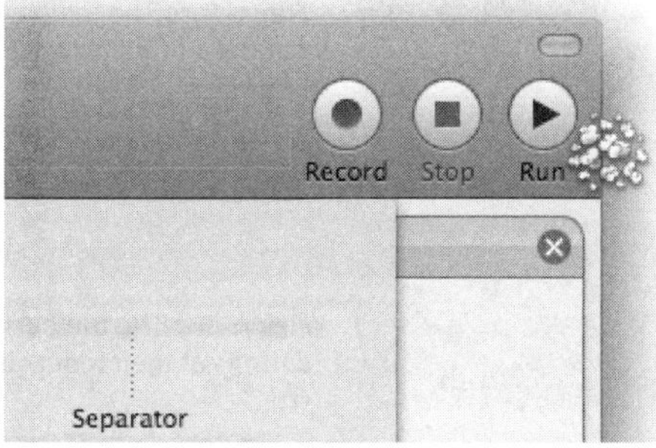

Figure 8.6 When customizing the toolbar, remove a button by simply dragging it off the toolbar.

Figure 8.7 A toolbar button can also be removed by choosing Remove Item from the contextual menu. To display the contextual menu, hold down Control and click the toolbar.

Adding and Removing Toolbar Buttons

Automator makes it easy to add or remove buttons in the toolbar and even provides a way to reset the toolbar back to its default buttons.

To add a toolbar button:

1. Follow the steps in the previous section to display the toolbar customization panel.
2. Drag the desired button from the customization panel to the toolbar (**Figure 8.4**).

   Automator moves any existing buttons out of the way and adds the new button to the toolbar.

Now, the button is available for you to use whenever you may need it (**Figure 8.5**).

✔ Tip

- Need to change the location of a button in the toolbar? No problem. Simply click the button and drag it to the desired location.

To remove a toolbar button:

- With the customization panel displayed, drag the button you want to remove off of the toolbar. With a puff of smoke, the button disappears (**Figure 8.6**).

  or

  Without the customization panel displayed, hold down ⌘, and drag the button off the toolbar. Again, one puff of smoke, and the button is gone.

  or

  Without the customization panel displayed, hold down the Control key, and click the button within the toolbar to display a contextual menu. Then, choose Remove Item from the menu (**Figure 8.7**). Automator removes the button.

To reset the toolbar buttons:

1. Display the toolbar customization panel.
2. Drag the default set of buttons to the toolbar (**Figure 8.8**).

   Any buttons you've added are removed, and the default buttons are displayed again (**Figure 8.9**).

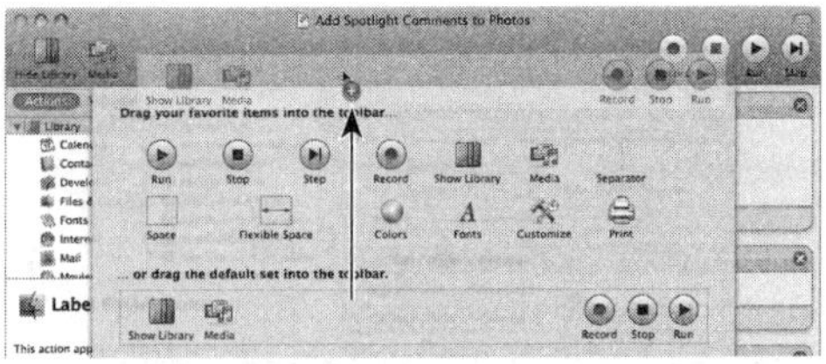

Figure 8.8 To reset the toolbar, simply drag the default set of buttons from the customization panel back to the toolbar.

Figure 8.9 When you drag the default set of buttons to the toolbar, any buttons you've added disappear and the original buttons are displayed.

Resizing Toolbar Buttons

The buttons in Automator's toolbar can be viewed in two sizes: small and large (**Figures 8.10** and **8.11**). Unless you have a lot of buttons in the toolbar, the default size of large is probably just fine. You can, however, change the size if you prefer.

To change the size of toolbar buttons:

1. Display the toolbar customization panel.
2. Click the Use Small Size checkbox (**Figure 8.12**).

or

1. Hold down Control and click the toolbar to display the contextual menu.
2. Choose Use Small Size from the menu.

To enlarge the buttons, deselect the Use Small Size checkbox in the customization panel, or deselect the Use Small Size menu item in the contextual menu (**Figure 8.13**).

Figure 8.10 The toolbar buttons at their normal, large size.

Figure 8.11 The toolbar buttons at their reduced size.

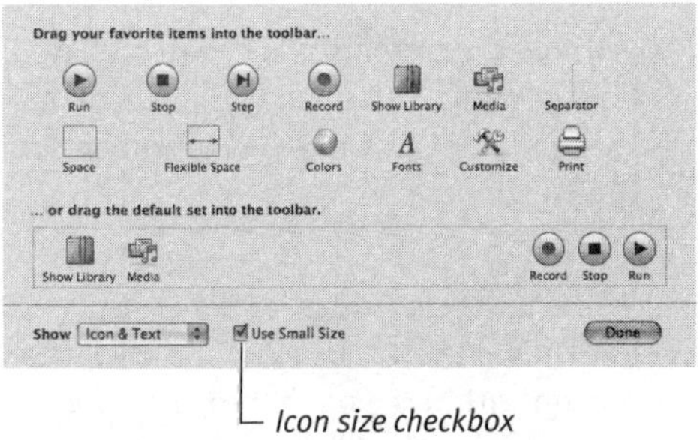

Figure 8.12 Click the Use Small Size checkbox to reduce the size of the buttons in the toolbar and gain slightly more space to build your workflows.

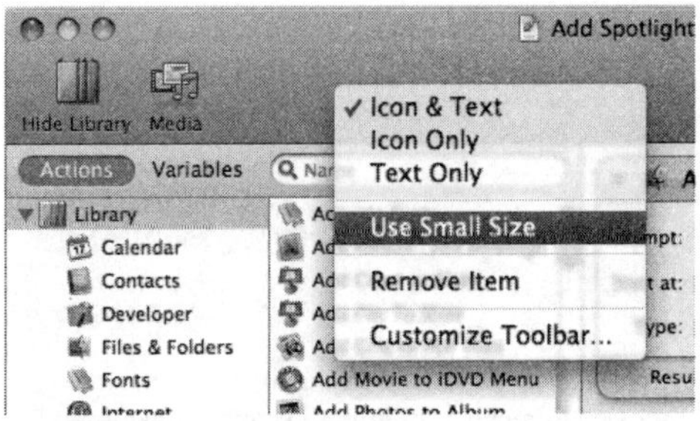

Figure 8.13 Reduce the size of toolbar buttons by choosing Use Small Size from the contextual menu. To display this menu, hold down Control and click the toolbar.

Figure 8.14 By default, toolbar buttons are displayed as icons and text.

Figure 8.15 To reduce the size of the toolbar ever so slightly, display toolbar buttons as icons only.

Figure 8.16 For the most screen real estate, display toolbar buttons as text only.

Changing the Style of Toolbar Buttons

By default, toolbar buttons are displayed as icons with text below them. If you want to maximize the amount of space available for creating workflows, however, you can display them as icons only or, even better, as text only. You won't gain a huge amount of extra space, but every little bit can help (**Figures 8.14**, **8.15**, and **8.16**).

To change the style of the toolbar buttons:

1. Display the toolbar customization panel.
2. From the pop-up menu at the bottom of the customization panel, choose Icon & Text, Icon Only, or Text Only (**Figure 8.17**).

or

1. Hold down Control and click the toolbar to display the contextual menu.
2. Choose Icon & Text, Icon Only, or Text Only (**Figure 8.18**).

   Automator updates the buttons in the toolbar to reflect the chosen style.

You now have a few millimeters of extra space to build your workflows.

Figure 8.17 To change the style of buttons, choose from the pop-up menu at the bottom of the customization panel.

Figure 8.18 You can also change the button style from the toolbar's contextual menu. Hold down Control and click the toolbar to display the contextual menu.

Hiding the Toolbar

Because many of the buttons in the toolbar have corresponding key commands, you may not need to see the toolbar all of the time. As you get more comfortable with Automator, you may start relying on key commands more and more. If you find yourself not using the toolbar much, you can hide it from view entirely.

To hide the toolbar:

- Click the oval-shaped button in the upper right of the toolbar (**Figure 8.19**).

  or

  Choose View > Hide Toolbar (**Figure 8.20**).

  The toolbar disappears, giving you more room to edit your workflow (**Figure 8.21**).

To display the toolbar again, click the oval-shaped button in the upper right of the workflow window, or choose View > Show Toolbar.

Figure 8.19 To hide the toolbar, click the oval-shaped button in its upper-right corner.

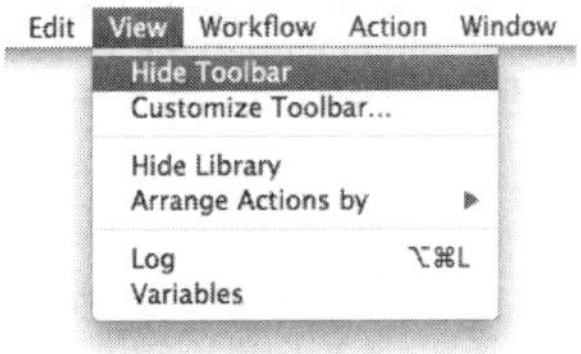

Figure 8.20 Hiding the toolbar from Automator's menu bar.

Figure 8.21 With the toolbar hidden, only the title of the workflow is visible at the top of the window. Now, there's more room to edit your workflow.

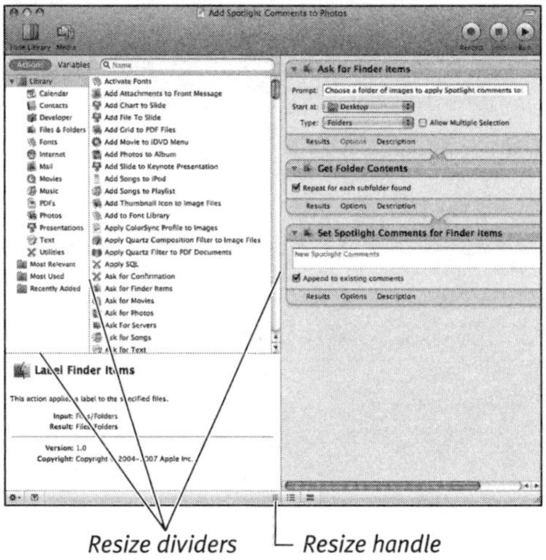

Figure 8.22 To prevent action names from appearing cropped, you can adjust the size of the Library list.

Customizing the Workflow Window

The toolbar isn't the only thing that's customizable in Automator. You can also change how the workflow window appears and functions. For example, you can resize the Library list or hide it entirely, hide the description area, show the log, and more.

Resizing the Library List

Action names are sometimes lengthy, causing them to appear cropped in the Library list. This can make it tough to find the action you're looking for. To reduce cropping, you can expand the size of Library list.

To resize the Library list:

- Click the handle in the lower right of the Library list, beneath the description area, and drag it to the left or right until you find the desired width.

  or

  Click and drag the divider line between the Library list and the workflow area to the left or the right until you find the desired width.

  or

  Click and drag the divider line between the columns of the Library list to the left or right to individually change the width of the columns.

  or

  Click and drag the divider line between the Library list and the description area until you find the desired height (**Figure 8.22**).

Hiding the Library List

When you finish adding actions to a workflow, you may not need to use the Library list again for a while. To give yourself more room to edit the actions in the workflow, you can hide the Library list (**Figure 8.23**).

To hide the Library list:

- Click the Hide Library button in the toolbar (**Figure 8.24**).

  or

  Choose View > Hide Library (**Figure 8.25**).

  The workflow area expands to the left, hiding the Library list. Now, you can focus all of your attention on the actions in your workflow, without getting distracted by unneeded interface elements.

You can bring back the Library list by clicking Show Library in the toolbar or by choosing View > Show Library (**Figure 8.26**).

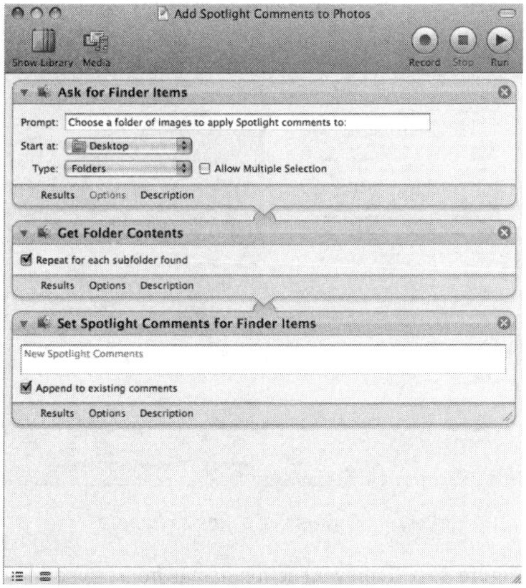

Figure 8.23 Automator enables you to hide the Library list entirely, giving you more room to view and edit your workflow.

Figure 8.24 Click the Hide Library button in the toolbar to hide the Library list.

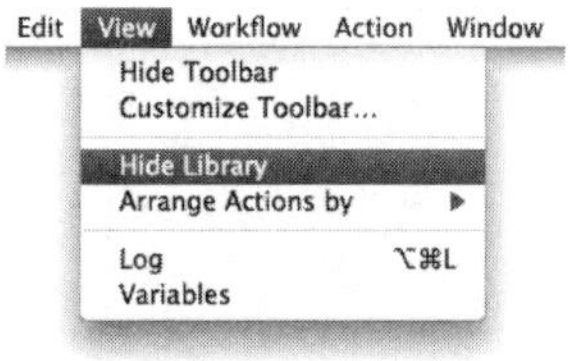

Figure 8.25 Choosing View > Hide Library to hide the Library list.

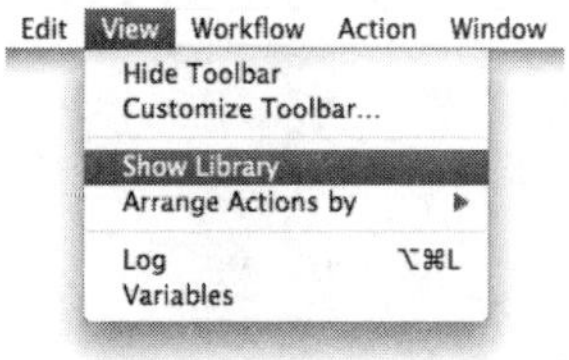

Figure 8.26 Choosing View > Show Library to view the Library list again.

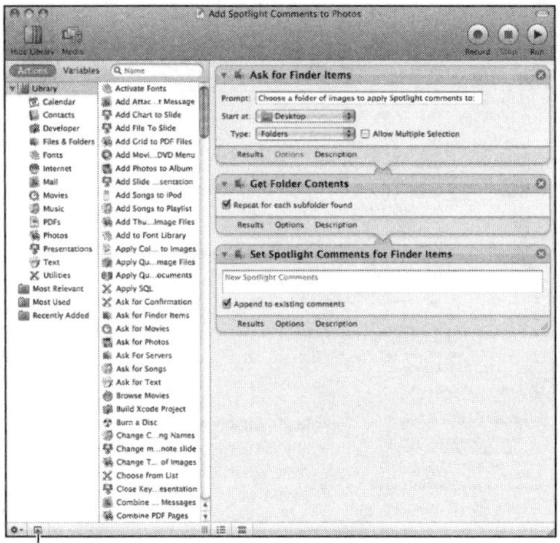

Hide/show description button

Figure 8.27 The description area beneath the Library list can be hidden from view to gain more room for the list of available actions.

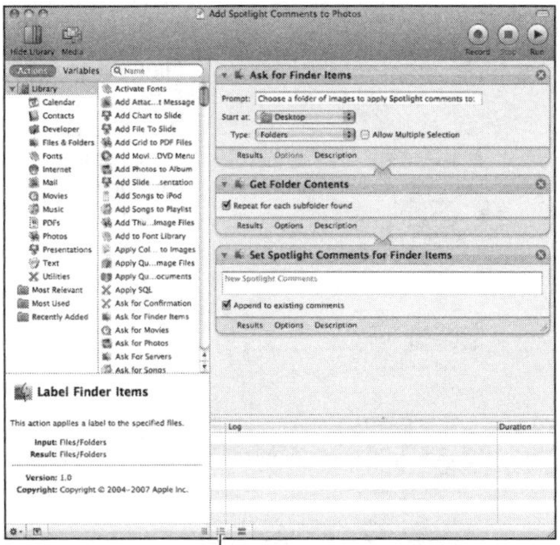

Show/hide log button

Figure 8.28 The log is a valuable troubleshooting tool. Consider keeping it visible at the bottom of your workflow window at all times.

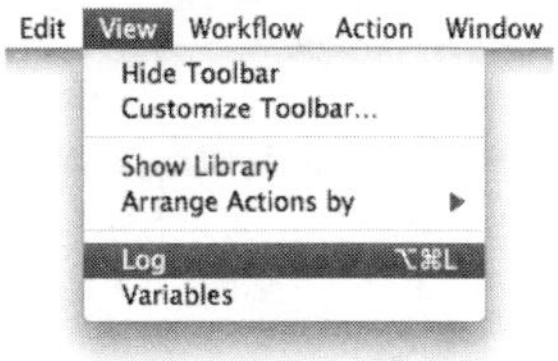

Figure 8.29 To display the log choose View > Log or press ⌘ Option L.

Hiding the Description Area

As you become more familiar with Automator actions, you may not need the description area as often. You may want to hide it.

To hide the description area:

- Click the button in the bottom left of the workflow window.

  The description area disappears, and the Library list now takes up the entire left side of the workflow window (**Figure 8.27**).

To redisplay the description area, click the button in the bottom left of the workflow window.

✔ Tip

- With the description area hidden, you can still view the description of an individual action within your workflow by clicking the Description button at the bottom of the action.

Showing the Log Area

As you know, the log is a valuable tool for troubleshooting workflow problems. It's wise to make it visible, so you see any problems right away.

To show the log area:

- Click the button beneath the workflow area (**Figure 8.28**).

  or

  Choose View > Log (**Figure 8.29**).

  or

  Press ⌘ Option L.

  The log area appears, and you can monitor the progress of your workflow as it runs within Automator.

✔ Tip

- For more on using the log, see Chapter 7, "Troubleshooting."

Showing the Workflow Variables Area

If your workflow uses variables, it's important to monitor their values to ensure your workflow is running smoothly. To do this, you can display a workflow variables area beneath the main workflow area (**Figure 8.30**).

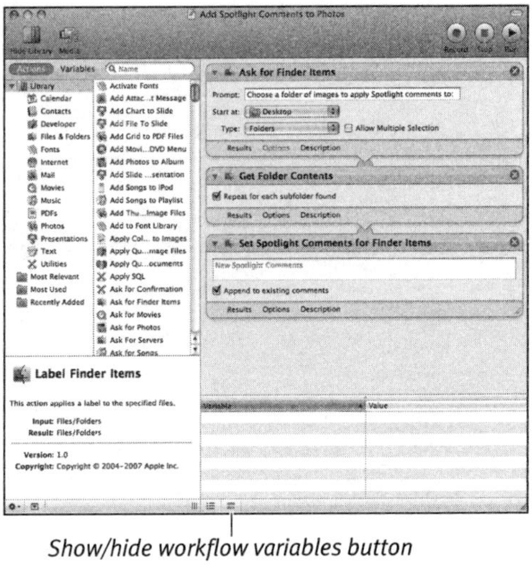

Figure 8.30 The workflow variables area allows you to monitor the values of variables used throughout your workflow.

To show the workflow variables area:

- Click the button at the bottom of the workflow area.

  or

  Choose View > Variables (**Figure 8.31**).

  The workflow variables area appears, and you can monitor the values of the variables used in your workflow as it runs within Automator.

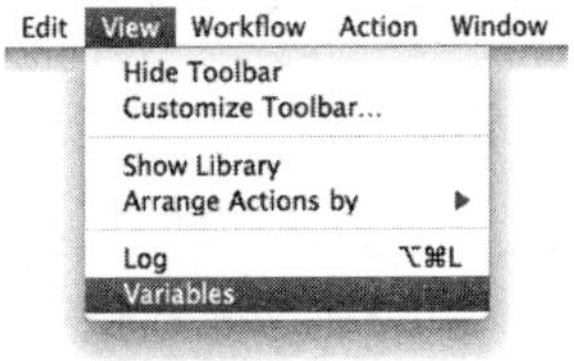

Figure 8.31 Choose View > Variables to display the workflow variables area.

✔ Tip

- You'll learn all about creating, using, and monitoring variables in Chapter 11, "Using Variables."

Changing the Default Window Size

Depending on the size of your monitor or the number of open windows, you may wish to change the Workflow window's size.

To change the default window size:

1. Click the handle in the lower right of the workflow window, and drag it left, right, up, or down until the window is the desired size.
2. Choose Window > Save As Default (**Figure 8.32**) to save the current window size.

Automator opens any future workflow windows at that size automatically.

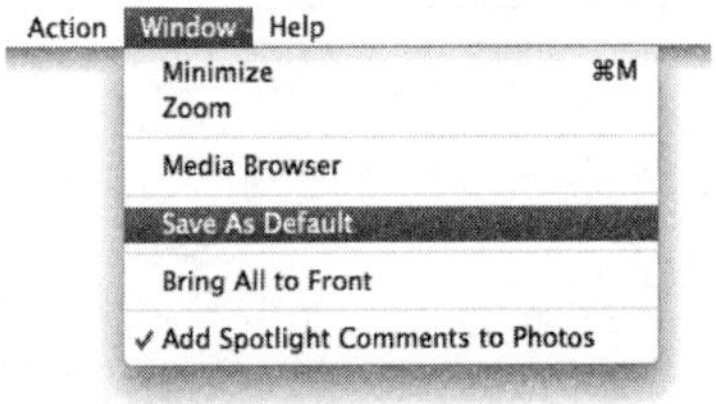

Figure 8.32 Saving the current workflow window size as the default size for future windows.

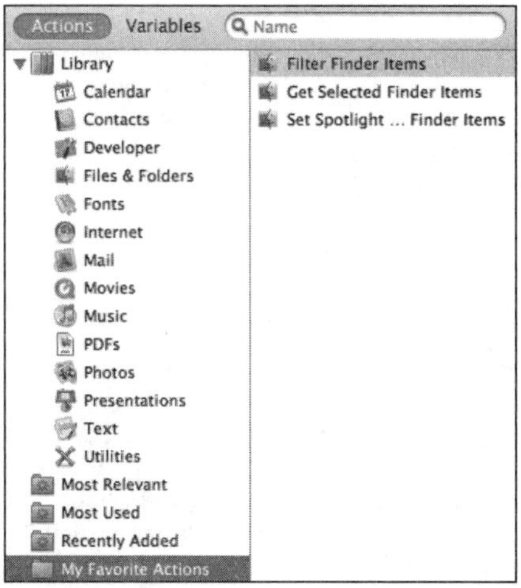

Figure 8.33 To easily find the actions you use most often, organize them into custom groups.

Figure 8.34 To create a custom group of actions, choose New Group from the pop-up menu in the bottom left of the workflow window.

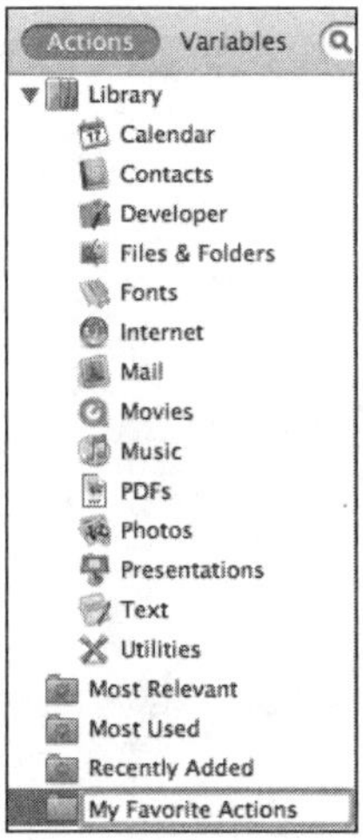

Figure 8.35 A newly created custom group, ready to be renamed to identify the actions it contains.

Figure 8.36 To add actions to a custom group, find them and drag them to the group.

Grouping Actions

The Library list's categories make it easy to locate an action with only a few mouse clicks. If you find yourself using the same actions over and over again, however, you may not want to have to click through these categories. Instead, you may want an easier way to access the actions and to differentiate them from other actions you don't use as often.

In Mac OS X, many applications allow you to organize items in custom ways. In the Finder, you can file things into folders. In iPhoto, you can add photos to albums. In iTunes, you can create playlists of songs. Automator is no different; in it, you can create custom action groups. For example, you might want to create a group for any third-party actions you've installed or for the actions you use most often (**Figure 8.33**).

To create a custom group of actions:

1. In the bottom left of the workflow window, click the button to display a pop-up menu.
2. From the pop-up menu, choose New Group (**Figure 8.34**).

   Automator creates an empty group at the bottom of the Library list, leaving the group's name selected.
3. Enter a name for the group, such as My Favorite Actions (**Figure 8.35**).
4. Find the actions you want to add and drag them to your custom group (**Figure 8.36**).

You now have a grouping of custom actions, which can be quickly accessed when creating workflows. In addition to residing within the group, the actions still reside within their original categories.

✔ Tip

- You can create groups of variables in the same way you can group actions.

To remove a custom group:

1. Select the custom group in the Library list.
2. Press Delete.

   or

   From the pop-up menu in the lower left of the workflow window, choose Remove Groups (**Figure 8.37**).

   Automator asks if you really want to remove the group.
3. Click OK to proceed with removing the group, or click Cancel to keep the group (**Figure 8.38**).

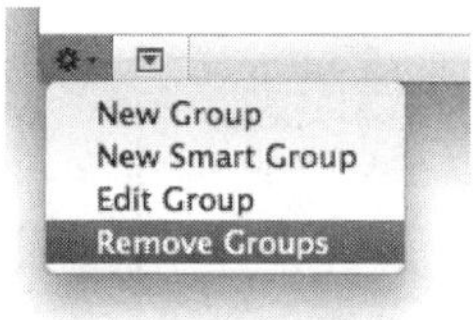

Figure 8.37 To remove a group, select the group and choose Remove Groups from the pop-up menu in the lower right of the workflow area.

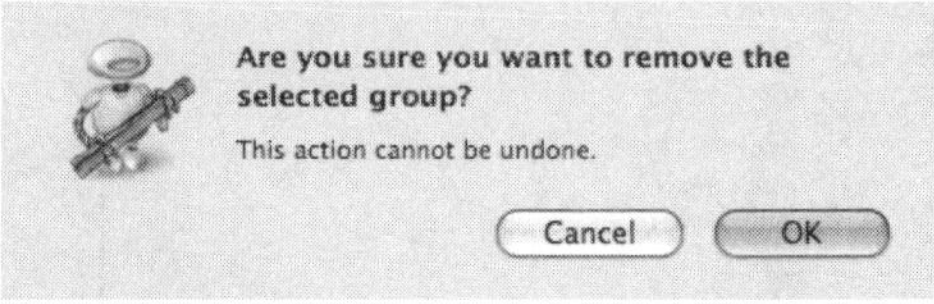

Figure 8.38 Automator makes sure you don't accidentally remove a group by displaying an alert asking for confirmation.

✔ Tip

- Removing a group deletes the group only, not the actions within it. The actions themselves are still listed in their original locations, too.

Creating Smart Groups of Actions

Many Mac OS X applications enable you to create smart groups, which are essentially saved searches matching criteria that you specify. For example, iPhoto allows you to create smart albums of photos, such as any photo with a keyword of "Vacation." In iTunes, you can create smart playlists of songs, such as any song recorded in the 1960s. In the Finder, you can create smart folders of items, such as any item whose modification date is in the current week. In Automator, you can create smart groups, too—smart groups of actions.

Unlike with custom groups of actions, you don't need to add anything into a smart group. Rather, you enter the desired search criteria, and then Automator automatically finds all actions matching those criteria. For example, you might create a smart group that finds all actions that accept text as input.

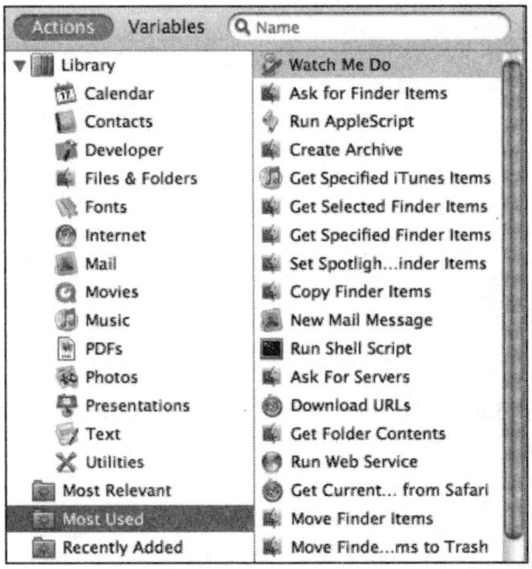

Figure 8.39 Smart groups display actions that meet specific criteria. The Most Used smart group displays the 25 actions you use most often.

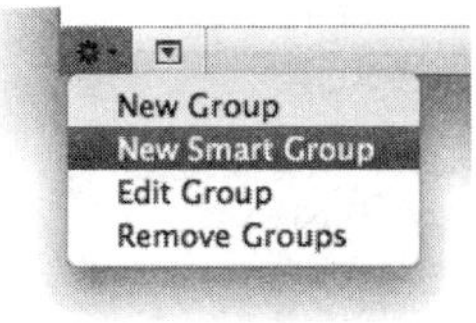

Figure 8.40 To create a smart group, choose New Smart Group from the pop-up menu in the lower left of the workflow window.

Several smart groups already exist in Automator's Library list (**Figure 8.39**):

- **Most Relevant.** Displays a list of actions that are most relevant to the actions within your workflow. As you add more actions to your workflow, the list of relevant actions changes.
- **Most Used.** Displays a list of the 25 actions you use most often.
- **Recently Added.** Displays a list of the 25 most recently added actions within the last 14 days. If you haven't installed new actions on your machine, then this list is empty.

To add a smart group:

1. From the pop-up menu at the bottom-left corner of the workflow window, choose New Smart Group (**Figure 8.40**).

   Automator displays a panel in which you can specify the desired search criteria.
2. In the Name field, enter a name for the smart group.
3. In the criteria area, choose the search criteria you want to use to fill the smart group. For example, suppose you use Mail and iCal to create most of your workflows. You can configure the smart group to display any actions that interact with those applications.
4. To reduce the number of actions that fill the Smart Group, click the "Limit number of items to" checkbox and enter a limit value into the following text field.
5. From the "Sort by" pop-up menu, choose how you'd like the actions to be sorted within the Smart Group. By default, actions are sorted by name.

continues on next page

6. Click OK (**Figure 8.41**).

   Automator creates a smart group at the bottom of the Library list. Click the group to display any actions matching the criteria you specified (**Figure 8.42**).

When you create a smart group, you're not locked in. You can change it in the future, if necessary, by adjusting its search criteria or adding new ones.

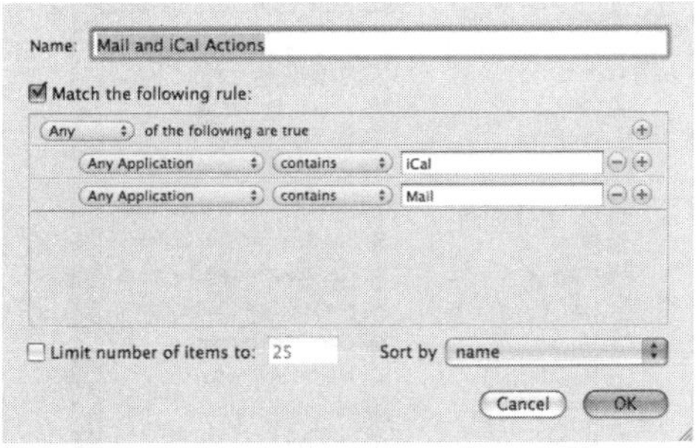

Figure 8.41 When configuring a smart group, specify the desired search criteria.

✔ Tips

- You cannot create a smart group for variables.
- To remove a smart group, follow the instructions earlier in this chapter for removing a custom group. The same steps apply to smart groups.

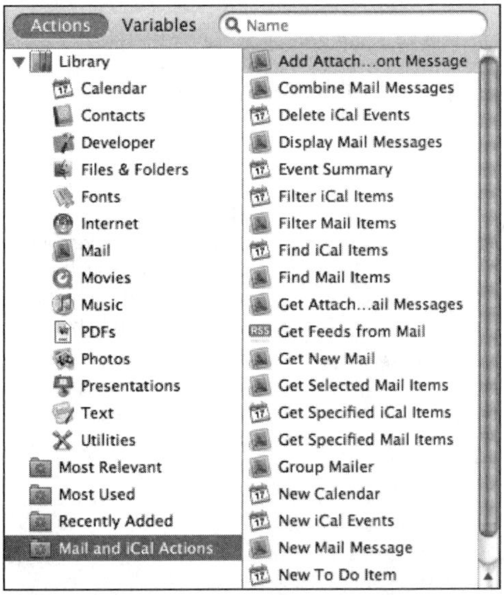

Figure 8.42 Click a smart group to display the actions matching the group's specified search criteria.

To edit a smart group:

1. Click the smart group in the Library list.
2. Choose Edit Group from the pop-up menu in the bottom left of the workflow window.

   Automator displays the smart group configuration panel again, and you can make any desired changes (**Figure 8.43**).

Figure 8.43 To edit a smart group, select the group in the Library list. Then, choose Edit Group from the pop-up menu in the bottom left of the Library list.

Saving Workflow Plug-Ins

9

As you know, an Automator workflow can be saved as a workflow file or a stand-alone application, which lets you use the workflow without launching Automator. Although these methods are both useful, Automator also offers a third, even more flexible option: You can save a workflow as a plug-in for another application or even for the system itself. A workflow plug-in can run in a more efficient or unique manner than a workflow file or application. It's like a way of adding your own features to applications, or even to the Finder.

For example, you can save a workflow as a Finder plug-in, allowing it to be run right from the Finder's contextual menu. Or, you can save a workflow as an iCal alarm, allowing it to run at scheduled intervals, such as at night or while you're at lunch. You can even create a plug-in that runs every time a file is added to a specified folder. You'll learn about these and other methods of saving workflows as plug-ins in this chapter.

Finder Plug-Ins

A workflow saved as a Finder plug-in appears in the Finder's contextual menu, allowing you to run it quickly from anywhere within the Finder. To display the Finder's contextual menu, hold down the Control key and click any file or folder (**Figure 9.1**).

When you trigger a Finder plug-in workflow via a contextual menu, any selected files and folders are passed to the first action in the workflow—much like dropping files onto a workflow application.

For example, if you trigger a Finder plug-in workflow after selecting a folder, then the path to that folder passes to the first action in the workflow as input. Running a Finder plug-in on an opened folder window passes the path to the window's folder to the first action in the workflow. Running it on the Desktop passes the path to the Desktop folder.

Building and Running a Finder Plug-in

To better understand the benefits, try creating an Automator workflow and saving it as a Finder plug-in. The example workflow you'll be building converts images from one type to another, such as from JPEG to TIFF.

Actions used:

- Copy Finder Items
- Change Type of Images

Figure 9.1 A workflow saved as a Finder plug-in appears in the Finder's contextual menu. The paths to any selected files and folders are passed to the first action in the workflow as input.

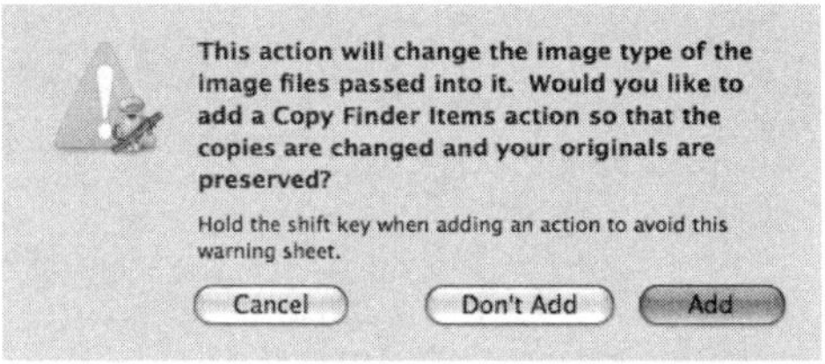

Figure 9.2 The Change Type of Images action modifies your image files in an irreversible manner. Automator alerts you to this when adding the action to your workflow and suggests inserting a Copy Finder Items action first.

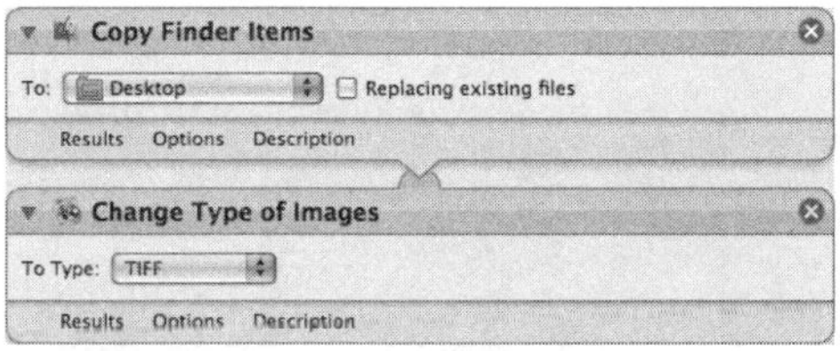

Figure 9.3 Your workflow should now consist of two actions: Copy Finder Items and Change Type of Images.

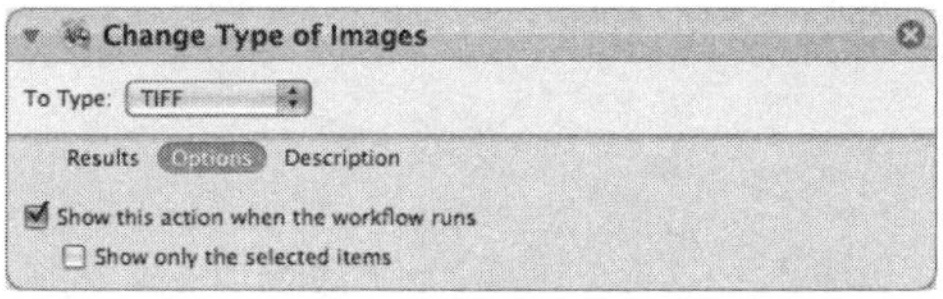

Figure 9.4 Set the Change Type of Images action to show when run. This will allow you to specify the desired type of image each time you run the workflow.

To build the workflow:

1. Create a new custom workflow by choosing File > New or pressing ⌘N. Click the Custom button in the Starting Points panel, and then click Choose.

   Starting Points creates an empty workflow window.

2. From the Photos category of actions, click the Change Type of Images action and drag it to the workflow area.

   This action modifies your original image files. Automator therefore displays an alert, suggesting that you insert a Copy Finder Items action prior to the Change Type of Images action to ensure that your original images remain untouched (**Figure 9.2**).

3. Click Add to insert the Copy Finder Items action as well.

   Automator adds both the Copy Finder Items action and the Change Type of Images action to the workflow. The Copy Finder Items action is set to copy the images to the Desktop by default. No additional configuration of this action is necessary (**Figure 9.3**).

4. At the bottom of the Change Type of Images action, click the Options button then click the "Show this action when the workflow runs" checkbox (**Figure 9.4**).

   When your workflow runs, it displays this action, allowing you to specify the desired type of image.

✔ Tips

- Using Starting Points to create a custom workflow is detailed in Chapter 3, "Workflow Creation Basics."
- Chapter 4, "Working with Actions," explains in detail how to locate an action and add it to a workflow.

To save the workflow as a Finder plug-in:

1. Choose File > Save As Plug-in (**Figure 9.5**).

   or

   Press Option ⌘ S.

   Notice that the resulting save panel is different from the one Automator displays when you save a workflow as a file or application. You may still enter a name for the saved workflow. Rather than specifying an output folder location, however, you will specify the type of plug-in that you would like to create from the "Plug-in for" pop-up menu (**Figure 9.6**).

2. Enter `Change Type of Images` into the Save Plug-in As text field.

3. Choose Finder from the "Plug-in for" pop-up menu.

4. Click Save.

   Automator saves the workflow and installs it in the appropriate location on your hard drive for the type of plug-in you specified, in this case a Finder plug-in.

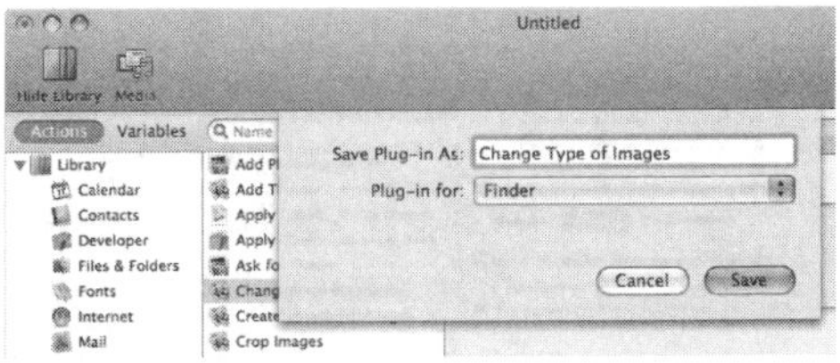

Figure 9.5 Choose File > Save As Plug-in to save your workflow as a Finder plug-in (or any other type of plug-in for that matter).

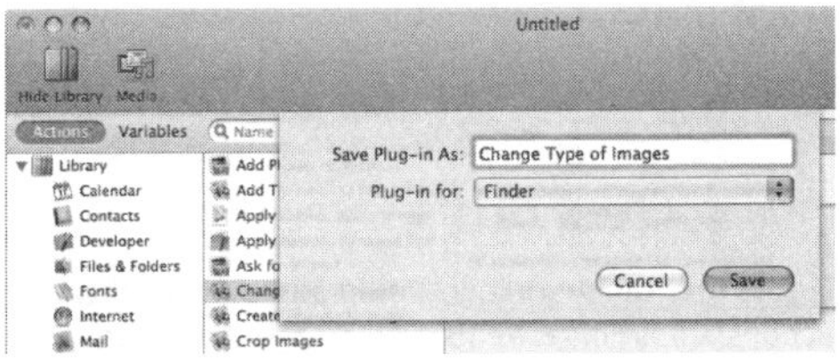

Figure 9.6 The Save As Plug-in panel allows you to enter a save name and specify the desired type of plug-in.

To trigger the Finder plug-in:

1. Locate and select some image files to process in the Finder.

2. Hold down Control and click the selected images.

   The Finder's contextual menu appears.

Figure 9.7 To trigger a Finder plug-in workflow, hold down Control and click the files and folders you want to process. Then, choose the workflow from the Finder's contextual menu.

Figure 9.8 When a workflow plug-in runs, the menu bar displays its status.

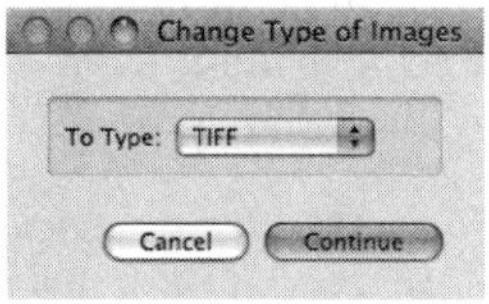

Figure 9.9 The Change Type of Images action displays when the plug-in workflow runs. Choose the desired type of image and click the Continue button to proceed.

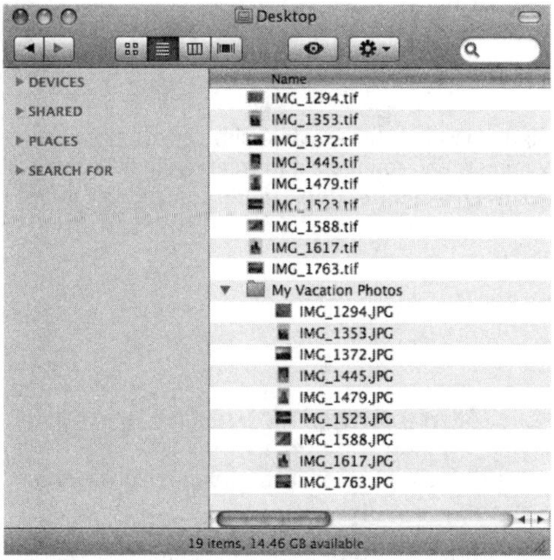

Figure 9.10 After your workflow runs, you'll find the processed image files on your Desktop.

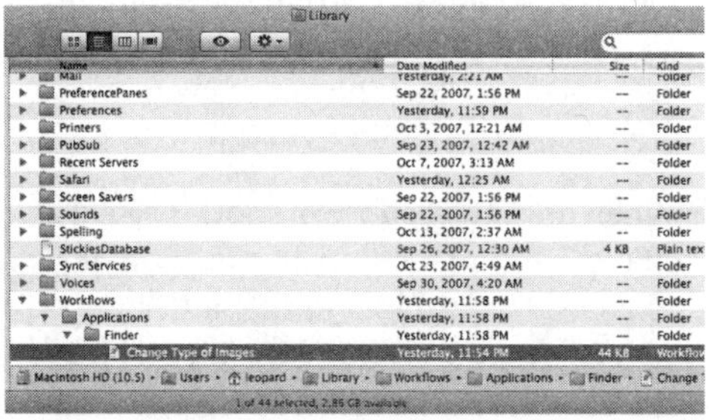

Figure 9.11 Finder plug-in workflows are saved as workflow files into a special folder on your hard drive. To edit a Finder plug-in workflow, locate it here and double-click it to open it within Automator.

3. Choose More > Automator > Change Type of Images from the contextual menu (**Figure 9.7**).

   The workflow begins running, and the menu bar displays its status (**Figure 9.8**).

   The selected images are first copied to your Desktop, leaving your originals intact. Next, the Change Type of Images action's window is displayed, allowing you to specify the desired image type.

4. Choose the desired type of images from the To Type pop-up menu. For example, if your images are JPEGs, you could choose TIFF.

5. Click Continue (**Figure 9.9**).

   The images on your Desktop are converted to the specified type (**Figure 9.10**). You're done. It's that easy.

✔ Tip

- Don't worry about losing your original images. Remember, the Copy Finder Items action copies the images to your Desktop before the images are processed.

Editing the Finder Plug-in

Finder plug-in workflows are saved as workflow files in the ~/Library/Workflows/Applications/Finder/ folder on your Mac (**Figure 9.11**).

To edit a Finder plug-in workflow, simply go to this folder and double-click the workflow file. The workflow opens in Automator, and you can edit it as you would any other workflow file.

✔ Tips

- A tilde (~) at the beginning of a folder path means that the folder resides in your user directory.
- To remove a Finder plug-in workflow, go to ~/Library/Workflows/Applications/Finder/, and delete the workflow.

Folder Action Plug-Ins

Need to create a watched folder workflow? To do so, save an Automator workflow as a Folder Action plug-in attached to a specified folder. A workflow saved this way automatically runs whenever files or folders are added to the folder.

For example, you could attach a Folder Action workflow plug-in to your incoming fax folder, to be triggered whenever a new fax arrives.

Building and Running a Folder Action Plug-in

In this section, you'll learn how to create a very simple Folder Action workflow that creates a zip archive of a file placed into the attached folder. Although this is pretty basic, you can apply these techniques to more complex workflows.

Actions used:

- Create Archive

To build the workflow:

1. Create a new custom workflow window.
2. From the Files & Folders category, drag the Create Archive action to the workflow area.
3. Enter `Archive` into the Create Archive action's "Save as" field.
4. Choose Desktop from the action's Where pop-up menu.
5. Click the action's "Ignore unreadable items" checkbox (**Figure 9.12**).

✔ Tips

- Make sure that your Folder Action workflow doesn't create or rename files in the attached folder. Otherwise, they may get processed by the workflow again.
- To improve Folder Action performance, it's good practice to remove items from your watched folder immediately after processing.

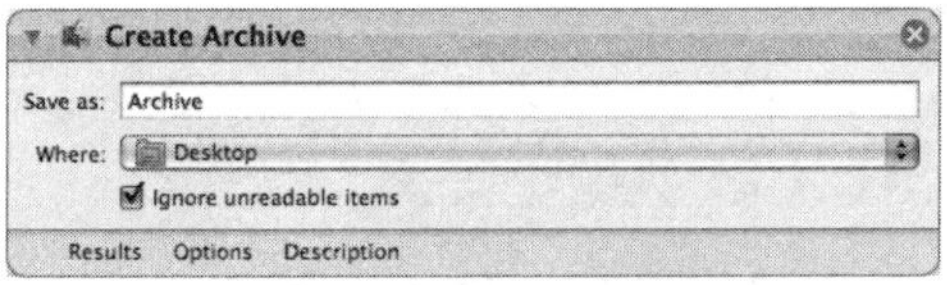

Figure 9.12 Add the Create Archive action to your workflow and configure it to create a zip file named Archive on your Desktop, ignoring unreadable items.

More About Folder Actions

A Folder Action is an AppleScript file that you can attach to a folder in the Mac OS X Finder. A Folder Action script can be configured to run when something specific happens to the watched folder: for example, when items are placed into the attached folder, when items are removed from the attached folder, when the folder's window is opened, or when the folder's window is closed.

When an Automator workflow is saved as a Folder Action plug-in, it is not actually attached to the folder itself. Rather, an AppleScript file is automatically created and attached to the folder. This AppleScript file launches your workflow when items are added to the folder and passes it the newly added items.

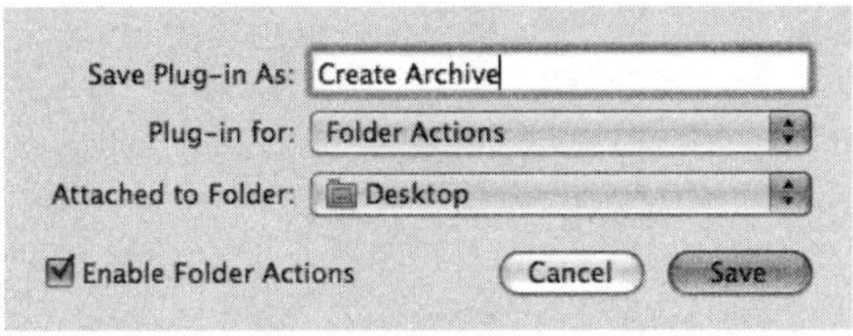

Figure 9.13 Additional options appear in the Save As panel when saving a workflow as a Folder Action plug-in.

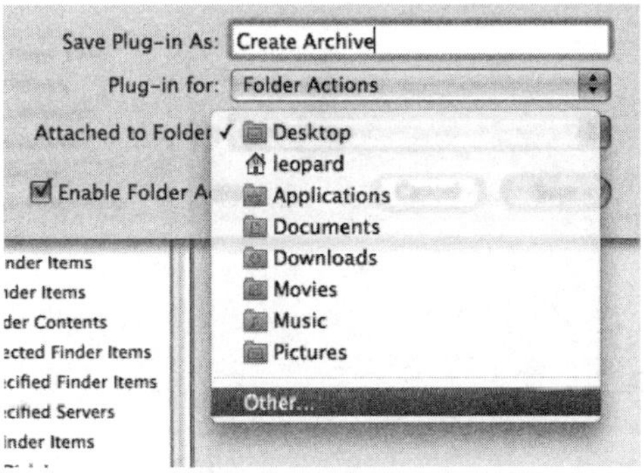

Figure 9.14 Choose Other from the Attached to Folder pop-up menu to select a folder to attach to the Folder Action workflow.

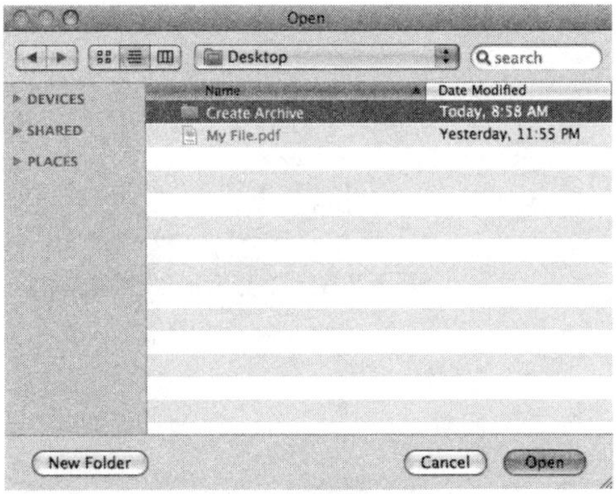

Figure 9.15 Choose Other from the "Attached to Folder" pop-up menu to display a folder selection window. Then, find and select the desired folder and click Open.

To save the Folder Action plug-in:

1. Create a new folder on your Desktop, named Create Archive.

   Your workflow will be attached to this folder, to be run whenever a file is placed into the folder.

2. Return to Automator and choose File > Save As Plug-in or press Option ⌘ S.

   The Save As Plug-in panel appears.

3. Enter `Create Archive` into the Save Plug-in As text field.

4. Choose Folder Actions from the "Plug-in for" pop-up menu.

   Some additional save options appear, including an "Attached to Folder" pop-up menu (**Figure 9.13**). This pop-up menu contains a list of several standard folders by default, from which you may choose, including the Desktop, your user folder, and your Documents folder.

5. For Folder Actions to function in Mac OS X, they must be enabled system-wide. If Folder Actions have not yet been enabled on your machine, then enable them by clicking the Enable Folder Actions checkbox.

   Please note that this checkbox will be shown in the Save panel only if Folder Actions are disabled on your machine.

6. Choose Other from the "Attached to Folder" pop-up (**Figure 9.14**).

   A folder selection window appears, allowing you to choose a folder that is not in the list of standard folders.

7. Locate and select the Create Archive folder you created on your Desktop.

8. Click Open (**Figure 9.15**).

   The folder selection window disappears, and the "Attached to Folder" pop-up menu contains the name of the chosen folder.

continues on next page

9. Click Save to attach the workflow to the specified folder (**Figure 9.16**).

   Now adding items to the folder will trigger the workflow.

To trigger the Folder Action plug-in:

- Select a file in the Finder, and drag it into the Create Archive folder on your Desktop (**Figure 9.17**).

  The Automator workflow runs, displaying its status in the menu bar. The file is archived as a zip file on the Desktop (**Figure 9.18**).

Disabling the Folder Action Plug-in

The Folder Actions Setup application, which can be found in /Applications/AppleScript/ (**Figure 9.19**), provides a central location to manage all Folder Actions that are configured on your machine. Here, you can enable or disable Folder Actions and more.

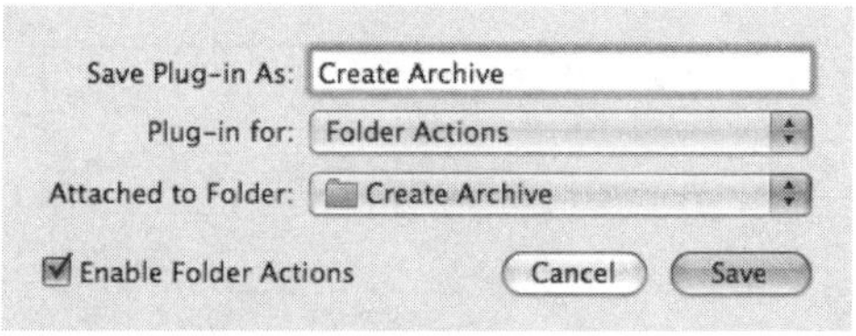

Figure 9.16 Click the Enable Folder Actions checkbox to enable Folder Actions on your Mac. If you don't see this checkbox, then Folder Actions are already enabled.

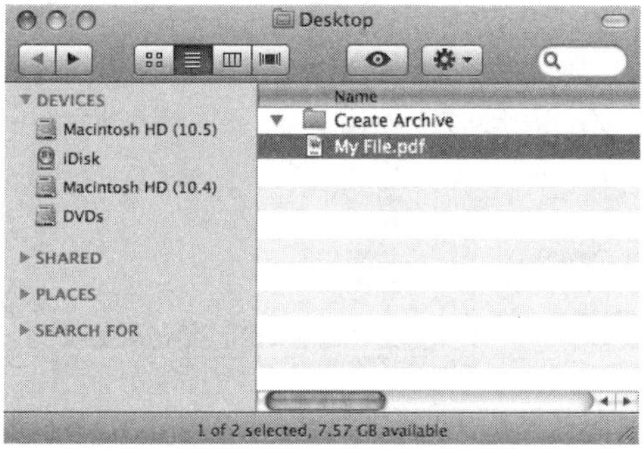

Figure 9.17 Select the file you want to process with the Folder Action workflow, and drag it into the Create Archive folder.

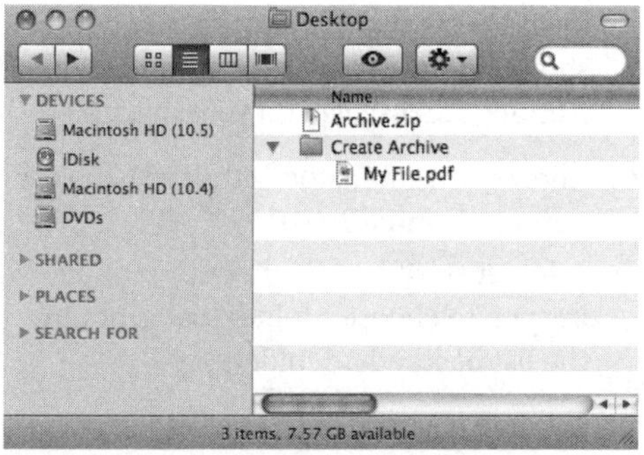

Figure 9.18 When a file is placed in the Create Archive folder, it is archived to the Desktop as a zip file.

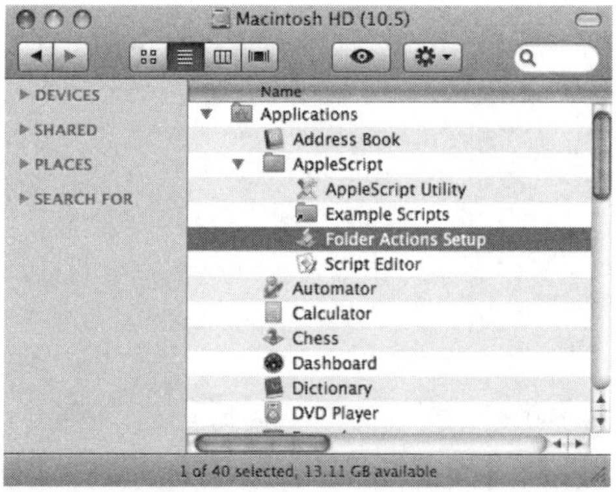

Figure 9.19 Folder Actions Setup, found in /Applications/AppleScript, is used to manage the Folder Actions on you Mac.

To disable the Folder Action plug-in:

1. Double-click the Folder Actions Setup application in the /Applications/ AppleScript/ folder.

   or

   Hold down the Control key and click the Create Archive folder on your Desktop to display the Finder's contextual menu. Choose More > Configure Folder Actions from the menu (**Figure 9.20**).

   The Folder Action Setup application launches and displays a list of all Folder Actions configured on your Mac.

2. In the left column of the Folder Actions Setup window, deselect the checkbox next to Create Archive (**Figure 9.21**).

   The Folder Action is now disabled. To enable it again, reselect the Folder Action's checkbox in the left column of the window.

As you configure additional Folder Action workflows on your Mac, use these steps to enable or disable them as needed.

Figure 9.20 Choose More > Configure Folder Actions from the Finder's contextual menu to launch the Folder Actions Setup application.

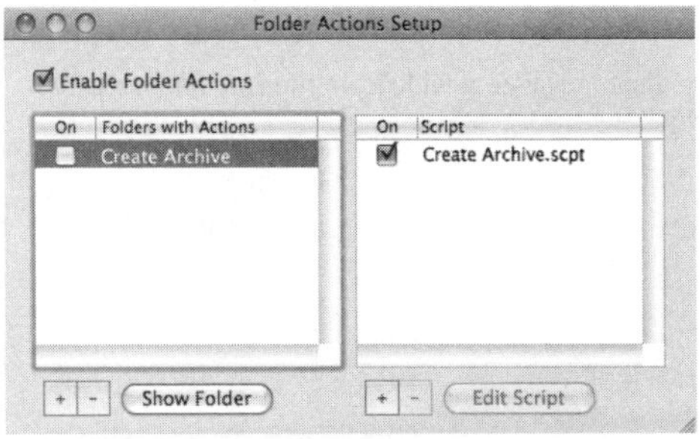

Figure 9.21 To disable a Folder Action, deselect it in the Folder Actions Setup application.

To disable all Folder Actions:

- Deselect the Enable Folder Actions checkbox in the Folder Actions Setup application (**Figure 9.22**).

  or

  Choose More > Disable Folder Actions from the Finder's contextual menu (**Figure 9.23**).

  Folder Actions are disabled system-wide on your Mac. To enable them again, select the Enable Folder Actions checkbox in Folder Actions Setup or choose More > Enable Folder Actions from the Finder's contextual menu.

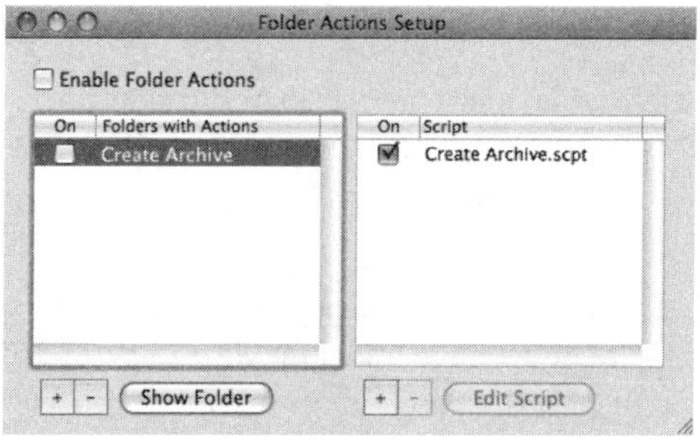

Figure 9.22 Deselect the Enable Folder Actions checkbox in the Folder Actions Setup application to disable all Folder Actions on your Mac.

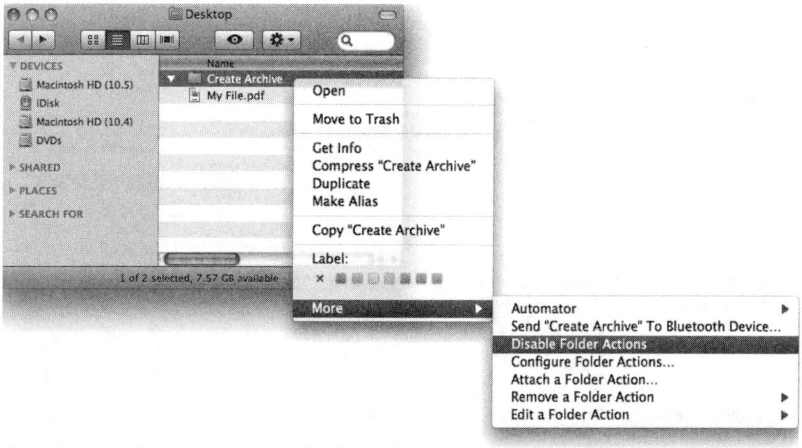

Figure 9.23 Folder Actions can also be disabled system-wide from the Finder's contextual menu. Choose More > Disable Folder Actions.

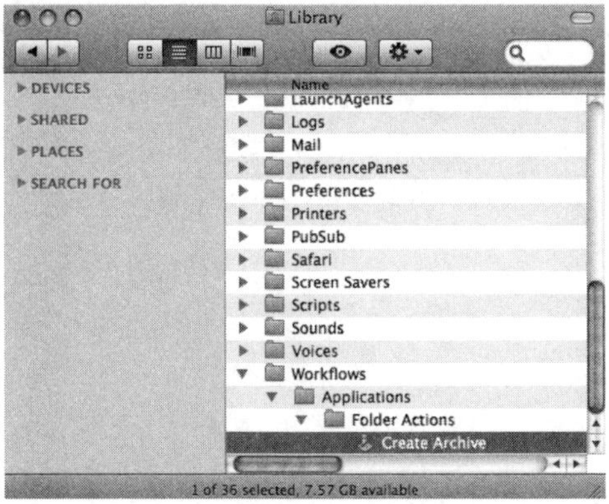

Figure 9.24 Folder Action workflow plug-ins are saved as workflow applications into the ~/Library/Workflows/Applications/Folder Actions/ folder.

Editing the Folder Action Plug-In

Folder Action plug-in workflows are saved as workflow applications in the ~/Library/Workflows/Applications/Folder Actions/ folder on your Mac (**Figure 9.24**).

To edit a Folder Action plug-in workflow, go to this folder, select the workflow application, and drag it onto the Automator icon in your Dock. The workflow opens in Automator, and you can edit it as you would any other workflow application.

There's More to Folder Actions Than Meets the Eye

Want to view the AppleScript code that triggers your Folder Action workflow? Hold down Control and click the Create Archive folder on your Desktop to display the Finder's contextual menu. Next, choose More > Edit a Folder Action > Create Archive.scpt.

Script Editor launches, and the Folder Action AppleScript code is displayed (**Figure 9.25**).

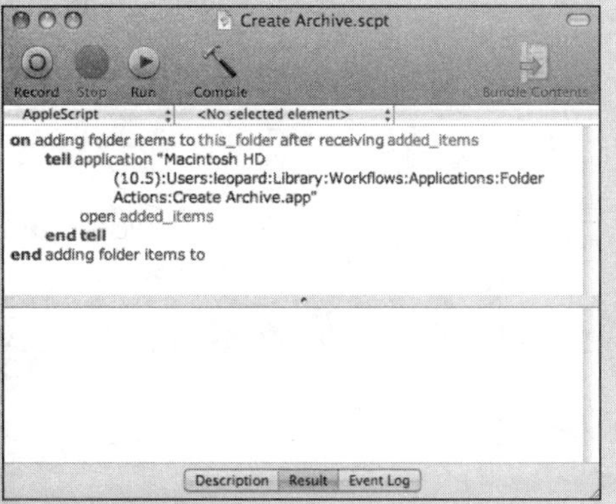

Figure 9.25 AppleScript code is the driving force behind Folder Action workflows.

To remove the Folder Action plug-in:

1. In the left column of the Folder Actions Setup window, select the Create Archive Folder Action and click the minus (–) button beneath the column.

   Automator displays an alert panel asking you to confirm you really want to delete the Folder Action. Click OK (**Figure 9.26**).

   or

   Hold down Control and click the Create Archive folder on your Desktop. Choose More > Remove a Folder Action > Create Archive.scpt from the menu (**Figure 9.27**).

   The Create Archive Folder Action AppleScript is deleted. You must now delete the corresponding Folder Action workflow.

2. Go to the ~/Library/Workflows/Applications/Folder Actions/ folder, and delete the Create Archive workflow application.

   The Folder Action and all associated files have now been removed.

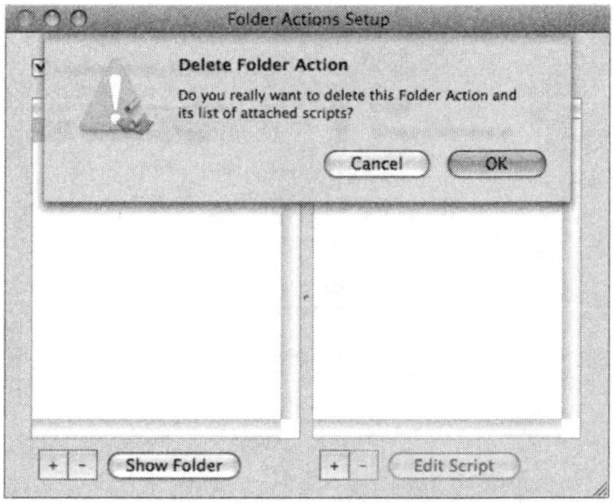

Figure 9.26 To remove a Folder Action using the Folder Actions Setup application, select the Folder Action and click the minus (–) button. You're then prompted to confirm that you want to remove the Folder Action.

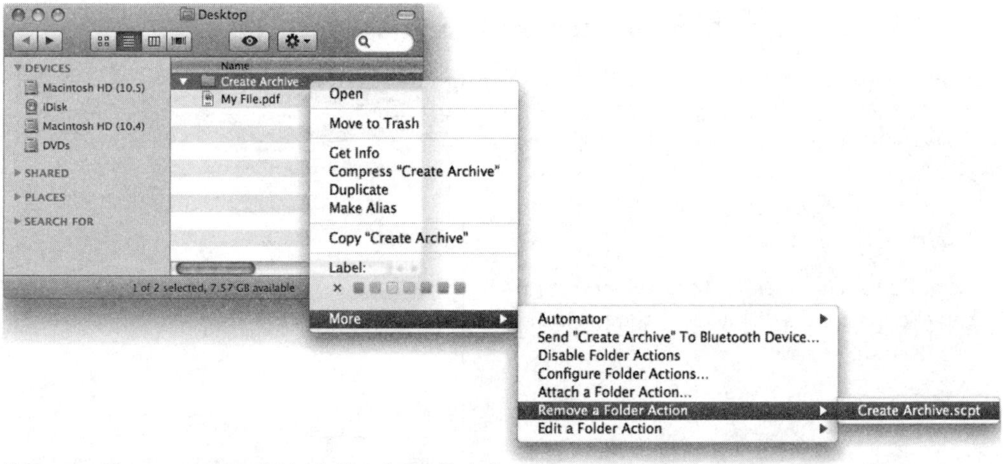

Figure 9.27 You can remove a Folder Action via the Finder's contextual menu as well. Choose More > Remove a Folder Action > Create Archive.scpt.

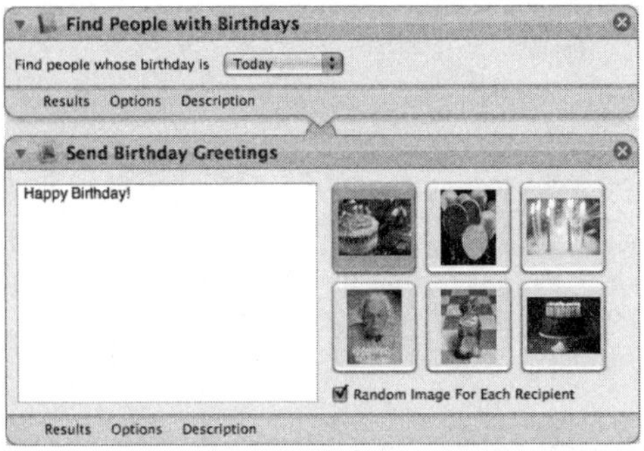

Figure 9.28 The iCal Alarm plug-in workflow consists of two actions: Find People with Birthdays and Send Birthday Greetings.

iCal Alarm Plug-Ins

You can save an Automator workflow as an iCal Alarm plug-in as well, enabling you to configure the workflow to run at a specific date and time. You can even set the alarm to trigger on a repeating schedule, such as every day at midnight.

Building and Running an iCal Alarm Plug-in

In Chapter 2, "Building Simple Workflows," you built a basic Automator workflow that sends daily birthday greetings to people in your Address Book. This is an excellent example of a workflow that could be saved as an iCal Alarm plug-in and configured to run automatically every morning.

Actions used:

- Find People with Birthdays
- Send Birthday Greetings

To build the workflow:

1. Create a new custom workflow window.
2. From the Contacts category, drag the Find People with Birthdays action to the workflow area. The action should already be configured to find people whose birthday is Today. No additional configuration is necessary.
3. From the Mail category, drag the Send Birthday Greetings action to the workflow area.
4. Click the Random Image For Each Recipient checkbox (**Figure 9.28**).

✔ Tips

- For this workflow to do anything, you must have birthdays and email addresses entered in your Address Book.
- To run this example workflow, you must have Mail configured on your machine.

To save the workflow as an iCal Alarm plug-in:

1. Choose File > Save As Plug-in or press Option ⌘ S.
   The Save As Plug-in panel appears.
2. Enter `Email Daily Birthday Greetings` into the Save Plug-in As text field.
3. Choose iCal Alarm from the "Plug-in for" pop-up menu (**Figure 9.29**).
   No additional plug-in options are displayed.
4. Click Save.
   iCal automatically launches and creates a new event named Automator that appears at the current date and time in the calendar. It is configured with an open file alarm, set to open the Automator workflow (**Figure 9.30**).
5. Adjust the date, time, and repeat settings for the event within iCal. For example, set the alarm to repeat every day at 9:00 AM (**Figure 9.31**).

There's no longer a need to manually trigger the workflow. The workflow now runs automatically each day when the iCal alarm triggers, finding people with birthdays and creating email greetings for them (**Figure 9.32**).

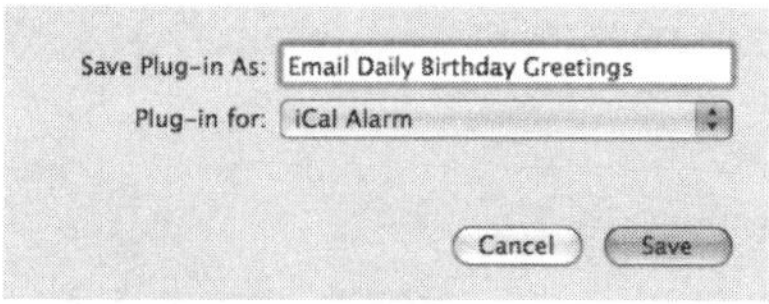

Figure 9.29 To save an iCal Alarm plug-in, choose iCal Alarm from the "Plug-in for" pop-up menu.

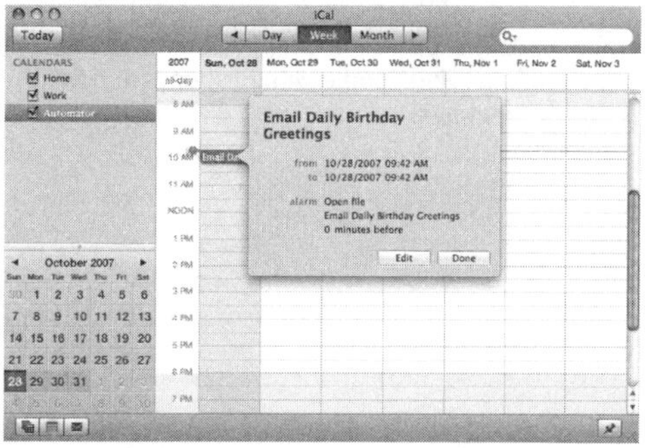

Figure 9.30 When you save an iCal Alarm plug-in, Automator automatically creates an event named Automator at the current date and time in a calendar. The event is configured with an alarm that opens the workflow.

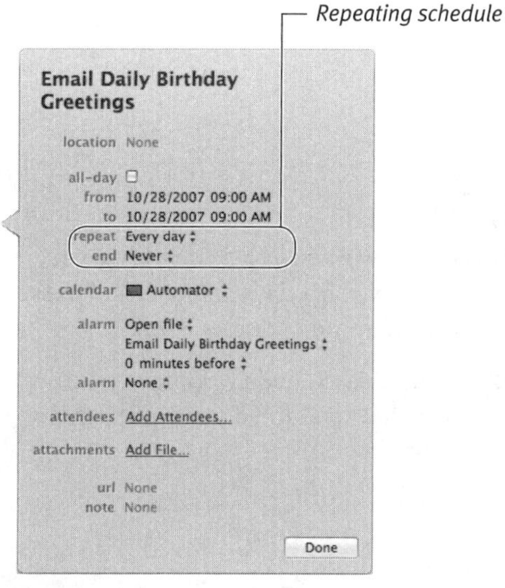

Figure 9.31 Adjust the date, time, and repeat settings for the event, to configure when and how often the workflow runs.

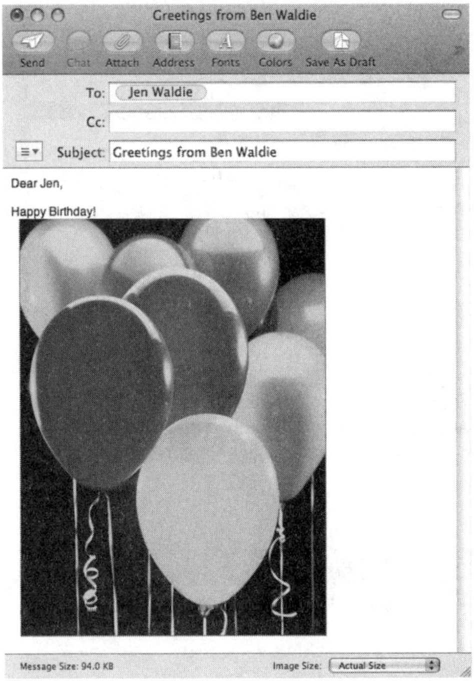

Figure 9.32 The iCal Alarm plug-in runs automatically according to schedule, finding people with birthdays and creating greetings for them in Mail.

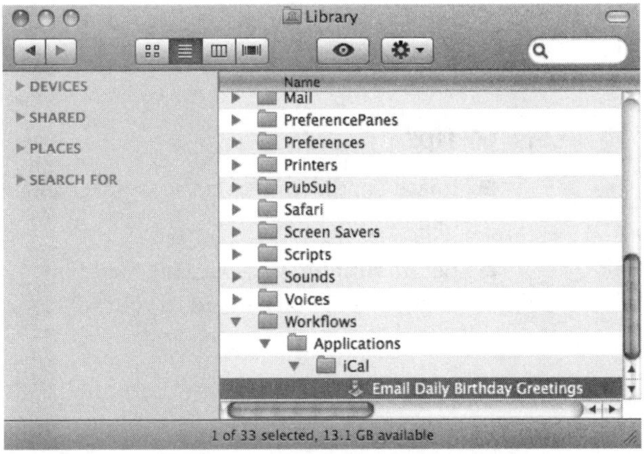

Figure 9.33 iCal Alarm plug-ins are saved as workflow applications in ~/Library/Workflows/Applications/ iCal/.

Editing an iCal Alarm Plug-in Workflow

Automator saves iCal Alarm plug-in workflows as workflow applications into the ~/Library/Workflows/Applications/iCal/ folder on your Mac (**Figure 9.33**).

To open and edit an iCal Alarm plug-in workflow, go to this folder, select the workflow application, and drag it onto the Automator icon in your Dock. The workflow opens in Automator, and you can edit it as you would any other workflow application.

✔ Tip

- To remove an iCal Alarm plug-in workflow, go to ~/Library/Workflows/Applications/iCal/ and delete the workflow. Then, delete the event in iCal that opens the workflow.

Image Capture Plug-Ins

A third type of plug-in that Automator supports is a plug-in for the Image Capture application. Saving an Image Capture plug-in causes the workflow to appear in Image Capture's Automatic Task pop-up menu when you import photos from your digital camera. If you choose the workflow from this pop-up menu, then images are passed to the workflow after downloading for further processing (**Figure 9.34**).

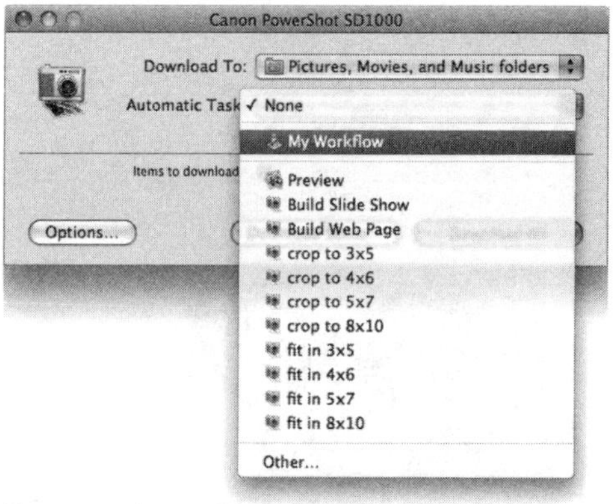

Figure 9.34 Image Capture plug-ins appear in the Automatic Task pop-up menu when you import camera images using Image Capture.

Building and Running an Image Capture Plug-in Workflow

Naturally, there are a lot of possibilities when it comes to Image Capture plug-ins. Any workflow that manipulates images makes a good candidate—resizing, renaming, converting images from one type to another, and so on. For this example, you'll create a workflow that prepares a PDF contact sheet of your images as you import them.

Actions used:

- New PDF Contact Sheet

To build the workflow:

1. Create a new custom workflow window.
2. From the PDF category, drag the New PDF Contact Sheet action to the workflow area.
3. Enter `My Latest Photos` in the "Save as" text field.

   The action should already be set to create a three-column contact sheet on the Desktop. No additional configuration is necessary (**Figure 9.35**).

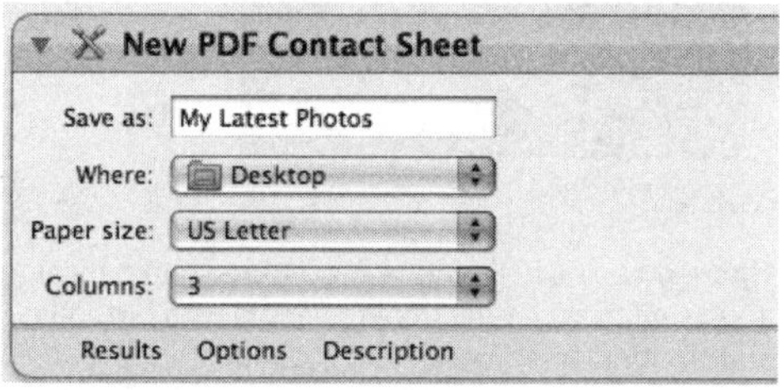

Figure 9.35 Configure the New PDF Contact Sheet action to create a three-column contact sheet named My Latest Photos on your Desktop.

✔ Tips

- Image Capture resides in the /Applications/ folder.
- Before running this example workflow, connect a digital camera to your Mac.

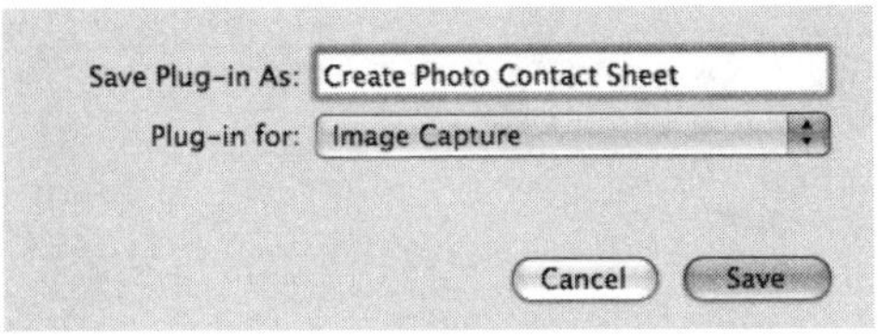

Figure 9.36 To save an Image Capture plug-in, choose Image Capture from the "Plug-in for" pop-up menu.

Figure 9.37 When downloading images, choose the Create Photo Contact Sheet workflow from the Automatic Task pop-up. After downloading, Image Capture will then pass images to the workflow for further processing.

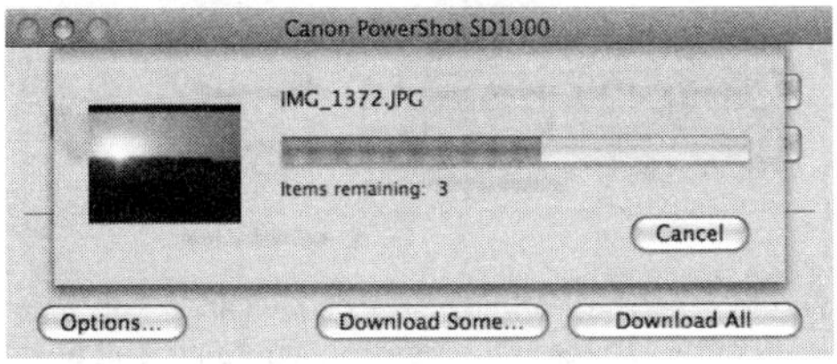

Figure 9.38 Image Capture displays a status panel when downloading images.

To save the workflow as an Image Capture plug-in:

1. Choose File > Save As Plug-in or press Option ⌘ S.

   The Save As Plug-in panel appears.

2. Enter `Create Photo Contact Sheet` into the Save Plug-in As text field.

3. Choose Image Capture from the "Plug-in for" pop-up menu (**Figure 9.36**).

   The panel does not display any additional plug-in options.

4. Click Save.

   The saved workflow will now appear in Image Capture.

To run the Image Capture plug-in workflow:

1. Launch Image Capture.

2. Connect your digital camera to your Mac.

   Image Capture recognizes that your camera is connected and displays an image download window.

3. From the Automatic Task pop-up, choose Create Photo Contact Sheet.

4. Click Download All to begin downloading the images (**Figure 9.37**).

   Image Capture begins downloading the images, displaying a progress bar as it proceeds (**Figure 9.38**).

continues on next page

After all images have been downloaded, Image Capture passes the paths to those images to the Create Photo Contact Sheet workflow for processing. The workflow then generates a contact sheet of the images and saves it to your Desktop (**Figures 9.39** and **9.40**).

✔ Tip

- To ensure that your images aren't permanently deleted from the camera after import, click Options in Image Capture's download window and verify that the "Delete items from camera after downloading" checkbox is *not* selected.

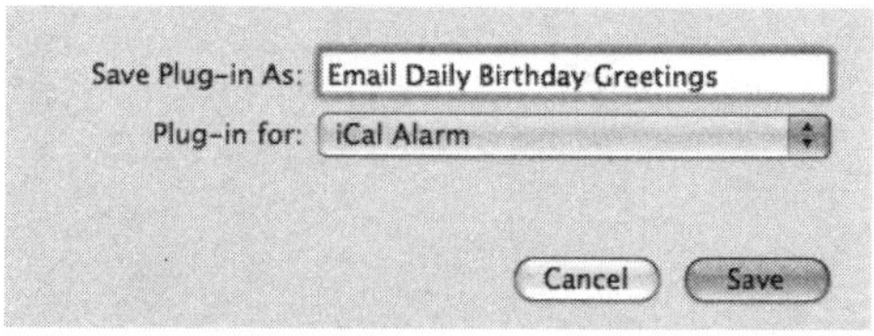

Figure 9.39 As the New PDF Contact Sheet action runs in the Automator workflow, it displays its own status window.

Figure 9.40 The workflow saves a My Latest Photos PDF contact sheet to the Desktop, containing all of the downloaded images.

Editing an Image Capture Plug-in Workflow

Image Capture plug-in workflows are saved as workflow applications in the ~/Library/Workflows/Applications/Image Capture/ folder on your Mac (**Figure 9.41**).

To open and edit an Image Capture plug-in workflow, go to this folder, select the workflow application, and drag it onto the Automator icon in your Dock. The workflow opens in Automator, and you can edit it as you would any other workflow application.

✔ Tip

- To remove an Image Capture plug-in workflow, go to ~/Library/Workflows/Applications/Image Capture/, and delete the workflow.

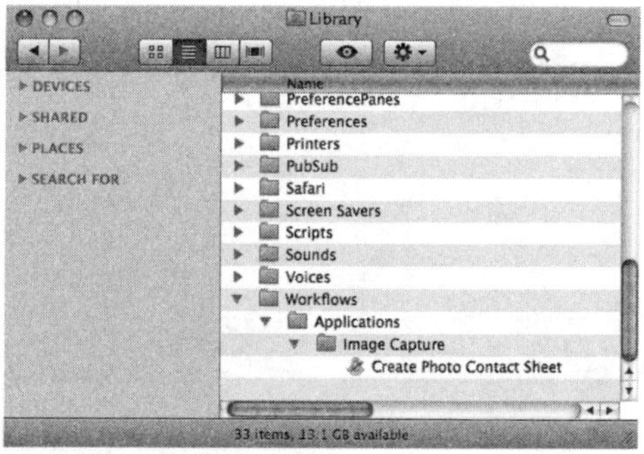

Figure 9.41 Image Capture plug-ins are saved as workflow applications in ~/Library/Workflows/Applications/Image Capture/.

Figure 9.42 Print Workflow plug-ins appear under the PDF pop-up menu in the Mac OS X Print dialog. When chosen, the document is saved as a PDF and passed to the workflow for processing.

Figure 9.43 Add the Move Finder Items action to your workflow. You should not need to adjust any of the action's settings.

Print Workflow Plug-Ins

You are probably already aware that you can convert any Mac OS X document to PDF format by selecting Save as PDF at the bottom of the print dialog. To further enhance your PDF conversion abilities, Automator allows you to save a workflow as a Print Workflow plug-in.

When you save a workflow as a Print Workflow plug-in, the workflow appears at the bottom of the print dialog in the PDF pop-up menu. When printing, choose the workflow to save the PDF and begin processing it (**Figure 9.42**).

Building and Running a Print Workflow Plug-in Workflow

As you may be aware, metadata, such as an author's name, copyright information, keywords, and more, may be embedded into PDF documents. This information can be useful for determining the source, content, or creator of a PDF.

For this example, you'll create a Print Workflow plug-in that can be triggered from the PDF pop-up menu in the Mac OS X print window in any application. Once triggered, the workflow will save your document as a PDF, move it to the Desktop, and add specified metadata to it.

Actions used:

- Move Finder Items
- Set PDF Metadata

To build the workflow:

1. Create a new custom workflow window.
2. From the Files & Folders category, drag the Move Finder Items action to the workflow area.

   The action should already be set to move files to the Desktop. No additional configuration is necessary (**Figure 9.43**).

continues on next page

3. From the PDFs category, drag the Set PDF Metadata action to the workflow area.
4. Click the checkbox next to the Author text field, and enter your name. Click the checkbox next to the Content Creator field, and enter some text, such as copyright information. If desired, enable other fields and enter values into them (**Figure 9.44**).
5. Click the Options button at the bottom of the action.

   The action expands to display additional options (**Figure 9.45**).
6. Click the "Show this action when the workflow runs" checkbox.

   When the workflow runs, it displays the Set PDF Metadata action, enabling you to modify the text fields, enter keywords, and more.

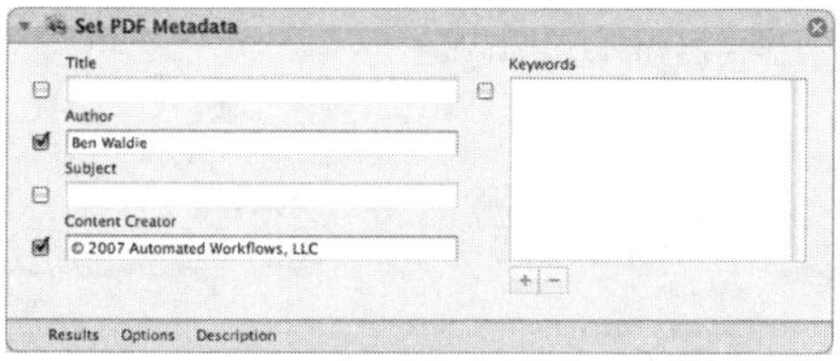

Figure 9.44 Add the Set PDF Metadata action to your workflow, then enable and populate the Author and Content Creator fields.

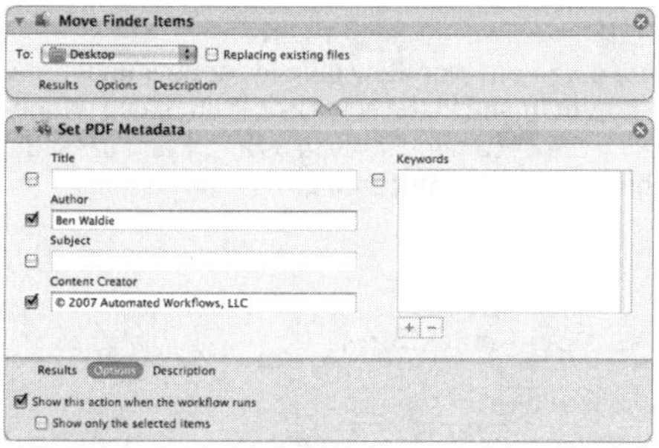

Figure 9.45 This workflow consists of the Move Finder Items action and the Set PDF Metadata action, which is configured to show when run.

To save the workflow as a Print Workflow plug-in workflow:

1. Choose File > Save As Plug-in, or press Option ⌘ S.

   The Save As Plug-in panel appears.
2. Enter `Insert PDF Metadata` into the Save Plug-in As text field.
3. Choose Print Workflow from the "Plug-in for" pop-up menu (**Figure 9.46**).

   No additional plug-in options are displayed.
4. Click Save.

   The saved workflow will now appear in the PDF pop-up menu of the Mac OS X Print dialog whenever you print something.

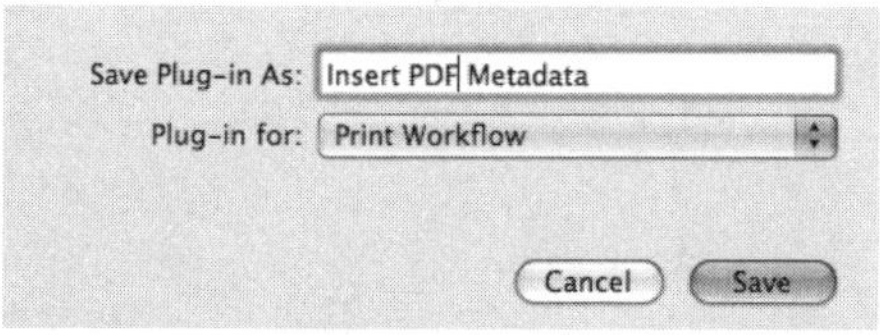

Figure 9.46 To save a Print Workflow plug-in, choose Print Workflow from the "Plug-in for" pop-up menu.

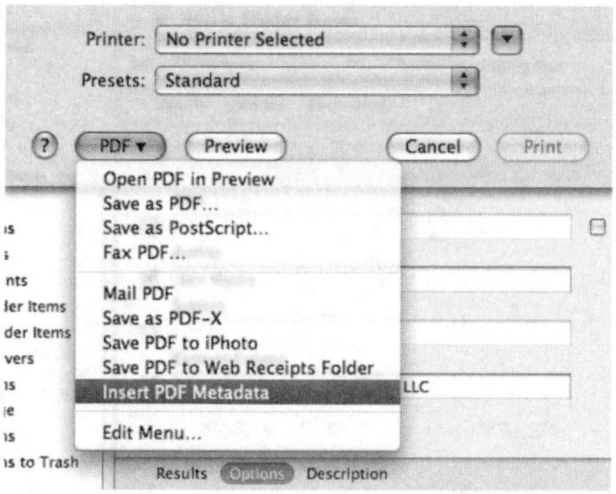

Figure 9.47 From the Mac OS X Print dialog, choose PDF > Insert PDF Metadata to trigger your workflow.

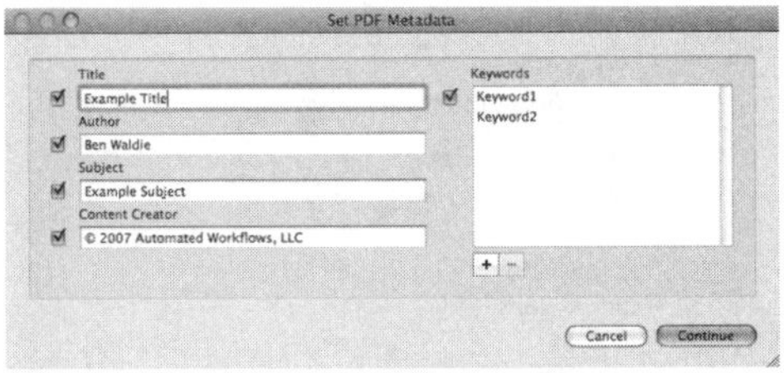

Figure 9.48 The Set PDF Metadata window displays when the workflow runs, allowing you to enter a title, subject, keywords, and more to be applied to the resulting PDF document.

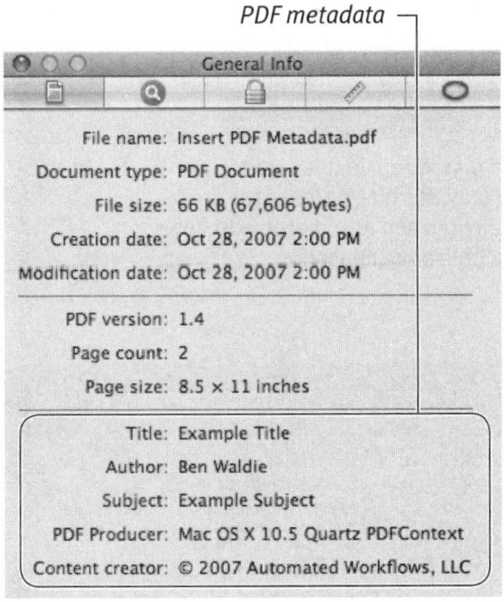

Figure 9.49 Open the PDF in Preview and view the Inspector window to verify that the specified metadata was successfully applied.

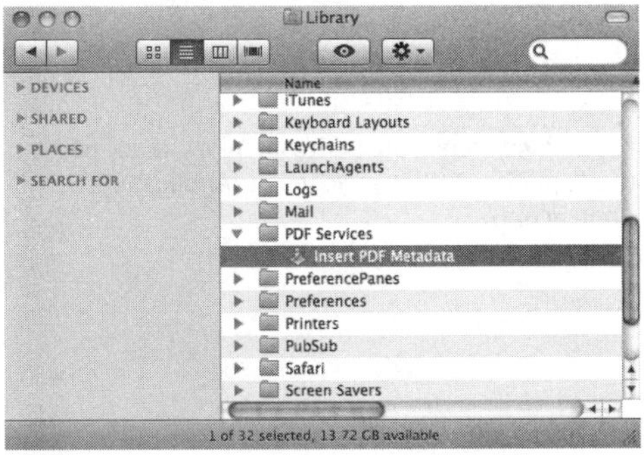

Figure 9.50 Print Workflow plug-ins are saved as workflow applications in ~/Library/PDF Services/.

To run the Print Workflow plug-in:

1. Open a document to print, such as a TextEdit document. Or, if desired, you can simply use your opened Automator workflow.
2. Choose File > Print.

   The Mac OS X Print dialog is displayed.
3. Choose Insert PDF Metadata from the PDF pop-up menu in the bottom left of the print dialog (**Figure 9.47**).

   The opened document is saved as a PDF to a temporary folder, and the Insert PDF Metadata Automator workflow triggers and begins to process the PDF.

   It moves the PDF to the Desktop, then displays the Set PDF Metadata window.
4. Enter the desired information into the Set PDF Metadata window, such as a title for the PDF, a subject, and keywords.
5. Click Continue (**Figure 9.48**).

   The workflow appends the specified metadata to the PDF.

To verify that the metadata was successfully applied, open the PDF in Preview and choose Tools > Inspector (or press [⌘][I]) to display an information window. The information window should list the metadata you specified when the workflow ran (**Figure 9.49**).

Editing a Print Workflow Plug-in Workflow

Automator saves Print Workflow plug-in workflows as workflow applications into the ~/Library/PDF Services/ folder on your Mac (**Figure 9.50**).

To open and edit a Print Workflow plug-in workflow, go to this folder, select the workflow application, and drag it onto the Automator icon in your Dock. The workflow opens in Automator, and you can edit it as you would any other workflow application.

Script Menu Plug-Ins

Mac OS X has a system-wide Script menu that, when enabled, appears in the menu bar at all times. The Script menu provides quick access to AppleScripts, PERL scripts, Shell scripts, and Automator workflows from within any application.

By default, this menu is disabled. It's enabled automatically when you save an Automator workflow as a Script Menu plug-in (**Figure 9.51**).

✔ Tip

- You can enable the system-wide Script menu manually with the AppleScript Utility application, located in /Applications/AppleScript/ (**Figure 9.52**).

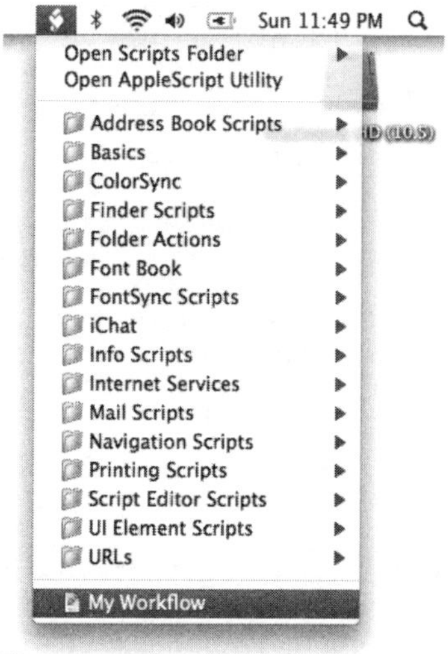

Figure 9.51 When enabled, the Script menu provides quick access to AppleScripts and Automator workflows from within any application.

Building and Running a Script Menu Plug-in Workflow

Need to quickly jot something down during a phone call? You could search your desk for a sticky note, open up a new Word document, or write on the back of your hand, but isn't there a better way?

For this example workflow, you'll create a simple workflow that can be run from the system-wide Script menu. The workflow will create and open a text file on your Desktop so you can start typing away.

Actions used:

- New Text File
- Open Finder Items

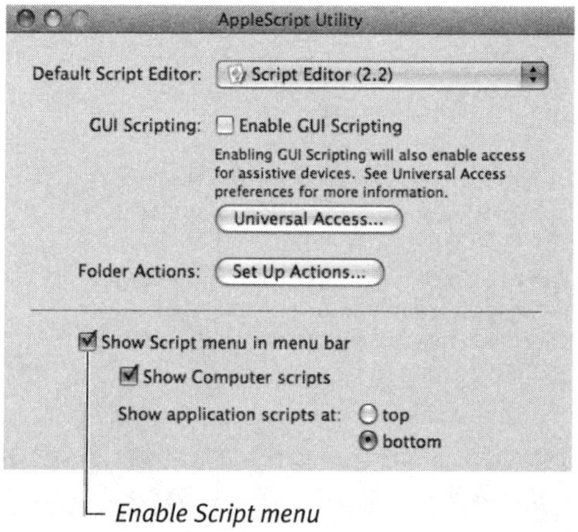

Figure 9.52 Enable the Script menu manually using the AppleScript Utility, located in /Applications/AppleScript/.

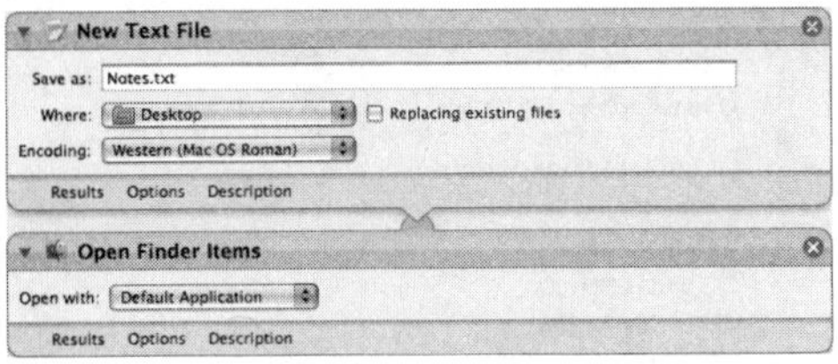

Figure 9.53 This example workflow consists of the New Text File action and the Open Finder Items action.

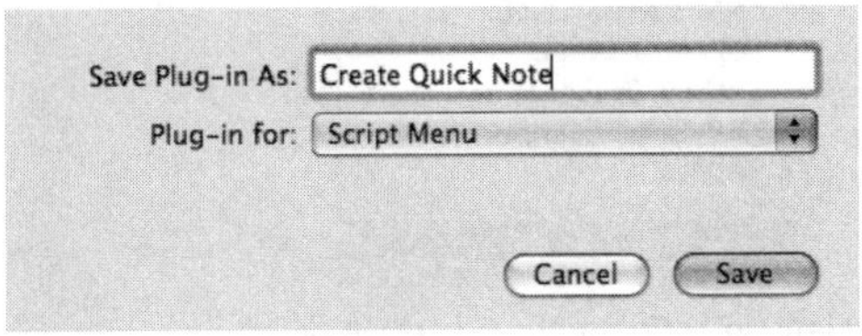

Figure 9.54 To save a Script Menu plug-in, choose Script Menu from the "Plug-in for" pop-up menu.

To build the workflow:

1. Create a new custom workflow window.
2. From the Text category, drag the New Text File action to the workflow area.
3. Enter `Notes.txt` into the "Save as" text field.

   No further configuration of this action is necessary.
4. From the Finder category, drag the Open Finder Items action to the workflow area.

   No further configuration of this action is necessary (**Figure 9.53**).

To save the workflow as a Script Menu plug-in:

1. Choose File > Save As Plug-in, or press Option ⌘ S.

   The Save As Plug-in panel appears.
2. Enter `Create Quick Note` into the Save Plug-in As text field.
3. Choose Script Menu from the "Plug-in for" pop-up menu (**Figure 9.54**).

   No additional plug-in options are displayed.
4. Click Save.

   The saved workflow will now appear in the system-wide Script Menu.

✔ Tip

- If the Script menu is not enabled, it automatically becomes enabled when you save a Script Menu plug-in.

To run the Script Menu plug-in workflow:

- Choose Create Quick Note from the Script menu in the Mac OS X menu bar (**Figure 9.55**).

  The workflow runs, creating and opening a Notes.txt file on the Desktop (**Figure 9.56**).

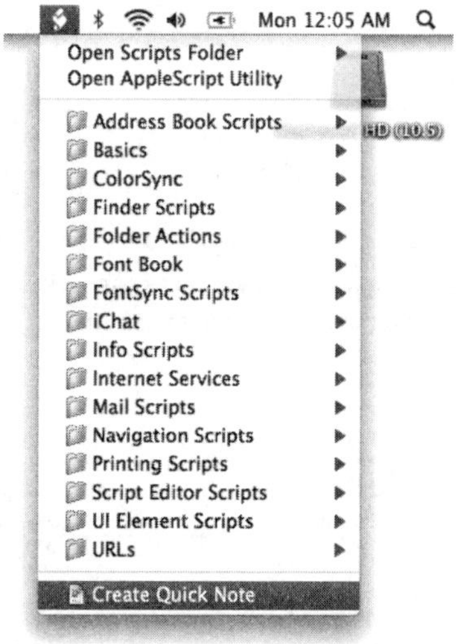

Figure 9.55 To run the Create Quick Note workflow, choose it from the Script menu in the menu bar.

Editing a Script Menu Plug-in Workflow

Automator saves Script Menu plug-in workflows as workflow applications into the ~/Library/Scripts/ folder on your Mac (**Figure 9.57**).

To open and edit a Script Menu plug-in workflow, go to this folder, select the workflow application, and double-click it. The workflow opens in Automator, and you can edit it as you would any other workflow file.

✔ Tip

- To remove a Script Menu plug-in workflow, go to ~/Library/Scripts/, and delete the workflow.

Figure 9.56 The newly created Notes.txt file is opened before you, ready for editing.

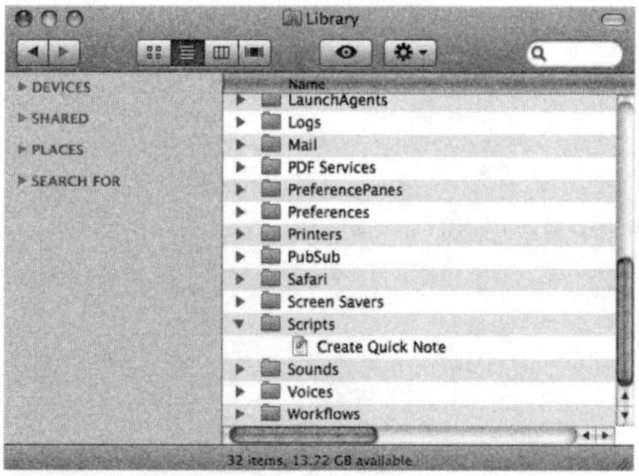

Figure 9.57 Automator saves Script Menu plug-ins as workflow files in ~/Library/Scripts/.

10

Workflow Looping

Until now, all of the Automator workflows you've created run in sequence from the first action in the workflow to the last—and then they're done. One time through, and that's it. In most cases, this type of workflow execution works just fine. In some cases, however, you may need something a bit more robust: a looping workflow that repeats a series of tasks over and over.

For example, suppose you want a workflow that takes a series of time-delayed screenshots for troubleshooting purposes, and then emails them to you for viewing on your iPhone. Sure, you could create this workflow without looping, but it would involve using the same actions over and over again and it would not continue running indefinitely.

In cases like this, it's generally much simpler to create a looping workflow that simply runs the same actions continually. This helps to keep your workflow manageable while providing the repeating functionality you need.

About Looping

One way to create a looping workflow is to save the workflow as an iCal Alarm plug-in and set it to run on a repeating schedule (see "iCal Alarm Plug-Ins" in Chapter 9). For simple workflows, however, this technique may be overkill, or it may not meet your specific needs. For example, you may want to run the workflow from the Script Menu or Image Capture, not from iCal. Or, you may want the workflow to loop only until you tell it to stop, to loop for a specific amount of time, and so forth.

In these situations, Automator's Loop action (located in the Utilities category) may be what you need. You can insert this action anywhere in your workflow to create a repeating workflow (**Figure 10.1**). When encountered at runtime, the Loop action causes your workflow to go back to the first action and start over again. This action has two main options:

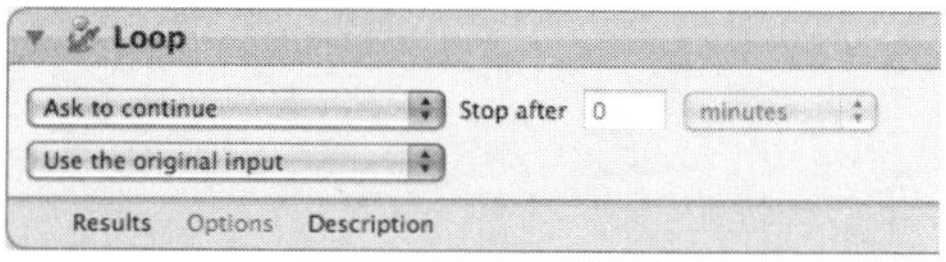

Figure 10.1 Use the Loop action to create a repeating workflow.

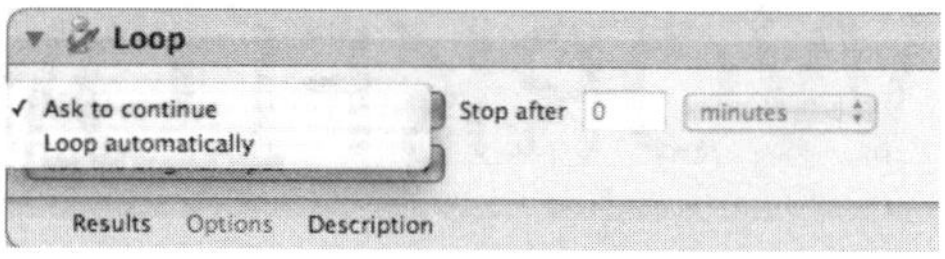

Figure 10.2 The Loop action can be set to ask you to continue before starting a loop or to loop automatically.

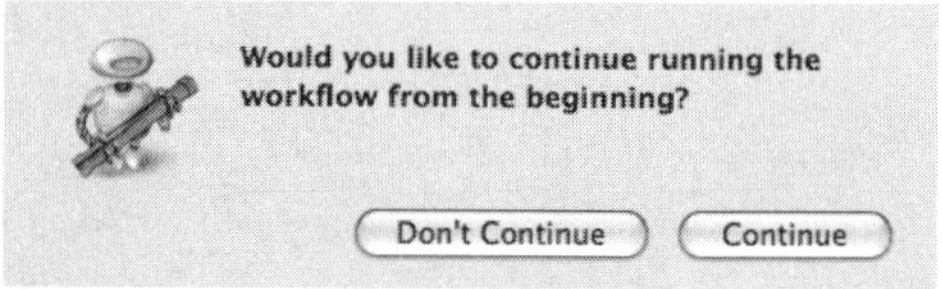

Figure 10.3 If the Loop action is set to ask to continue, then Automator displays an alert when the workflow runs.

Looping Method

The Loop action's first pop-up menu allows you to specify the looping method: whether the workflow should ask to continue looping or loop automatically (**Figure 10.2**). It contains two choices:

Sorry Tiger Users

The Loop action is available in Mac OS 10.5 (Leopard) only. It is, however, still possible to create a looping workflow in Mac OS X 10.4 (Tiger). Here are some options:

- **Run Workflow.** Consider inserting this action (located in the Automator category) at the end of your workflow. Configure it to run your workflow again, thus creating a never-ending loop.
- **Automator Loop Utility.** Google this little gem, and you should find an AppleScript-based application that you can use to create looping workflow applications.
- **iCal Alarm Plug-In.** Consider saving your workflow as an iCal Alarm plug-in and configuring it to run on a repeating schedule. In many cases, this may work just fine.

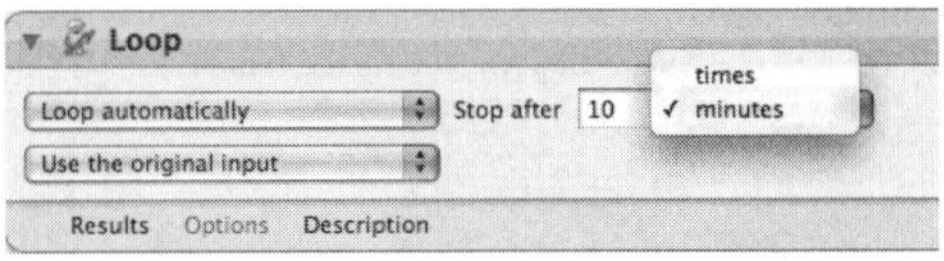

Figure 10.4 When looping automatically, you can choose to loop a specified number of times or for a specified number of minutes.

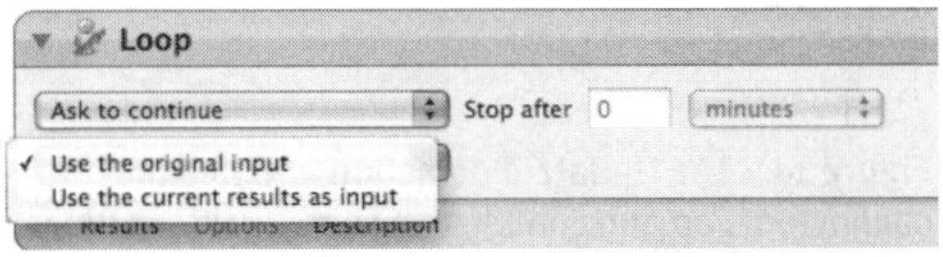

Figure 10.5 Setting the Loop action to use the original input rather than the current results as input during each loop.

- **Ask to continue.** Instructs the Loop action to display an alert asking if you'd like to continue looping. You can choose to continue looping or stop looping and run any remaining actions in the workflow (**Figure 10.3**).

  When you choose this option, the action disables the "Stop after" text field and pop-up menu in the Loop action.

- **Loop automatically.** Instructs the Loop action to loop a specified number of times or for a specified period of time.

  When you select this option, the action enables the "Stop after" text field and pop-up menu. You can now specify whether the workflow should stop after a certain number of times or a certain number of minutes (**Figure 10.4**).

Input Handling

The Loop action's second pop-up menu enables you to specify whether the original input or current results should be used each loop (**Figure 10.5**). It contains two choices:

- **Use the original input.** Instructs the Loop action to pass the workflow's original input back to the first action to be processed again.

- **Use the current results as input.** Instructs the Loop action to pass the results of the previous action to the first action in the workflow.

✔ Tip

- If you add actions to your workflow after a Loop action, those actions run after Automator exits the loop.

Basic Looping Workflows

Most of the looping workflows you create are likely to be normal Automator workflows that are simply configured to run a specified number of times, for a specified amount of time, or until you tell the workflow to stop looping. Typically, these workflows will start fresh with each new loop, processing their original input time and time again.

Building and Running a Basic Looping Workflow

iPods are wonderful things. They allow you to carry your music, photos, contacts, calendars, and more wherever you go. To send such information to your iPod, you must perform a sync. You can do this manually by clicking a Sync button in iTunes, or you can configure iTunes to sync your iPod automatically whenever it's connected.

Once synced, however, what if you modify your music, photos, contacts, or calendars? iTunes doesn't automatically update your iPod with these changes until the next sync occurs. For this example, you'll create a looping workflow that updates your connected iPod once per minute, allowing you to ensure it contains the most current data. Once the loop exits, the iPod is then ejected.

✔ Tip

■ To run this workflow, you must have an iPod connected to your Mac.

Actions used:

- Update iPod
- Pause
- Loop
- Eject iPod

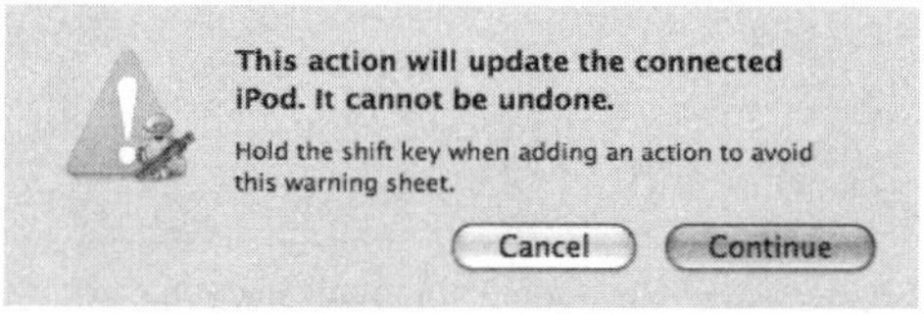
This action will update the connected iPod. It cannot be undone.
Hold the shift key when adding an action to avoid this warning sheet.
Cancel
Continue

Figure 10.6 The Update iPod action displays an alert when added to a workflow indicating that it cannot be undone.

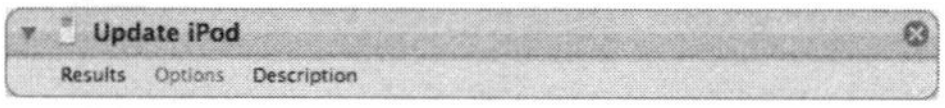
Update iPod
Results
Options
Description

Figure 10.7 The Update iPod action updates the connected iPod and contains no configurable settings.

Looping Through Files

Unfortunately, Automator's Loop action does not allow you to individually process files through a workflow. If you pass 700 files to the first action in the workflow, all 700 of those files are passed through the workflow as a group. Depending on the workflow, this may be problematic.

For example, suppose your workflow consists of four actions that perform four separate tasks: open a file, modify the file, save the file, and close the file. If you send 700 files through the workflow for processing, the first action opens all 700 files, then the workflow modifies all 700 files, saves all 700, and closes all 700.

Naturally, it's not practical to process files in this manner. For starters, most applications would not even allow you to open 700 files at one time. As a workaround, I have developed a freeware AppleScript application that you can use to individually send dropped files to an Automator workflow application. You can download the Automator Multi-Item Processing Utility from www.automatedworkflows.com/software/automator_actions/automator_tools.html.

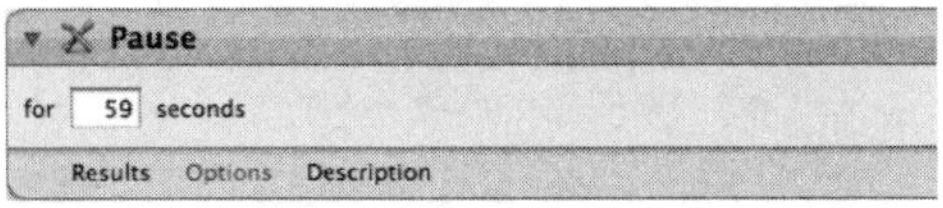

Figure 10.8 Use the Pause action to delay a workflow for a specified amount of time.

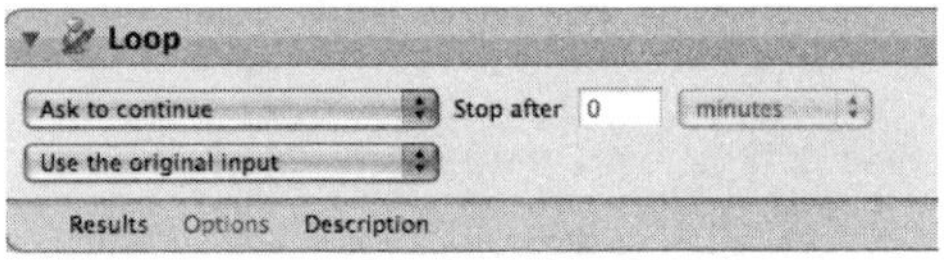

Figure 10.9 The Loop action causes the workflow to run over and over again.

Figure 10.10 The Eject iPod action runs after looping has finished, ejecting the connected iPod.

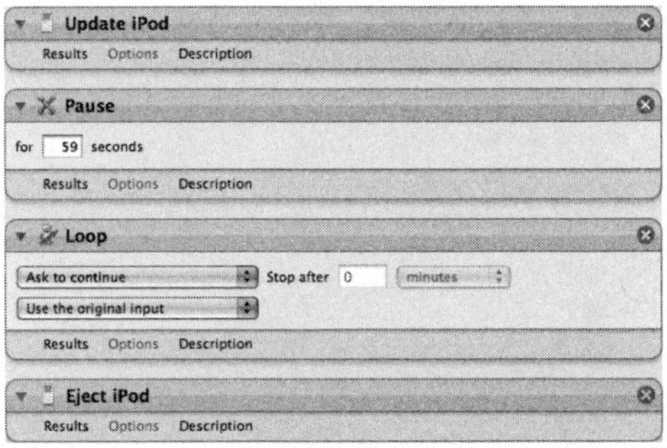

Figure 10.11 The completed workflow contains four actions: Update iPod, Pause, Loop, and Eject iPod.

To build the workflow:

1. Create a new custom workflow window.
2. From the Music category, drag the Update iPod action to the workflow area.

   Automator displays an alert letting you know that the action will update your iPod and cannot be undone (**Figure 10.6**).
3. Click Continue to proceed with adding the action.

   Automator inserts the Update iPod action to the workflow area. This action has no configurable settings (**Figure 10.7**).
4. From the Utilities category, drag the Pause action to the workflow area.
5. Type 59 into the Pause action's text field.

   This instructs the workflow to delay for 59 seconds after your iPod has been updated (**Figure 10.8**).
6. From the Utilities category, drag the Loop action to the workflow area.
7. From the first pop-up menu in the Loop action, choose "Ask to continue."

   The "Stop after" text field and pop-up menu should be disabled.
8. Choose "Use the original input" from the second pop-up menu in the Loop action (**Figure 10.9**).
9. From the Music category, drag the Eject iPod action to the workflow area.

   This action has no configurable settings (**Figure 10.10**).

Consisting of four actions—Update iPod, Pause, Loop, and Eject—the workflow is now complete and is ready to be run. (**Figure 10.11**).

To run the workflow:

1. Launch iTunes.
2. Connect an iPod to your Mac.

   Depending on your iTunes settings, your iPod may sync at this time.
3. Click the Run button in Automator's toolbar, or press (⌘ R) to run the workflow.

   The workflow begins running. The connected iPod syncs, the workflow pauses for 59 seconds, then asks you if you'd like to continue looping (**Figure 10.12**).
4. To continue looping, click Continue. To stop looping, click Don't Continue.

   When you click Continue, the workflow begins again: It updates the iPod, pauses for another 59 seconds, and asks if you'd like to continue looping. The workflow proceeds in this manner until you click Don't Continue.

   When you click Don't Continue, the workflow stops looping and runs the Eject iPod action. The iPod ejects, and the workflow finishes.

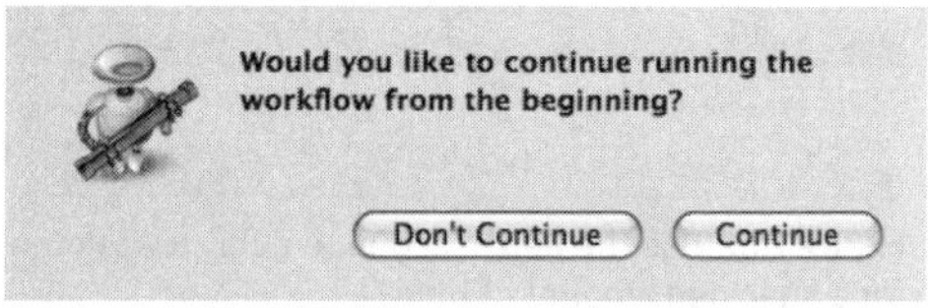

Figure 10.12 When the workflow reaches the Loop action, it asks if you want to continue looping.

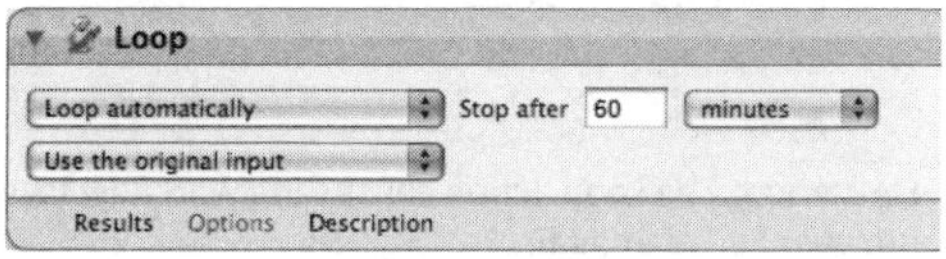

Figure 10.13 Configuring the Loop action to loop automatically for 60 minutes then stop.

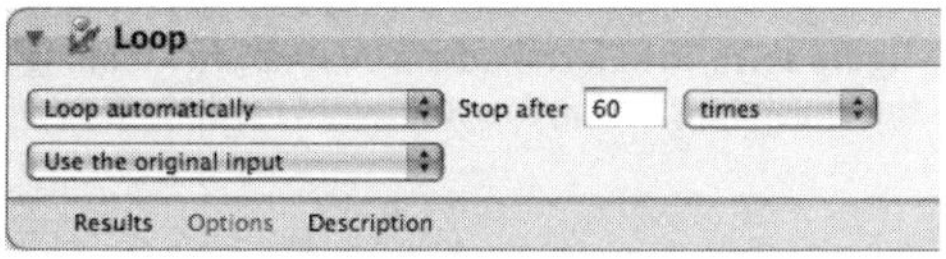

Figure 10.14 Configuring the Loop action to loop automatically 60 times then stop.

Other Looping Options

This example workflow runs fine, but what if you prefer to configure the workflow to loop automatically, rather than ask you each time if you want to continue? Making the change is easy.

To loop the workflow automatically:

1. Choose Loop Automatically from the first pop-up menu in the Loop action.
2. To loop for a specified amount of time, enter the desired number of minutes, such as **60**, into the "Stop after" text field. Then, choose "minutes" from the "Stop after" pop-up menu (**Figure 10.13**).

   To loop a specified number of times, enter the desired number of cycles into the "Stop after" text field, and choose "times" from the pop-up menu (**Figure 10.14**).

Advanced Looping Workflows

Automator's Loop action also enables you to create a more advanced type of looping workflow—one that passes the last looped action's result as input to the first action in the workflow. For example, you might need to create a workflow application that accepts a dropped folder as input, renames the folder, gets a list of subfolders within the folder, and then performs the same process again on those subfolders. Workflows of this nature are likely to be pretty rare, but Automator is ready to help if you need to create one.

Building and Running an Advanced Looping Workflow

For this example, you'll create a workflow application that accepts a dropped image file as input. Once triggered, the workflow copies the image to the Desktop, scales it to 50 percent of its original size, and renames it to Scaled Image.

The workflow then loops, passing the resulting Scaled Image file back to the beginning of the workflow. Again, Automator copies the image to the Desktop, scales it to 50 percent of its already diminished size, and renames it Scaled Image 2.

The result is two images on the desktop: Scaled Image, which is 50 percent the size of the original dropped image, and Scaled Image 2, which is 50 percent the size of Scaled Image. A workflow of this nature might come in handy when preparing images for inclusion on a website.

Actions used:

- Copy Finder Items
- Scale Images
- Rename Finder Items
- Loop

To build the workflow:

1. Create a new custom workflow window.
2. From the Files & Folders category, drag the Copy Finder Items action to the workflow area.

   This action should be configured to copy items to the Desktop by default. No further adjustments are necessary (**Figure 10.15**).
3. From the Photos category, drag the Scale Images action to the workflow area.
4. Choose By Percentage from the Scale Images action's pop-up menu.
5. Enter `50` into the Scale Images action's text field (**Figure 10.16**).
6. From the Files & Folders category, drag the Rename Finder Items action to the workflow area.

   Automator displays an alert suggesting that you insert a Copy Finder Items action first to preserve the names of your original images (**Figure 10.17**).

   Because the first action in the workflow is already Copy Finder Items, this is unnecessary.
7. Click Don't Add.

   Automator adds the Rename Finder Items action to the workflow.
8. Choose Name Single Item from the first pop-up menu in the Rename Finder Items action.

   The action's interface changes to display some new options.
9. Choose "Basename only" from the Name pop-up menu, and enter a value of `Scaled Image` into the To text field (**Figure 10.18**).

   The basename is the name of the image minus its file extension.

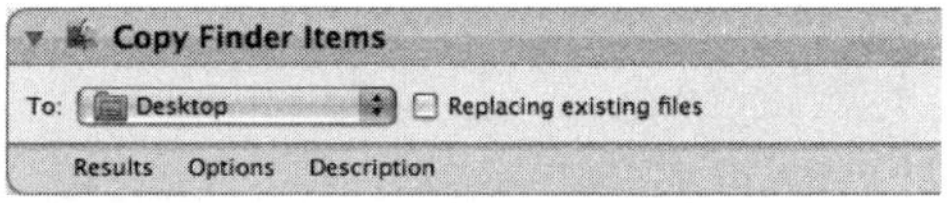

Figure 10.15 The Copy Finder Items action copies items passed to the workflow to the Desktop.

Figure 10.16 Set the Scale Images action to resize images to 50 percent.

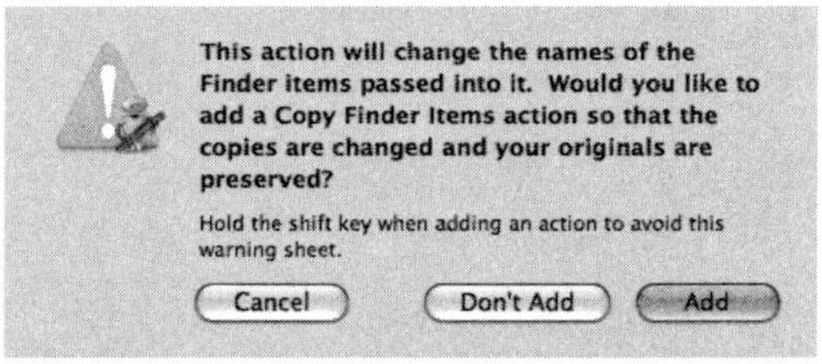

Figure 10.17 The Rename Finder Items action's alert suggests inserting a Copy Finder Items action to preserve your original image names.

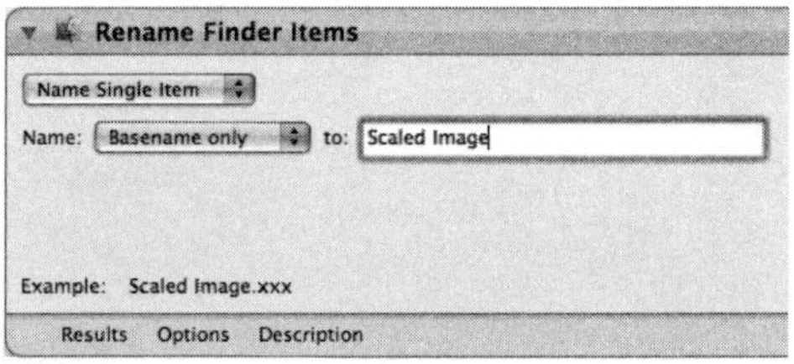

Figure 10.18 Configuring the Rename Finder Items action.

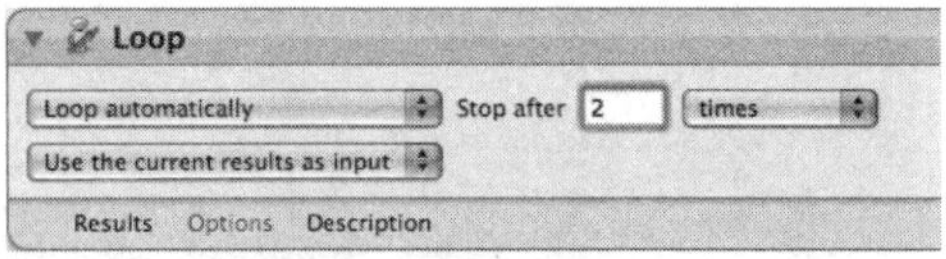

Figure 10.19 Configuring the Loop action to loop automatically twice and to use the current results as input.

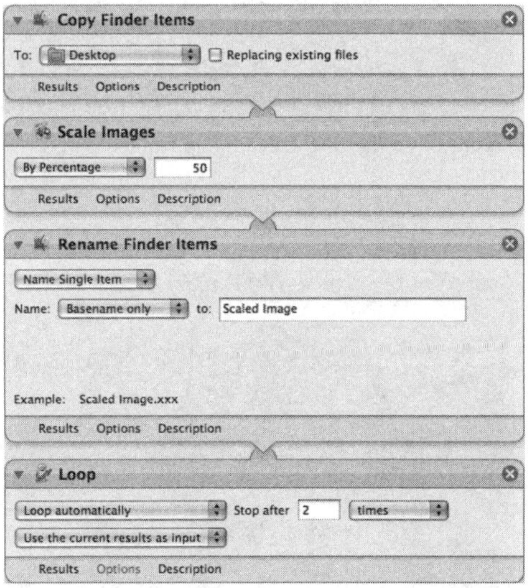

Figure 10.20 The completed workflow consists of four actions: Copy Finder Items, Scale Images, Rename Finder Items, and Loop.

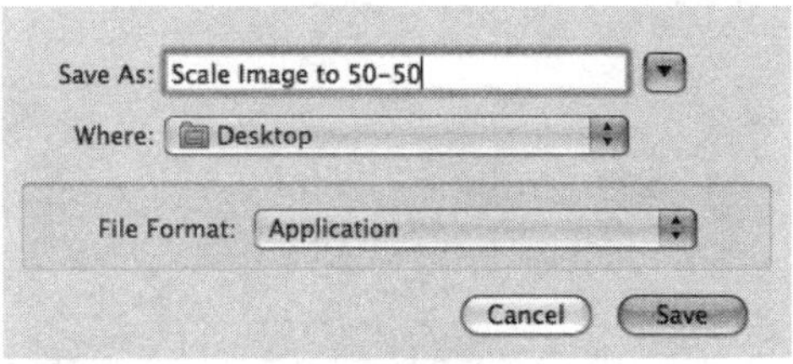

Figure 10.21 Save the workflow to your Desktop as an application named Scale Image to 50-50.

10. From the Utilities category, drag the Loop action to the workflow area.
11. Choose "Loop automatically" from the first pop-up menu in the Loop action.

    Automator enables the "Stop after" text field and pop-up menu.
12. Type 2 into the "Stop after" text field, and choose "times" from the "Stop after" pop-up menu.
13. Choose "Use the current results as input" from the second pop-up menu (**Figure 10.19**).

    Your workflow is now complete and ready to be saved. It consists of four actions: Copy Finder Items, Scale Images, Rename Finder Items, and Loop (**Figure 10.20**).

To save the workflow:

1. Choose File > Save As (or press [⇧Shift][⌘][S]).

   The save panel appears.
2. Type `Scale Image to 50-50` into the Save As text field.
3. Choose Desktop from the Where pop-up menu.
4. Choose Application from the File Format pop-up menu.
5. Click Save (**Figure 10.21**).

   Automator saves the workflow as an application named Scale Image to 50-50 on your Desktop. It's now ready to run.

To run the workflow:

- Locate an image file and drag it onto the Scale Image to 50-50 workflow application on your Desktop.

  The workflow begins running.

  As the workflow runs, it copies the dropped image file to the Desktop, scales it to 50%, and renames it as Scaled Image.

  The Loop action then runs the workflow a second time. This time, the first action receives the newly scaled image file as input, copies it to the Desktop, and resizes it to 50%. Because there's already a file on the Desktop named Scaled Image, the Rename Finder Items action names the new image Scaled Image 2.

  You now have two scaled images on your Desktop. The first, Scaled Image, is resized to 50% of the original dropped image. The second, Scaled Image 2, is resized to 50% of the first scaled image (**Figures 10.22**, **10.23**, and **10.24**).

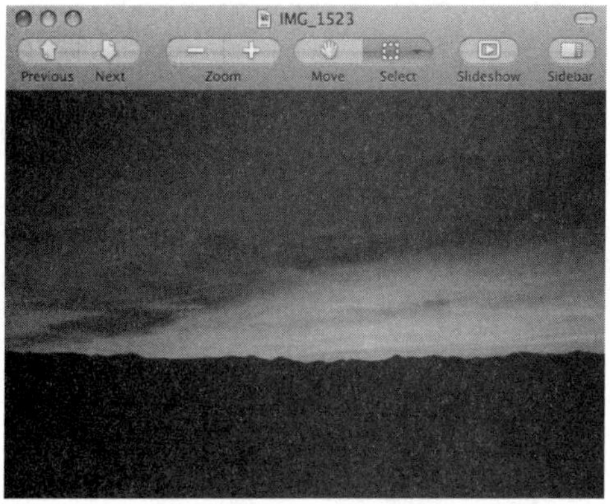

Figure 10.22 The originally dropped image is at its full size.

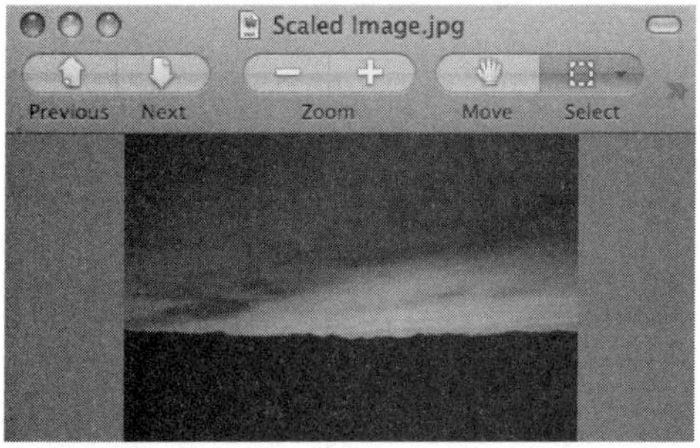

Figure 10.23 The first resized image, named Scaled Image, is 50% of the original.

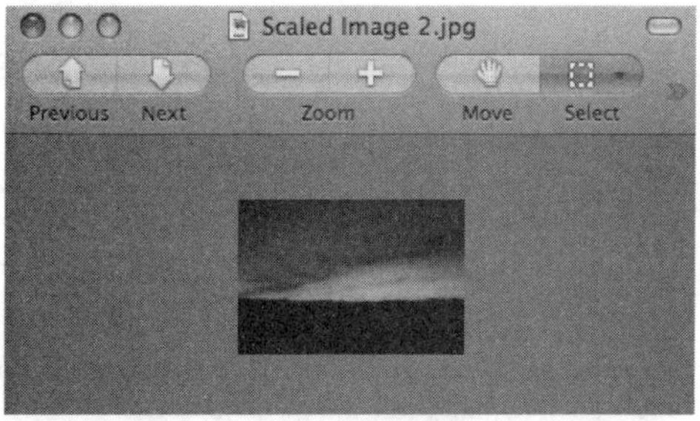

Figure 10.24 The second resized image, named Scaled Image 2, is 50% of the first resized image.

11

Using Variables

The way information passes through an Automator workflow is fairly simple: It passes in sequence from action to action. Sometimes, however, problems occur—actions don't produce a result, or actions need information from an action much earlier in the workflow. Although such scenarios are less likely to occur in simple workflows, they can severely limit your ability to create complex workflows. Automator in Leopard's introduction of workflow variables helps avoid this tremendously.

Variables allow you to store information (such as an action's result) at one point in a workflow and then refer back to it at a later point. They also allow you to retrieve dynamic content (such as the current date or time, or the current user's name) and use it when your workflow runs. In essence, a variable is nothing more than stored information; it can be a reference to a file or folder, some text, or almost anything else.

In this chapter, you'll learn how to incorporate variables into your workflows, including storing and retrieving action results, using variables to reference dynamic content, and more. You'll also create some example workflows that incorporate variables, including one that downloads images from a Safari webpage into a dated folder on your Desktop.

Types of Variables

Like actions, variables are organized into categories within Automator's Library list (**Figure 11.1**). The available categories of variables are:

- **Date & Time.** These variables enable your workflow to retrieve and use information, such as the current day, current month, and current time. For example, you could use a Date & Time variable to append the current time to the name of a file created by your workflow.
- **Locations.** These variables enable your workflow to easily reference folders on your Mac, such as when saving a file, backing up files and folders, and more. Predefined variables exist for commonly accessed folders, including Applications, Documents, and Favorites. The category's New Path variable also enables you to create a custom location mapped to the folder of your choice.
- **System.** These variables enable your workflow to retrieve information about the current system configuration, including IP address, operating system version, and the amount of time the computer has been running. These variables could be useful in a workflow that emails troubleshooting information to a system administrator.
- **Text & Data.** These variables enable your workflow to store and retrieve text values, as well as other types of data, such as file and folder paths, iPhoto items, and Mail messages. Generally, the variables in this category are likely to be used for storing and retrieving action results.

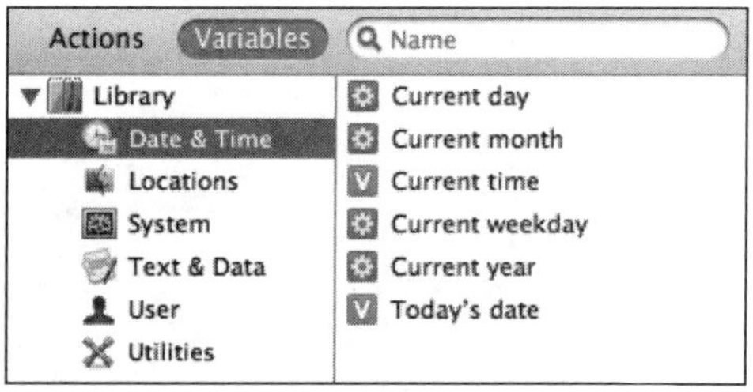

Figure 11.1 Displayed in Automator's Library list, variables are organized into categories by their type.

Help for Tiger Users

Workflow variables are new to Mac OS X 10.5 (Leopard). In Mac OS X 10.4 (Tiger), however, you can still store and retrieve information through the use of third-party actions. To find these actions, use Google to search for "Temporary Storage Actions for Automator."

- **User.** These variables enable your workflow to retrieve information about the current user, such as the first name, last name, full name, or homepage. This information could be appended to an email message, added to a TextEdit document, and so forth.
- **Utilities.** These variables enable your workflow to retrieve random numbers and text, which you can use, for example, to ensure that file names do not conflict with one another. Also included in this category are AppleScript and Unix variables, which can be used to execute code at various points within a workflow. These particular variables are fairly advanced and are probably likely to be used only by advanced Automator users.

✔ Tip

- For an introductory overview of variables, see "About Variables" in Chapter 1, "Getting Started."

Adding Variables to Workflows

Automator includes dozens of variables. To use one, you must first add it to your workflow, like an action. Unlike an action, however, a variable doesn't immediately appear as part of the workflow itself. Rather, a variable initially appears in the workflow variables area. You can then insert the variable into different parts of your workflow whenever you want to retrieve its value. You'll learn how to retrieve the value of a variable shortly.

To add a variable to your workflow:

1. At the top of the Library list within a workflow window, click the Variables button.

   The list of categories and variables appears (**Figure 11.2**).

2. Find the variable you want to add to your workflow, such as "My name" in the User category.

   You locate a variable in the same way you locate an action: by clicking through the categories or entering a keyword into the Library list's search field (**Figure 11.3**).

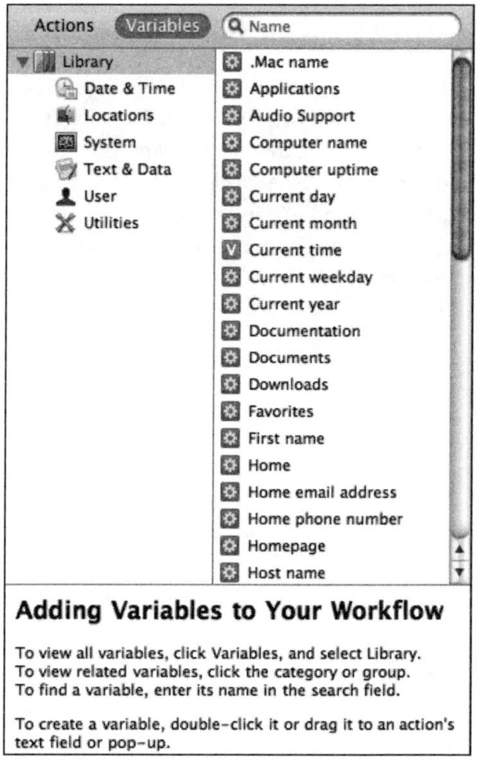

Figure 11.2 To display a list of categories and variables, click Variables at the top of the Library list.

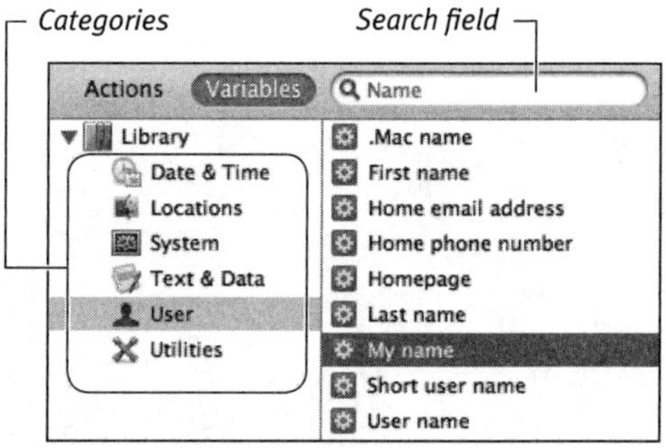

Figure 11.3 Click through the categories or enter a search term to find a variable to meet your needs.

3. Double-click the desired variable.

   The workflow variables area, containing the variable, displays at the bottom of the workflow window (**Figure 11.4**).

As indicated by the empty Value column in the workflow variables area, a variable has no value when initially added to a workflow. It gets its value when you run the workflow. For example, the "My name" variable gets the name of the current user when the workflow runs.

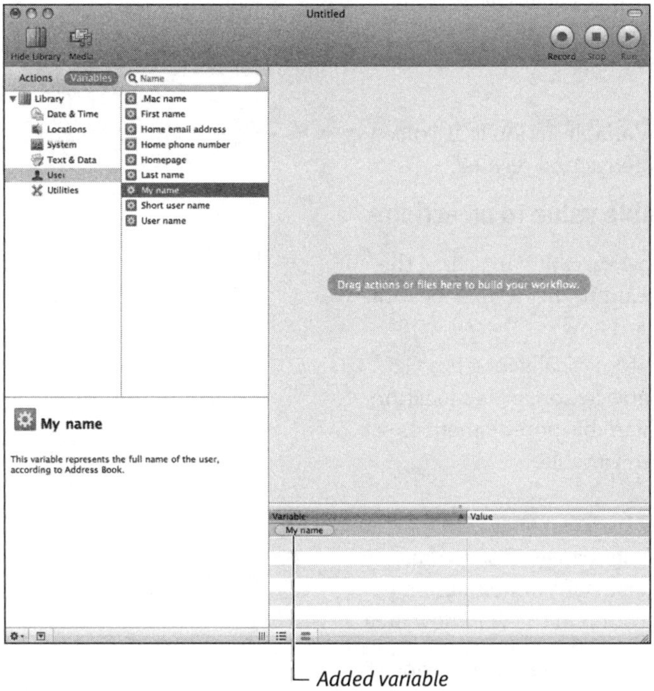

Figure 11.4 Double-click a variable in the Library list to add it to the Workflow Variables area of your workflow window.

Using Variables as Action Input

Once a variable has been added to your workflow, its value can be passed as input to an action. To do so, you use the Get Value of Variable action, which is found in the Utilities category of actions. This action retrieves the value of the specified variable, and then passes it as input to the next action in the workflow.

For example, you could create a workflow that uses a variable to retrieve the current user's name and passes it to an action that inserts that name into a new TextEdit document or Mail message.

✔ Tip

- Get Value of Variable action is also used to retrieve stored action results.

To pass a variable value to an action:

1. In the workflow variables area, drag the variable you want to the desired location within your workflow.

   Automator automatically inserts a Get Value of Variable action at that location. The action's Variable pop-up menu is set to the specified variable.

or

1. From the Utilities category of actions, drag the Get Value of Variable action to the desired location in the workflow area.
2. From the Variable pop-up menu, choose the desired variable (**Figure 11.5**).

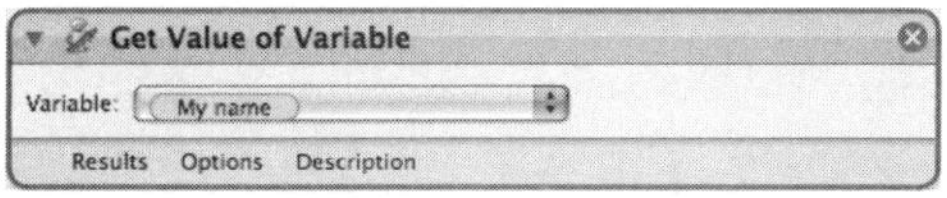

Figure 11.5 The Get Value of Variable action retrieves the value of the specified variable and passes it to the next action in the workflow.

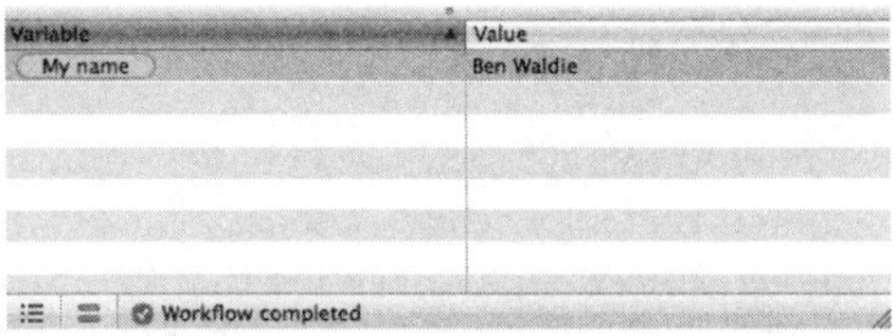

Figure 11.6 When a workflow runs, the workflow variables area updates to display the values of any variables used within the workflow.

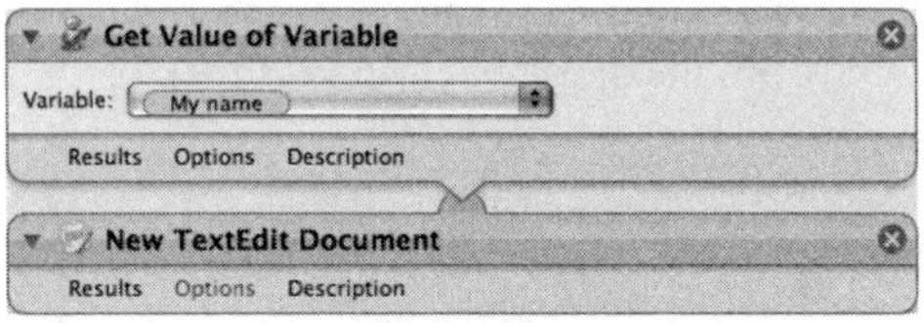

Figure 11.7 In this example, the Get Value of Variable action retrieves the value of the "My name" variable and passes it to the New TextEdit Document action for processing.

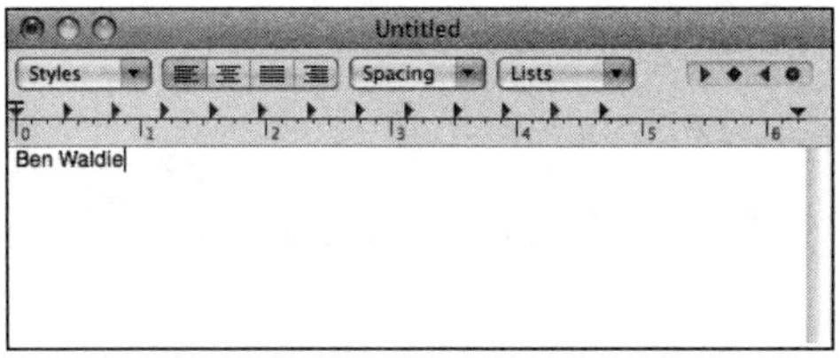

Figure 11.8 The New TextEdit Document action creates a new document in TextEdit and inserts the variable value passed as input, in this case, the name of the current user.

When you run the workflow, the Get Value of Variable action retrieves the value of the specified variable. That value is now reflected in the workflow variables area at the bottom of the workflow window (**Figure 11.6**).

The variable's value is then passed as input to the next action in the workflow for processing. In this example, the Get Value of Variable action retrieves the value of the "My name" variable and passes it to the New TextEdit Document action. This action then creates a new TextEdit document containing your name (**Figures 11.7** and **11.8**).

Inserting Variables in Action Fields

Variables don't just have to be passed as input to actions. They can also be inserted into text fields and path pop-up menus within actions. This gives you a lot of flexibility when creating workflows, and it can allow for some interesting possibilities.

As an example, you could insert the "My name" variable in the Create Archive action's "Save as" text field. Now when the action runs, it automatically appends your name to the name of the archive. You could also insert a Location variable, such as a variable pointing to the current user's Shared folder, to the action's Where pop-up menu (**Figure 11.10**).

✔ Tip

- Not every text field accepts variables. It's up to the action's developer to add this capability. If you drag a variable to a text field that doesn't accept variables, then the variable simply is not added to the field.

What's a Path Pop-up Menu?

Many Automator actions include pop-up menus that allow you to choose a file or folder. For example, an action that saves a file may let you choose an output folder. Typically, these types of pop-up menus include a list of default files or folders, such as the Desktop, your Documents folder, and so on. Often, these menus also include an Other option, allowing you to choose a custom file or folder (**Figure 11.9**).

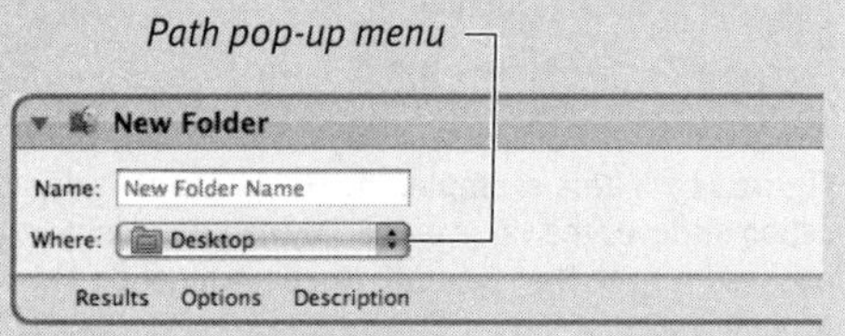

Figure 11.9 The New Folder action contains a path pop-up menu, allowing you to choose an output location for the folder.

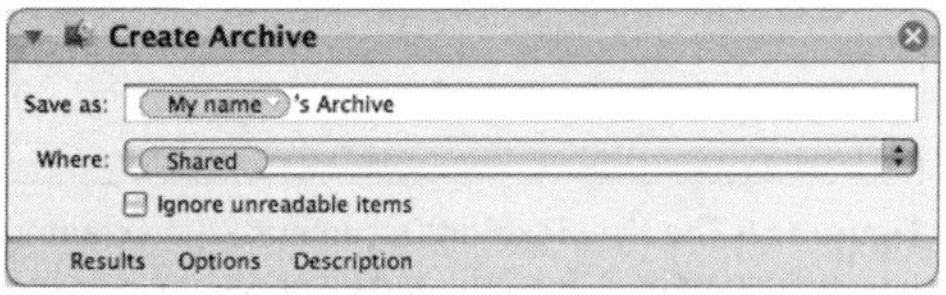

Figure 11.10 You can insert variables into text fields and path pop-up menus, allowing actions to use dynamic content in their settings. This example uses the "My name" variable to add the current user's name to the newly created archive's name. It also uses the Shared Location variable to create the archive in the current user's Shared folder.

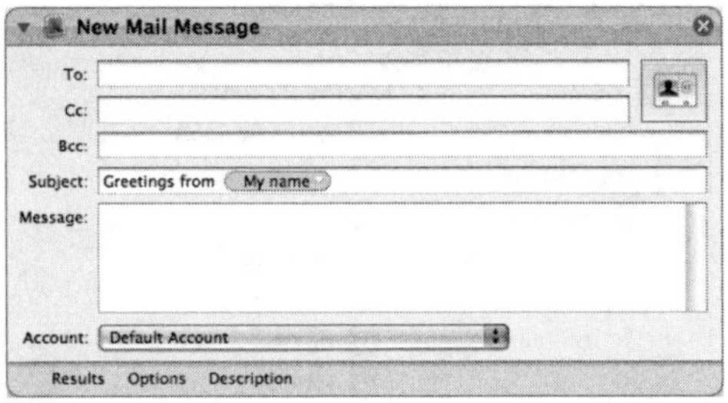

Figure 11.11 Here, the "My name" variable is added, along with some specified text, to the Subject field of the New Mail Message action.

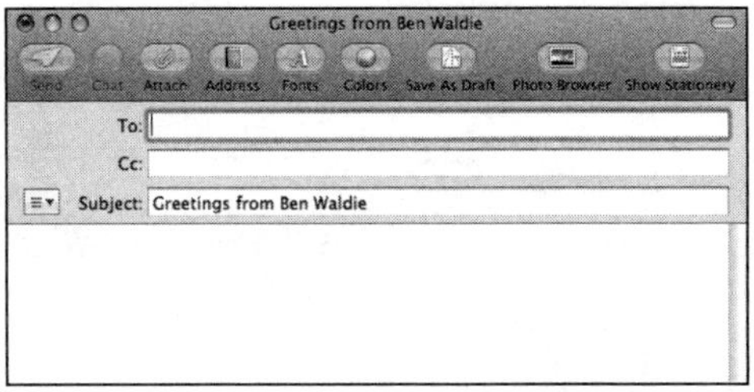

Figure 11.12 The New Mail Message action creates a new email message and inserts the value of the "My name" variable, along with specified text, into the Subject field.

To insert a variable in an action field:

1. Drag the variable you want from the workflow variables area to the text field or path pop-up in the action's interface.

   or

   Drag the desired variable from the Library list to the text field or path pop-up in the action's interface. When you do this, the variable also appears in the workflow variables area.

2. If you added the variable to a text field, you can insert additional text around the variable, if desired.

   For this example, the "My name" variable is added, along with some additional text, to the Subject field of the New Mail Message action (**Figure 11.11**).

When the action runs within the workflow, the value of the variable is retrieved first, and then the action uses that value. In this example, your name is appended to the specified subject of the newly created Mail message (**Figure 11.12**).

Storing and Retrieving Action Results

Variables are powerful because they enable you to store an action's result and use it later in the workflow.

Depending on the type of result being stored, you use one of the following variables:

- **New Path.** Found in the Locations category, this variable stores a reference to a file or folder output by an action (**Figure 11.13**).
- **New Storage.** Found in the Text & Data category, this variable stores the result of an action regardless of its type. For example, it could be used to store references to iPhoto items, Mail messages, iCal events, multiple file or folder paths, and so forth.
- **New Text.** This variable, also located in the Text & Data category, stores text output from an action (**Figure 11.14**).

To store an action's result:

1. Determine the type of action result you want to store, such as text, files and folders, Mail messages, and so forth.

   To determine the type of result for an action, look at the action's description area (**Figure 11.15**).

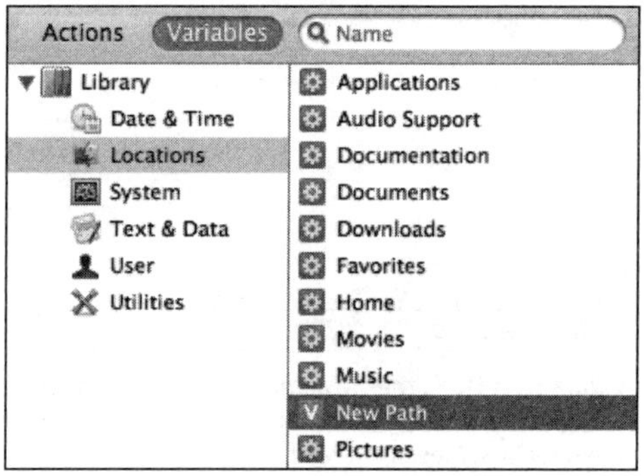

Figure 11.13 Found in the Locations category, the New Path variable can be used to store files and folder output from an action.

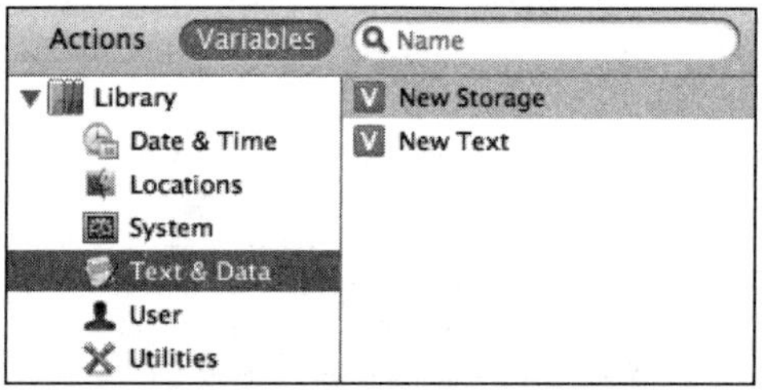

Figure 11.14 Found in the Text & Data category, the New Storage variable can be used to store any action result, whereas the New Text variable stores text from an action.

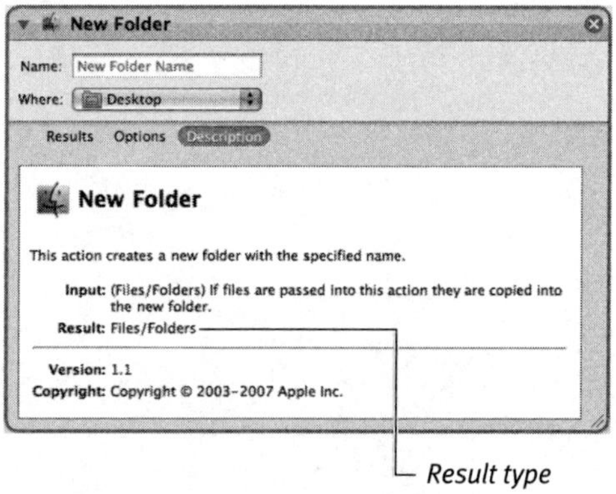

Figure 11.15 Check an action's description to find out its result type.

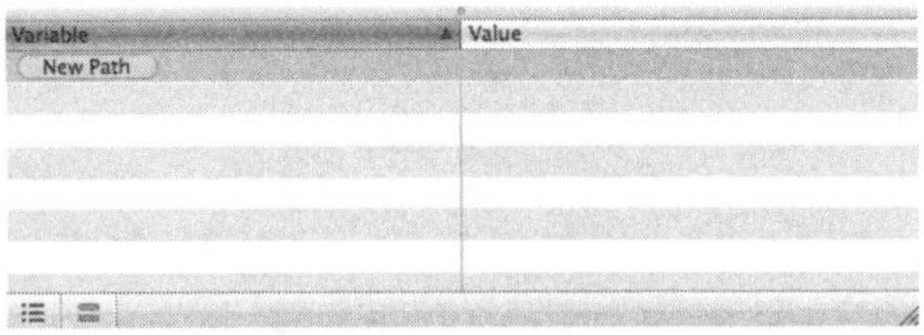

Figure 11.16 Add a variable, such as New Path, to your workflow for the result you want to store.

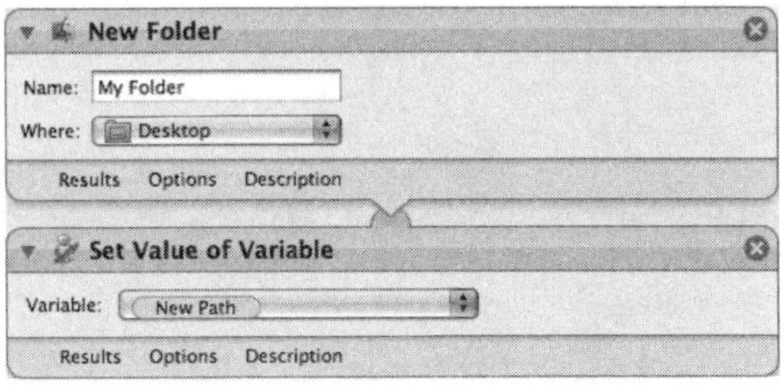

Figure 11.17 The Set Value of Variable sets a variable's value to the preceding action's result. In this example, the New Folder action's result is the path to the newly created folder, which is then stored in the New Path variable.

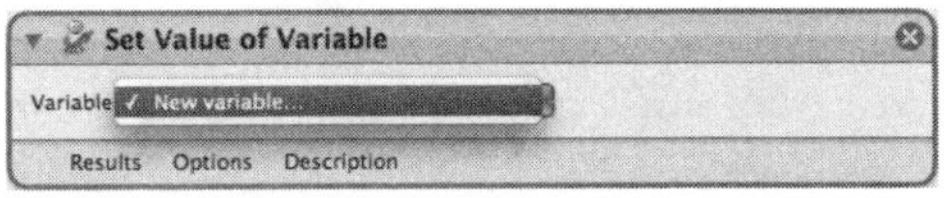

Figure 11.18 Create a New Storage variable by choosing "New variable" from the Set Value of Variable action's Variable pop-up menu.

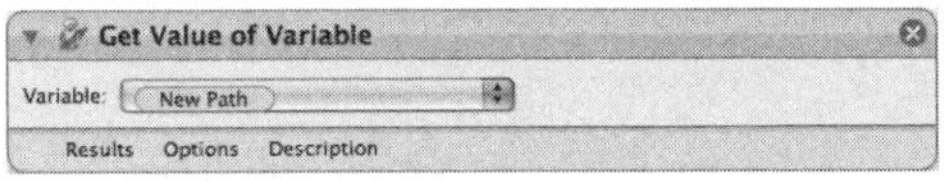

Figure 11.19 Use the Get Value of Variable action to retrieve an action result stored in a variable and pass it to an action for processing.

2. Add a variable to your workflow for the result type you would like to store.

   For example, if the action's result is files and folders, then add a New Path variable to your workflow (**Figure 11.16**).

3. From the Utilities category of actions, drag Set Value of Variable after the action whose result you want to store.

4. From the Variable pop-up menu, choose the variable you added to the workflow, in this case New Path (**Figure 11.17**).

When the workflow runs, the result of the action is passed to the Set Value of Variable action, which stores it in the specified variable. In this example, the New Path variable stores the New Folder action's result, the path to the newly created folder.

✔ Tip

- You can also create a New Storage variable by choosing "New variable" from the Set Value of Variable action's Variable pop-up menu (**Figure 11.18**).

To retrieve a stored action result:

1. Drag the variable to the desired location within the workflow.

   A Get Value of Variable action is inserted for you.

2. Choose the variable from the Variable pop-up menu (**Figure 11.19**).

   When you run the workflow, the Get Value of Variable action retrieves the value of the variable. The workflow variables area shows the variable's value and passes it to the next action for processing.

   or

   Drag the variable to a text field or pop-up menu within an action's interface (**Figure 11.20**).

continues on next page

When you run the workflow, Automator retrieves the variable's value and uses it in the action's setting.

In this example, the New Path variable stores the result of the New Folder action, the newly created folder. This variable is then referenced in the Where field of the New Text File action. When the workflow runs, Automator first creates a folder named My Folder is on the Desktop. Next, it creates a text file within that folder. The workflow variables area displays the value of the New Path variable, which is the path to the newly created folder (**Figures 11.21** and **11.22**).

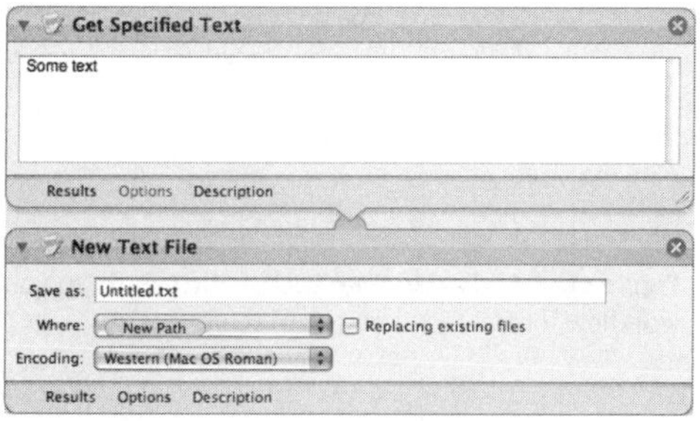

Figure 11.20 You can use a variable containing a stored action result in action text fields and pop-up menus.

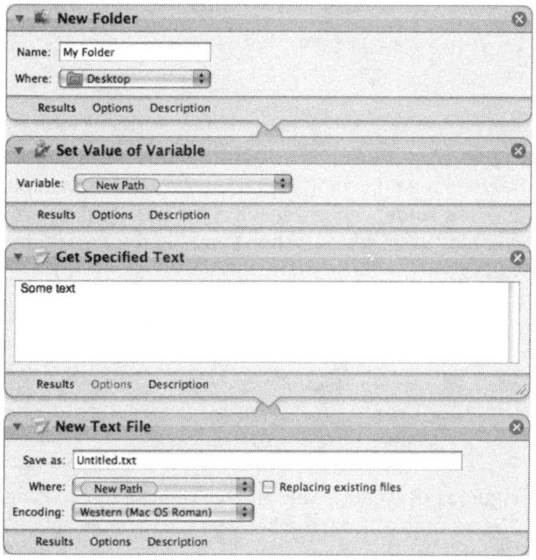

Figure 11.21 In this example, the result of the New Folder action is stored in the New Path variable. It's then later referenced in the Where pop-up menu of the New Text File action.

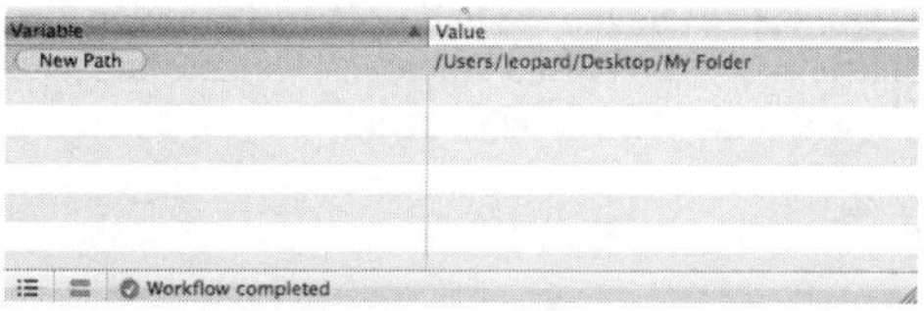

Figure 11.22 The workflow variables area in the workflow shows that the New Path variable contains the path to the newly created folder.

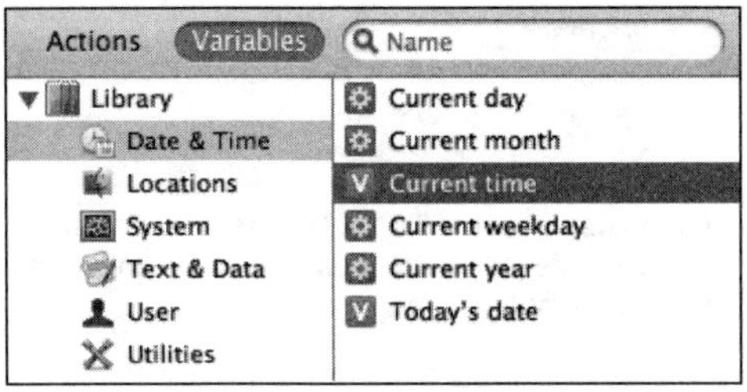

Figure 11.23 Within the Library list, customizable variables are denoted by blue icons, and noncustomizable variables are denoted by purple icons.

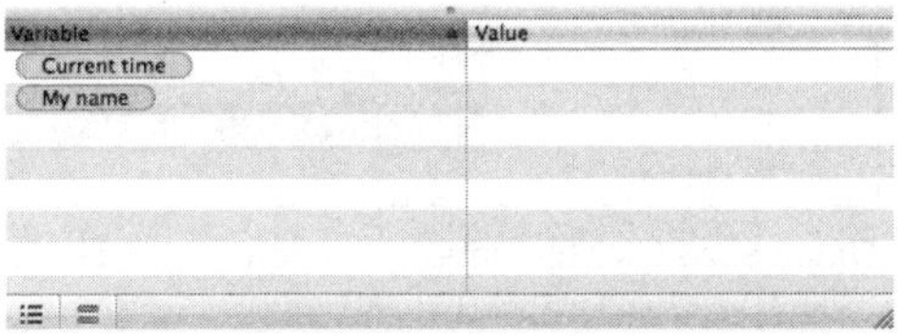

Figure 11.24 Within the workflow variables area at the bottom of the workflow window, customizable variables appear blue and noncustomizable variables appear purple.

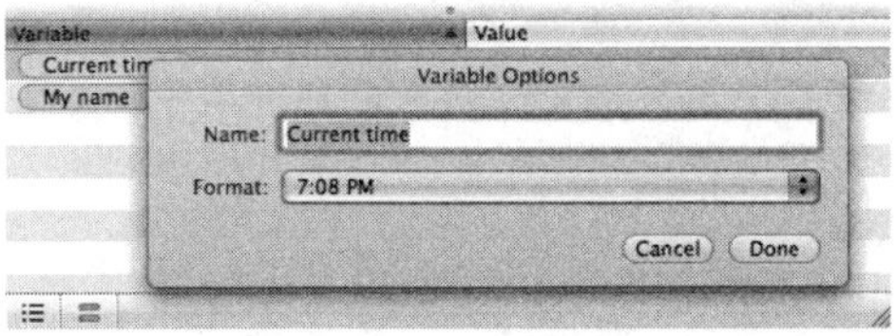

Figure 11.25 Double-click a blue variable in the workflow variables area to display the Variable Options window.

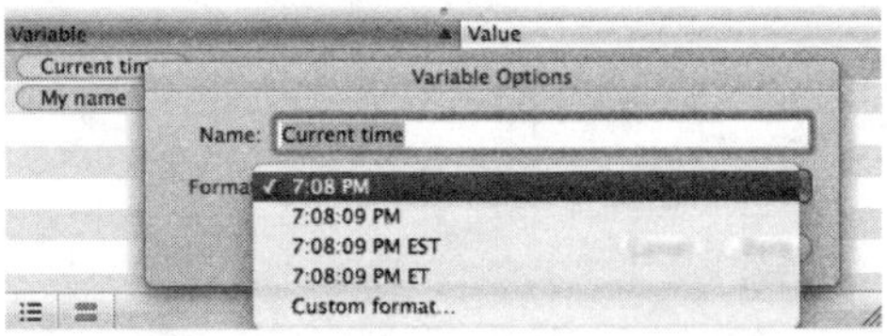

Figure 11.26 In the Variable Options window, you can adjust how the variable behaves when the workflow runs.

Adjusting Variable Options

Some Automator variables are customizable, allowing you to change the variable's name or behavior when run within a workflow. "Current time" is one such variable. When you add it to a workflow, you may want to specify the format in which the time is retrieved. For example, in some instances, you may want hours and minutes; in others, you may want hours, minutes, and seconds.

Within the Library list and the workflow variables area, variables are color-coded to indicate whether they have modifiable options: blue variables have modifiable options; purple ones do not. Within the Library list, icons are also used to denote whether a variable is customizable; the V icon indicates a customizable variable, and the icon indicates a noncustomizable variable (**Figures 11.23** and **11.24**).

To adjust the options for a variable:

1. Double-click the desired variable in the workflow variables area at the bottom of the workflow window.

   A Variable Options window opens (**Figure 11.25**).

2. If you'd like, enter a new name for the variable.

3. Make any changes to the variable's options (**Figure 11.26**).

4. Click Done.

   The Variable Options window closes. When you run the workflow, the variable retrieves its value using the options you specified.

✔ Tip

- A variable's options are different depending on the variable's function. The "Current time" variable, for example, allows you to specify the format of the retrieved time. The New Path variable, however, allows you to specify a custom folder path.

Creating a Simple Variable Workflow

A great way to become acquainted with variables is to create a workflow that uses one. This example walks through creating a very simple workflow using a single predefined variable to create a dated folder on the Desktop. The example then demonstrates adjusting the variable's options to change the date formatting in the folder's name.

Actions used:

- New Folder

Variables used:

- Today's date

To build the workflow:

1. Create a new custom workflow window.
2. From the Files & Folders category, drag the New Folder action to the workflow area.

   This action is configured to create a folder on your Desktop. Do not enter a name into the action's Name field (**Figure 11.27**).
3. At the top of the Library list, click the Variables button.

   A categorized list of variables appears, replacing the categorized list of actions (**Figure 11.28**).
4. From the Date & Time category, drag the "Today's date" variable into the New Folder action's Name field (**Figure 11.29**).

   The variable appears in the Name field of the action, and the workflow variables list is displayed at the bottom of the workflow area (**Figure 11.30**).

The workflow is now complete and ready to be run.

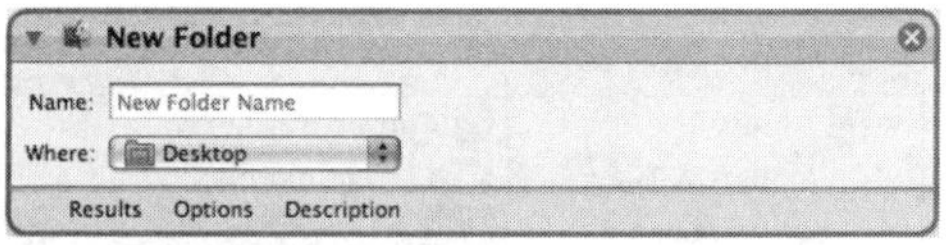

Figure 11.27 From the Files & Folders category, drag the New Folder action to the workflow. Do not adjust any of its default settings.

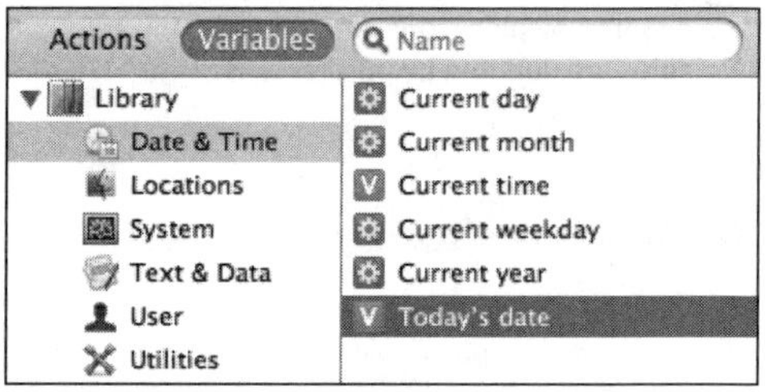

Figure 11.28 Click the Date & Time category to display a list of variables within that category.

Figure 11.29 From the Date & Time category, drag the "Today's date" variable to the New Folder action's Name field.

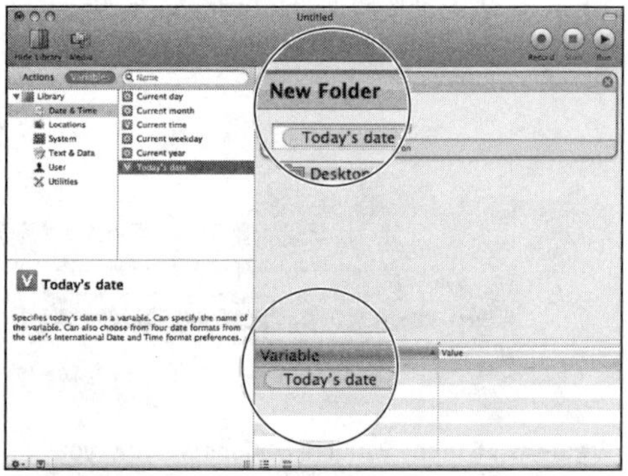

Figure 11.30 The "Today's date" variable now appears in the Name field of the New Folder action, as well as in the workflow variables area at the bottom of the workflow window.

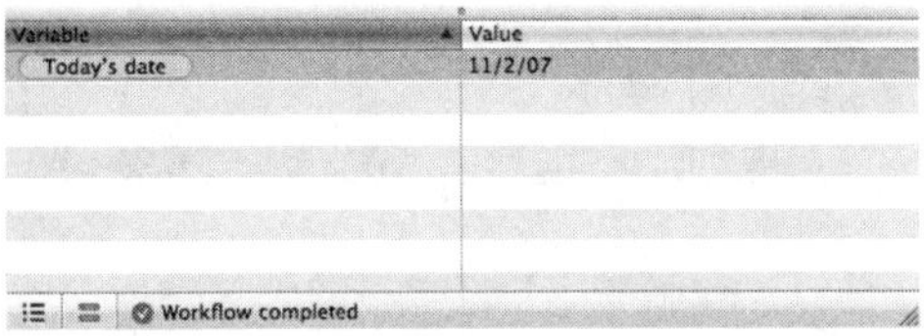

Figure 11.31 As the workflow runs, the value of the "Today's date" variable is indicated in the workflow variables area at the bottom of the workflow window.

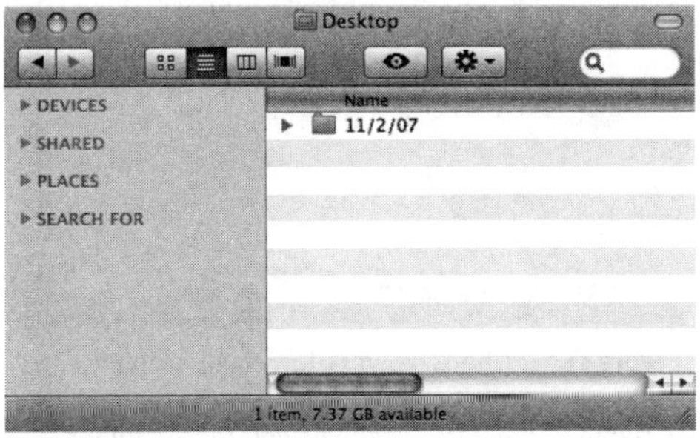

Figure 11.32 The New Folder action creates a folder named with the current date on the Desktop.

Figure 11.33 Click the triangle on the right side of the "Today's date" variable in the New Folder action's text field, and choose Edit.

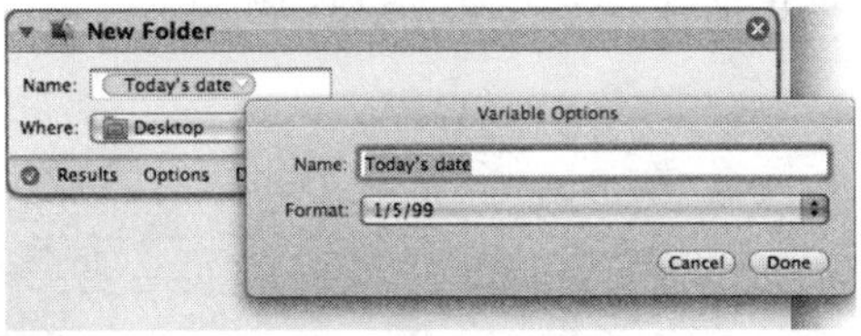

Figure 11.34 When you edit the "Today's date" variable, a Variable Options window opens.

To run the workflow:

- Click the Run button in Automator's toolbar, or press ⌘R.

  The workflow begins running. When it's done, the workflow variables area displays the value of the "Today's date" variable, and a new folder, named with the current date, is on your Desktop (**Figures 11.31** and **11.32**).

Changing the Today's date Variable Format

As you've learned, you can modify the options of some variables. One such variable, "Today's date," lets you modify the format in which the date is retrieved. For example, you may want the date to be retrieved as a short date, such as 1/5/99, or you may want it to be retrieved as a long date, such as January 5, 1999.

To change the Today's date variable format:

1. In the New Folder's Name field, click the triangle on the right side of the "Today's date" variable.

   A contextual menu appears.

2. Choose Edit from the menu (**Figure 11.33**).

   A Variable Options window opens; here you can configure the variable's behavior (**Figure 11.34**).

3. If desired, enter a new name for the "Today's date" variable.

continues on next page

4. Choose the desired date format from the Format pop-up menu, such as January 5, 1999 (**Figure 11.35**).
5. Click Done.

   The Variable Options window closes.

Now, when you run the workflow, Automator applies your custom date format to the folder created by the New Folder Action (**Figure 11.36**).

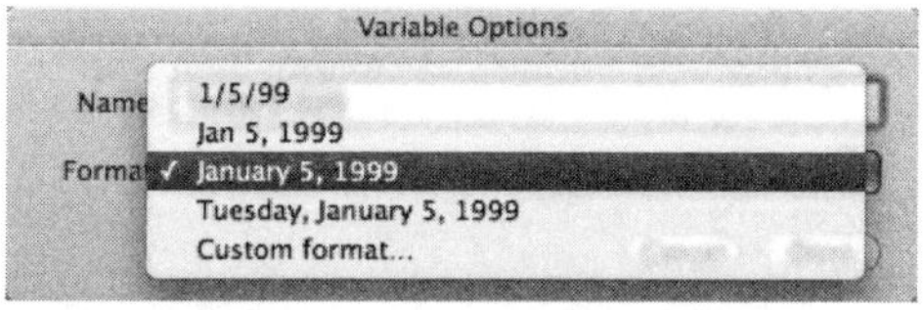

Figure 11.35 From the Format pop-up menu, choose the desired format for the "Today's date" variable.

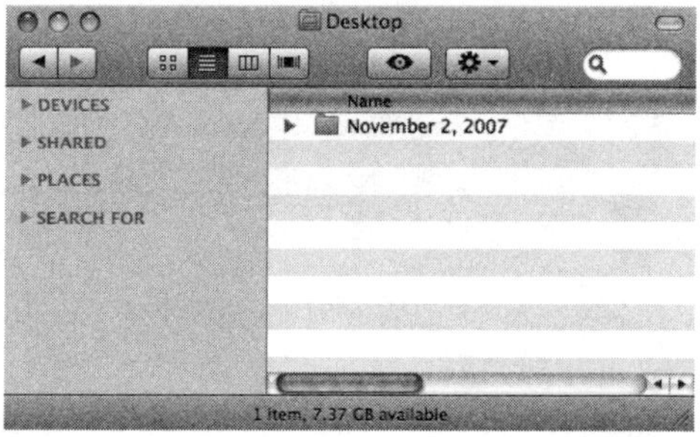

Figure 11.36 When the workflow runs, Automator applies the specified format for the "Today's date" variable to the name of the newly created folder.

Customizing the Today's date Variable

Although the "Today's date" variable has several formatting options available, you may prefer a more customized format. No problem. You can do that, too.

To customize the Today's date variable:

1. In the New Folder's Name field, click the triangle on the right of the "Today's date" variable.

   A contextual menu appears.
2. Choose Edit from the contextual menu.

   A Variable Options window opens.
3. Choose "Custom format" from the Format pop-up menu.

   The Variable Options window expands to show some additional options, including a customization field and date elements (**Figure 11.37**).
4. Drag the desired date elements into the customization field (**Figure 11.38**).

   For example, to include the month, day, and year, drag the Month, Day of Month, and Year date elements into the customization field.

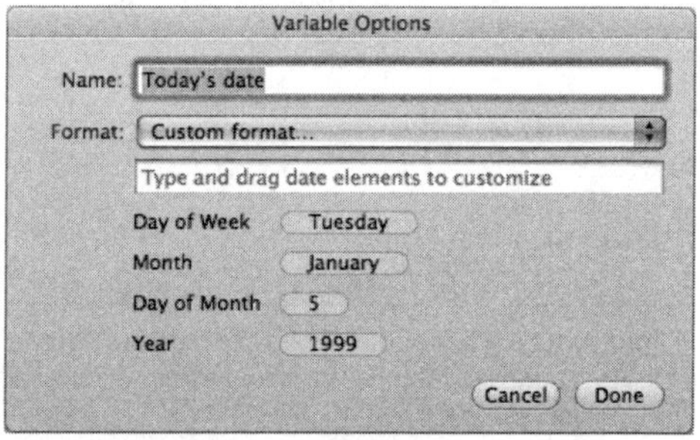

Figure 11.37 To customize the "Today's date" variable, choose "Custom format" from the Format pop-up menu in the Variable Options window.

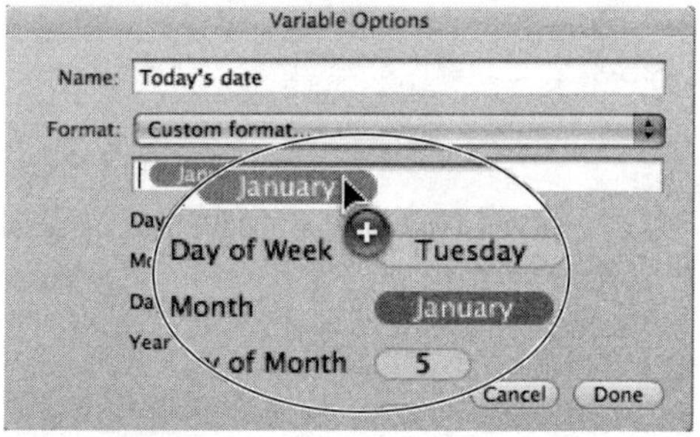

Figure 11.38 Drag the desired date elements to the customization field in the Variable Options window.

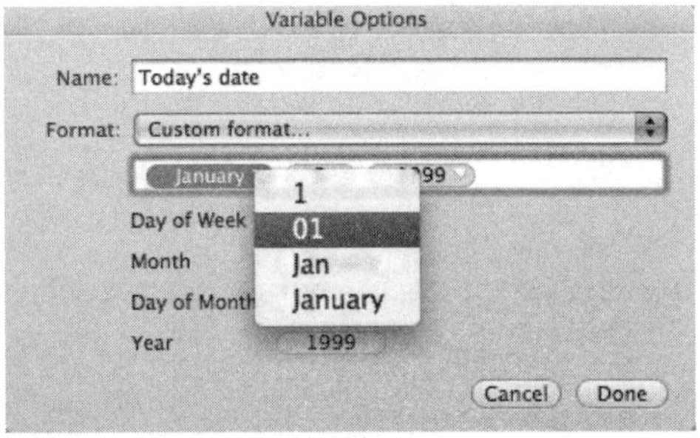

Figure 11.39 If desired, click the triangle to the right of each date element in the customization panel to customize its format.

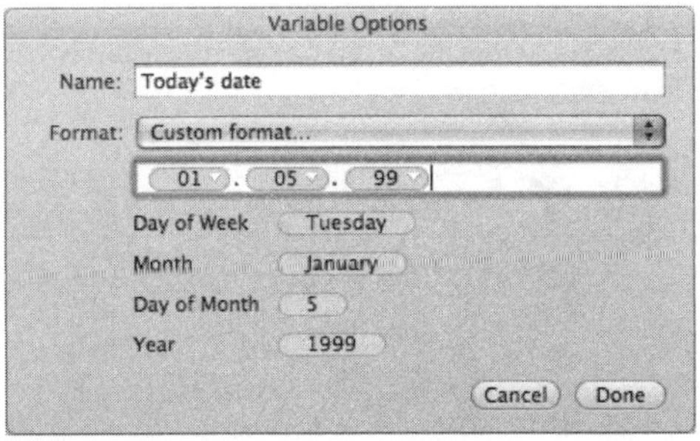

Figure 11.40 The customization field also allows you to enter text to be incorporated with the specified date elements.

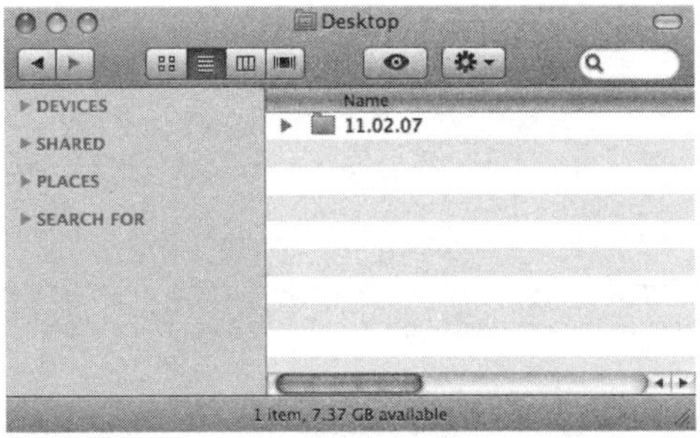

Figure 11.41 When the workflow runs, Automator applies the custom format for the "Today's date" variable to the name of the newly created folder.

5. To customize a specific date element, click the triangle on its right within the customization field.

   A contextual menu appears, containing several formatting options for the date element (**Figure 11.39**).

6. Choose the desired format from the menu.

   For example, for the Month date element, you could choose 01 to display the month as a two-digit month.

7. If desired, repeat steps 5 and 6 for any other date elements you've added to the customization panel.

8. If desired, enter into the customization field any text to appear as part of the formatted date, such as a delimiter.

   For example, you may want each date element to be separated by a period (**Figure 11.40**).

9. Click Done.

   The Variable Options window closes.

Now, when you run the workflow, Automator applies your custom date format to the newly created folder (**Figure 11.41**).

Creating an Advanced Variable Workflow

The following example workflow is a bit more advanced. It creates a dated folder on the Desktop and then downloads any linked images from the currently opened Safari webpage into that folder. The workflow makes use of two variables: one that retrieves a predefined variable value and one that stores and retrieves the result of an action within the workflow.

Actions used:

- New Folder
- Set Value of Variable
- Get Current Webpage from Safari
- Get Image URLs from Webpage
- Download URLs

Variables used:

- Today's date
- New Path

To build the workflow:

1. Create a new custom workflow window.
2. At the top of the Library list, click the Variables button.

   The list of categories and variables displays.
3. In the Date & Time category, double-click the "Today's date" variable.

   The workflow variables area, containing the "Today's date" variable, displays at the bottom of the workflow window (**Figure 11.42**).
4. In the Locations category, double-click the New Path variable.

   The New Path variable appears in the workflow variables area (**Figure 11.43**).
5. Double-click the New Path variable in the workflow variables area.

   The Variable Options window appears.

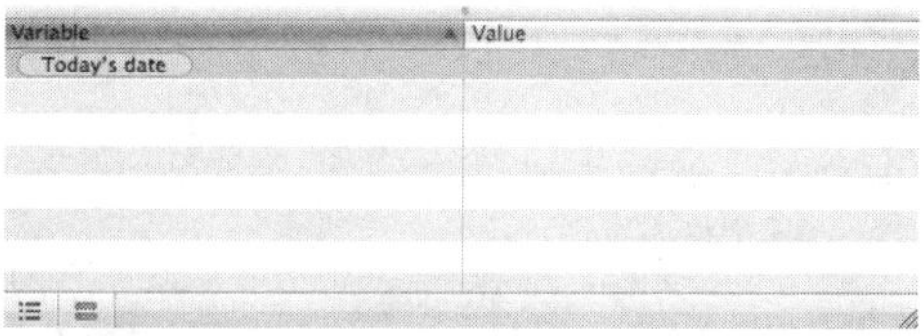

Figure 11.42 From the Date & Time category, add the "Today's date" variable to your workflow.

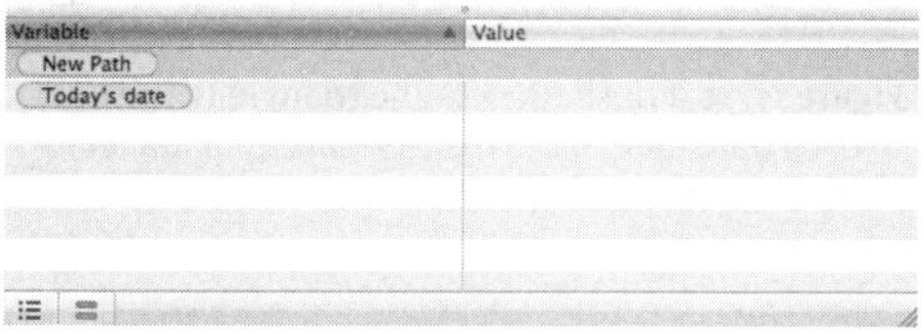

Figure 11.43 From the Locations category, add the New Path variable to your workflow.

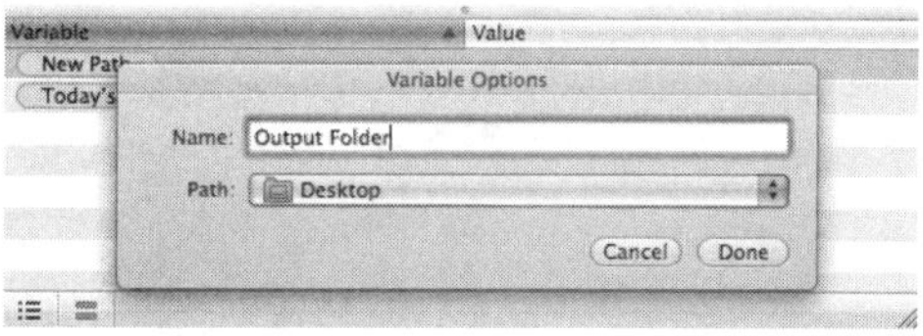

Figure 11.44 Double-click the New Path variable in the workflow variables area to display the Variable Options window. Change the name of the variable to Output Folder.

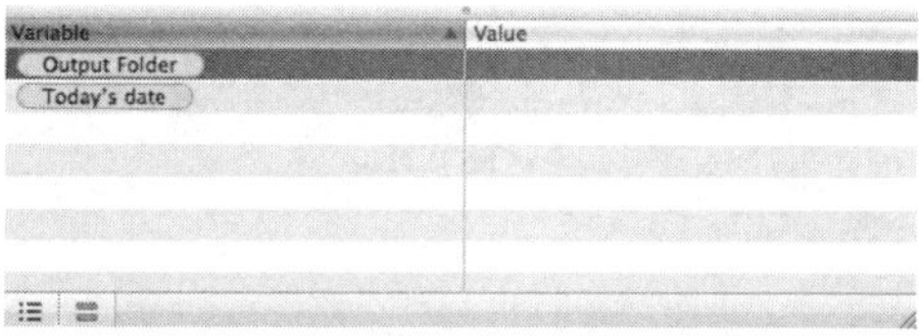

Figure 11.45 The workflow variables area displays a list of the variables you've added to your workflow.

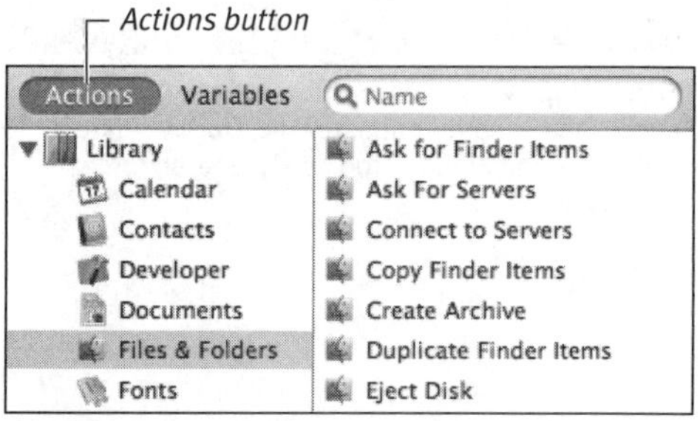

Figure 11.46 Click the Library list's Actions button to display the list of categorized actions.

6. Enter `Output Folder` into the Name field (**Figure 11.44**).

7. Click Done.

   The Variable Options window closes, and the workflow variables area displays the variable's new name (**Figure 11.45**).

8. At the top of the Library list, click the Actions button.

   The list of categories and actions displays (**Figure 11.46**).

9. From the Files & Folders category, drag the New Folder action to the workflow area.

   Enter `-Website Photos` into the action's Name field. No additional configuration is necessary (**Figure 11.47**).

10. From the workflow variables area, drag the "Today's date" variable to the beginning of the New Folder action's Name field (**Figure 11.48**).

11. From the Utilities category, drag the Set Value of Variable action to the workflow area.

12. From the action's Variable pop-up menu, choose the Output Folder variable (**Figure 11.49**).

13. From the Internet category, drag the Get Current Webpage from Safari action to the workflow area (**Figure 11.50**).

14. From the Internet category, drag the Get Image URLs from Webpage action to the workflow area.

15. From the "Get URLs of Images" pop-up menu, choose "linked from these webpages" (**Figure 11.51**).

16. From the Internet category, drag the Download URLs action to the workflow area.

continues on next page

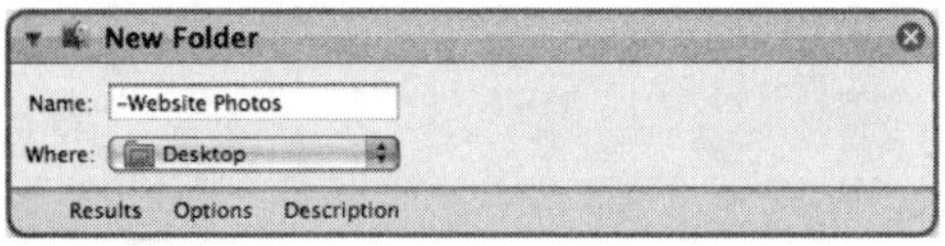

Figure 11.47 From the Files & Folders category, add a New Folder action to the workflow and enter `-Website Photos` into the Name field.

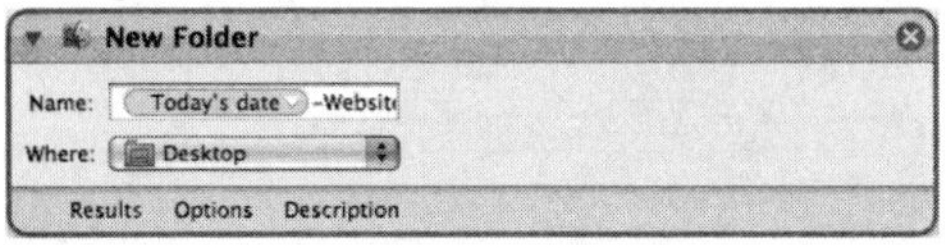

Figure 11.48 Drag the "Today's date" variable to the beginning of the New Folder's Name field.

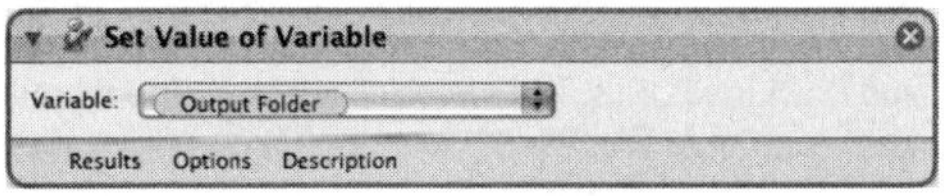

Figure 11.49 From the Utilities category, add the Set Value of Variable action to the workflow and choose Output Folder from the Variable pop-up menu.

Figure 11.50 From the Internet category, add the Get Current Webpage from Safari action to the workflow.

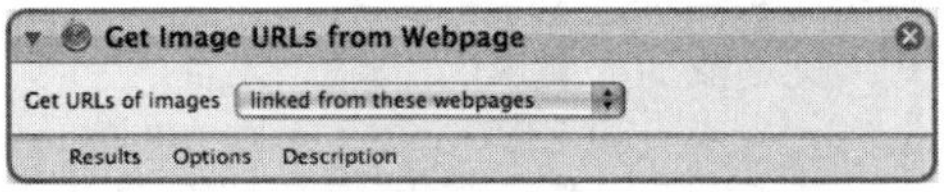

Figure 11.51 From the Internet category, add the Get Image URLs from Webpage action to the workflow and choose "linked from these webpages" from the "Get URLs of images" pop-up menu.

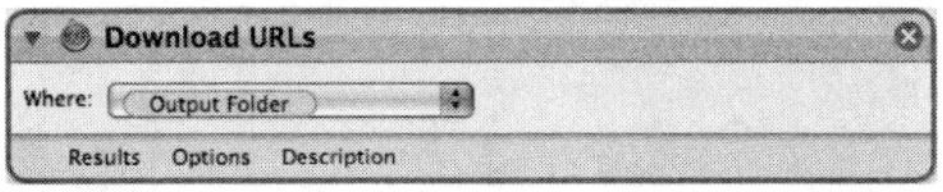

Figure 11.52 From the Internet category, add the Download URLs action to the workflow. Next, drag the Output Folder action from the workflow variables area to the Where pop-up menu.

17. From the workflow variables area, drag the Output Folder variable to the beginning of the Download URLs action's Where pop-up menu (**Figure 11.52**).

The workflow is now complete and ready to be run. It should consist of two variables—Output Folder and "Today's date"—and five actions—New Folder, Set Value of Variable, Get Current Webpage from Safari, Get Image URLs from Webpage, and Download URLs (**Figure 11.53**).

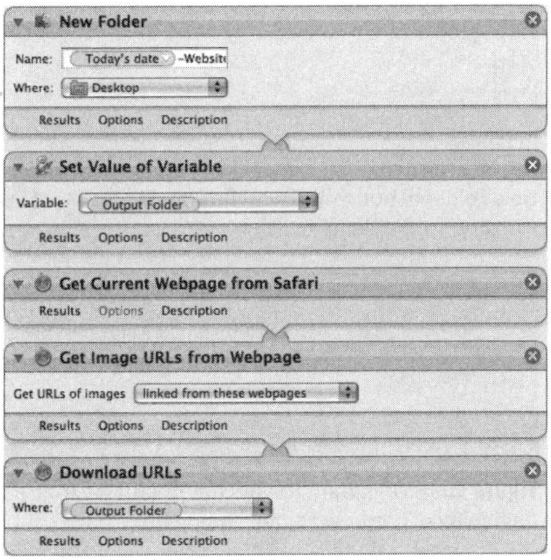

Figure 11.53 The completed workflow consists of five actions: New Folder, Set Value of Variable, Get Current Webpage from Safari, Get Image URLs from Webpage, and Download URLs. Two variables are used throughout this workflow.

To run the workflow:

1. Launch Safari and go to a webpage containing linked images.

   For this example, you can use the test site www.automatedworkflows.com/demos/photos/ (**Figure 11.54**).

2. Click the Run button in Automator's toolbar, or press ⌘R.

   The workflow runs. When it's done, the workflow variables area displays the value of the Output Folder and Today's date variables, and a dated Website Photos folder is on your Desktop, containing the downloaded photos (**Figures 11.55** and **11.56**).

Figure 11.54 Open a webpage in Safari containing linked images.

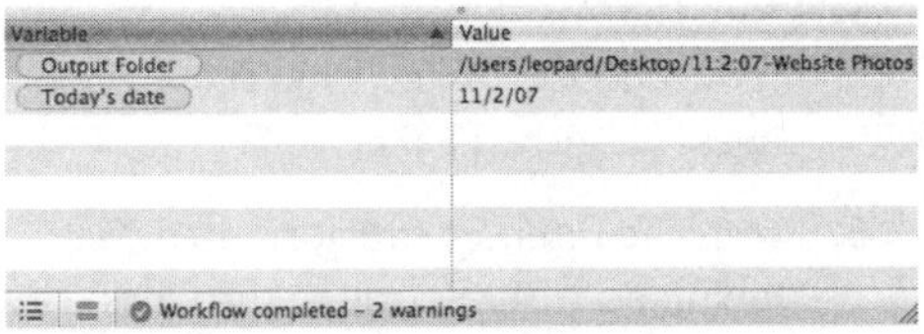

Figure 11.55 The values of the Output Folder and "Today's date" variables appear in the workflow variables area when the workflow runs.

Figure 11.56 In this example, a dated Website Photos folder is created on the Desktop, containing any downloaded images.

Sharing Actions and Workflows

12

Automator is a truly amazing technology that can benefit virtually every Mac user. Unfortunately, people are often intimidated by it and are unsure of how to get started. But you can help spread the good word about Automator by showing others what it can do and how easy it is to use. If you've created a useful workflow, send it to friends so they can use it, too. Once they've seen the benefits of Automator firsthand, they're sure to begin adopting it themselves.

This chapter explores various ways of sharing actions and workflows with friends and colleagues, including emailing workflows, locating action files in the Finder, importing actions on your own machine, and printing workflows.

Distributing Workflows

Automator workflows that have been saved as applications or workflow files are just like any other file on the Mac. They can be moved or copied anywhere on your machine, and they can also be sent to other users.

Emailing Workflows

Probably the simplest way to distribute workflows is to send them as email attachments. Just be sure that the recipients have installed the correct versions of the actions required by the workflow. Otherwise, as mentioned in Chapter 7, "Troubleshooting," they will get an error message when opening or running the workflow indicating that required actions cannot be found. If a user doesn't have the required actions, then consider sending them as well.

✔ Tip

- To reduce file size and reduce the possibility of corruption, archive workflows when emailing them to friends. To archive a workflow as a zip file, select it in the Finder and choose File > Compress "Name of File."

Publicly Distributing Workflows

If you've created a really useful workflow, you may want to make it available to a larger audience. As you'll learn in Chapter 14, "Automator Resources," there are a number of websites that cater to hosting user-contributed workflows, including Automator World (http://automatorworld.com/) and MacScripter (http://macscripter.net). Feel free to submit your workflow for inclusion on one of these sites.

Action Distribution Limitations

Treat Automator actions like any software application. Although many third-party actions are available as freeware, some may be commercial. Keep this in mind, and before sending an action to a friend or colleague, consult the action's documentation. If a license is included, make sure you're not going to violate it by distributing the action. If the license restricts distribution or is unclear, consider sending a URL to the developer's website instead.

Locating Action Files

If you intend to send an action to a friend or colleague, you need to find it first. Because actions can be located within an application's bundle or within one of several folders on your Mac, this can sometimes be a challenge.

Where Action Files Reside

As mentioned above, an action may reside in one of several locations on your machine:

- **Application bundle.** Some applications don't put their actions in a folder somewhere. Rather, the actions are included within the application itself. When Automator launches, it scans the bundled applications on your Mac and looks for actions like this.
- **/System/Library/Automator.** This folder contains actions for applications installed with Mac OS X, such as iCal, Mail, and TextEdit. It's highly unlikely that third-party actions would ever be in this folder.
- **/Library/Automator.** This folder is probably the most likely location to hold third-party actions that you installed. Any actions contained within this folder are available to all user accounts on your machine.
- **/Users/YourUserName/Library/Automator.** This folder may also contain third-party actions. Any actions in this folder are available to you only and not to other user accounts.

Although you can certainly spend time scanning these locations for an action, Automator provides a much easier way to find the one you're looking for.

What's a Bundle?

A bundle is a directory in Mac OS X that contains a group of related files and folders. Often, bundles are "packaged" to look like a single file to the user. Many applications in Mac OS X are packaged bundles, containing components necessary for the application to function. When you double-click a bundled application, executable code within the bundle runs and the application launches.

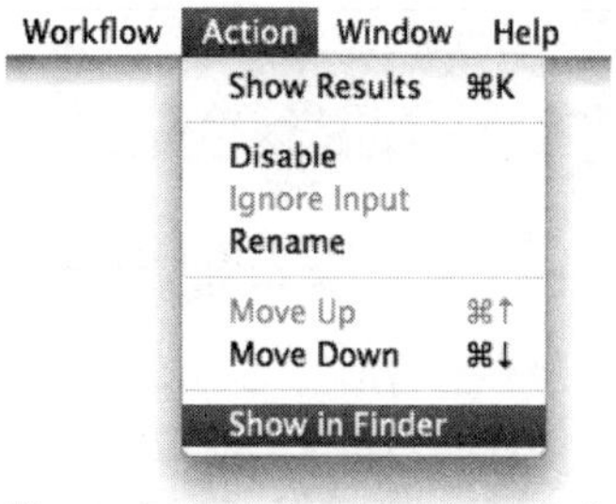

Figure 12.1 To locate an action's file in the Finder, select the action in your workflow and then choose Action > Show in Finder.

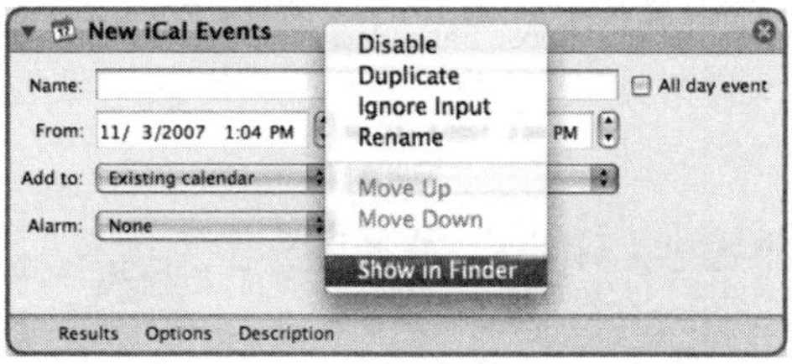

Figure 12.2 To locate an action's file in the Finder, choose Show in Finder from the contextual menu.

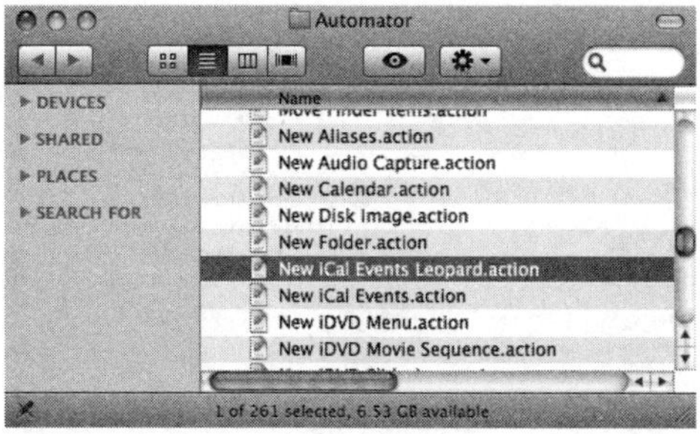

Figure 12.3 When you choose to show an action in the Finder, a new window opens, displaying the selected action.

To locate an action file using Automator:

1. In an opened workflow, select an action in the workflow area.
2. Choose Action > Show in Finder (**Figure 12.1**).

   or

   Press Control, and click the title bar of the action. From the resulting contextual menu, choose Show in Finder (**Figure 12.2**).

   The Finder comes to the front and a new window opens, displaying the selected action (**Figure 12.3**).

✔ Tip

- This procedure works even for actions embedded within an application's bundle.

To manually locate actions within an application's bundle:

1. Find the application that may contain the action you want.

   This example uses Keynote, which contains embedded actions within its bundle.

2. Press Control, and click the application in the Finder to display the contextual menu.

3. Choose Show Package Contents from the menu (**Figure 12.4**).

   A new Finder window opens and displays the contents of the application's bundle. If the application contains Automator actions, they can be found in the bundle's /Contents/Library/Automator/ folder (**Figure 12.5**).

✔ Tip

- This example is meant only to show you where actions reside within an application's bundle. It's not recommended to remove actions, or any other components for that matter, from an application's bundle.

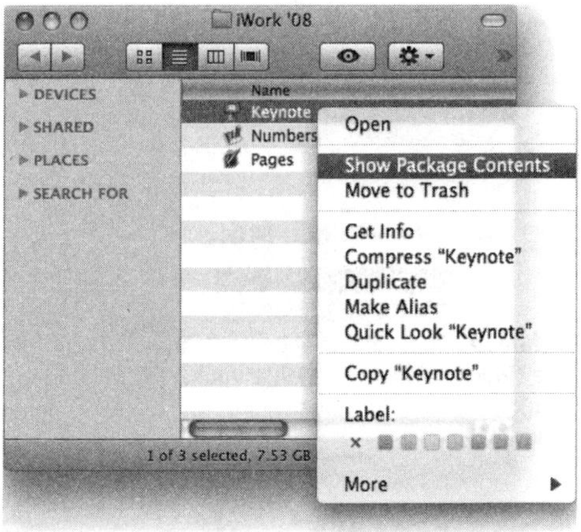

Figure 12.4 To display the contents of a bundled application, choose Show Package Contents from the application's contextual menu.

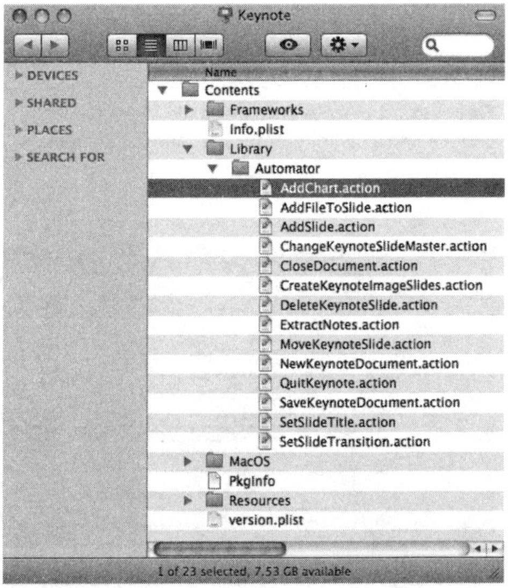

Figure 12.5 Actions stored within an application's bundle are in the bundle's /Contents/Library/Automator/ folder. This example shows the actions within Keynote's bundle.

Importing Actions

Sharing Automator workflows is a two-way street. In addition to distributing workflows you've created, you may also receive some workflows from others or download some from the Web. To run workflows that you've acquired, you must first install any required third-party actions.

As you've learned, some actions are installed within applications. For these, you just need to install the required application; you'll need it anyway for the workflow to function.

Some third-party actions may come with a stand-alone action installer. Simply run it to automatically install the actions into the correct location on your machine.

Of course, you can also manually install actions by moving them into one of the /Library/Automator/ folders on your machine—at the root level of your hard drive for all users on your machine or within your user folder for only yourself.

Actions can also be installed from within Automator itself. If you're installing actions that don't have an installer of their own, use this method.

✔ Tip

- You may need to relaunch Automator to see third-party actions you've installed.

To import third-party action files from within Automator:

1. Choose File > Import Actions (**Figure 12.6**).

   An Import Automator Action window appears.

2. Locate and choose the actions you want to import.

3. Click Import (**Figure 12.7**).

   The chosen actions are imported into the ~/Library/Automator/ folder within your user folder (**Figure 12.8**).

There's no need to relaunch Automator this time. Assuming you have any applications and other resources required by the imported actions, you should see the new actions in Automator's Library list immediately. Go ahead and begin adding them to your workflows (**Figure 12.9**).

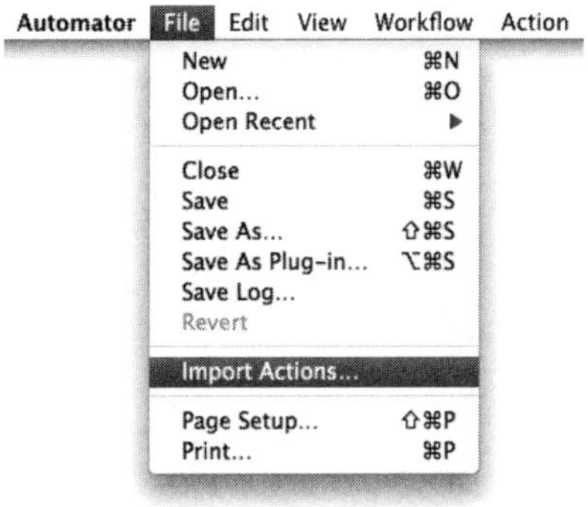

Figure 12.6 To import third-party actions into Automator, choose File > Import Actions.

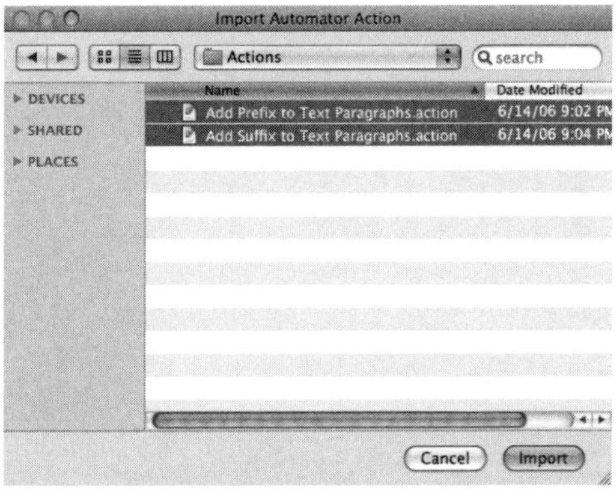

Figure 12.7 When prompted, locate the actions you want to import and click Import.

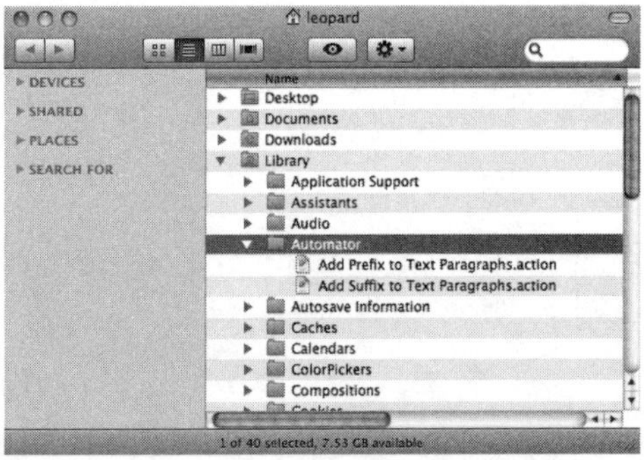

Figure 12.8 Imported actions are added to the ~/Library/Automator/ folder. They are available only for you and not in other user accounts on your machine.

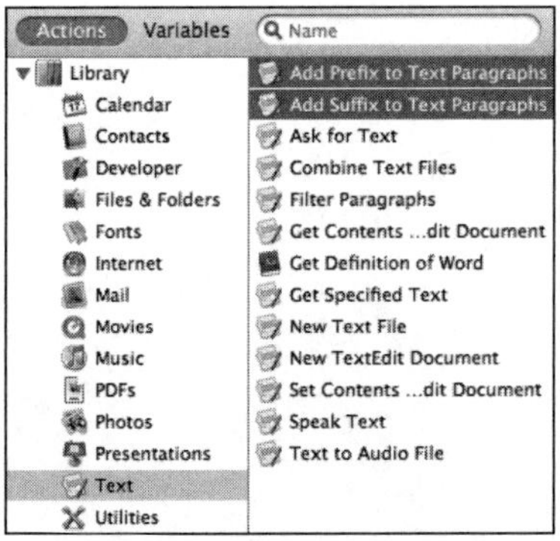

Figure 12.9 Imported actions appear in Automator right away, assuming any required applications are installed.

Printing a Workflow

Another way to share workflows with others is in print format. One advantage of sharing a printed workflow is that it doesn't require the recipient to have the workflow's actions installed. In fact, they don't even need to have a Mac! You may just want to show off what Automator can do to some of your PC buddies at work.

Printing a workflow can also be helpful when you are creating a workflow. It allows you to place the entire workflow on paper right in front of you, which may be useful with lengthy workflows. You can now review the actions and their settings all at once in order to ensure that things are configured properly. You can also consider potential areas for improvement or additional actions that you may wish to add to the workflow.

To print a workflow:

1. Open the workflow.
2. Choose File > Print (**Figure 12.10**).

   or

   Press ⌘P.

   A print panel appears, attached to the workflow window (**Figure 12.11**).
3. Click Print.

   The workflow prints.

A printed workflow shows what you see onscreen when viewing the workflow in Automator—previews of all of the workflow's actions, including their settings (**Figure 12.12**).

✔ Tips

- To modify the page setup prior to printing, choose Print > Page Setup or press Shift⌘P.
- To save the workflow as a PDF, choose Save as PDF from the PDF menu at the bottom of the print panel.

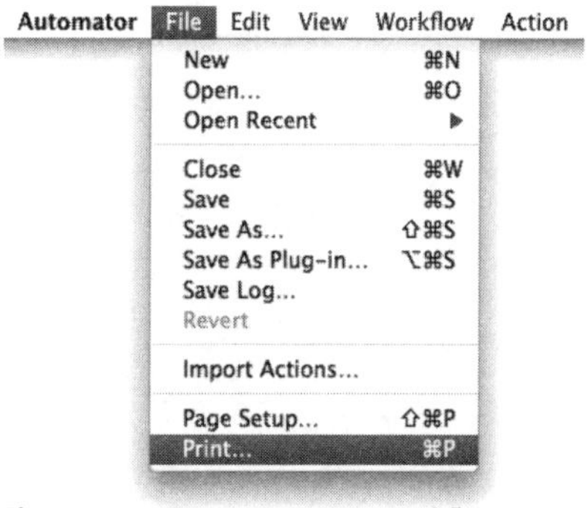

Figure 12.10 To print an open workflow in Automator, choose File > Print or press ⌘P.

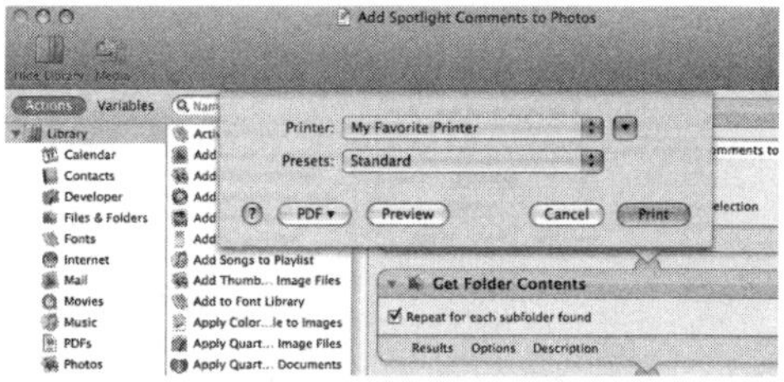

Figure 12.11 When printing a workflow, a print panel is displayed attached to the workflow. Here, you can specify the target printer and adjust other print options.

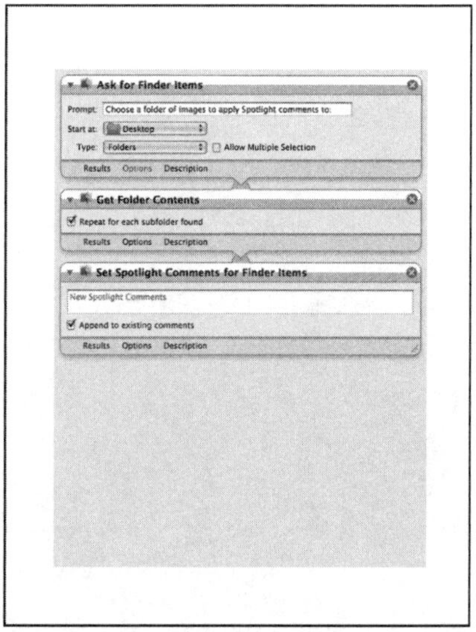

Figure 12.12 A printed workflow shows previews of all of the actions within the workflow.

BUILDING ADVANCED WORKFLOWS

13

You now know how to create some pretty powerful workflows using a combination of actions and variables. You can, however, take your workflows even further by implementing some advanced techniques that leverage the power of AppleScript, UNIX, and more.

In this chapter, you'll learn about actions and variables that allow you to execute AppleScript and shell script code as part of a workflow, giving you direct access from within a workflow to countless scriptable applications and processes that may not otherwise be directly accessible in Automator. You'll also learn how to write AppleScripts to automate repetitive tasks within Automator itself.

Don't let needing to understand AppleScript and shell scripting put you off; learning these techniques will give you insight into ways of building more complex workflows and expanding Automator's capabilities—two results well worth the effort.

Running AppleScript Commands

Although many Automator actions are available, they don't exist for everything. In situations where an action to do what you need isn't available, you may be able to write an AppleScript to do the job and run it within your workflow. For example, suppose you want your workflow to change your iChat status message. Presently, Automator doesn't include an action for this. You could try looking for a third-party action to do the job, or you could use AppleScript.

Built into Mac OS X, AppleScript is a scripting language that you can use to control applications on your machine—much like Automator does—as long as they are scriptable. Although not every Mac application is scriptable, many are. Even if an application doesn't have Automator actions available, it may still be AppleScriptable.

Generally, you write AppleScripts in a script editing application, and then save and run them as applications. Using the Run AppleScript action (from the Utilities category), you can also run scripts from within Automator workflows, meaning you can control any scriptable application from directly within your workflow (**Figure 13.1**).

The Run AppleScript action can even accept input from a previous action in the workflow. If you'd like, you can write your AppleScript code to process that input, and pass a new value to the next action in the workflow.

✔ Tip

- AppleScript may seem like a pretty complex topic, but it can be self-taught. Appendix C, "Developer Resources," lists websites, books, and other aids to get you started.

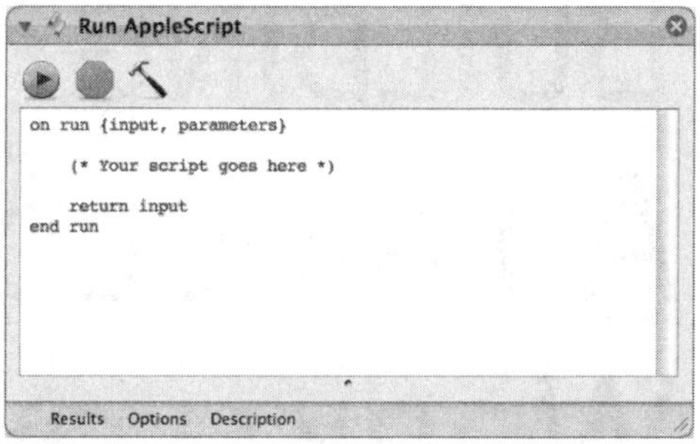
Run AppleScript
on run {input, parameters}
(* Your script goes here *)
return input
end run
Results
Options
Description

Figure 13.1 The Run AppleScript action allows you to execute AppleScript code as part of an Automator workflow.

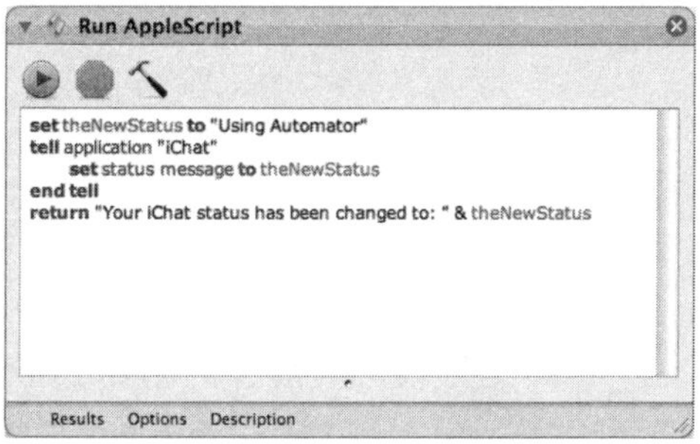
Run AppleScript
set theNewStatus to "Using Automator"
tell application "iChat"
set status message to theNewStatus
end tell
return "Your iChat status has been changed to: " & theNewStatus
Results
Options
Description

Figure 13.2 Insert the Run AppleScript action into your workflow, and enter the specified AppleScript code into the code field.

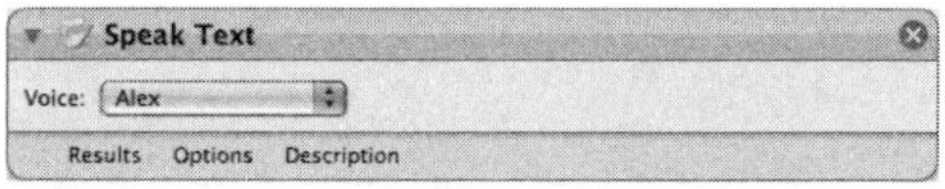
Speak Text
Voice:
Alex
Results
Options
Description

Figure 13.3 Add the Speak Text action to the workflow. Leave the Voice pop-up menu set to Alex.

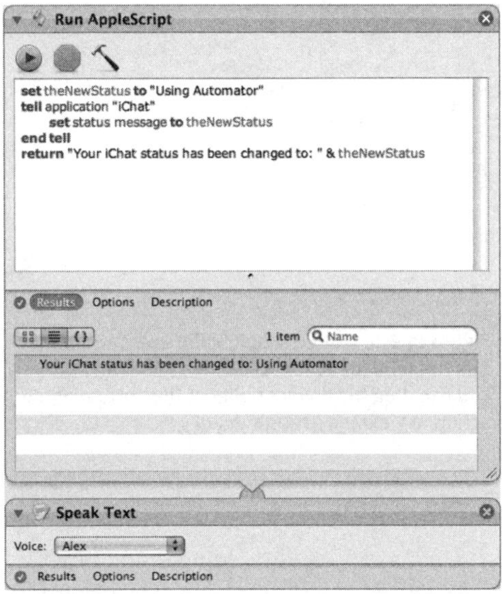

Figure 13.4 This example workflow uses AppleScript to change your iChat status to Using Automator. A message indicating that the status was changed is returned as the result of the action, and is read aloud by the Speak Text action.

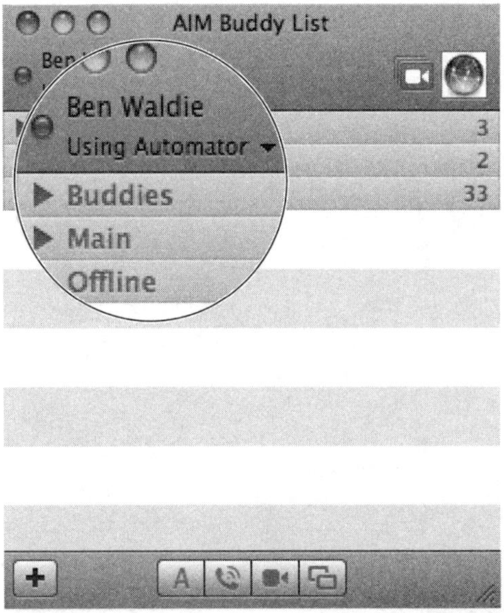

Figure 13.5 Your status message in iChat is now set to Using Automator.

Using the Run AppleScript Action

This example workflow runs AppleScript code to change the status message in iChat. A message indicating that the status has been changed is then spoken for you to hear.

Actions used:

- Run AppleScript
- Speak Text

To build the workflow:

1. Create a new custom workflow window.
2. From the Utilities category in the Library list, drag the Run AppleScript action to the workflow area.
3. Within the Run AppleScript action's code area, enter (**Figure 13.2**):

```
set theNewStatus to "Using
→ Automator"
tell application "iChat"
   set status message to theNewStatus
end tell
return "Your iChat status has been
→ changed to: " & theNewStatus
```

4. From the Text category in the Library list, drag the Speak Text action to the workflow area.
5. Leave the Speak Text action's Voice pop-up menu set to Alex (**Figure 13.3**).

When you run the workflow, the Run AppleScript action executes your specified AppleScript code. In this example, your iChat status message changes to Using Automator. Next, the text "Your iChat status has been changed to: Using Automator"is passed to the Speak Text action, which uses Mac OS X's speech synthesizer to read it aloud (**Figures 13.4** and **13.5**).

Testing the Run AppleScript Action's Code

You can test your AppleScript code using the Run AppleScript action, which is a good idea, because it allows you to ensure that the code works properly before running it as part of the entire workflow.

To test your Run AppleScript code:

1. Click the Run button at the top of the action.
2. Drag the divider bullet at the bottom of the action up to reveal a script result area.

   Here, you can view the result of your script code, and make sure it worked as expected (**Figure 13.6**).

✔ Tip

- For complex scripts, it's a good idea to use Script Editor (found in /Applications/AppleScript/) to write the code you intend to run within the Run AppleScript action. Doing so gives you access to more robust AppleScript development and troubleshooting features, such as code completion, an event log, and more. When your code is working, you can then copy and paste it into the Run AppleScript action within your workflow.

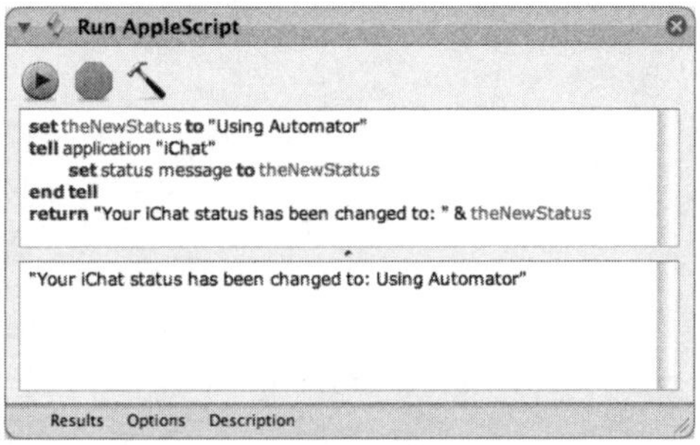
Run AppleScript
set theNewStatus to "Using Automator"
tell application "iChat"
set status message to theNewStatus
end tell
return "Your iChat status has been changed to: " & theNewStatus
"Your iChat status has been changed to: Using Automator"
Results
Options
Description

Figure 13.6 To test the AppleScript code within the Run AppleScript action, click the green Run button. You can drag the divider bullet at the bottom of the action to view the action's result.

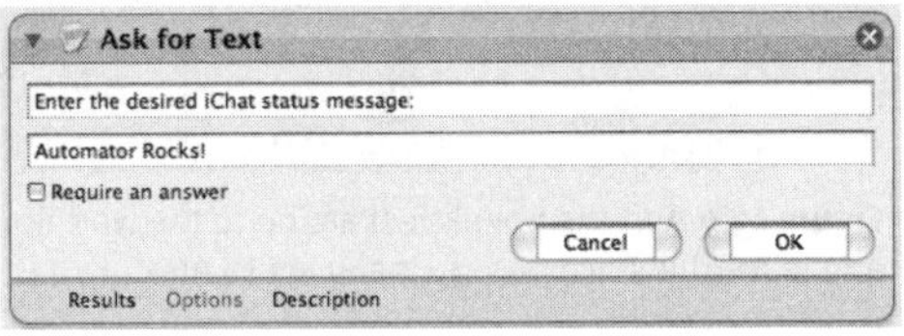

Figure 13.7 From the Text category, drag the Ask for Text action to your workflow. In the first text field, type `Enter the desired iChat status message:`. In the second text field, enter `Automator Rocks!`.

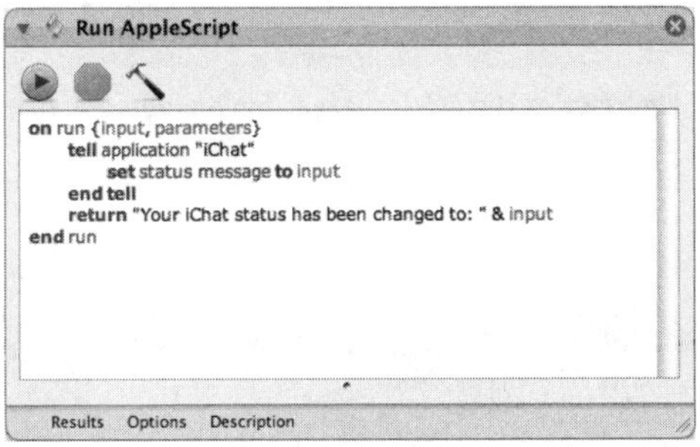

Figure 13.8 Insert the Run AppleScript action into your workflow and enter the specified AppleScript code into the code field.

Using the Run AppleScript Action to Process Input

This example workflow prompts the user to enter a new iChat status message. It then runs AppleScript code to change iChat's status to the specified message. Text indicating that the status has been changed is then spoken by the workflow.

Actions used:

- Ask for Text
- Run AppleScript
- Speak Text

To build the workflow:

1. Create a new custom workflow window.
2. From the Text category in the Library list, drag the Ask for Text action to the workflow area.
3. In the Ask for Text action's first text field, type `Enter the desired iChat status message:`.
4. In the Ask for Text action's second text field, enter `Automator Rocks!` (**Figure 13.7**).
5. From the Utilities category in the Library list, drag the Run AppleScript action to the workflow area.
6. In the Run AppleScript action's code area, enter the following demonstration code (**Figure 13.8**):

```
on run {input, parameters}
  tell application "iChat"
    set status message to input
  end tell
  return "Your iChat status has been
  → changed to: " & input
end run
```

continues on next page

When your workflow runs, this code instructs iChat to change its status to the text entered in the Ask for Text action.

7. From the Text category in the Library list, drag the Speak Text action to the workflow area.

8. Leave the Speak Text action's Voice pop-up menu set to Alex (**Figure 13.9**).

When you run the workflow, the Ask for Text action prompts you to enter the desired iChat status message. Enter your message and click OK. The workflow passes the specified text to the Run AppleScript action, which changes the status message in iChat. Finally, the Speak Text action reads a completion message aloud (**Figures 13.10** and **13.11**).

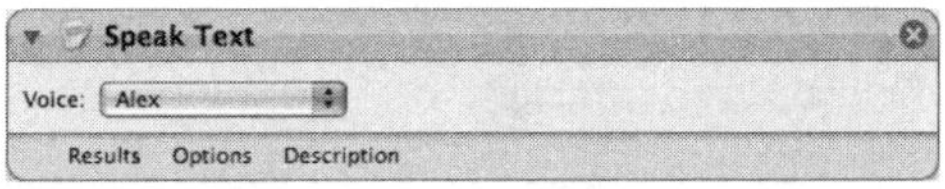

Figure 13.9 Add the Speak Text action to the workflow and leave the Voice pop-up menu set to Alex.

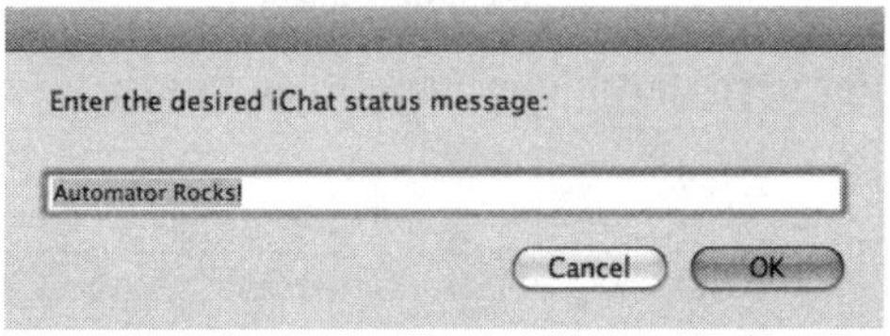

Figure 13.10 The Ask for Text action prompts you to enter the desired iChat status message. Enter a message, and click OK.

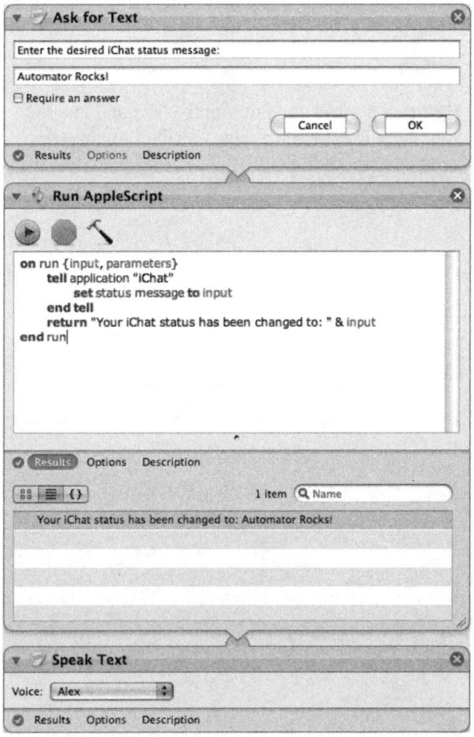

Figure 13.11 This example workflow uses AppleScript to change your iChat status to the text passed from the Ask for Text action. A message indicating that the status was changed is returned as the result of the action and is read aloud by the Speak Text action.

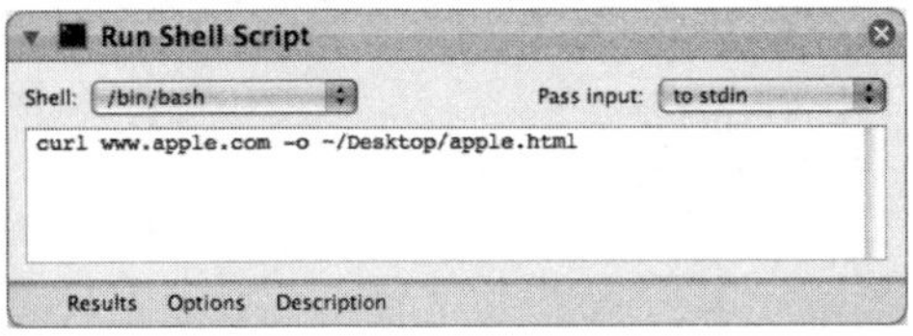

Figure 13.12 The Run Shell Script action allows you to execute shell scripts as part of an Automator workflow. This example uses `curl` to download the Apple homepage to a file named apple.html on your Desktop.

Running UNIX Commands

One of the great things about Mac OS X is that it is built upon UNIX. Although the UNIX underpinnings in Mac OS X are hidden from the casual user, you can use them if you want to. Mac OS X offers a command-line environment, where you can run command-line utilities, shell scripts, and more.

If you're interested in integrating UNIX with Automator, the news is even better. Automator's Run Shell Script action (from the Utilities category) enables you to execute UNIX commands as part of a workflow. Of course, the use of this action goes beyond the regular Automator skill set, requiring at least a minimal understanding of UNIX (**Figure 13.12**).

Like the Run AppleScript action, the Run Shell Script action can accept information as input from a previous action. This information can then be passed as arguments to your shell script code for further processing. Because the action's input type is Text, you'll need to ensure that the preceding action outputs text or something that can be changed to text by a conversion action, such as file or folder paths. The result of the shell script code, if any, is returned as the result of the Run Shell Script action itself.

✔ Tips

- A shell script is a script that is written for the Mac OS X command line. It may consist of a single command or multiple commands strung together to perform a larger function.
- A Shell Scripting Primer is available from Apple at http://developer.apple.com/documentation/OpenSource/Conceptual/ShellScripting/index.html.

Changing the Shell

A shell is a command-line environment in which you can execute commands. There are several shells available for you to use, each of which has its own syntax.

By default, the Run Shell Script action runs your code in the `bash` shell. If desired, however, you can change this by selecting a different shell from the Shell pop-up menu. Other options include `csh` and `tcsh`. You can even use the Run Shell Script action to execute Perl, Python, or Ruby scripts (**Figure 13.13**).

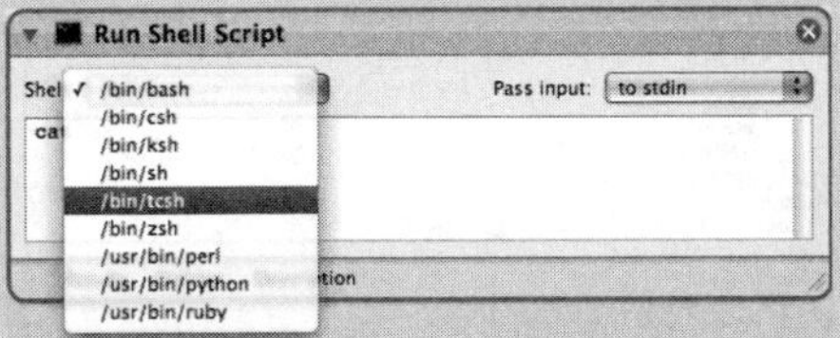

Figure 13.13 The Run Shell Script action uses the `bash` shell by default. Other shells, as well as Perl, Python, or Ruby, are also available.

Using the Run Shell Script Action

This simple example workflow uses the `ls` command to retrieve a list of items within your Applications folder. The workflow then inserts the list of items into a new TextEdit document.

Actions used:

- Run Shell Script
- New TextEdit Document

To build the workflow:

1. Create a new custom workflow window.
2. From the Utilities category in the Library list, drag the Run Shell Script action to the workflow area.
3. Leave the Run Shell Script action's Shell pop-up menu set to `/bin/bash`, and the "Pass input" pop-up menu set to "to stdin" (a.k.a. standard input).
4. In the Run Shell Script action's code area, enter `ls /Applications/` (**Figure 13.14**).
5. From the Text category, drag the New TextEdit Document action to the workflow area (**Figure 13.15**).

When you run the workflow, the Run Shell Script action executes the specified code. In this example, a list of items in the Applications folder is retrieved. The workflow then passes this information as input to the New Text Edit Document action, which creates a new document in TextEdit and inserts the list of items (**Figures 13.16** and **13.17**).

✔ Tip

- `ls` is a UNIX command that is used to list the contents of a directory.

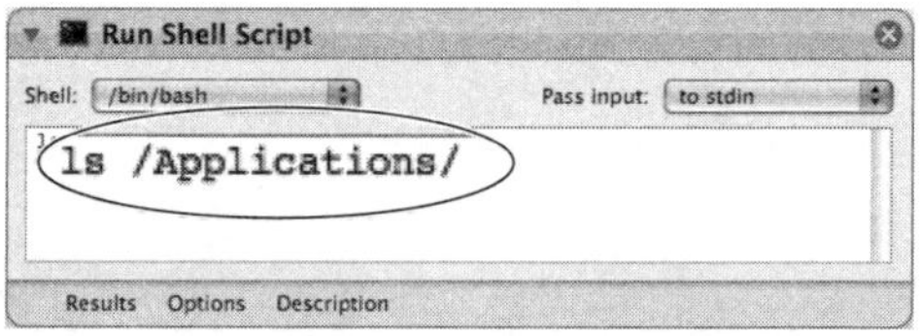

Figure 13.14 Insert the Run Shell Script action in your workflow, and enter `ls /Applications/` in the code field.

Figure 13.15 Add the New TextEdit Document to the workflow.

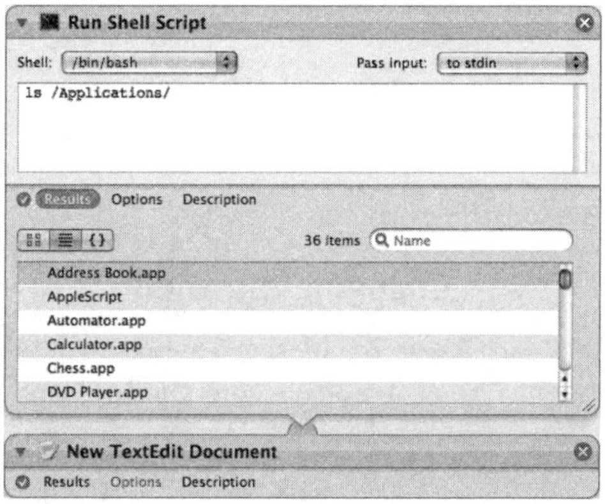

Figure 13.16 This simple example uses the `ls` command to retrieve a list of items in your Applications folder. The list of items is then passed to the New TextEdit Document for further processing.

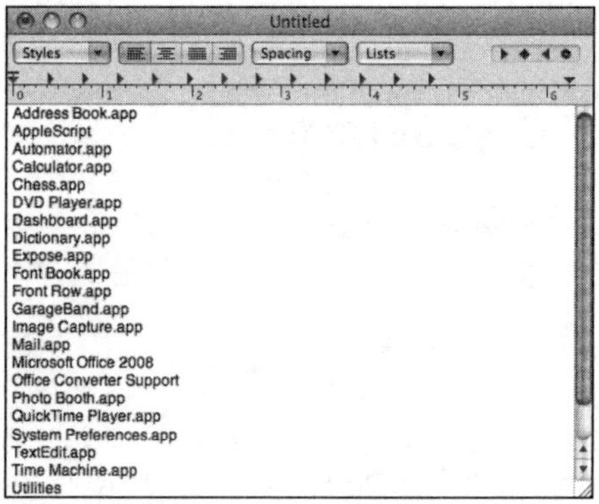

Figure 13.17 The New TextEdit Document action creates a document in TextEdit and inserts the list of items retrieved by the Run Shell Script action.

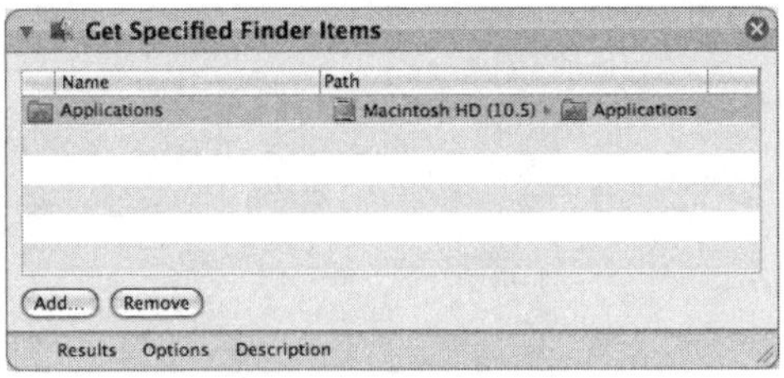

Figure 13.18 Add the Get Specified Finder Items action to your workflow and configure it to get the Applications folder on your machine.

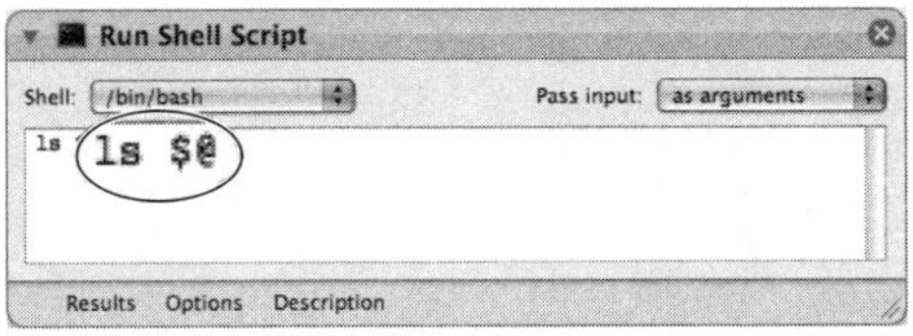

Figure 13.19 Insert the Run Shell Script action into your workflow and enter `ls $@` in the code field. Choose "as arguments" from the "Pass input" pop-up menu, and leave the Shell pop-up menu set to `/bin/bash`.

Figure 13.20 Add the New TextEdit Document to the workflow.

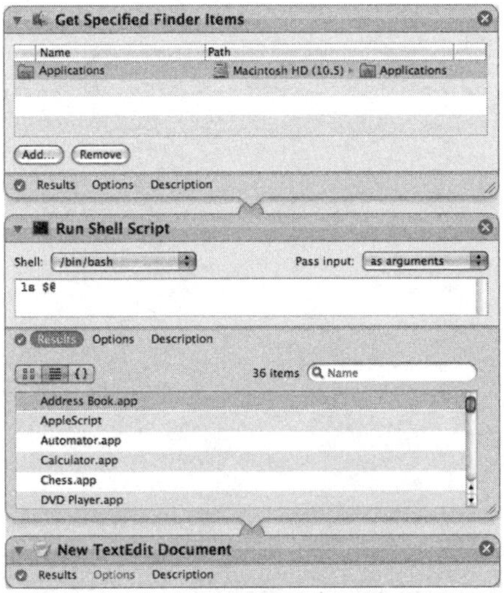

Figure 13.21 In this example, the Run Shell Script action uses the folder passed as input as an argument for the `ls` command. The result is a list that's passed to a New TextEdit Document.

Using the Run Shell Script Action to Process Input

This example workflow uses the `ls` command to retrieve a list of items in a folder from the previous action. The workflow then inserts the list of items into a new TextEdit document.

Actions used:

- Get Specified Finder Items
- Run Shell Script
- New TextEdit Document

To build the workflow:

1. Create a new custom workflow window.
2. From the Files & Folders category in the Library list, drag the Get Specified Finder Items action to the workflow area.
3. Click Add, then add a folder, such as your Applications folder, to the Get Specified Finder Items action (**Figure 13.18**).
4. From the Utilities category in the Library list, drag the Run Shell Script action to the workflow area.
5. Leave the Run Shell Script action's Shell pop-up menu set to `/bin/bash`.
6. From the Run Shell Script action's "Pass input" pop-up menu, choose "as arguments."
7. In the Run Shell Script action's code area, enter `ls $@` (**Figure 13.19**).
8. From the Text category, drag the New TextEdit Document action to the workflow area (**Figure 13.20**).

When you run the workflow, the Get Specified Finder Items action passes the Applications folder to the Run Shell Script action as input. The specified shell script code retrieves a list of items in the Applications folder, then passes the list to the New TextEdit Document action, which inserts it into a new TextEdit document (**Figure 13.21**).

Using AppleScript Variables

AppleScript code doesn't have to run just within the Run AppleScript action. You can insert it into the New AppleScript variable as well, causing the code to run whenever the variable is used within your workflow. The result of the AppleScript code then serves as the variable's value.

Although Automator includes numerous built-in variables for dates, times, user data, and such, it doesn't include variables for everything. This is where the New AppleScript variable can come into play. You could, for example, use it to retrieve a list of opened InDesign documents, get your current iChat status, create and return a reference to a new folder, and much more.

Using the Run AppleScript Variable

This example workflow uses an AppleScript variable to check for the existence of a folder on the Desktop named My Video Snapshots. If the folder doesn't exist, then the script creates it. The result of this code is a reference to the folder, which is used as the output folder for the Take Video Snapshot action. This action uses your built-in iSight camera to take a video snapshot of you, and saves it into the folder.

Actions used:

- Take Video Snapshot

Variables used:

- New AppleScript

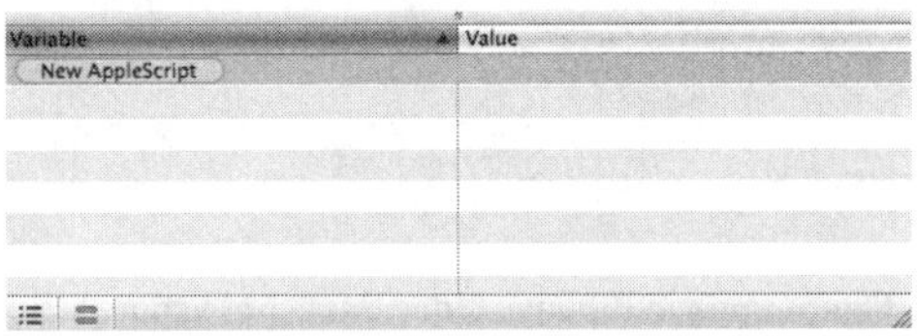
Variable
Value
New AppleScript

Figure 13.22 Double-click the New AppleScript variable in the Utilities category to add it to the workflow variables area.

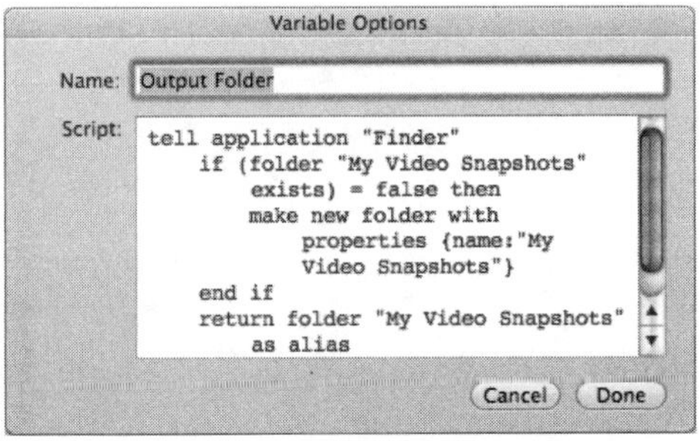
Variable Options
Name:
Output Folder
Script:
tell application "Finder"
if (folder "My Video Snapshots"
exists) = false then
make new folder with
properties {name:"My
Video Snapshots"}
end if
return folder "My Video Snapshots"
as alias
Cancel
Done

Figure 13.23 In the Variable Options window, rename the New AppleScript variable to Output Folder, and enter the specified AppleScript code.

To build the workflow:

1. Create a new custom workflow window.
2. At the top of the Library list, click the Variables button.

   The list of categories and variables is displayed.
3. In the Utilities category, double-click the New AppleScript variable.

   The workflow variables area, containing the New AppleScript variable, is displayed at the bottom of the workflow window (**Figure 13.22**).
4. Double-click the New AppleScript variable in the workflow variables area.

   The Variable Options window opens.
5. Enter `Output Folder` into the Name field.
6. In the Script field, enter (**Figure 13.23**):

```
tell application "Finder"
   if (folder "My Video Snapshots"
   → exists) = false then
      make new folder with properties
      → {name:"My Video Snapshots"}
   end if
   return folder "My Video Snapshots"
   → as alias
end tell
```

7. Click Done.

   The Workflow Variables window closes.
8. At the top of the Library list, click the Actions button to display the list of categories and actions.
9. From the Photos category, drag the Take Video Snapshot action to the workflow area.

continues on next page

10. Leave the Take Video Snapshot action's "Save as" field set to Video Snapshot.tiff.

11. From the workflow variables area, drag the Output Folder variable to the Take Video Snapshot action's Where pop-up menu.

12. Click the "Take picture automatically" checkbox (**Figure 13.24**).

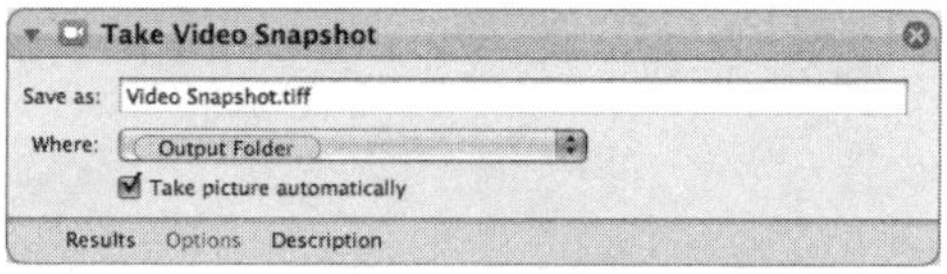

Figure 13.24 In the Take Video Snapshot action, leave the "Save as" text field set to Video Snapshot.tiff, drag the Output Folder variable to the Where pop-up menu, and click the "Take picture automatically" checkbox.

When you run the workflow, the AppleScript code of the Output Folder variable executes, checking for a folder named My Video Snapshots, and creating it if it does not already exist. The Take Video Snapshot action then takes a snapshot with your built-in iSight camera, and saves it into the My Video Snapshots folder (**Figures 13.25** and **13.26**).

Figure 13.25 The Take Video Snapshot automatically takes a snapshot of you when the workflow runs.

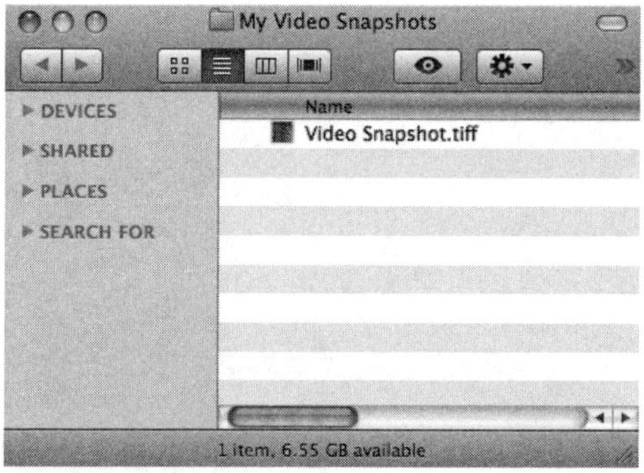

Figure 13.26 The workflow saves the new snapshot into the My Video Snapshots folder.

Using UNIX Variables

Shell script code can also be executed from a variable using the New Shell Script variable (found in the Utilities category). Like the New AppleScript variable, the New Shell Script variable runs shell script code whenever your workflow uses the variable. The result of the shell script code is returned as the variable's value.

Using the Run Shell Script Variable

Remember the days of dot matrix printers and large ASCII banners that said "Happy Birthday!" and the like? If you thought those days were over, think again. This example workflow uses the Run Shell Script variable to create ASCII banner text that reads `Automator Rocks!`. The workflow then writes the text to a file and opens it for you to view. If you like, you can print it and hang it in your office to remind yourself that Automator rocks!

Actions used:

- Get Value of Variable
- New Text File
- Open Finder Items

Variables used:

- New Shell Script

To build the workflow:

1. Create a new custom workflow window.
2. At the top of the Library list, click the Variables button to display the list of categories and variables.
3. In the Utilities category, double-click the New Shell Script variable.

   The workflow variables area, containing the New Shell Script variable, displays at the bottom of the workflow window (**Figure 13.27**).
4. Double-click the New Shell Script variable in the workflow variables area.

   The Variable Options window opens.
5. Enter `Banner Text` in the Name field.
6. In the Script field, enter `banner 'Automator Rocks!'` (**Figure 13.28**).
7. From the workflow variables area, drag the Banner Text variable to the workflow area.

   Automator adds a Get Value of Variable action to the workflow and sets the action's Variable pop-up menu to Banner Text (**Figure 13.29**).
8. At the top of the Library list, click the Actions button to display the list of categories and actions.
9. From the Text category, drag the New Text File action to the workflow area.

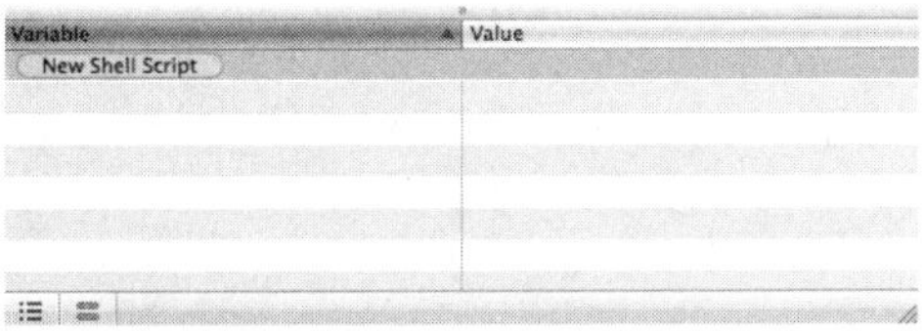

Figure 13.27 Double-click the New Shell Script variable in the Utilities category to add it to the workflow variables area.

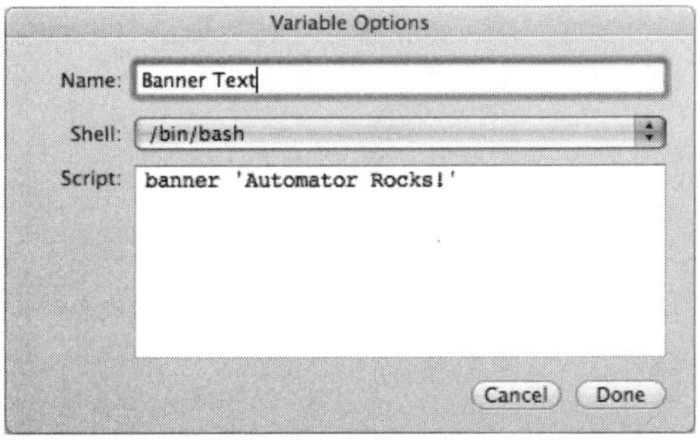

Figure 13.28 In the Variable Options window, rename the New Shell Script variable to Banner Text, and enter `banner 'Automator Rocks!'` in the Script field.

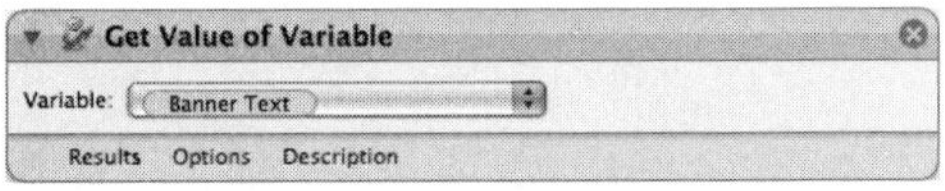

Figure 13.29 When you drag the Banner Text variable into your workflow, Automator automatically adds a Get Value of Variables action that is configured to retrieve the variable's value.

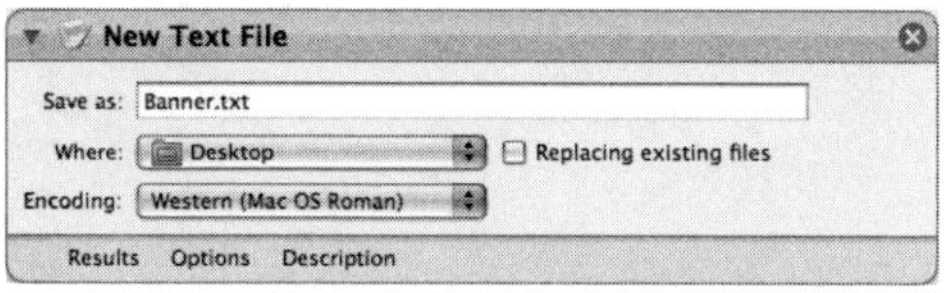

Figure 13.30 From the Text category of actions, drag the New Text File action to your workflow and enter `Banner.txt` into the "Save as" field.

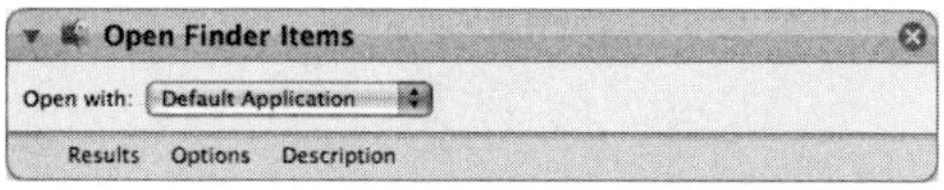

Figure 13.31 Add an Open Finder Items action to the workflow.

10. Enter `Banner.txt` into the New Text File's "Save as" field.

    You should not need to adjust any other settings for this action (**Figure 13.30**).

11. From the Files & Folders category, drag the Open Finder Items action to the workflow area.

    You should not need to configure any settings for this action (**Figure 13.31**).

When you run the workflow, the Banner Text variable executes the specified shell script code, creating Automator Rocks! as ASCII banner text. This information is then passed to the New Text File action, where it is written to a text file named Banner.txt. The Open Finder Items action opens the resulting file (**Figures 13.32** and **13.33**).

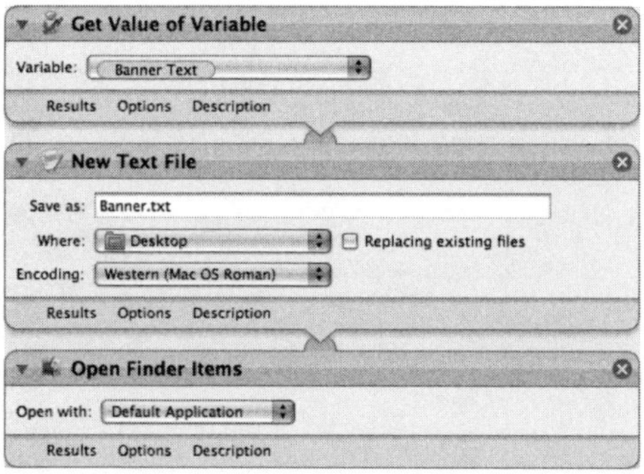

Figure 13.32 The completed workflow runs the shell script code of the Banner Text variable and passes the result to the New Text File action.

Figure 13.33 The resulting file contains an ASCII banner that reads Automator Rocks!

Watch Me Do and AppleScript

As you may recall from Chapter 5, Automator can record manual events, such as mouse clicks and key presses and insert them into your workflow in the form of a Watch Me Do action. When the workflow runs, the Watch Me Do action plays these events as part of the workflow.

Did you know, however, that AppleScript is a major driving force behind the playback of these recorded sequences? Every recorded event within the Watch Me Do action is actually nothing more than AppleScript code, which runs as part of the workflow. Automator even allows you to view the AppleScript code of a recorded event, which can be a great way to get some insight into how recorded events function.

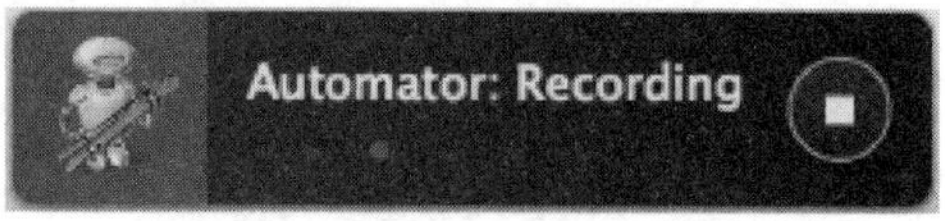

Figure 13.34 When you begin recording, your workflow disappears and a small recording window displays.

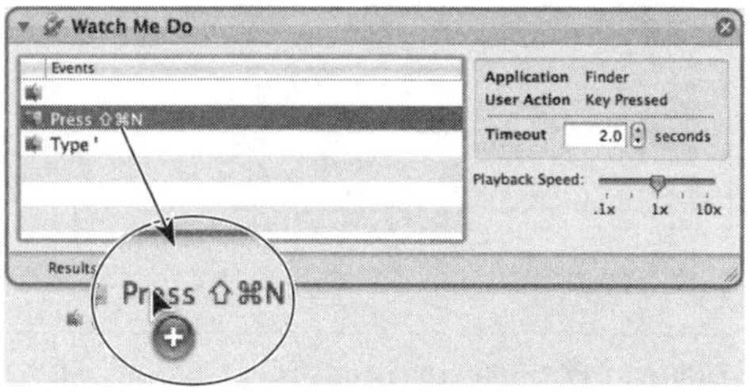

Figure 13.35 Drag a recorded event from the Watch Me Do action to the end of your workflow.

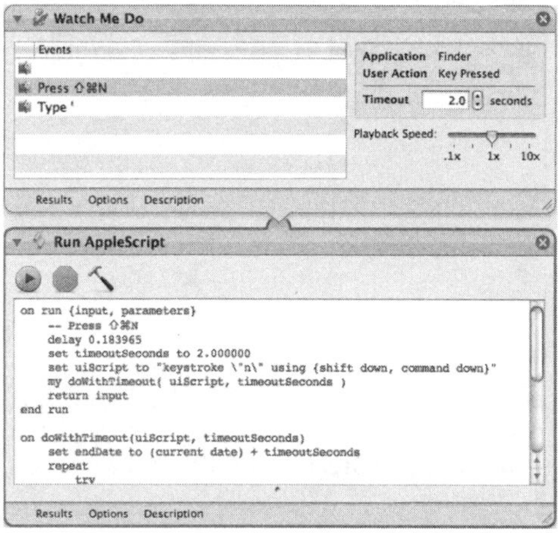

Figure 13.36 When you drag an event from the Watch Me Do action to your workflow, Automator inserts a Run AppleScript action that contains the AppleScript code behind the event.

To view the AppleScript code behind a recorded event:

1. Within an opened workflow, click Record in the toolbar.

   Automator enters recording mode (**Figure 13.34**).

2. Begin performing some manual events; for example, go to the Finder, press ⇧Shift ⌘ N to create a new folder, and give it a name.

3. Go back to Automator and click the Stop button.

   Recording stops, and you return to your workflow. Automator inserts a Watch Me Do action containing the recorded events into your workflow.

4. Select an event in the Watch Me Do action and drag it to the end of your workflow (**Figure 13.35**).

   Automator inserts a Run AppleScript action into your workflow. It contains the AppleScript code behind the recorded event (**Figure 13.36**).

You can now explore the AppleScript code to learn how it works, use it as part of the workflow, insert it into another AppleScript, and so forth.

AppleScripting Automator

Automator is a scriptable application itself, meaning you can control it with AppleScript. It has a comprehensive AppleScript dictionary, allowing you to write code to perform almost any task you can do manually, including building, saving, and running workflows, configuring actions, and more (**Figure 13.37**).

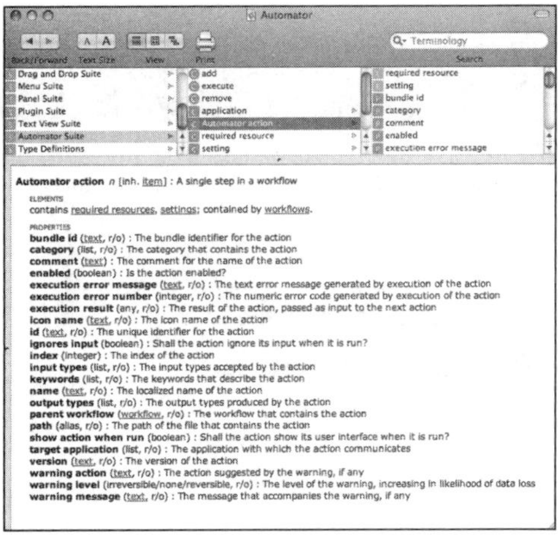

Figure 13.37 Automator's AppleScript dictionary is extensive, enabling you to write scripts to automate repetitive tasks within Automator itself.

If you know AppleScript, then you can use this capability to automate repetitive tasks you do within Automator itself. For example, suppose you frequently save workflows to your Desktop as applications. Rather than doing this manually each time, you could create an AppleScript script to do it. You could then run the script whenever you want to save a workflow (**Figure 13.38**).

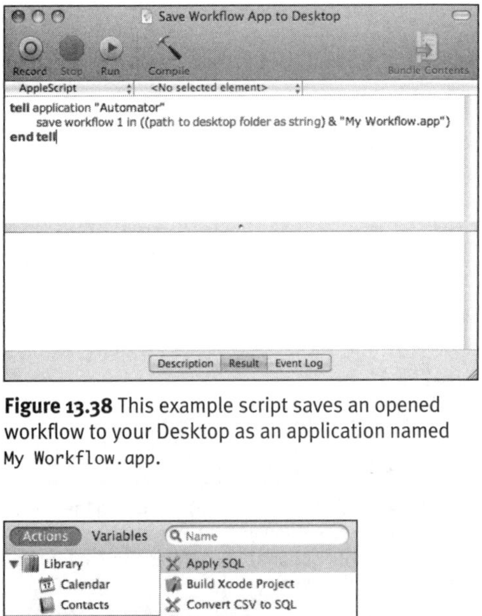

Figure 13.38 This example script saves an opened workflow to your Desktop as an application named `My Workflow.app`.

Developer-Related Actions

For Mac OS X application developers, a number of Automator actions are installed with Xcode. These actions allow you to automate time-consuming tasks typically involved in the application development process. For example, you can use the Build Xcode Project action to batch build and install specified Xcode projects. The Create Package action enables you to batch create installation packages, using a number of custom default settings. Look for these actions and more in the Developer category of Automator's Library list (**Figure 13.39**).

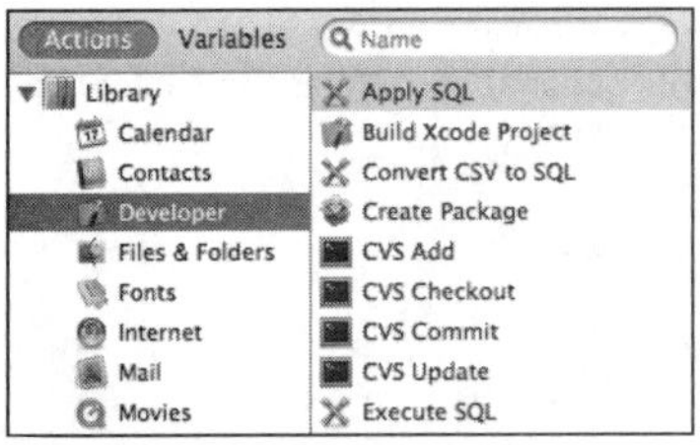

Figure 13.39 Actions are installed with Xcode to help with developer-related tasks, such as batch building Xcode projects, creating installation packages, and more.

14

AUTOMATOR RESOURCES

You're now ready to begin using Automator on your own. Along the way, you may encounter obstacles or questions. Remain calm. Loads of available resources can help you through tough situations and take you to the next level with Automator.

Numerous websites provide detailed Automator information, including tutorials, tips, and example workflows. Hundreds of third-party actions are available for download, enabling you to expand the list of actions installed on your machine. Mailing lists and forums provide an excellent opportunity to meet other Automator users, ask questions, and find answers.

This chapter provides a comprehensive list of these and other valuable Automator resources. Of course, be sure to keep this book handy, too, and use it regularly as a quick reference guide for creating workflows, saving plug-ins, looping, using variables, and more.

Automator's Help

Like many applications in Mac OS X, Automator contains built-in help documentation. You can use it while building your workflows to find basic information about actions, variables, workflows, and other important topics.

To access Automator's help documentation:

1. Choose Help > Automator Help (**Figure 14.1**).

   or

   Press Help.

   A window appears, displaying Automator's help documentation.

2. Browse the topics listed, or enter a query into the search field in the window's toolbar (**Figure 14.2**).

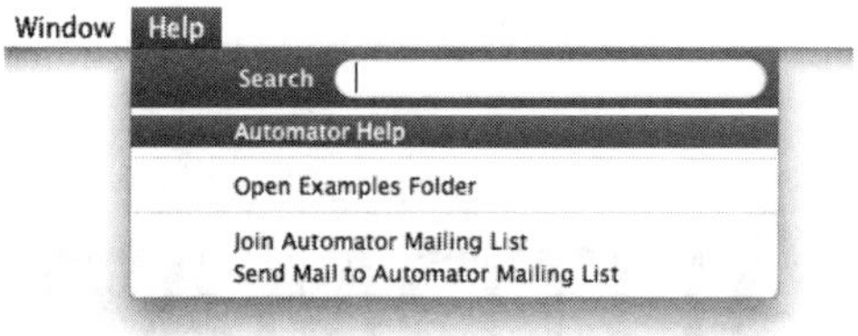

Figure 14.1 Choose Help > Automator Help to display Automator's help documentation.

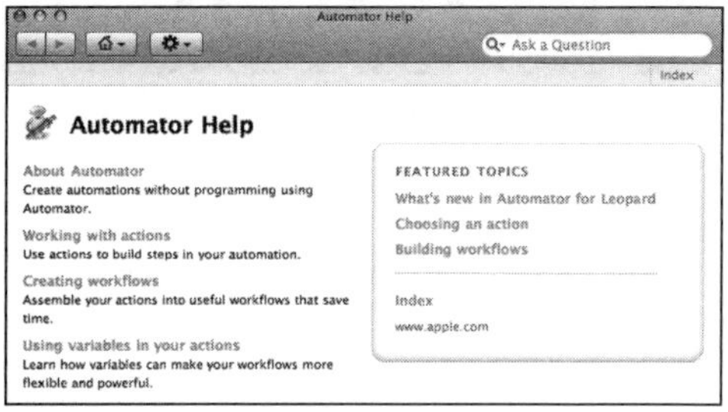

Figure 14.2 Automator's help documentation provides quick access to basic information about workflows, actions, and more.

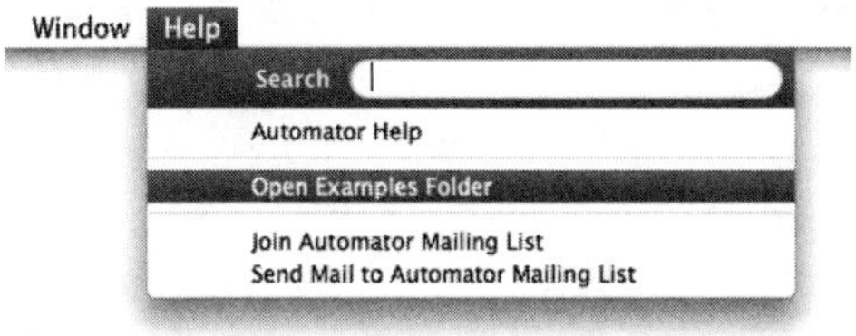

Figure 14.3 Choose Help > Open Examples Folder to display the example workflows that are installed with Mac OS X.

Figure 14.4 Automator's example workflows provide a good starting point for Automator. Open them, see how they work, and adjust them to meet your own needs.

Automator's Example Workflows

An excellent way to learn Automator is to look at examples of completed workflows. Although you can find numerous example workflows online, Apple includes a few with Automator to get you started. You're encouraged to open these workflows and study them to see how they work. Use them to get ideas for your own workflows, and don't be afraid to adjust them to meet your needs.

To view Automator's example workflows:

1. Choose Help > Open Examples Folder Feedback (**Figure 14.3**).

   or

   Open /Library/Application Support/Apple/Automator/Workflows/.

   The Workflows folder opens to display several example workflows (**Figure 14.4**).

2. Double-click the desired workflow to open it in Automator.

   You may now study the workflow, modify it, or run it.

Websites

Although Mac OS X includes hundreds of actions, and even more are bundled with Apple and third-party applications, these actions don't do everything. Fortunately, hundreds of additional actions—and the list is constantly growing—are available for download from third-party developers. Although some of these actions are available commercially, you can download many for free.

For an excellent way to jump-start your adoption of Automator, check out the loads of prebuilt workflows online. Before building a workflow, consider looking for an existing one to use as-is or modify to meet your needs.

The following websites are excellent resources for learning more about Automator, as well as expanding your library of actions and workflows.

Apple.com

www.apple.com/automator

This, obviously, is Apple's corporate website and contains information about Automator and everything else Mac.

Automator.us

http://automator.us

This website is the definitive resource for all things Automator. Here, you'll find Automator tips, tricks, tutorials, and videos, as well as downloadable actions, workflows, and much more. This website is updated often, so be sure to check it regularly.

Apple's Mac OS X Downloads

www.apple.com/downloads/macosx/automator/

Apple's Mac OS X Downloads website is an excellent resource, containing an entire category specifically for third-party Automator actions and workflows. Of course, you'll find lots of other great downloads here, as well, including Mac applications, Dashboard widgets, and much more.

Automator World

http://automatorworld.com

This website is a great place to go for the latest Automator information, news, and tips. It also hosts a large repository of user-contributed actions and workflows. It's a great place to share workflows that you create, too!

MacScripter

http://macscripter.net

Although the primary focus of this website is AppleScript, you'll also find a wealth of information here about Automator, including articles and links. An Automator Actions section also includes hundreds of downloadable actions and workflows.

Mac OS X Automator Video Training

By Jesse Feiler

www.vtc.com/products/Mac-OS-X-Automator-tutorials.htm

VTC (Virtual Training Company) offers a ton of high-quality Mac-related video tutorials, including a course on Automator. The first three chapters of this course are available online for free viewing, or you can purchase the complete course as a CD or via VTC's Online University.

✔ Tip

- VTC's Online University gives you unlimited access to hundreds of video tutorials, making it an excellent way to get low cost video-based training.

Automated Workflows, LLC

www.automatedworkflows.com

This is my site. I've written numerous Automator tutorials and articles for Apple.com, *Macworld* magazine, and more. I have also released shareware Automator actions for such applications as InDesign, Photoshop, and QuarkXPress. Visit my website to access my Automator actions, example workflows, articles, tips, and lots of other great Automator content.

Automator for Mac OS X 10.5 Leopard: Visual QuickStart Guide Companion Website

www.peachpit.com/vqs/automator

Visit the companion website for this book to access downloadable versions of the example workflows, as well as any errata information that may be provided in the future.

Mailing Lists and Forums

User-to-user support is perhaps the best way to receive quick Automator assistance when you need it, and there are several mailing lists and forums available to help. Typically, these resources are host to hundreds, if not thousands of other users who are usually more than happy to provide a quick answer to any question you may have. Participant skill level varies from extreme novice to super geek, so don't be afraid to ask a question, no matter how simple or complex it may seem. As you become an expert on Automator yourself, don't forget to offer your expertise, too.

Apple's Automator Users Mailing List

http://lists.apple.com/mailman/listinfo/automator-users

Many people may be unaware that Apple provides mailing lists for dozens of Mac-related topics, including Aperture, QuickTime, and—you guessed it—Automator. These mailing lists provide an excellent opportunity to network with other Mac users, as well as get quick answers to your burning questions. Automator even includes menu items to aid you in signing up and sending messages to this valuable list.

To join the Automator Users Mailing List:

1. Choose Help > Join Automator Mailing List (**Figure 14.5**).

   The Automator Users Mailing List webpage opens in your web browser.

2. Enter your name, email address, and a password, and follow the instructions to subscribe (**Figure 14.6**).

   You are sent an email requesting confirmation of your subscription.

After confirming your subscription, you will receive regular emails from other users subscribed to the list. Feel free to email your own Automator-related questions to the list, and be sure to answer questions from others if you are able to do so.

✔ Tips

- To reduce the number of emails you receive, subscribe to the list as a daily digest.
- Consider setting up a mail rule to autofilter mailing list emails into a specific mailbox, allowing you to review them at your leisure.
- You can manage your mailing list subscription or unsubscribe from the Automator Users Mailing List webpage at http://lists.apple.com/mailman/listinfo/automator-users.

To email the Automator User's Mailing List:

1. Choose Help > Send Mail to Automator Mailing List.

   A new email message is created, addressed to the mailing list.

2. Type a subject and your question, and send the email.

   Now, just sit back and wait for a response.

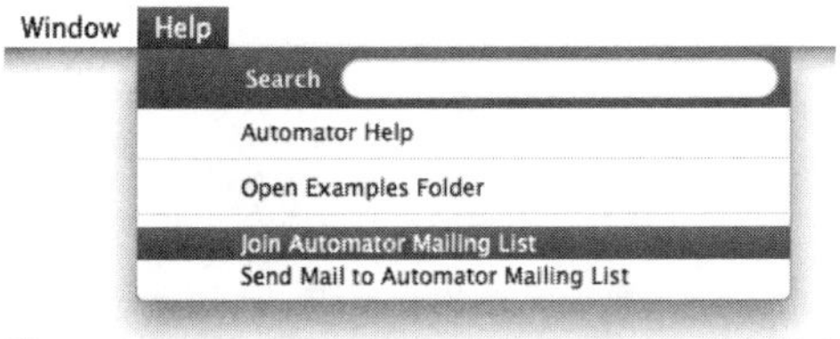

Figure 14.5 Choose Help > Join Automator Mailing List to open a subscription page in your web browser.

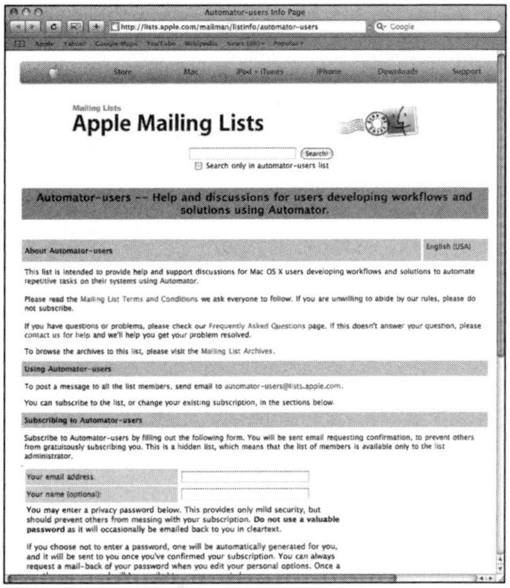

Figure 14.6 Apple's website allows you to subscribe to dozens of Mac-related mailing lists, including the Automator Users Mailing list.

✔ Tip

- For help with other Apple technologies, check out the other mailing lists available at http://lists.apple.com/.

Apple's Automator Discussion Board

http://discussions.apple.com

If you prefer not to clutter your inbox with email from a mailing list, Apple also offers dozens of online discussion forums, including one for Automator. If you're stuck on something, search the Apple discussion boards for advice. If you can't find an existing post that helps with your problem, go ahead and post a question.

Automator World Forum

http://automatorworld.com/forum/

In addition to providing news, tips, and downloadable actions and workflows, Automator World also hosts a popular Automator forum. Use it to network with other Automator users and find quick answers to your burning questions.

MacScripter BBS

http://bbs.applescript.net/

Although the MacScripter BBS is primarily an AppleScript forum, it does have an Automator category, which can be an excellent resource for getting expert Automator advice.

Sending Feedback to Apple

Apple values customer input, and takes it into consideration when updating their software. Please let them know if you encounter any problems with Automator or if you have suggestions for features or actions you'd like to see. You never know; your suggestions just might make it into a future Automator release.

To provide Automator feedback:

1. Choose Automator > Provide Automator Feedback (**Figure 14.7**).

   Automator's feedback webpage opens in your web browser.

2. Enter your comments, and click Send Feedback (**Figure 14.8**).

Apple won't respond to your input directly. Rest assured, however, that your input is entered safely in their database and will be taken into consideration.

✔ Tip

- You can provide feedback about any Apple product via Apple's website at www.apple.com/feedback.

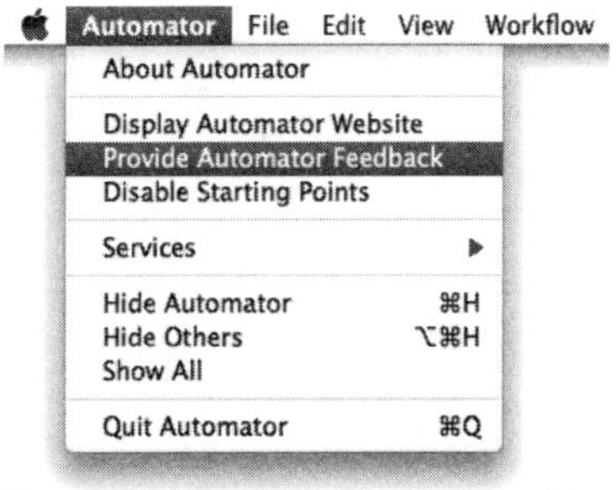

Figure 14.7 Choose Automator > Provide Automator Feedback to send Apple your input about Automator.

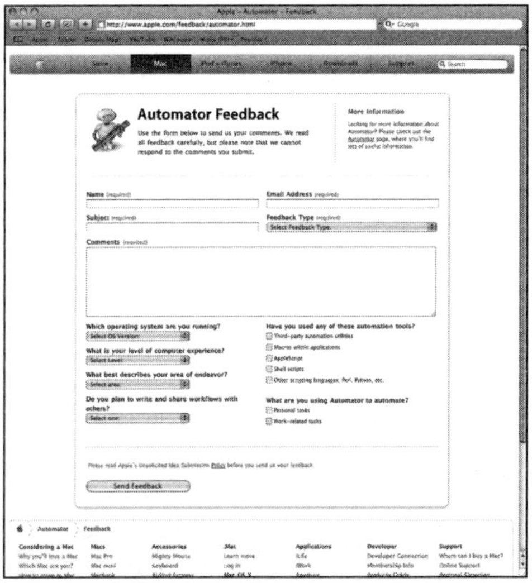

Figure 14.8 Use Apple's feedback webpage to let Apple know about bugs you encounter and features you'd like to see.

Glossary

This glossary serves as a quick reference guide for many key Automator terms. Additional terms are explained within the text of *Automator for Mac OS X 10.5 Leopard: Visual QuickStart Guide*. Please consult the Index if you are unable to locate a specific term.

- **Action.** An action is a building block within Automator. Each action is responsible for performing a single, specific automated task, and actions are placed together in sequence to form a workflow. Most actions have modifiable settings, allowing you to specify how they should behave when run within a workflow.
- **Folder action.** An Automator workflow can be saved as a Folder action plug-in and attached to a specified folder. When items are placed in the attached folder, the workflow runs and the newly added items are passed to the workflow for processing.
- **Input.** Most actions in Automator accept information from the previous action in the workflow as input. This information is generally processed by the action when the workflow runs. The type of input accepted by an action depends on the task the action performs. In some actions, input can be ignored.

- **Library.** The list of installed actions and variables, organized into categories, is known as Automator's Library. The Library is displayed along the left side of every workflow window, although it may be hidden from view, if desired.
- **Log.** Automator's log can be displayed at the bottom of a workflow window. When a workflow runs, the log provides a list of the events performed by the workflow, including any actions that have run, their duration, and a list of any errors that may have occurred.
- **Output.** Information that an action passes to the next phase of a workflow is known as the action's output (see Result).
- **Plug-in.** Automator workflows can be saved as plug-ins for certain applications and processes in Mac OS X, including the Finder, iCal, and Image Capture. Plug-ins offer a way to more tightly integrate Automator workflows into a daily routine, without the need to launch Automator. For example, a Finder plug-in workflow can be run from within the Finder's contextual menu to quickly and easily process selected files and folders.
- **Recording.** Automator in Leopard offers the ability to record manual tasks, such as mouse clicks and key presses. Recorded events are inserted into a workflow in the form of a Watch Me Do action. When the workflow runs, the recorded events are played back as part of the workflow.
- **Result.** Information an action passes to the next phase of a workflow is known as the action's result or output. The type of result an action produces varies depending on the function of the action. Typically, an action's result is passed to the next action in the workflow (which receives it as input) for further processing.

- **Script menu.** Mac OS X includes a system-wide script menu, which provides quick access to AppleScripts and Automator workflows from within any application. By default, the Script menu is disabled. It can be enabled via the AppleScript Utility application, found in /Applications/AppleScript/ or by saving an Automator workflow as a Script menu plug-in.
- **Timeout.** The amount of time allowed for a recorded manual event (within the Watch Me Do action) to be performed when run within an Automator workflow is known as a timeout. By default, recorded events are given a timeout of two seconds. This can be increased or decreased for recorded events on an individual basis, if desired.
- **Variable.** Variables provide a way to store and retrieve values as a workflow runs. A number of predefined variables are available, allowing a workflow to retrieve and use such dynamic information as the current time, current date, current user, system version, and more. Custom variables can also be used to store and retrieve action results, text, and more. Variables are new to Automator in Leopard.
- **Watch Me Do.** Used to insert recorded events into a workflow (see Recording).

Workflow Creation Step-by-Step Guide

A

1. Determine the job you want to automate. Look for repetitive and time-consuming things you do on a regular basis.
2. List the steps needed to accomplish the job. You can do this in your head or as a written outline. Try to associate each step with an action in Automator.
3. Use Starting Points to create a new Custom, Files & Folders, Music & Audio, Photos & Images, or Text workflow. Depending on the type of workflow you create, certain actions may be inserted automatically.
4. Locate the necessary actions in the Library list, and drag them to your workflow. To locate actions, try clicking through the different categories or entering keywords into the Library list's search field. If you can't find an action to accomplish a task, look online for a third-party action that can help.
5. Configure any action settings. To configure an action's settings at runtime, enable the "Show when run" option (if available).
6. Determine whether any variables are necessary for your workflow to function. If so, insert them into the workflow and configure them.

continues on next page

7. Test the workflow by running it within Automator.
8. Check the status area and workflow log for errors. If errors occurred, troubleshoot and resolve them. Check action results to make sure the correct information is being passed through the workflow.
9. Save the workflow as a file, application, or plug-in.
10. Run the workflow and become more efficient.

B

Example Workflows

To supplement the numerous examples throughout the book, this appendix provides three additional workflows that demonstrate creation techniques, using variables, saving plug-ins, and more:

- **Backup Safari Data.** To be saved as an iCal Alarm plug-in, this workflow finds items named Safari in your user folder and archives them as a zip file into a dated Safari Backups folder in your Documents folder.
- **Make Dated Subfolder.** To be saved as a Finder plug-in, this workflow creates a subfolder, named with the current date, within the currently selected folder.
- **Clean Up Desktop.** To be saved as a Script Menu plug-in, this workflow moves all files and folders from your Desktop to a dated subfolder within your Documents folder.

These workflows are quite a bit longer than the ones you've seen so far. If you have trouble following along, remember that all of the workflows in this book are included in this book's companion files. Visit www.peachpit.com/vqs/automator to access them.

Backup Safari Data

This workflow is designed to be saved as an iCal alarm and to be run on a repeating schedule, such as once per week. When it runs, it creates a folder named Safari Backups in your Documents folder. It then finds all of the Safari data in your user folder and archives it into the Safari Backups folder, naming it with the current date (**Figure B.1**).

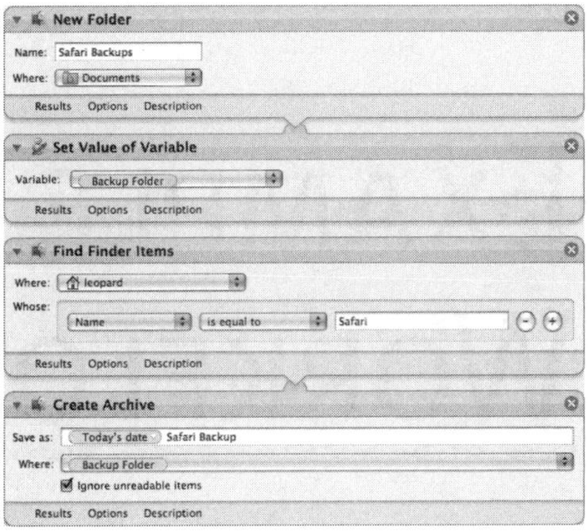

Figure B.1 The Backup Safari Data workflow.

Building the Workflow

Actions used:

- New Folder
- Set Value of Variable
- Find Finder Items
- Create Archive

Variables used:

- New Path
- Today's date

To build the workflow:

1. Create a new custom workflow window.
2. At the top of the Library list, click the Variables button.

   The list of categories and variables displays.
3. In the Locations category, double-click the New Path variable.

   The workflow variables area, containing the New Path variable, displays at the bottom of the workflow window (**Figure B.2**).
4. Double-click the New Path variable in the workflow variables area to open the Variable Options window.

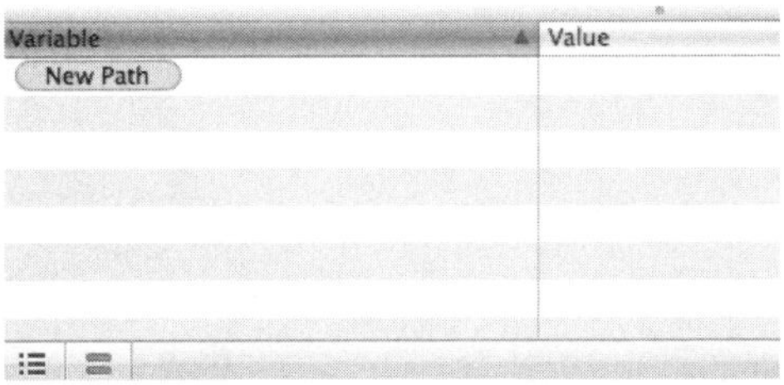

Figure B.2 Double-click the New Path variable in the Locations category to add it to the workflow variables area.

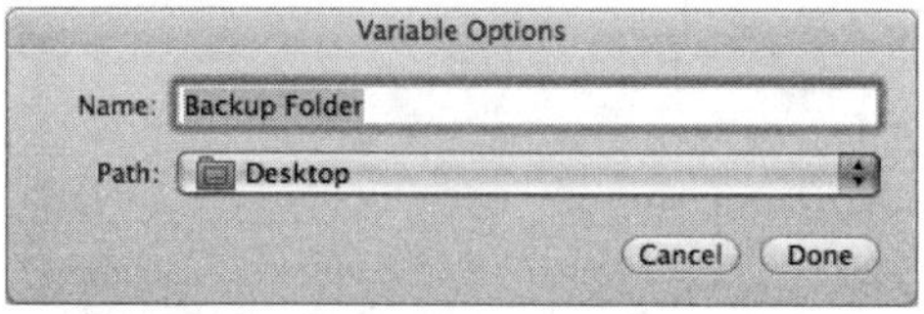

Figure B.3 In the Variable Options window, rename the New Path variable to Backup Folder.

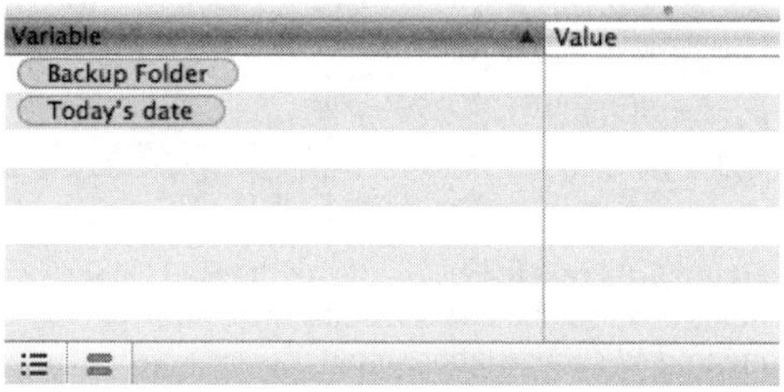

Figure B.4 Double-click the "Today's date" variable in the Date & Time category to add it to the workflow variables area.

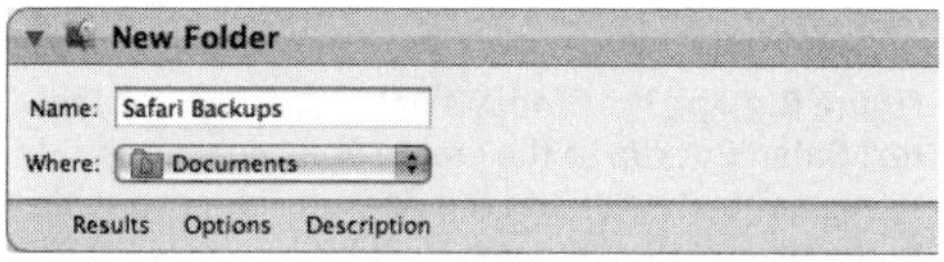

Figure B.5 From the Files & Folders category, add a New Folder action to the workflow and enter `Safari Backups` into the Name field.

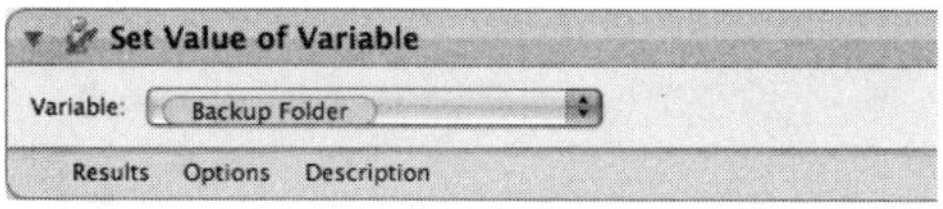

Figure B.6 From the Utilities category, add the Set Value of Variable action to the workflow and choose Backup Folder from the Variable pop-up menu.

5. Enter `Backup Folder` in the Name field (**Figure B.3**).

   Leave the Path pop-up menu set to Desktop. This folder won't be used when the workflow runs. Rather, the variable will receive a new value: a backup folder that the first action in the workflow will create.

6. Click Done.

   The Workflow Variables window closes.

7. In the Date & Time category, double-click the "Today's date" variable.

   Automator adds the variable to the workflow variables list (**Figure B.4**).

8. At the top of the Library list, click the Actions button to display the list of categories and actions.

9. From the Files & Folders category, drag the New Folder action to the workflow area.

10. Enter `Safari Backups` in the New Folder action's Name field.

11. Choose Documents from the New Folder action's Where pop-up menu. (**Figure B.5**).

12. From the Utilities category, drag the Set Value of Variable action to the workflow area.

13. From the Set Value of Variable action's Variable pop-up menu, choose Backup Folder (**Figure B.6**).

14. From the Files & Folders category, drag the Find Finder Items action to the workflow area.

15. From the Find Finder Items action's Where pop-up menu, choose your user folder.

continues on next page

16. Choose Name from the first pop-up menu in the Find Finder Items action's Whose field.

17. Choose "is equal to" from the second pop-up menu in the Find Finder Items action's Whose field.

18. Enter `Safari` in the text field in the Find Finder Items action's Whose field (**Figure B.7**).

19. While holding down Control, click the title of the Find Finder Items action in the workflow area and choose Ignore Input from the resulting contextual menu (**Figure B.8**).

20. From the Files & Folders category, drag the Create Archive action to the workflow area.

21. From the workflow variables area, drag the "Today's date" variable to the beginning of the Create Archive action's "Save as" text field.

22. Enter `Safari Backup` into the Create Archive action's "Save as" text field, following the "Today's date" variable.

23. From the workflow variables area, drag the Backup Folder variable to the Create Archive action's Where pop-up menu.

24. Click the Create Archive action's "Ignore unreadable items" checkbox (**Figure B.9**).

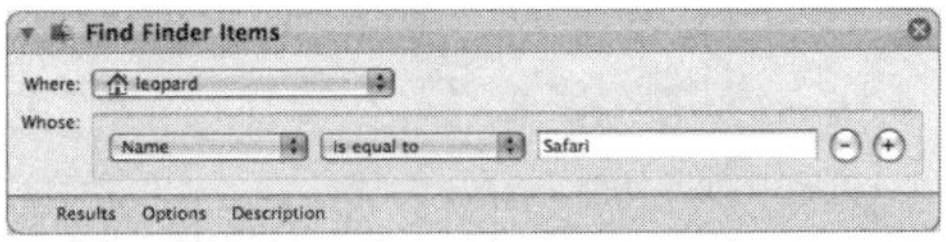

Figure B.7 Configure the Find Finder Items action to search your user folder for any items whose name is equal to Safari.

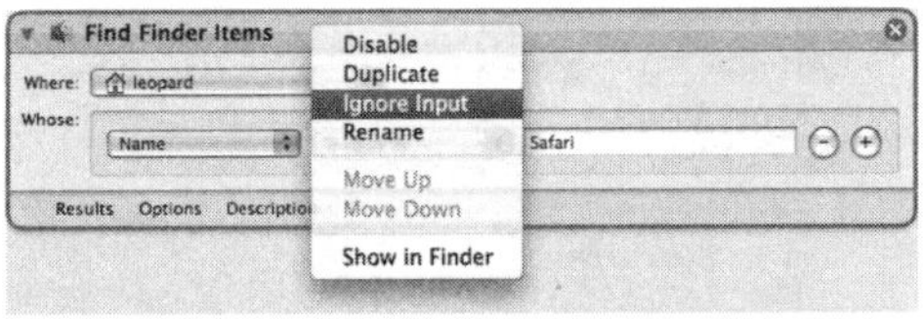

Figure B.8 Press Control and click the Find Finder Items action's title bar to display the contextual menu, and choose Ignore Input.

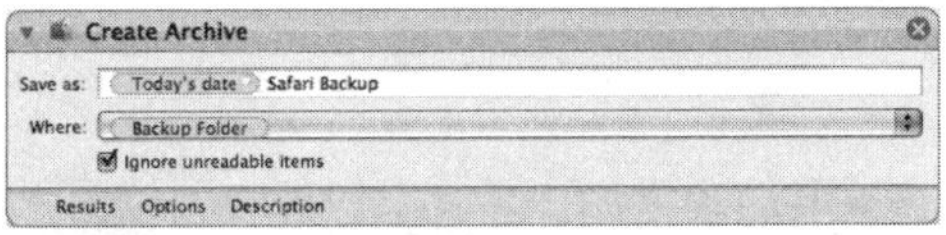

Figure B.9 Add the "Today's date" variable and the text Safari Backup to the Create Archive action's "Save as" text field. Add the Backup Folder variable to the Where pop-up menu.

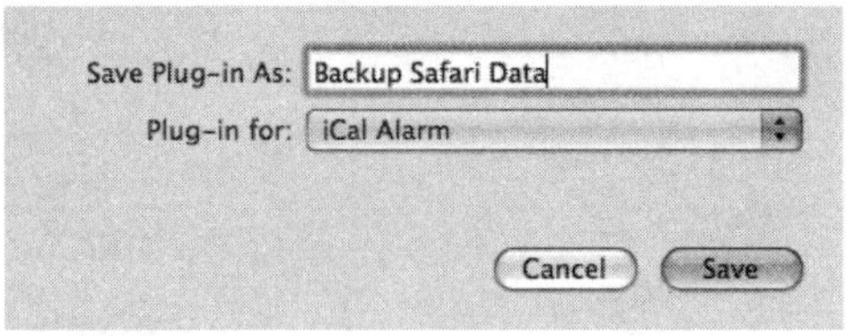

Figure B.10 Choose iCal Alarm from the "Plug-in for" pop-up menu.

Figure B.11 Adjust the date, time, and repeat settings for the event.

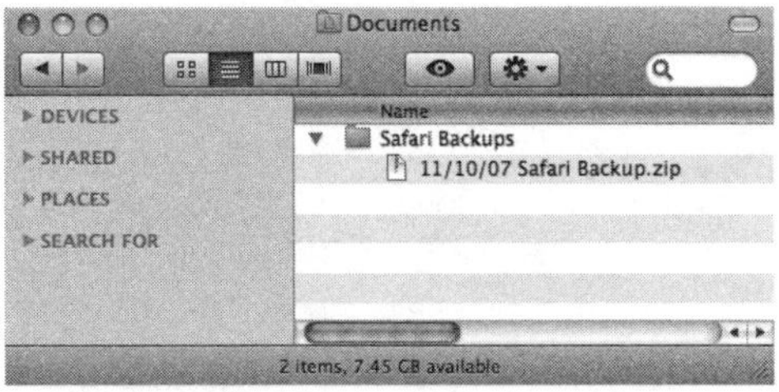

Figure B.12 The workflow runs automatically at the scheduled times, backing up your Safari data to a Safari Backups folder in your Documents folder.

Saving the Workflow

1. Choose File > Save As Plug-in, or press Option ⌘ S to open the Save As Plug-in panel.
2. Enter `Backup Safari Data` in the Save Plug-in As text field.
3. Choose iCal Alarm from the "Plug-in for" pop-up menu (**Figure B.10**).

   No additional plug-in options are displayed.
4. Click Save.

   iCal launches and creates a new event.
5. Adjust the date, time, and repeat settings for the event. For example, set the alarm to repeat every Saturday at 8:00 AM (**Figure B.11**).

Running the Workflow

There's no need to lift a finger. This workflow runs automatically according to the alarms scheduled in iCal, backing up all of the Safari data in your user folder (**Figure B.12**).

Make Dated Subfolder

Designed to be saved as a Finder plug-in, this workflow can be run from the Finder's contextual menu to create a subfolder in the currently selected folder. The new folder is named with the current date (**Figure B.13**).

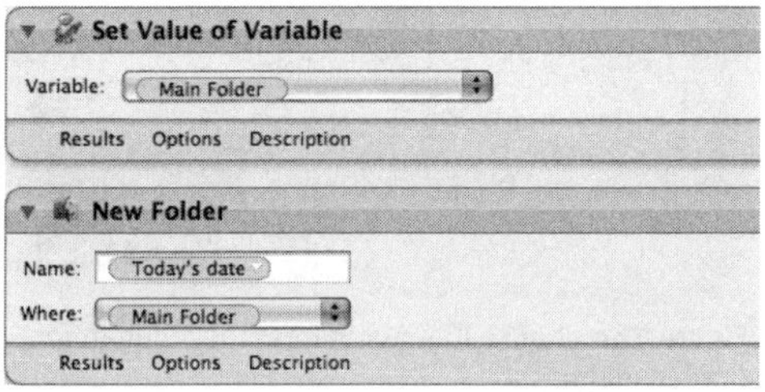

Figure B.13 The Make Dated Subfolder example workflow.

Building the Workflow

Actions used:

- Set Value of Variable
- New Folder

Variables used:

- New Path
- Today's date

To build the workflow:

1. Create a new custom workflow window.
2. At the top of the Library list, click the Variables button to display the list of categories and variables.
3. In the Locations category, double-click the New Path variable.

   The workflow variables area, containing the New Path variable, displays at the bottom of the workflow window.
4. Double-click the New Path variable in the workflow variables area to open the Variable Options window.
5. Enter `Main Folder` in the Name field.

   Leave the Path pop-up menu set to Desktop. This folder won't be used when the workflow runs. Rather, the variable will receive a new value: the folder on which the workflow is run.
6. Click Done to close the Workflow Variables window.

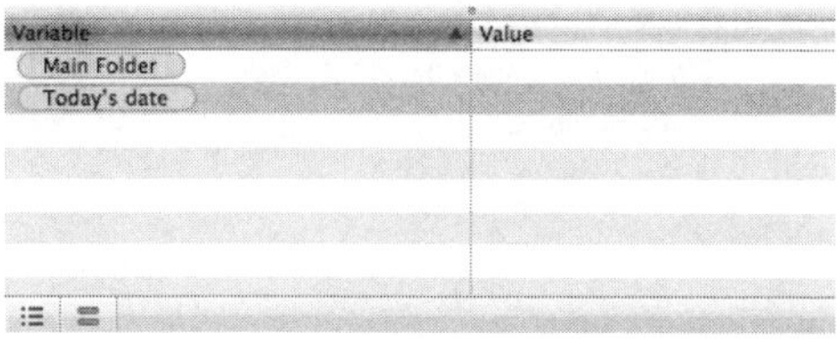

Figure B.14 The workflow variables area now contains two variables: Main Folder (originally New Path) and "Today's date."

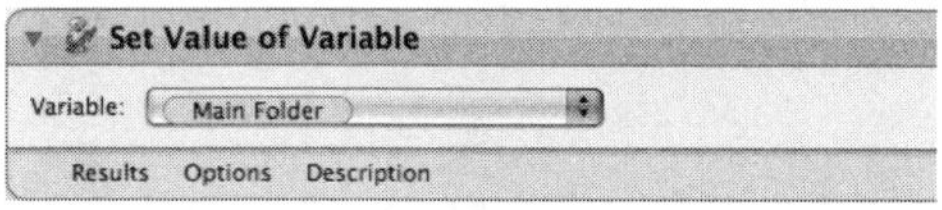

Figure B.15 From the Set Value of Variable action's Variable pop-up menu, choose Main Folder.

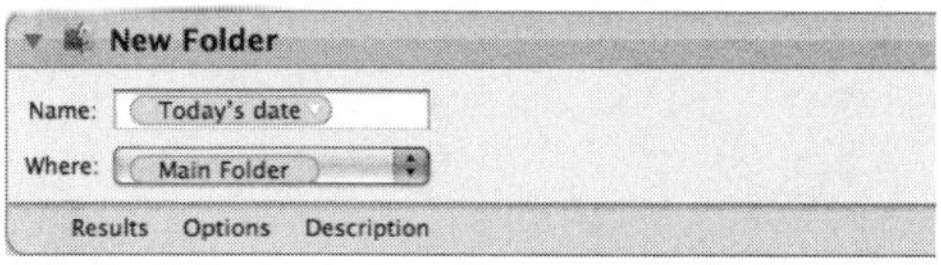

Figure B.16 From the workflow variables area, drag the "Today's date" variable to the New Folder action's Name field and the Main Folder variable to the Where pop-up menu.

7. In the Date & Time category, double-click the "Today's date" variable to add it to the workflow variables list (**Figure B.14**).

8. At the top of the Library list, click the Actions button to display the list of categories and actions.

9. From the Utilities category, drag the Set Value of Variable action to the workflow area.

10. From the Set Value of Variable action's Variable pop-up menu, choose Main Folder (**Figure B.15**).

    Because this workflow will be saved as a Finder plug-in, the selected folder in the Finder will be passed to this action as input when the workflow runs.

11. From the Files & Folders category, drag the New Folder action to the workflow area.

12. From the workflow variables area, drag the "Today's date" variable to the New Folder action's Name text field.

13. From the workflow variables area, drag the Main Folder variable to the New Folder action's Where pop-up menu (**Figure B.16**).

14. While holding down Control, click the title of the New Folder action in the workflow area and choose Ignore Input from the resulting contextual menu.

Saving the Workflow

1. Choose File > Save As Plug-in, or press Option ⌘ S to open the Save As Plug-in panel.
2. Enter `Make Dated Subfolder` in the Save Plug-in As text field.
3. Choose Finder from the "Plug-in for" pop-up menu (**Figure B.17**).

   No additional plug-in options are displayed.
4. Click Save.

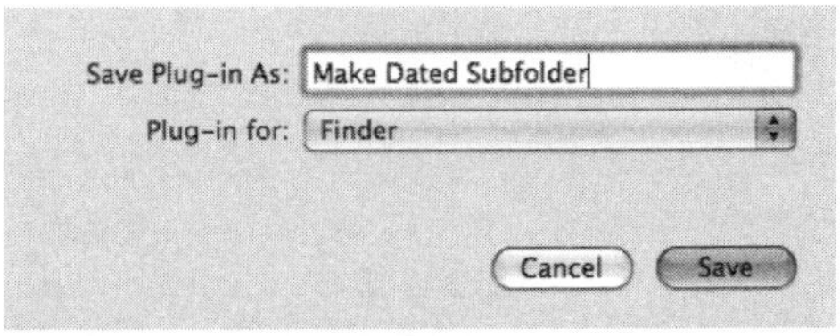

Figure B.17 Choose Finder from the "Plug-in for" pop-up menu.

Running the Workflow

1. Select a folder in the Finder.
2. Hold down Control and click the folder to display the Finder's contextual menu.
3. Choose More > Automator > Make Dated Subfolder (**Figure B.18**).

   The workflow runs and creates a subfolder in the selected folder, naming it with the current date (**Figure B.19**).

Figure B.18 Hold down Control, click a folder and choose More > Automator > Make Dated Subfolder from the Finder's contextual menu.

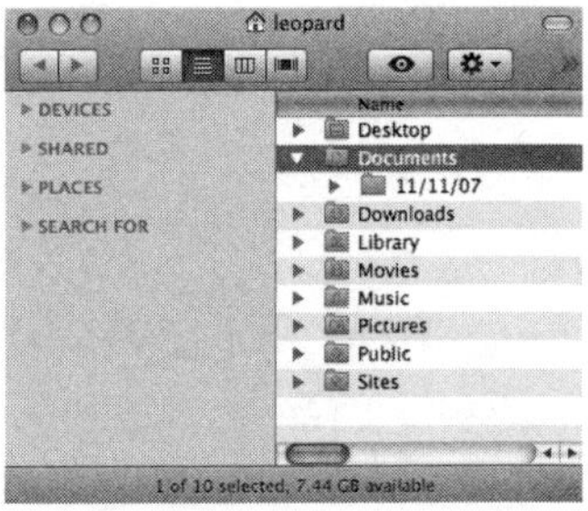

Figure B.19 The workflow runs and creates a dated subfolder in the selected folder.

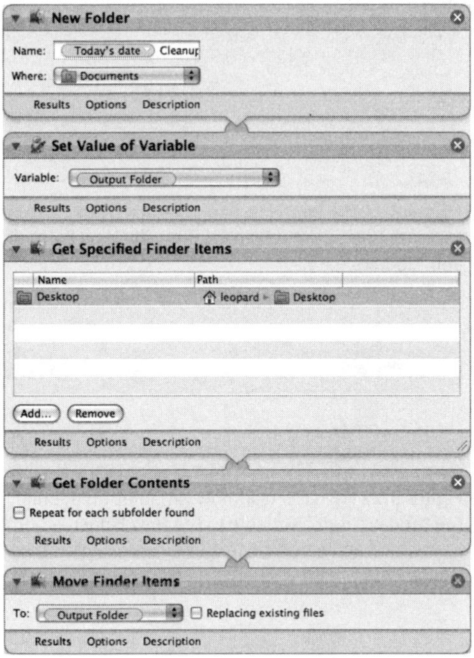

Figure B.20 The Clean Up Desktop example workflow.

Clean Up Desktop

Saved as a Script Menu plug-in, this workflow can be run at any time by selecting it in the system-wide Script menu. When you run it, any files and folders on your Desktop will be moved automatically to a dated subfolder in your Documents folder. (**Figure B.20**).

Building the Workflow

Actions used:

- New Folder
- Set Value of Variable
- Get Specified Finder Items
- Get Folder Contents
- Move Finder Items

Variables used:

- New Path
- Today's date

To build the workflow:

1. Create a new custom workflow window.
2. At the top of the Library list, click the Variables button to display the list of categories and variables.
3. In the Locations category, double-click the New Path variable.

   The workflow variables area, containing the New Path variable, displays at the bottom of the workflow window.
4. Double-click the New Path variable in the workflow variables area to open the Variable Options window.
5. Enter `Output Folder` in the Name field.

   Leave the Path pop-up menu set to Desktop. The variable will receive a new value when the workflow runs.

continues on next page

6. Click Done to close the Workflow Variables window.
7. In the Date & Time category, double-click the "Today's date" variable.

   Automator adds the variable to the workflow variables list (**Figure B.21**).
8. At the top of the Library list, click the Actions button to display the list of categories and actions.
9. From the Files & Folders category, drag the New Folder action to the workflow area.
10. From the workflow variables area, drag the "Today's date" variable to the New Folder action's Name text field.
11. Enter `Cleanup` in the New Folder action's Name text field, following the "Today's date" variable.
12. From the New Folder action's Where pop-up menu, choose Documents (**Figure B.22**).
13. From the Utilities category, drag the Set Value of Variable action to the workflow area.
14. From the Set Value of Variable action's Variable pop-up menu, choose the Output Folder variable (**Figure B.23**).
15. From the Files & Folders category, drag the Get Specified Finder Items action to the workflow area.
16. Click the Get Specified Finder Items action's Add button.

    A folder selection window opens.
17. Locate and choose the Desktop folder (**Figure B.24**).

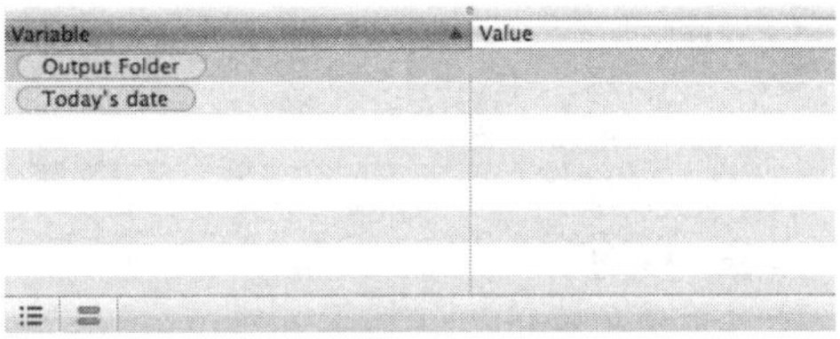

Figure B.21 The workflow variables area now contains two variables: Output Folder (originally New Path) and "Today's date."

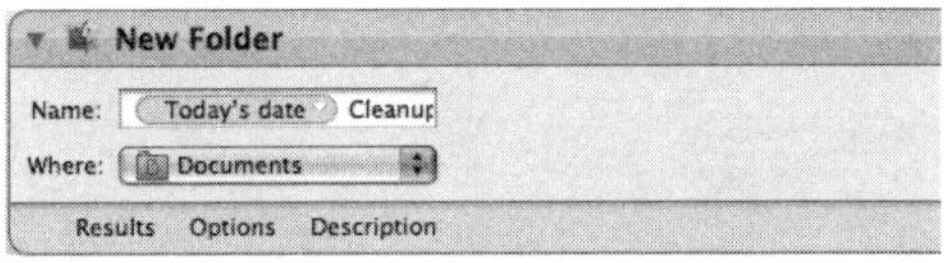

Figure B.22 From the workflow variables area, drag the "Today's date" variable to the New Folder action's Name field and enter the text `Cleanup`. Choose Documents from the Where pop-up menu.

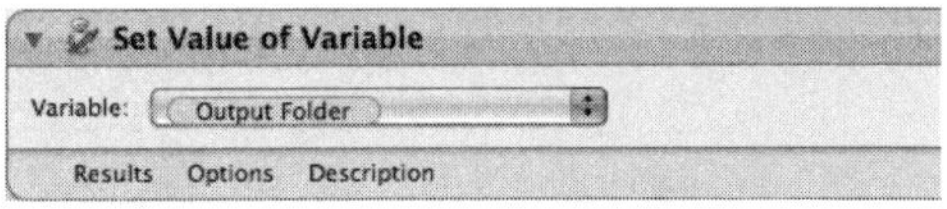

Figure B.23 From the Set Value of Variable action's Variable pop-up menu, choose Output Folder.

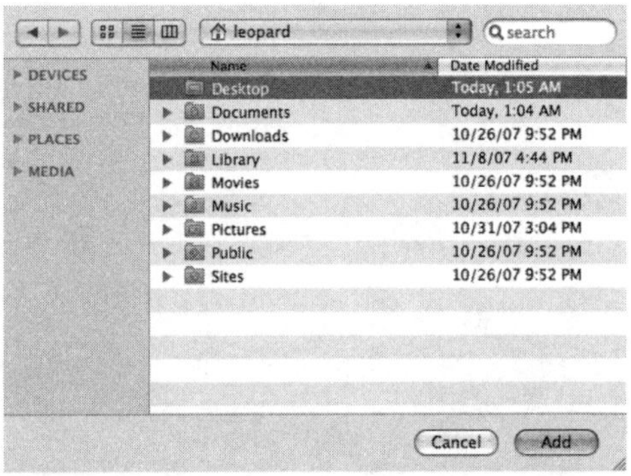

Figure B.24 Locate and choose the Desktop folder.

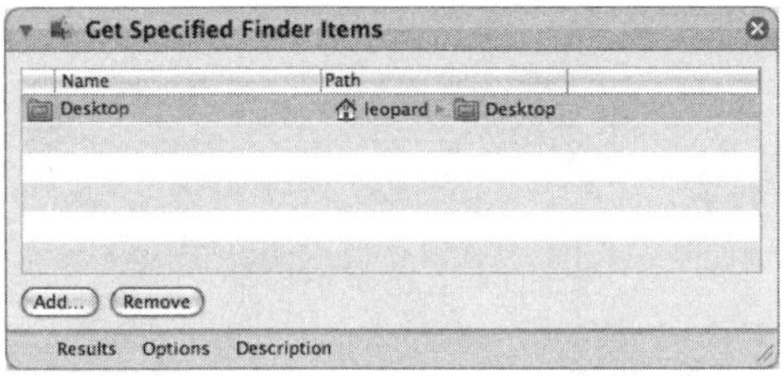

Figure B.25 Configure the Get Specified Finder Items action to get the Desktop folder.

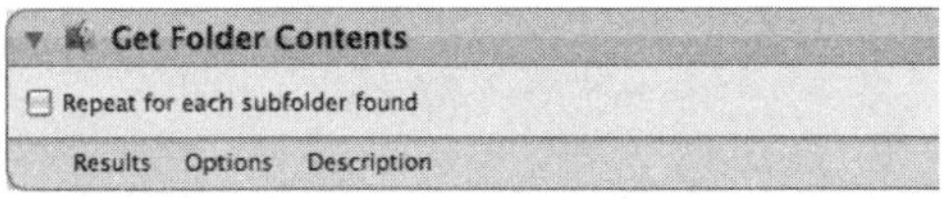

Figure B.26 Make sure the Get Folder Contents action's "Repeat for each subfolder found" checkbox is deselected.

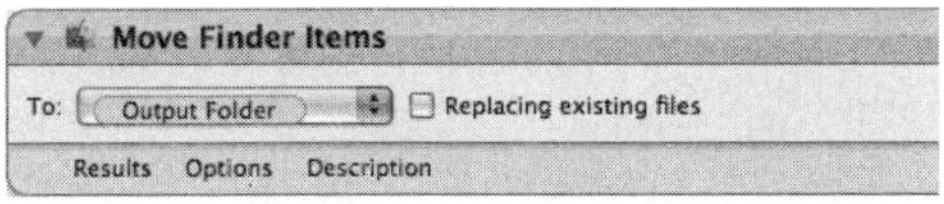

Figure B.27 From the workflow variables area, drag the Output Folder variable to the Move Finder Items action's To field and verify that the "Rename existing files" checkbox is deselected.

18. Click Add.

Automator adds the Desktop folder to the Get Specified Finder Items action (**Figure B.25**).

19. While holding down Control, click the title of the Get Specified Finder Items action in the workflow area.

A contextual menu displays.

20. Choose Ignore Input from the contextual menu.

21. From the Files & Folders category, drag the Get Folder Contents action to the workflow area.

22. Verify that the Get Folder Contents action's "Repeat for each subfolder found" checkbox is deselected (**Figure B.26**).

23. From the Files & Folders category, drag the Move Finder Items action to the workflow area.

24. From the workflow variables area, drag the Output Folder variable to the Move Finder Items action's To pop-up menu.

25. Verify that the Move Finder Items action's "Replace existing files" checkbox is deselected (**Figure B.27**).

Saving the Workflow

1. Choose File > Save As Plug-in, or press Option ⌘ S.

   The Save As Plug-in panel appears.

2. Enter `Clean Up Desktop` in the Save Plug-in As text field.

3. Choose Script Menu from the "Plug-in for" pop-up menu (**Figure B.28**).

   No additional plug-in options are displayed.

4. Click Save.

Running the Workflow

Choose Clean Up Desktop from the Script menu to run the workflow (**Figure B.29**). The workflow moves all files and folders on your Desktop into a dated subfolder in your Documents folder (**Figure B.30**).

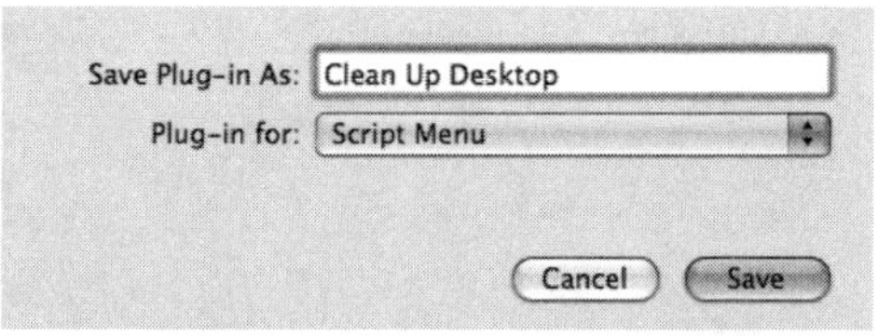

Figure B.28 Choose Script Menu from the "Plug-in for" pop-up menu.

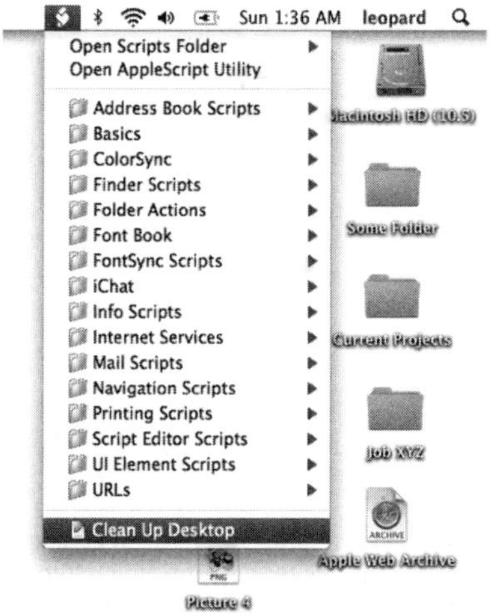

Figure B.29 Choose Clean Up Desktop from the Script menu.

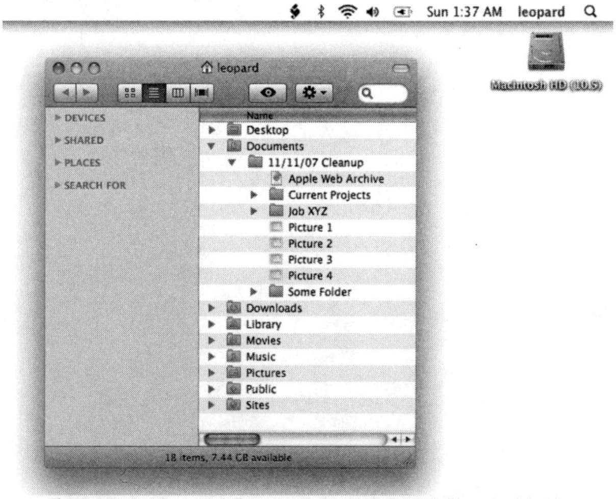

Figure B.30 The workflow runs and moves all files and folders from your Desktop to a dated subfolder in the Documents folder.

C

Developer Resources

Are you interested in creating your own custom Automator actions? If so, then you're in luck. Mac OS X includes the tools you need to get started, and dozens of websites, books, and forums are ready to help, too.

Automator involves a number of technologies, including AppleScript, Cocoa, Interface Builder, Objective-C, and Xcode. You'll need to become familiar with these in order to begin developing actions of your own. Once you understand these, however, building actions is a snap. This appendix outlines some valuable resources to put you on the right course.

Apple Developer Connection

http://developer.apple.com/

The Apple Developer Connection is the best resource around for information about development in Mac OS X. Here, you can find extensive documentation and lots of examples for developing virtually anything for Mac OS X. Detailed documentation is available for developers interested in creating Automator actions in AppleScript, Objective-C, and more, including:

- **Automator Programming Guide.** This document provides a fairly comprehensive walkthrough of the development process for AppleScript, Objective-C, and Shell Script Automator actions.
- **Automator AppleScript Actions Tutorial.** This document walks developers through the steps involved in the creation of AppleScript-based actions for Automator.
- **AppleScript Studio Terminology Reference.** This document outlines the terminology used in the development of AppleScript Studio applications. If you plan to develop AppleScript-based actions, this document is priceless.
- **AppleScript Studio Programming Guide.** This document provides detailed instructions for creating AppleScript Studio projects in Xcode. It includes a number of tutorials that walk through the complete process of project creation.
- **Objective-C Programming Guide.** This document provides a complete introduction to the Objective-C programming language. Also covered in detail is an introduction to object-oriented programming.

This list is just a taste of the documentation you'll find in the Apple Developer Connection Reference Library, which is installed with the Xcode developer tools and is also available online. To ensure access to the latest documentation and developer resources, consider joining the Apple Developer Connection. An online membership is free!

Websites

Although Apple's Developer Connection provides much of what you need to know to learn how to develop for Automator, it doesn't tell you everything. Don't worry; numerous third-party websites are also available to help with Automator development, AppleScript, and Objective-C. Here are some good places to get started.

Automator.us

http://automator.us

Primarily geared toward Automator users, this website contains some gems for developers, too, including links to Automator developer resources and tools to aid with action development. The site is updated regularly, so be sure to check it often.

Apple's AppleScript Web Page

www.apple.com/applescript/

This website is an excellent resource for anyone interested in learning AppleScript. Here, you'll find AppleScript documentation, links to third-party resources, and other important information. In addition, you'll find countless downloadable scripts that are fully editable for you to view, modify, and even incorporate into your own AppleScript projects.

MacScripter

http://macscripter.net/

This is perhaps the most comprehensive AppleScript resource available on the Web. Maintained by a handful of experienced scripters as well as the overall AppleScript community, this site serves as a repository for AppleScript articles, tips, links, forums, and much more. You'll also find thousands—and I mean thousands—of user-contributed scripts here. Although some of these are commercial and contain locked code, many are freeware and fully editable.

Objective-C Beginner's Guide

www.otierney.net/objective-c.html

This website offers a nice tutorial of the Objective-C programming language, complete with practical example code.

Automated Workflows, LLC

www.automatedworkflows.com

My website provides lots of great information for anyone interested in AppleScript or Automator development. In the Tips section, you'll find numerous developer resources, including my MacScripter and *MacTech* columns on AppleScript, AppleScript Studio, and Automator.

Apple Mailing Lists

http://lists.apple.com

Offering a way to ask questions and network directly with other developers, mailing lists and online forums provide an unparalleled learning experience for developers. Apple hosts a variety of developer mailing lists that may be of interest to Automator developers, including:

- Automator Developers List

  http://lists.apple.com/archives/automator-dev
- AppleScript Studio List

  http://lists.apple.com/mailman/listinfo/applescript-studio
- AppleScript Users List

  http://lists.apple.com/mailman/listinfo/applescript-users
- Carbon Developer's List

  http://lists.apple.com/mailman/listinfo/carbon-dev
- Cocoa Developer's List

  http://lists.apple.com/mailman/listinfo/cocoa-dev
- Objective-C Language List

  http://lists.apple.com/mailman/listinfo/objc-language
- Xcode User's List

  http://lists.apple.com/mailman/listinfo/xcode-users

Third-Party Mailing Lists and Forums

You're not just limited to Apple's mailing lists. Many third-party options are available, too. Here are a few that should prove beneficial to Automator developers.

Macintosh Scripting Systems Mailing List

http://listserv.dartmouth.edu/archives/macscrpt.html

This email list, which is hosted by Dartmouth, is host to thousands of AppleScript developers who can provide answers to virtually any AppleScript-related question you may have.

MacScripter's AppleScript BBS

http://bbs.applescript.net/

This online forum provides yet another excellent resource for asking questions about AppleScript and Finder scripting. Much like the email lists, this forum is frequented by thousands of developers who are always willing to share their scripting knowledge.

Objective-C Newsgroup

news://comp.lang.objective-c

This newsgroup focuses on discussions of the Objective-C programming language.

Books and Tutorials

Numerous books and tutorials can help you in your quest to develop Automator actions. Here are some good places to start.

Danny Goodman's AppleScript Handbook: Mac OS X Edition

Danny Goodman

SpiderWorks, LLC *www.spiderworks.com*

Originally written shortly after AppleScript's debut, then updated for Mac OS X, this book is an excellent study guide for anyone interested in learning AppleScript. Great for beginners, the book is also a useful reference guide for experienced scripters.

AppleScript: The Definitive Guide

Matt Neuburg

O'Reilly *www.oreilly.com*

Sure to be found on the bookshelf of many AppleScript developers, this book provides a truly comprehensive guide to AppleScript in Mac OS X. It covers all the ins and outs of the AppleScript, from core language principles to developing applications with AppleScript Studio.

Learn Objective-C on the Macintosh

Mark Dalrymple and Scott Knaster

SpiderWorks, LLC *www.spiderworks.com*

This book offers an in-depth look at programming with Objective-C, including inheritance, composition, and memory management, to name a few topics. It also includes an introduction to object-oriented programming. All in all, it's an excellent way to become acquainted with Objective-C.

AppleScript 2006 Video Training Course

Ben Waldie

VTC, Virtual Training Company
www.vtc.com

This AppleScript course, authored by yours truly, provides a solid introduction and foundation for anyone looking to learn AppleScript. Each video-based lesson allows you to follow along onscreen at your own pace. The first few chapters are available for free online viewing, and the complete course is available on CD or through VTC's Online University.

AppleScripting the Finder and *Mac OS X Technology Guide to Automator*

Ben Waldie

Automated Workflows, LLC
www.automatedworkflows.com

Visit the books section for a list of all of my books, including *AppleScripting the Finder* and my previous Automator book, the *Mac OS X Technology Guide to Automator*, which covers the process of developing AppleScript- and Objective-C-based Automator actions in Mac OS X 10.4 Tiger.

✔ Tip

- My August 2005 *MacTech* column, available online, explains how to build Automator actions with AppleScript.

Action Templates and Example Code

Action templates included with Xcode provide an excellent way to get started constructing your own actions. When you create a new Xcode project, you'll see these templates listed in the project creation window (**Figure C.1**).

Apple also provides some fully editable functional example action projects. Look for these example projects in the /Developer/Examples/Automator/ folder. Examples include demonstrations of AppleScript-, Cocoa-, and Shell-Script-based actions (**Figure C.2**).

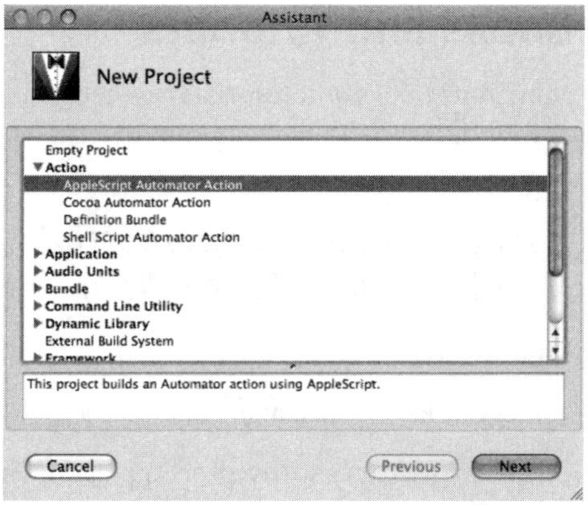

Figure C.1 Xcode includes a number of prebuilt template projects ready to get you started developing custom Automator actions of your own.

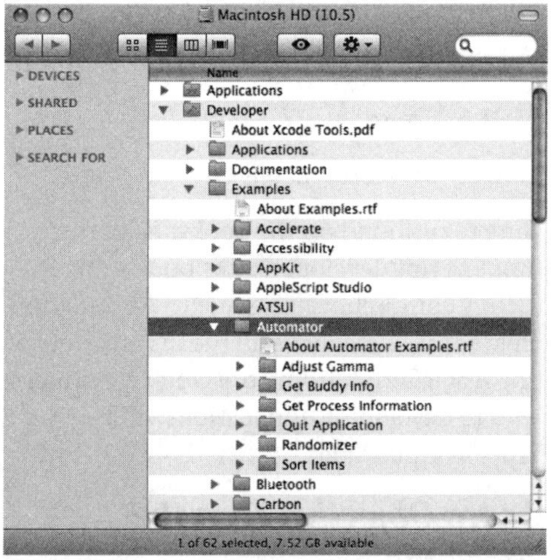

Figure C.2 When you install the Mac OS X Developer tools, you can find several example Automator action Xcode projects in /Developer/Examples/Automator/.

INDEX

INDEX

N

O

P

R

S